The Social Construction
of Ancient Cities

The Social Construction
of Ancient Cities

EDITED BY
MONICA L. SMITH

SMITHSONIAN BOOKS
WASHINGTON AND LONDON

Copy editor: Vicky Macintyre
Production editor: Duke Johns
Designer: Brian Barth

Library of Congress Cataloging-in-Publication Data
The social construction of ancient cities / edited by
Monica L. Smith.
    p. cm.
  Includes bibliographical references and index.
  ISBN 1-58834-098-8 (alk. paper)
    1. Cities and towns, Ancient. 2. Civilization,
Ancient. I. Smith, Monica L.
HT114.S635 2003
307.76'09'01—dc21   2002030436

British Library Cataloguing-in-Publication Data
available

Manufactured in the United States of America
10 09 08 07 06 05 04 03
5 4 3 2 1

♾ The paper used in this publication meets the
minimum requirements of the American National
Standard for Information Sciences—Permanence
of Paper for Printed Library Materials ANSI
Z39.48-1984.

Contents

Figures

Tables

Contributors

CHRISTOPHER J. ATTARIAN

Department of
Anthropology
University of California
Los Angeles, CA 90095

MARK CHILD

Department of
Anthropology
Yale University
P. O. Box 208277
New Haven, CT
06520-8277

GEORGE L. COWGILL

Department of
Anthropology
Arizona State University
Tempe, AZ 85287-2402

GEOFF EMBERLING

Museum of
Anthropology
University of Michigan
Ann Arbor, MI 48109-
1079

HÉCTOR ESCOBEDO

33 Avenida, 22-76

Zona 5, 01005
Guatemala City,
Guatemala

CHARLES GOLDEN

Department of
Anthropology
University of
Pennsylvania
33rd and Spruce Streets
Philadelphia, PA 19104

STEPHEN D. HOUSTON

Department of
Anthropology
Brigham Young
University
Provo, UT 84602

KATHRYN KEITH

Department of
Anthropology
Boise State University
Boise, ID 83725

RODERICK J. McINTOSH

Department of
Anthropology-MS 20
Rice University
6100 Main Street
Houston, TX 77005-
1892

SUSAN KEECH McINTOSH

Department of
Anthropology-MS 20
Rice University
6100 Main Street
Houston, TX 77005-
1892

JERRY D. MOORE

Department of

Anthropology
CSU Dominguez Hills
1000 E. Victoria St.
Carson, CA 90747

RENÉ MUÑOZ

Department of
Anthropology
University of Arizona
Tucson, AZ 85721-0030

CHEN SHEN

Department of Near
Eastern and Asian
Civilizations
Royal Ontario Museum
100 Queen's Park
Toronto, ON M5S 2C6

MONICA L. SMITH

Department of
Anthropology
University of California
Los Angeles, CA 90095

JASON YAEGER

Department of
Anthropology
5440 Social Science
Building
1180 Observatory Drive
University of Wisconsin
Madison, WI 53706-1393

MELINDA A. ZEDER

Department of
Anthropology
National Museum of
Natural History
Smithsonian Institution
Washington, DC 20560

The Social Construction
of Ancient Cities

ONE

Introduction

The Social Construction of Ancient Cities

In both ancient and modern cities, the vast majority of urban dwellers are not elites, but members of ordinary households. Their production and consumption patterns form the basis of the city's economy; their participation in ceremonies affirms the effectiveness of an organizing authority; their labor permits the manifestation of an urban ethos as constructed through both fanciful monuments and practical infrastructure. This volume explores the role of cities for those inhabitants and provides archaeological case studies of the complexities of urban formation and urban continuities in both the Old and New Worlds. As the meeting ground for immigrant populations from the immediate hinterlands as well as from distant territories, a city represents a new social order, in which numerous different groups must coexist. The resultant social networks, economic activities, and political opportunities are concentrated in a locus of relatively dense population, where the process of daily life takes place as part of the physical landscape that forms and is formed by the negotiated consensus between groups.

In the past three decades, the archaeological study of the city has focused mainly on cities' hinterlands and territories, emphasizing settlement patterns, catchment analysis, and long-distance exchange. Since the early 1990s, there has been a return to the heart of cities, and to the integration of the city and its hinterland. New data on households, neighborhoods, markets, and other domestic venues indicate that ancient cities were not merely the result of leaders' directives, and that the city was constructed by all those who lived in the urban core as well as its hinterlands. As the authors of the following chapters illustrate, the form and function of cities are brought about by a variety of groups (leaders, migrants, ritual specialists, economic specialists, neighborhood associations, and other types of social configurations) that crosscut the space of the city.

Urban centers may come into existence for a variety of reasons, such as trade, ceremony, strategic placement, or administrative demands. Cities can also be legislated into existence, although they cannot be sustained through coercion; especially at the incipient stages of sociopolitical complexity, any attempt to compel urban residence would have outstripped finite central resources and left political systems vulnerable to competition. Even at a state level of sociopolitical organization, planning alone is not sufficient to make cities thrive, as Joffe (1998) has observed in his study of ancient West Asian disembedded capitals. These cities were founded by charismatic elites but many failed to retain a central role afterward, and some disappeared altogether. Similarly, "planned capitals" and developments in the modern world are often not as successful as other cities (Peiser and Chang 1999; Potter 1985).

Given the lack of resources to compel residence in a center of concentrated population and the potential disadvantages of city life, the key to the success of cities must lie in their social aspects and the way in which they are configured by different, often competing groups. Rather than seeing cities as fundamentally changed by the advent of the Industrial Revolution and the global connections of the modern world, new anthropological research suggests that both ancient and modern cities are the result of a limited range of configurations that structure human action in concentrated populations.

PREMODERN AND MODERN URBANISM:
A FUNDAMENTAL DIFFERENCE?

Urban sociologists seek to understand and explain the development and growth of contemporary cities, and their assessment of the effect that cities have upon their inhabitants has historically oscillated from pessimistic to exuberant. A negative view of city life was proposed by early theorists such as Louis Wirth (1938:12), who argued that cities are places where the individual is disconnected from former ties and where human contacts are "impersonal, superficial, transitory, and segmented." In the same negative vein, critiques based on Marxist analyses of class struggle saw cities as the physical locus of alternating rejections of, and acquiescence to, capitalist domination (Castells 1977; Gottdiener 1985; Lefebvre 1979). With the increasing ecological awareness of the 1960s and 1970s, cities in addition came to be seen as having a disastrous impact on the environment and on human health. Titles gracing works on urbanism intoned that cities were "doomed," "dying," and "dysfunctional," and that city life was inherently damaging, inefficient, and wasteful.

But despite an academic undertanding of cities as disastrous places to live, urban zones have continued to grow and have become the dominant residential mode in many parts of the world. Anthropologists and sociologists have had to reconcile a philosophical understanding of the autocratic role of leadership and the rootlessness of city life with observations showing that residents actively view cities as places of community and opportunity (Jacobs 1961; Khalat and Kongstad 1973; Lewis 1952; Penvenne 1997). In urban environments, kinship ties are reaffirmed and augmented, rather than destroyed; social contacts are diversified; and neighborhoods become the principal geographic anchor of social interaction (Dike 1979; Khalat and Konstad 1973; Schweizer et al. 1998). More recently, analysts have also begun to see the city form as a potentially efficient nexus of environmental management and a crucible of opportunity and positive change (e.g., Inoguchi et al. 1999; Keating and Krumholz 1999; O'Meara 1999).

Bolstered by an appreciation of individual agency and the reality of a complex social configuration, these new anthropological and sociological approaches are evaluating the interrelated changes that occur in a city and beyond its boundaries from the point of view of the individual and household. While analysts of modern cities often use the configurations that they see as indicators that the Industrial Revolution brought irreversible and substantial changes to the phenomenon of concentrated populations, archaeological evidence indicates that these same types of transformations are visible in the premodern world, and that the components of cities in the past and present are similar (Potter 1985). These similarities are not limited merely to physical configurations, such as the juxtaposition of public and private space, or the architectural identifiers of hierarchy. They also include the fundamental transformations in human relations as exclusively kin-based social networks become supplemented or supplanted by other types of social networks, and the way in which a perception of improved opportunities draws individuals and households into urban locales.

Consider a straightforward problem shared by studies of both modern and premodern urbanism: the delineation of the city's boundaries. In the view of contemporary urban analysts, the concepts of sprawl, spread, and endless suburbia are a tremendous liability of the modern city (Gottdiener 1985; Vagale 1973; Williams 1985; Wirth 1938). Mark Gottdiener (1985:4) uses the term "deconcentration" to describe the regional dispersal of people, commerce, and industry into a giant polynucleated sprawl, which he contrasts with "the compact city form which once represented a historical process years in the making." The modern city's spread is often blamed on wasteful transportation policies, and while urban sociologists emphasize that there is a social as well as technological component to these developments, they still see the physical configuration of the post-Industrial Revolution city as radically different from its predecessors.

However, archaeological investigations suggest that there has perhaps never been a clear distinction between the urban edge and its hinterland, and that cities are interdigitated with their surrounding communities even when physical walls and embankments suggest a clear-cut perimeter. As the authors in this volume observe, the distinction between the exterior edge of the city and its hinterlands is not a salient one for ancient cities. The effective boundaries of a city may be quite different depending on the criterion in use, with economic boundaries (e.g., the territory representing the source of most comestibles) differing from social boundaries (e.g., the catchment area of ethnic groups drawn into the city).

Since they are linked to identity, these social boundaries fluctuate because a variety of criteria are applied by inhabitants as well as by outsiders (Davidson 1972; Katten 1999; Penvenne 1997; Rubertone and Thorbahn 1985; see also Yaeger, this volume). The concept of a firm "rural-urban" divide is also problematic when the same individuals move back and forth from one setting to another, a phenomenon especially apparent at the inception of large urban centers (e.g., Andersson 2001; Dike 1979; Khalat and Kongstad 1973). Even when cities are well established, continued economic interdependence with their hinterlands means that seasonally required manual labor can be brought into the city from the countryside or can be drawn from an urban labor pool (Grieco 1995).

By contrast, formal, recognized boundaries are likely to result from specific requirements imposed by political entities for the sake of internal management such as revenue-collection, or as the result of disputes with a rival political entity; in either case, they can shift in response to changed internal or external circumstances. Nor are official boundaries and definitions all-encompassing, even when they are in place and become part of the textual record. As Penvenne (1997) observed in her study of migrant Mozambican women, cultural perceptions about appropriate work for women meant that official documents seldom acknowledged their many urban-based sources of income. In urban Padang, official documents about the prescribed and prohibited locations of marketplaces were often the opposite of economic activities as they were actually practiced (Colombijn 1994).

The city and its distant hinterland present another important point of comparison between modern and ancient exemplars. Unlike towns, whose hinterlands are relatively limited in scope, cities have economic hinterlands as far away as the most distantly traded good in the marketplace. In modern times, this has resulted in the "world city," with its global economic ties (Knox 1995; see also Gottdiener 1985; Lefebvre 1979). Paul Knox (1995:13) sees these global cities as socially constructed domains in which the inhabitants "define themselves through globally oriented, populist value systems and through possession of high-end consumer goods." The complexities of modern manufacturing, including fluctuating costs and availability of raw materials and labor, mean that these display items may have origins in multiple locales.

The use of exotic goods in large quantities as social markers is also evident in premodern cities, as we can see from the presence of nonlocal stone in pre-Columbian Mesoamerican cities (Healan 1993); ostrich feathers, tea, and diamonds in medieval Paris (Kurin 1997); and jade in the Chinese cities of the T'ang era (Schafer 1963:225–226). Cities of the late Roman period had changing relationships with their farthest hinterlands since urban bishops controlled economic resources hundreds of kilometers away (Heath 1999). Long-distance trade relationships could also be sustained through permanent enclaves of traders from distant locales, good examples of which can be found in chalcolithic Anatolia (Stein et al. 1996) as well as in precontact Mesoamerica (summarized in Marcus 1998). The inhabitants of ancient cities certainly made use of economically scarce resources from distant regions through a variety of economic and social ties. Modern means of transportation and communication have accelerated, but not fundamentally altered, the city's ability to pull in a vast economic hinterland.

Another point to consider is the attraction of city life for individuals in both modern and ancient cities. A description of London in the nineteenth century provides a vivid picture of why people migrated into the seething, sometimes dangerous world of the Victorian city: "London grew by sucking in provincial migrants because jobs were either better paid there or thought to be so; it also offered a more liberal array of charities, richer rewards for crime, a more persuasive legend of opportunity than could be found anywhere in the country" (Dyos and Reeder 1973:362). Other studies of modern cities show that for those who are economically disadvantaged in the countryside, the diversified and specialized economy of the city promises more niches in which even casual laborers and the disenfranchised may be able to make a living (e.g., Christopher 1979; El-Bushra 1989; El-Shakhs 1979; Penvenne 1997; Vagale 1973).

Although textual evidence for marginal gorups in antiquity is limited, ancient peoples' motives for migration to the city appear to have been similar. In ancient Rome, city distribution agents provided basic subsistence goods such as grain to appease the disenfranchised (Garnsey 1983), a move that probably added to the city's appeal in the minds of immigrants. Juvenal, the Roman satirist, complained that the wealth of the city drew in beggars and thieves, and that the grain dole brought in a torrent of partakers (*Satires,* III). The *Perumpanatrupadai,* a Tamil South Indian poem of the early centuries A.D., similarly describes the city of Kanchipuram as a place with "gates not shut against poor mendicants / Who need no patron else" (Chelliah 1985:129).

In this book, it is argued that the similarities between modern and ancient cities are not limited to these comparative formal properties of economic opportunity, fluid rural-urban boundaries, and the consumption of luxury goods as social markers. More fundamentally, it appears that the capacities for human interaction in concentrated locations are exercised within a limited set of parameters, an observation that may make us distinctly uncomfortable given our tendency to view modern *Homo sapiens* as highly inventive and innovative. People developed cities in many parts of the world independently, yet the resulting urban form exhibits similarities in the organization of space (broad avenues and open plazas), the placement of symbolic architecture in prominent locations, and the development of neighborhoods around occupational specialties. Even more striking, cities in the Old World and the New World, without contact between them, developed into the most complex and densely occupied type of human population center, with remarkably similar configurations. In the view of this volume's authors, the physical similarities noted above are only a manifestation of underlying principles that prove fundamental to the organization of concentrated populations. These include the manipulation of perceived short-term and long-term benefits, investment in the physical realms of portable objects and space to signify social action, and the use of networks to increase information transfer.

The cognitive formulation of urban centers provides numerous occasions for contacts that enable individuals and households to engage in more complex social behavior. Although the speed of transportation and communication has changed, a city's social role, as conceived by modern analysts, fits ancient cities as well as modern ones:

> Their significance lies in their role as centres of *authority*, as places that are able to generate and disseminate discourses and collective beliefs, that are able to develop, test, and track innovations, and that offer "sociable" settings for the gathering of high-level information (economic, political, cultural) and for establishing coalitions and monitoring implicit contracts. (Knox 1995:8–9)

These "implicit contracts" crosscut the social space of the city, with the result that social relations are built across the political and class spectrum, a series of links interwoven with social distinctions. A cohesive force of these relations is the way in which information and decisions about shared long-term goals are managed. As Colombijn (1994) notes, information management among these groups is achieved through shared long-term goals. While simple commands may be expedient, they are the most politically expensive form of decision making; by contrast, "the least expensive decision is consensual, but attaining such a consensus is a long process" (Colombijn 1994:18). Where theorists such as Lefebvre, Gottdiener, and Castells concentrate on power relations that exclude the vast majority of urban inhabitants, Colombijn believes that the success or failure of a city is transcribed in the thousands of daily household-level negotiations for food, shelter, and access to land. To achieve the ultimately more cost effective consensual mode of decision making requires a significant investment of time and a shared belief that those who are invested in the system (either as individuals or through corporate groups such as households and nonkin associations) will, *in the long run,* be better off than if they had not participated.

In a city, the long-term investment in consensus is manifested at all levels of the physical environment: in the monuments designed by leaders and built by followers; in the juxtaposition and accommodation reached within neighborhoods; and within the domestic sphere in the architecture of houses, courtyards, and burial places. For both elites and nonelites, the physical environment includes not only what is fixed but also what is portable: ornaments, clothing, utensils, and other manufactured and traded items. The authors in this volume show that through archaeologically documentable aspects such as portable goods (Attarian chapter 8), space (Moore chapter 4), food preferences (Zeder chapter 7), and the production of labor-intensive products such as metals (Shen chapter 12), we can document social changes in premodern urban settings and the transformation of social groups to an urban configuration. These transformations, signaling the development of a new identity that is expressed in material terms, further suggest other types of ideological and sociological changes that we cannot document archaeologically but that we know must also have taken place in the transition to urbanism (Houston et al. chapter 9).

DEFINING THE "CITY"

The threshold at which a population center becomes truly "urban" is more difficult to determine than it might appear, even for modern cities (Adedeji and Rowland 1973; Potter 1985; Smith 1972; Trigger 1972; Zeder 1991). In the contemporary world, the threshold of "urbanism" is the basis upon which further classifications and social components are intertwined, such as the census and proposals for economic development. To those studying ancient cities, the conferral of "urban" status upon a site establishes an implicit judgment of size and importance in the landscape. For both modern and ancient cities, minimal definitions based on any single quantitative criterion (such as physical size or number of inhabitants) are bound to fail because they nearly always exclude one or more sites that appear to have an urban ethos (Weber 1958:65; R. McIntosh and S. McIntosh, this volume). Static definitions also conceal the dynamic nature of urban activities and urban formations, the sometimes explosive growth of population centers from villages to towns to cities, and the changes undergone by even well-established cities from one era to another. Urban centers are social formations manifest in a physical surrounding that is always changing, while definitions serve archaeologists best when applied to entities that are fixed or are found within relatively fixed parameters.

However, the lack of a definition is equally problematic since without one, researchers rely on their qualitative judgment about any particular site under the assumption that while we cannot define cities, we intuitively "know one when we see one." Some recent work on the origins of urbanism, in failing to define what a city is, has produced nothing more than gazetteers of sites whose comparability is weakened by a lack of formal criteria (see Shaffer 1996). Definitions based on multiple characteristics, rather than a single static criterion such as population size or areal extent, appear more likely to resolve this difficulty. Since V. G. Childe's (1950) list of 10 criteria has, implicitly or explicitly, served as the basis for evaluating premodern urbanism, it is worth revisiting this list. Regardless of the specific determinants of urbanism, it is clear that cities are the most complex form of human population aggregation, but a reexamination of Childe's urban criteria provides a threshold for discussion and a set of parameters within which comparisons can be made.

Childe (1950:3) saw cities as both a result and a symbol of an "urban revolution" that signified the "culmination of a progressive change in the economic structure and social organisation of communities that caused, or was accompanied by, a dramatic increase in the population affected." He wrestled with the awkward fact that cities appeared in both the New and Old Worlds, though with vastly different technologies and apparatus; many characteristics such as the wheel and draft animals that might have been identified as critical and integral components of Old World cities were not present among the cities of the New World. Childe saw the minimum definition of a city as "impoverished" by having to include groups such as the Maya, yet this dilemma prompted the acknowledgment that social, rather than physical, infrastructure is the key to identifying the city (Adams 1966). Childe's 10 criteria are all thus rather elastic and stress *relative* degrees of population density, economic specialization, taxation/tribute to a central authority, monumental buildings "to symbolize the concentration of the social surplus," social stratification, and record-keeping. In sum, Childe did not provide an analytic framework, but a descriptive one serving as an index to identifying the components of the most complex form of aggregated populations. His criteria are not fundamentally different from those used to describe cities today, as Robert Potter has observed (1985:30).

Within this descriptive framework, all of the components are interrelated; however, some components, such as the economy, provide a highly accessible way to identify and monitor the scale of these relationships. In a city, individuals and households become interdependent in an economy that is complex, integrated, and large in scale (Zeder 1991:19–21). Population centers the size of cities are beyond the capacity of the household to efficiently manage a number of tasks simultaneously; they *must* specialize in order to take advantage of economies of scale in production as well as to obtain a larger variety of goods and services. At the household level, this usually means that its members specialize in certain social, civic, and economic tasks. As Zeder (chapter 7) further observes, the specialization of the urban economy occurs at different rates and applies to different types of goods. The factors that affect the development vary with the commodity being produced: sometimes changes in political structure affect the organization of production, as Shen (chapter 12) shows for the production of metal goods in the Zhou-period cities of China; sometimes changes were made because of the physical nature of the commodity, as Zeder discusses with reference to the different fodder and pasture needs of cattle, sheep, goats, and pigs.

Another way to define the city is in oppositional terms, making use of apparent disbalances between an urban zone and its hinterland. When cities bring people together into a locus of dense habitation and specialized economy, the surrounding countryside also experiences a restructuring, as seen in examples from cities of both the premodern (Yoffee 1995) and modern periods (de Oliveira and Roberts 1996). City fashions and the demand for certain types of products, including foodstuffs and building material, as well as a demand for labor, have an effect upon economic and social configurations in the surrounding countryside. This dependence is not unidirectional, since city fashions are also emulated by those in the hinterlands who desire to signal their urban ties through material goods and architectural styles (see Yaeger chapter 6). These goods and styles may consist of a variety of previously existing elements in the surrounding area, which city-dwellers transform to new patterns and structures.

Anthropological understanding of the close association of human actions and material goods lets us evaluate archaeological sites in places where social changes are visible in artifacts. At the early modern West African city of Elmina in Ghana, urban residents distinguished themselves both from interior peoples and from foreigners, often using goods that came from those outside sources (DeCorse 2001). In Elmina, the traditional practice of graves under houses was retained, but the burials began to include European ceramics. Architectural forms in the city underwent change as local African inhabitants learned European building techniques in stone. Foodways remained largely unchanged in terms of preferred forms of comestibles such as stews, but food began to be served in imported bowls with new types of decoration. Christopher Attarian's discussion in this volume (chapter 8) examines the process of urbanization in pre-Columbian Peru, making use of the concept of ethnogenesis as the manner by which an urban population marks a distinction from both hinterlands and surrounding traders. Similarly, Jason Yaeger (chapter 6) examines the way in which rural households emulated urban models in architecture and portable objects of domestic use and ornamentation among the ancient Maya.

In sum, the definition of cities in both the modern and premodern world is subject to a variety of criteria whose applicability depends on the particular questions asked of the data set. Quantified indices such as population size, density, or areal extent provide what may appear to be useful measures, but these data are difficult to unambiguously obtain for ancient cities. The difficulties of establishing a simple numerical threshold for "urban" status even in the modern world is likewise an indicator that qualitative criteria must also be utilized; these include the perceptible difference between urban and hinterland activities.

THE ORIGIN OF CITIES

A quest to identify an exact catalyst for city formation poses not only an intractable problem of "firsts" but also obscures a more interesting question of sustainability. Much of the scholarly tradition of looking for the "first" city is linked to the study of the ancient Near East as the distant ancestor of European culture. Sites such as Jericho and Çatal Höyük have been the focus of such investigations (see Emberling chapter 10). This search for firsts presupposes clear criteria for defining a city, with the implicit establishment of a checklist and then the application of that checklist to the archaeological site in question. In this way, the question of how to define a city and how to determine its origins are intimately linked. But just as single-criterion definitions are inadequate, so too are monocausal explanations of origins. No single factor of opportunity or compulsion appears to explain voluntary relocation to urban areas, and a variety of "push" as well as "pull" factors seem to affect the pace of relocation: the development of employment economies of scale in the city, drought or flooding in the countryside, warfare and civil unrest, the opportunity to use the city as a base of transit to other regions, and cultural shifts resulting in selective disenfranchisement from rural family or land ties. All of these factors may be present in the initial development of a city, although the specific historical circumstances of a given locale may be a combination of political, demographic, social, and environmental circumstances that may not be exactly replicated elsewhere. Cities, as the focal point of concentrated populations seeking improved opportunities for communication, social ties, and economic gain, appear instead to be generated by a combination of uncertainty mingled with opportunity, what Herzog (1997:13) has called the "constellation of circumstances" that bring a city into being.

The relationship between urban form and political authority is also complex, since cities can be found within a variety of political parameters: as entities comprising urban functions in an otherwise politically underorganized landscape, as units that integrate with the countryside to form a small state, and as a primate city or as one among many cities within the expansive territory of a single state. The presence of cities can serve political agents as the nodes in a cost-effective linked chain of hierarchies, but it is important to recognize that cities do not require a state level of political authority to exist and thrive. This assessment marks a sharp digression from earlier theories of ancient urbanism, which generally assumed that cities and states occur simultaneously (e.g., Adams 1966, 1972; Storey 1992:28; Trigger 1972:592; Zeder 1991). The duality became structured into a causal relationship, with some theorists declaring that "cities are found only in societies that are organized as states" (Fox 1977:24). We can trace this conflated nature of cities and state-level political organizations back to Childe (1950) as well. He used the now-disfavored term "civilization" to denote a condition in which states were marked by cities. Childe's observations were quickly applied in reverse since it was also assumed that cities were marked by states. As a result, subsequent theorizing about urbanism has often really been about states rather than cities, as noted perhaps most succinctly by Robert McC. Adams in his volume *The Evolution of Urban Society* (1966:90), wherein he proclaims that his "central concern is the growth of the state."

Another reason for the conflation of cities and states is that the terms "urban," "urbanism," and "urbanization" are often used interchangeably. These terms are distinct in meaning, as noted by Fox (1977:14–15; 39–41), who proposed that "urbanism" refers to the form of the city and that urbanization is the process in which people move from rural areas to cities. Another way to preserve the significant nuances of these terms is to clearly articulate the aspects implied by their use. We should reserve the term "urban" for the characteristics of a city in its geographic and territorial locale; it is a reflexive term, used primarily to distinguish a population locus at a particular point in its historical trajectory and/or in relation to a nonurban hinterland. "Urbanism," by extension, is the general phenomenon of cities in their political, social, and economic aspects, again with reference to cities as assessed by those living in and around them. By contrast, "urbanization" refers to a whole territorial expanse becoming linked with an center-dominated ethos: a territorial expanse such as a state that is marked by the presence and effects of urban locales. Only the phenomenon of "urbanization" implies a territorial expanse; once again, these semantic differences illustrate why cities and states can, and should, be conceptualized as distinct entities, complex phenomena that often—but not always—occur together.

These distinctions may help to clarify the definition of "states" as well. Though it remains a complex issue, some theorists have proposed that political, ritual, and economic activities be used as defining criteria, rather than the presence or role of cities (e.g., Marcus and Feinman 1998:4–7; Possehl 1998:264–268, 275–276). Nor are they convinced that cities require states for their existence (Possehl 1998:286–287). If anthropologists are willing to forgo the idea that cities are a critical component of ancient states, then it is also time for the understanding of cities to be uncoupled from the necessary presence of states. By breaking this pairing of cities and states, we allow cities to be understood on their own terms as centers of political, economic, and social organization that may be considerably more complex than the territories and regions in which they are located.

Three types of city configurations help us to further unpack the relationship between cities and states: ports, cities in place before states, and cities between periods of large-scale state-level territorial integration. These cases illustrate that cities as centers of concentrated human activity can be acted upon by political leaders seeking to pull together numerous population centers into a territorial expression of authority, but that the city form is developed first.

Ports constitute an urban type in which the impact of hinterland political structures is tangential to the success of the city form, since ports can survive and thrive in a political configuration no more complex than that of a tribe (e.g., Connah 1987; Sedov 1996). Ports are located where environmental zones meet (water and land, or desert and forest) to form a nexus of economic and social interaction that can be described as a "complex interplay of physical, geographical and socio economic phenomena" (Ray 1996:2). Ports present a flexible political environment in which contacts are managed by disparate groups for commercial gain; these commercial activities are also often intertwined with the social and religious activities of persons passing through ports to sites elsewhere. The presence of a rigid state ideology and practice may actually be detrimental to the health of a port, as Boone and Redman (1982) observe in their study of cities in medieval North Africa. Although these specialized cities may have leaders whose actions have an impact on infrastructure and overall urban design, the observation that a port functions as a nexus of communication and transfer means that a high proportion of actions are undertaken by disparate groups without a central leader either in the city itself or in the surrounding territory.

Another way to explain the distinction between urban centers and urbanized states is to consider the historical trajectory of cities within states. Archaeologists frequently examine cities when the urban form is already well established and contains a literary or iconographic tradition highlighting the role of rulers. As a result, it is difficult to ascertain political actions at the inception of the city form, when leadership roles may have been multiple and overlapping, and when overt signs of leadership may not be apparent except as they are manifested in communal activities. The development of corporate or group-level interaction may well precede the development of individualizing leadership, as Blanton and his colleagues (1996) note in their discussion of corporate and network styles of group dynamics in Mesoamerica. While they caution that the two categories describe cyclical processes and not an evolutionary progression, many archaeologically derived examples of social complexity show that individualizing leadership develops only after a period of group-based interaction (e.g., Renfrew 1974; Trubitt 2000). Cities may provide a similar background of communal activity against which individual leaders exercise their authority. At the pre-Columbian site of Tikal in present-day Guatemala, differences in elites (including better relative health and longevity, as well as distinctly elaborate tombs) make it possible to separate upper- and lower-class individuals only by the last hundred years B.C., which is several centuries *after* the first large-scale public architecture (a solar observatory) was constructed (Haviland and Moholy-Nagy 1992:57).

As Elizabeth Stone (1995) observes, the exact causes for the origins of Mesopotamian cities is uncertain, and temples preceded palaces as a focus of urban activity by as much as half a millennium. These early temples functioned like large households and held land worked by sharecroppers; they also provided rations in return for work by otherwise disenfranchised individuals such as widows and orphans (Robertson 1995). In the Classical world, the large states of the Hellenistic and Roman periods incorporated cities that had previously been politically independent (Weber 1958:99). On the Indian subcontinent, large fortified cities appear in the archaeological record of the Ganges Valley several centuries before the historical or archaeological documentation of state-level political structure, which suggests that these cities were the largest consistent unit of territorial integration (Smith chapter 11). Roderick McIntosh and Susan McIntosh (chapter 5) propose that in West Africa, the state was never forthcoming; in the Niger Delta, the configuration of environment and social structure may even have combined to produce cities in which power relations were consciously negotiated *away* from territorial integration.

Nonstate configurations are also evident in cities that continue to be occupied and to thrive during conditions of state collapse and disintegration. Modern examples of such cities abound: Lagos, Khartoum, Bogotá, Phnom Penh, Kinshasa. Examples from the ancient world include the cities (or city-states; see Baines and Yoffee 1998) of Mesopotamia as loci of habitation that were often incorporated into larger units. Throughout any individual city's centuries of occupation, alliances were created with a variety of other units in a larger territory; "the epigraphic literature of Early Dynastic Mesopotamia provides dozens of examples of rulers who temporarily united two, three or even more small polities into a larger unit" (Marcus 1998:86; see also Stone 1997). Similarly, Mesoamerica was the scene of repeated coalitions of smaller political units into larger territorial entities (Feinman and Nicholas 1991:244; see also Hodge 1994; Webster 1997). As Hodge (1994:61) observes for the Valley of Mexico, the Triple Alliance's use of preexisting centers "provided the benefits of hierarchy without the cost of creating and maintaining many levels of administrators and administrative centers." But cities in the ancient world could still survive when large-scale political systems dissolved, as illustrated in southern France at the end of the Roman period (Heath 1999). These transformations did not mean the demise of population centers; instead, the notion of a city as a locus of shared identity and obligation became the preferred metaphor for bishops as they built the organization of the Christian churches on a Roman bureaucratic model.

As these examples indicate, cities in the premodern world did not require a state level of political organization, only an initial impetus for settlement, some level of highly visible labor investment, and a sustainable social network afterward. The social development of cities does not, however, mean that leaders were absent from the process of urban organization; rather, city leadership was composed of complex configurations of power relations between political and religious entities as well as other groups such as neighborhood groups and voluntary associations that also used the city form to establish authority and compete for symbolic leadership through the administration of territory.

What about city-states? This configuration could be argued to be the most pronounced coupling of political and urban systems. But are they cities first, or states first? In a recent volume, Charleton and Nichols (1997:5) have observed that they find city-states to be "one of two or three major forms of early states" (an assessment also made in Hansen 2000). These researchers tend to emphasize the "state" portion of the term, highlighting the analytic value of a political unit that consists of a small, politically independent state with a capital city as distinct from the types of states with extensive territory and numerous population centers (for an alternate view that doubts the utility of the city-state concept, see Marcus and Feinman 1998:8–10). By these parameters, the city-state may be a subset of the types of states, but the workings of the urban center should be considered similar.

URBAN TRANSFORMATIONS

Regardless of the subsequent political entities that might capture cities within state-level hierarchies, the city form represents the physical manifestation of social transformations. The city form can be distinguished from other types of concentrated populations by transformations in leadership, in spatial organization, and in economic organization. These fundamental transformations can be assessed through the archaeological remains of ancient cities.

Leadership

Urban life is certainly facilitated by centrally sponsored inputs such as markets, roads, and sanitation. Yet these are not essential to the functioning of a city. In many Third World cities today, people come together and subdivide land in sprawling shanty towns in which no services are centrally provided (Myers 1996). In some cities, urban growth is regulated by market forces, rather than by central planning agencies, which may be weakened by corruption, ineffective management, confusion caused by multiple overlapping agencies, or a lack of funds (e.g., El-Bushra 1989; Khalat and Kongstad 1973). A city may also consist of distinct parts that do not necessarily harmonize and whose configurations and activities are not dictated by any form of leadership, as Emberling observes (chapter 10).

Leadership can develop in a variety of ways. At the inception of cities, priests and other ritual specialists may provide a supernatural setting and sense of purpose to the urban social and physical landscape. These ideologically based mediations are the most difficult to trace in the archaeological record; yet, as Cowgill (chapter 2) suggests for Teotihuacan and Houston and others (chapter 9) document for Piedras Negras, they probably played a strong role in establishing and maintaining the ideology of the city (see also Adams 1966:121). Political leaders are likely to associate themselves with religious activities and architecture, and the link between religious and political authority is often subsequently taken over by political leaders (see Moore chapter 4). These activities serve to distinguish between different groups of elites clamoring for respect; at the same time, this competition enables nonelites to form alliances within networks to achieve communally what would otherwise be difficult to achieve at a smaller scale.

In the urban context, individuals and households can increase their network of contacts through a variety of groups whose organizing principle is based on self-selection of members acting on shared criteria such as religion, occupation, or ethnicity. Such associations allow a restructuring or re-creation of power relations within a city, whether created as a guild, cooperative, neighborhood association, religious group, or other voluntary society. The opportunity for nonelites to participate in alternative sources of authority-making structures draws a large number of people into these groups, whether they seek to be selected for office or merely seek "the authority that derives from the ability to define" who their associates will be (Coutin 1994:297; Walker-Ramisch 1996). Once formed, an association can wield more influence than individual members, allowing it to act on behalf of members who seek to maintain or expand their ability to appropriate resources (Colombijn 1994:16).

Group investments in authority have an impact on the physical layout of the city as well as on members' social identity and economic success. Attracted by city life, numerous individuals may participate in the construction of city monuments, amenities, and other types of sponsored projects. Examples can be drawn from the Roman world, in which building programs were commemorated through inscriptions. As Di Segni's (1995) study of monuments in Byzantine cities shows, an individual's civil status could affect the way that donations were credited in a building's inscriptions. Municipal officials would record their occupational status if they were donating to civil buildings, but not if they were donating to religious buildings such as churches where they presented themselves as private citizens. In other cases, the profession of the person was mentioned (such as lawyer or doctor) even when the construction project did not involve them in their professional capacity but merely as a donor (Di Segni 1995). This illustrates that people in cities could compartmentalize their civic activities: as members of a professional group, as private individuals, as appointed or elected officials, and as members of a particular religious affiliation. While the recognition achieved in one sphere undoubtedly influenced the individual's standing in other spheres, there were multiple groups into which those with elite ambitions could place themselves.

For those without ambitions of improving their social status, the city still represented gains. There were opportunities for different kinds of jobs, better employment, or the possibility of escaping penury or family troubles in the countryside. Those in the low-paying jobs of the city also risked the most in that if they failed there might not be lands to fall back upon, but the diversity of employment and economic niches provided more choices than the distant hinterlands. Those who had the fewest economic options of all could also find a place in the city as beggars, thieves, and prostitutes, all occupations more easily practiced in areas of concentrated populations. Thus, while the aggregate of network connections and the perception of long-term gains built a momentum for continuity in city life, short-term gains were also anticipated by those moving into the urban zone.

The ability to address short-term needs as well as collectively manage long-term investments is another reason why associations become valued as the individual and household strive to function in the urban setting. On the immediate level, associations can provide information about basic services, assist newcomers with employment, and assuage feelings of disorientation and loneliness. On the cognitive level, these associations may serve as repositories of collective memory. As Cox et al. (1999:370) have recently observed, memory is an important aspect of the evolution of cooperative behavior; in their simulations, they note that "a simple memory for past encounters is sufficient to allow stable cooperation to evolve even when the number (or frequency) of interactions is relatively low." In urban zones characterized by frequent relocation and migration (e.g., as individuals go back and forth to the hinterlands), associations and groups can serve as a repository of members' memories for the benefit of any individual who requires such information.

The benefit of greater information flow works to the mutual advantage of different social classes, including those balanced within hierarchical relations. For example, from the point of view of an employer, dealing with well-established groups is more efficient than dealing with individuals seeking work. As observed in a variety of modern social settings, hiring institutions actively seek the presence of habitual or regular contracts with groups (even if individual workers change). This phenomenon is associated with large institutions and habitual work contracts that are perceived as efficient *because of* their consistent social content (Granovetter 1985). The urban-based need for consistent work forces may well mirror similar preexisting work relationships in the countryside. For example, the desired consistency of social interaction can be seen in work parties among the agricultural Kofyar people of Nigeria, in which laborers who are neighbors are preferred to unknown hired hands (Netting 1993:72–80). The Kofyar present a particularly interesting case because they occupy regions of high-quality land at densities up to 200 per square kilometer. Although population is unevenly distributed between these highly productive rural areas, factors of reliability are still more important in arranging work contracts than the mere presence of able-bodied workers. In growing cities as well, the need for an adequate work force is critical (for support services as well as for manufacturing activities), but hiring institutions and workers both seek to maneuver the terms of work to their advantage.

Space

Space within cities ranges from private to public in design and use and is configured by inhabitants at numerous levels (Carr et al. 1992; Colombijn 1994). Public, social space is shaped in a variety of ways, often connected with the symbolic manipulation of access by crowds of people. This space may be constrained through the use of partitions and inner courtyards that direct the flow of traffic within and between buildings, as shown by Keith (chapter 3) and Moore (chapter 4). Space can be constrained vertically as well as horizontally, as Yaeger (chapter 6) shows in his discussion of the diminishing platform sizes of pyramids set in central urban courtyards. While this suggests that the configurations of public space are largely guided by elites, the response to the provision of public space can be manipulated and altered by residents if they fail to use the space for its intended purpose, for example, by shunning elaborately planned plazas and marketplaces, or by converting wasteland into informal gathering places (e.g., Colombijn 1994; Streicker 1997).

Similarly, private and semipublic space in a city is shaped by regular social and economic transactions. Patterns of communication and interaction as measured in material culture can be discerned through a variety of activities that produce archaeological data sets: investigation of production sites to determine the scale and distribution of manufacturing, excavations of waste deposits to see what is discarded and at what periodicity, and examination of households to determine patterns of lived material culture. The advantage of using households as an archaeological unit of investigation is that a whole physical household is more likely to be excavated in detail than an entire neighborhood; households are also tied to the economic life of the city, and their transformations can signal the city's general economic health (Smith 1987). These economic changes are matched by household adjustments, including the reconfiguration of space. An example is provided by the modern city of Cairo, where rural-style kitchens are redesigned to conform to the restricted space of urban dwellings, and semipublic open space such as rooftops and courtyards are eventually covered over and converted to private use (Abu-Lughod 1969; El-Shakhs 1979).

A similar process can be seen in archaeologically documented cities. The early medieval city of Koumbi Saleh (Mauretania) shows signs of the development of domestic architectural forms and decorations that replicate a well-defined urban model from one dwelling to the next (Berthier 1997:45). This includes the continued subdivision of rooms into smaller and smaller spaces and the covering of courtyards, as though the domestic spaces of the city were being reconfigured to accommodate increasing numbers of inhabitants and different types of tasks, with the result that quarters became more cramped even as the city was prospering. This may have been the result of immigrants crowding into smaller living quarters to take advantage of the city's opportunities. A similar process can be seen in the Old Babylonian period, where texts show the buying and selling of houses and rooms as new individuals come into the city (Yoffee 1988). Thus, what is deduced by archaeologists as a decline in urban inhabitants' absolute standard of wealth may simply be the result of urban wealth being enjoyed by a larger proportion of the population. A city perceived as being attractive to migrants can produce the paradox of a lowered collective standard of living, a fact that does not seem to deter continued migration, as Storey (1992) observed for the ancient city of Teotihuacan.

In both modern and premodern cities, collections of houses become forged into neighborhoods, a distinctly urban type of social group in which proximity and geography become the defining characteristics of membership (Hallman 1984; Henig 1982). Through regular interactions, the neighborhood also becomes an economic community (Khalat and Kongstad 1973). While formal rules of access may not apply (as they do in ceremonial spaces, for example), neighborhoods and districts serve to circumscribe inhabitants by a shifting conceptual geography. The neighborhood becomes a political and social community, a "cell within a larger settlement" that provides a frame of reference for the individual and a venue for the exchange of skills, emergency assistance, and mutual protection (Hallman 1984:11). The neighborhood can also take action as a group, and its ability to serve as a collective nexus for action is visible in both ancient and modern urban zones. Textual records of Old Babylonian cities, for example, show the workings of neighborhood associations *(babtum)* as a level at which contacts were mediated between the household and the city bureaucracy (Keith, chapter 3).

These neighborhoods may mirror the space of preexisting village links as well as providing cognitive groupings of a similar size. In Mesopotamian cities such as Eshnunna and Mashkan-shapir, grids of major thoroughfares divide the urban zone into blocks about 1 hectare in size, and it "may not be coincidental that one hectare is both the average size of small Mesopotamian village sites and the size of residential neighborhoods—the face-to-face communities that served as the building blocks of those preindustrial cities outside Mesopotamia which have been studied" (Stone 1995:240). Other neighborhood-level configurations can be seen in the "ethnic neighborhoods" of Teotihuacan (Cowgill 1992) and the development of newcomers' settlements in Chinese cities of the late first millennium B.C. (Shen 1994).

The connection between urban neighborhoods and kinship ties is strong, since neighborhoods at least initially tend to be comprised of persons sharing kinship or extended-kinship ties retained from rural settlements (see, e.g., Abu-Lughod 1969; Khalat and Kongstad 1973; Lewis 1952; Perlman 1976). As with neighborhoods, kinship relations present the individual with a group in which information can be obtained and through which actions can be successfully undertaken. The same family functions are apparent in archaeologically documented sites of the historic period: in the Early Dynastic period in Mesopotamia, lineage groupings continued to be strong even within cities, since they corporately held title to agricultural lands and played a role in organizing corvée labor and craft production (Adams 1966, 1972:743).

Within the space of the household and neighborhood, activities are signaled materially through the consumption of portable goods and shared space (Gottdiener 1995; Miller 1987). Differential consumption activities signaling individual and household participation in community activities are seen in the smallest social groups and hardly require an urban setting, but an examination of consumption activities in cities suggests a dramatically increased consumption of material goods (Fine and Leopold 1993; Gottdiener 1995; Knox 1995; Miles and Paddison 1998). While increased numbers of possessions may be a marker of hoarding or of political instability (cf. Hamilton and Lai 1989), they are more often the means by which participation in diverse activities can be signaled (Smith 1999).

Increased consumption in cities is linked to the greater impetus for individuals and the household to communicate their participation in neighborhood and voluntary associations, as well as their status achieved through economic activity, political organizations, and religious affiliations. Urban markets and the potential for increased disposable income provide city dwellers with additional opportunities for consumption, not only directly but by proxy when their income is transferred to rurally based relatives (El-Bushra 1989). The increased proportion of per capita consumption of durable goods is clearly visible in ancient cities, where occupations are marked by immense quantities of debris, including new types of goods added to the repertoire of items that are seen in hinterland settlements. This observation of increased urban consumption in premodern cities counters the confident statements by modern sociologists that a high level of urban consumption is a product of post-Fordist, late-twentieth-century society (e.g., McCracken 1988; Miles and Paddison 1998).

Economic Interactions

A high level of economic interdependence between a variety of economic and social groups is evident in the city. At its most basic level, this includes the mutual exploitation of haves and have-nots. "Haves" rely on a competitive, often underpaid, labor pool for the labor-intensive inputs that make upper-class life distinct; the "have-nots" jockey for patronage, handouts, and favors in an atmosphere where prestige is awarded to those with the largest circle of dependents. Exchange relations between these groups may consist of exchanging goods for prestige or patronage rather than strict goods-for-goods trade (see Clark and Blake 1994 on prestige relations). Charity as a civic concern, whether in modern San Francisco or Victorian London, can be a marker of urban identity; this is seen in premodern cases as well, for example, in the provision of grain for the poor in Rome (Garnsey 1983).

More complex relationships of dependency can also evolve, as when rural inhabitants and urban-based merchants buy and sell agricultural produce to each other in transactions that depend on mutual exploitation of cycles of debt (Harris 1989). Dependency relations in antiquity could take place on a very local scale, especially when elites and nonelites lived in close proximity in the same neighborhood (see Stone 1995). In the cities of the Khabur plain, for example, elites and nonelites did not have access to the same quality of meat resources, as assessed through archaeologically recovered faunal remains (Zeder chapter 7). But elites and nonelites did rely on each other in their economic networks, since the commerce of animals probably took place within the city itself where poorer residents raised animals that were afterward consumed by elites. As Zeder shows, even the basic demands of subsistence can take on a socially charged aspect within the concentrated population of the city.

Mutual dependence may be an expedient strategy for both short-term and long-term gain, but the proliferation of resource managers and perceptions of disadvantage can also provoke discord between social groups in the close quarters of the city. While the concept of "resistance" is a very Western and postcolonial one relating to the tremendous imbalances in center-directed resources that can be used against underprivileged groups, it is important to recognize that in premodern times, force may have been mustered against city-dwellers by factions competing for authority and resources. Examples of intraurban factionalism can be documented in the cities of the Roman world, where voluntary associations such as trade guilds sometimes came into conflict with local governments. In Ephesus in the second century A.D., the state responded to a bakers' strike with an edict regulating the future conduct of the organization (Remus 1996:148). Actions such as this, and the requirement that voluntary associations (even burial societies and other mutual-aid groups) seek imperial permission for existence, point to the state's interest in controlling potential sources of conflict within cities (Remus 1996; Walker-Ramisch 1996).

Chen Shen (chapter 12) also discusses the potential for conflict between political authorities and economic agents such as merchants and producers, in which proprietary interests over technology and marketing may have been a flashpoint for violence. The presence of a mass grave at Yan-Xiadu, he notes, may have resulted from conflicts between rulers and ruled over economic rights within the city walls. Even in the modern world, groups assembled for one purpose can be used as a block against a central authority when the groups evolve to confront new issues and social developments (Coutin 1994). In the close quarters of the city, the disenfranchised can resort to violence to achieve their ends, although it is more straightforward for them to "vote with their feet" and simply leave. This appears to have been the strategy when populations did not have particular incentives to stay beyond the demands of the elite, or when incentives of food provisioning and services no longer outweighed the disadvantages of staying.

ARCHAEOLOGICAL EXAMINATIONS OF
SOCIAL IDENTITY AND CITY FORMATION

The transformations of leadership, space, and economic activity are all interdependent in the urban environment, where the close proximity of individuals and groups means that changes are effected at a number of levels simultaneously. In view of the complexities of these actions, an elite-dominated explanatory model for urban organization and growth is inadequate: elite actions and decisions can affect, but not fundamentally *cause,* urban transformations without the active participation of the majority of city-dwellers. Furthermore, transformations in leadership, space, and economic activity have material correlates. As such, they are visible in the archaeological record of premodern cities, as well as in the physical realm of modern cities.

A word about the characteristics of archaeological data sets may have a sobering yet insightful effect at this juncture. As the largest type of archaeological site, cities are marked by an abundance of archaeological remains, but usually on such a large scale that traditional methods of investigation such as excavation can expose only a tiny proportion of an ancient site. Artifacts can be assessed for production, distribution, and use, while architecture on both the domestic and monumental scale makes it possible to calculate labor time requirements and spatial configurations. Faunal, skeletal, and botanical studies tell us about the transformation of the biological realm in cities, enabling us to evaluate everything from human health to local environmental conditions.

But the ability to assess all the types of archaeological remains found in excavations—from fish bones and cooking pots to temples, palaces, and broad avenues—gives us what may be a misleading precision of information, since large portions of ancient sites will always remain out of reach of excavators' time and budgets. An alternative method of investigating ancient sites is to conduct a surface survey, by tallying and mapping the remains found on the surface of the site. Though comprehensive in terms of spatial coverage, this technique limits an investigator to what may be highly variable data sets affected by the vagaries of postoccupational processes ranging from vegetation to modern habitation and bulldozing. In sum, as archaeologists dealing with the material remains of cities, we must be aware that we are evaluating a highly complex human phenomenon with a less-than-comprehensive data set—a point made by many authors in this volume. Although our theories are therefore more robust than our data sets, by framing our questions in terms of the social interactions that produce the material patterns that we see, we are able to provide insights into the reasons and mechanisms by which concentrated populations thrive.

Each chapter in this volume examines a different aspect of social configurations in ancient cities: neighborhoods and daily household provisioning, mundane as well as monumental architecture, communal and private space, markets and manufacturing areas. Starting at the most local scale of social interaction, the authors look at the architectural forms and social dynamics that comprise neighborhoods and residential quarters. Leading off, George Cowgill explains the sacred underpinnings of the urban form at the pre-Columbian urban site of Teotihuacan in central Mexico, and the way in which ritually ordained configurations were integral to the city's organization; urban dwellers' basic needs were also affected by ritual as necessary elements such as water became sanctified. As this discussion clearly illustrates, ritual knowledge and expectations were integrated into daily life and actions at Teotihuacan, and the city became a locus for activities that were simultaneously economic and religious in character.

Kathryn Keith (chapter 3) examines socially integrative mechanisms but from the perspective of individual households and neighborhoods in Mesopotamia, where documentary sources and household-level excavations provide data about the way in which domestic groups were linked with one another and with their kin in the countryside. In physical terms, these groupings included not just physical households but also neighborhoods, in which craft workshops, bakeries, and shops were located. In social terms, neighborhoods were the place where people of different statuses interacted, and where some decision-making and dispute-settling authority was exercised.

In chapter 4, Jerry Moore considers a similar relationship between ideology and the lived spaces of the city for the Chimú culture on the north coast of Peru, where the relationships of the rulers and the ruled are evident in architectural configurations within the urban zone. Walled compounds can be interpreted as a symbolic statement of social order and a physical manifestation of rules for interaction. These rules for interaction in Chimú culture, which Moore compares with later Inka principles of organization, provided both a mechanism for the separation and management of urban populations and a shared ideology in which walled compounds were the physical containers for both royal and commoner households.

Chapter 5 by Susan McIntosh and Roderick McIntosh further explores urban dynamics from a perspective of power relations. In contrast to many studies of power that find elites maintaining and dominating their environments, they present a radically different picture based on data drawn from West Africa. The cities in this case are not only without states, but also have no visible form of hierarchy as demonstrated through traditionally understood archaeological markers such as monumental architecture. These authors illustrate the potential richness of urbanism away from the biases of Western-based comparanda for archaeological remains and bring to mind other regions of the world, such as the Indus Valley, where cities exist without the evidence of specifically elite-based social configurations.

The relationship between the city and its hinterland and between urban-dwellers and the surrounding community is the subject of chapter 6, by Jason Yaeger. The focal point here is the Maya city of Xunantunich, which served as a source of prestige, stylistic motifs, and physical goods found in the surrounding communities. Far from being a unidirectional radiation of an urban ethos to a passive but receptive countryside, Yaeger argues, the city requires the continued input of the hinterland population to create and maintain an urban identity, and hinterland residents actively sought to translate their adoption of an urban ethos into their rural social relations.

In chapter 7, Melinda Zeder provides a different perspective on urban and urban-hinterland economic interactions, using data from the Khabur region in Syria. Economic change, she argues, is due not only to social changes, but also to the nature of the "raw materials" and technological requirements of production intensification (in this case, the different management strategies used in the raising of cattle, sheep, goats, and pigs). Herds and flocks were managed by pastoralists whose activities were instrumental in making cities a locus for specialized production and exchange. Within cities, both wealthy and poorer residential districts show differential distributions of other kinds of production strategies, including the small-scale raising of animals such as pigs, which indicate that elites and nonelites probably had complex relationships of subsistence dependency.

In chapter 8, Christopher Attarian asks how an urban ethos is formed, and how its progression can be evaluated through archaeologically recoverable material remains. Using survey data from the Peruvian site of Mocollope and the concept of ethnogenesis, he demonstrates how a city provides a new environment and a new identity for residents who move in from the surrounding countryside. As indicated by a comparison of sites in the Chicama Valley before and during the process of urban growth, numerous fortified settlements were abandoned in favor of urban residence. Once in the city, as is evident from stylistic changes in material culture such as pottery, these urban communities participated in new economic and social networks that supplanted their previous rural ties.

The next chapters examine how such interactions between groups occur, focusing on the city as a nexus for communication and as the repository of a shared urban ethos defined and maintained by its residents. As Stephen Houston and his colleagues note in chapter 9, the Maya site of Piedras Negras provides abundant textual and archaeological evidence of rulers' investments in architecture and ceremony at a dynastic center. This urban center was a mosaic of economic, ritual, and social opportunities unavailable elsewhere; moreover, both rulers and residents defined the city as a "moral" community with collective values. With the city's rapid growth and subsequent precipitous decline, goals shared by rulers and ruled were expressed in actions including migration and the establishment of new cities.

Using recent research at the fourth-millennium site of Tell Brak, Geoff Emberling (chapter 10) also focuses on the establishment of cities and social actions that crosscut and thus transcend the apparent dichotomy of elite/nonelites. Although (like many cities examined in this volume) Brak is in a relatively marginal zone for agriculture, its location at an intersection of ecological zones facilitated exchange. The substantial and early investment in temples, however, suggests that city life also encompassed significant ritual activity. Such activity was undertaken at a household level as well as at centralized locations, as shown by archaeological recovery of eye amulets in domestic contexts and at the Eye Temple, where thousands of such amulets have been found.

In chapter 11, I turn to the formation of cities in a politically fragmented environment, as seen in data from excavations and surveys of Early Historic sites on the Indian subcontinent. Walled cities of the early centuries B.C./A.D. show a significant investment of labor in a context where both leaders and followers gained protection and a symbolic demarcation of the urban zone. Cities achieved success in this era of political uncertainty and population growth principally by maintaining consensus in these concentrated loci of population. I propose that cities are fostered and thrive because of the social and economic networks created and maintained by households and groups.

The final case study further explores this relationship and the wide range of social interactions encompassed by economic interaction. Chapter 12, by Chen Shen, focuses on the royal city of Yan-Xiadu in eastern China, which was initially created as an administrative site and then transformed into a complex urban community through a variety of production and consumption activities. Markets were the locus of interaction between elites and nonelites, in which lower-status individuals were not only the suppliers of goods but also the purchasers of a wide variety of goods, including labor-intensive ornaments. Over time, the relationship between central authorities and market-based activity underwent various changes, ranging from facilitation to restriction of certain manufacturing processes and finished goods.

CONCLUSION

From the point of view of the individual and household, there are considerable similarities between modern and ancient cities. Composed of concentrated populations, diverse economies, and specialized social and ritual events, cities are a dynamic and evolving fixture in any cultural landscape. Individuals migrating into cities selectively retain their social, ethnic, and economic identities; upon entering the city, they also can choose from a greater variety of crosscutting groups in which to belong. The transformations to urban life effected in the spheres of both public and private space result in particular configurations of households and neighborhoods, as well as markets, shrines, and rulers' compounds. Changes in the built environment reinforce the diversification of social roles, so that individuals use space as both the mirror and arbiter of action.

As the authors in this volume show, archaeological evidence and historical data let us evaluate social organization in the spaces of the ancient city, from the level of the household to the most public of arenas. The study of spatial organization and artifacts provides a way to assess the city-dweller's multiple roles in the household, the neighborhood, and the wider realm of the city. Choices in material culture are framed by a variety of economic, social, and technological parameters and signal the changing activities, identities, and social alliances that occur in the urban realm. Cities are thus fully social constructions, manifested in tangible remains.

ACKNOWLEDGMENTS

Many thanks are due to the volume participants for their stimulating contributions and ongoing discussions about the nature of urbanism and the means by which we can understand archaeologically known cities. Special appreciation is extended to Robert McC. Adams and Richard Leventhal for their comments on the collection of papers. I would also like to thank Elizabeth Brumfiel, George Cowgill, Steve Houston, and Susan McIntosh for their careful reading and comments on this chapter.

REFERENCES

Abu-Lughod, J.

    1969   Migrant Adjustment to City Life: The Egyptian Case. In *The City in Newly Developing Countries,* edited by G. Breese, pp. 376–388. Prentice Hall, Englewood Cliffs, N.J.

Adams, R. McC.

    1966   *The Evolution of Urban Society: Urban Mesopotamia and Prehispanic Mexico.* Aldine, Chicago.

    1972   Patterns of Urbanization in Early Southern Mesopotamia. In *Man, Settlement and Urbanism,* edited by P. J. Ucko, R. Tringham, and G. W. Dimbleby, pp. 735–749.

Adedeji, A., and L. Rowland (editors)

    1973   *Management Problems of Rapid Urbanization in Nigeria.* University of Ife Press, Ile Ife.

Andersson, Jens A.

    2001   Reinterpreting the Rural-Urban Connection: Migration Practices and Socio-Cultural Dispositions of Buhera Workers in Harare. *Africa* 71(1):82–112.

Baines, J., and N. Yoffee

    1998   Order, Legitimacy, and Wealth in Ancient Egypt. In *Archaic States,* edited by G. M. Feinman and J. Marcus, pp. 199–260. School of American Research, Santa Fe, New Mexico.

Berthier, S.

    1997   *Recherches archéologiques sur la capitale de l'empire de Ghana: Etude d'un secteur d'habitat à Koumbi Saleh, Mauritanie.* Campagnes II-III-IV-V (1975–1976)–(1980–1981). BAR International Series 680. Cambridge Monographs in African Archaeology.

Blanton, R. E., G. M. Feinman, S. A. Kowalewski, and P. N. Peregrine

    1996   A Dual-Processual Theory for the Evolution of Mesoamerican Civilization. *Current Anthropology* 37(1):1–14.

Boone, J. L., and C. L. Redman

    1982   Alternate Pathways to Urbanism in the Medieval Maghreb. *Comparative Urban Research* 9:28–38.

Carr, S., M. Francis, L. G. Riulin, and A. M. Stone

    1992   *Public Space.* Cambridge University Press, Cambridge.

Castells, M.

    1977   *The Urban Question: A Marxist Approach.* Translated by Alan Sheridan. Edward Arnold, London.

Charleton, T. H., and D. L. Nichols

    1997   The City-State Concept: Development and Applications. In *The Archaeology of City-States: Cross-Cultural Approaches,* edited by D. L. Nichols and T. H. Charleton, pp. 1–14. Smithsonian Institution Press, Washington D.C.

Chelliah, J. V. (translator)

    1985   *Pattupattu: Ten Tamil Idylls.* Tamil University, Thanjavur.

Childe, V. G.

    1950   The Urban Revolution. *Town Planning Review* 21:3–17.

Christopher, G.

1979 Urbanization, Rural and Urban Migration and Development Policies in the Ivory Coast. In *Development of Urban Systems in Africa,* edited by R. A. Obudho and S. El-Shakhs, pp. 157–176. Praeger, New York.

Clark, J. E., and M. Blake

1994 The Power of Prestige: Competitive Generosity and the Emergence of Rank Socie-ties in Lowland Mesoamerica. In *Factional Competition and Political Development in the New World,* edited by E. M. Brumfiel and J. W. Fox, pp. 17–30. Cambridge University Press, Cambridge.

Colombijn, F.

1994 *Patches of Padang: The History of an Indonesian Town in the Twentieth Century and the Use of Urban Space.* Centre of Non-Western Studies, Leiden University, Leiden.

Connah, G.

1987 *African Civilizations.* Cambridge University Press, Cambridge.

Coutin, S. B.

1994 Enacting Law Through Social Practice: Sanctuary as a Form of Resistance. In *Con-tested States: Law, Hegemony and Resistance,* edited by M. Lazarus-Black and S. F. Hirsch, pp. 282–303. Routledge, New York.

Cowgill, G. L.

1992 Social Differentiation at Teotihuacan. In *Mesoamerican Elites: An Archaeological Assess-ment,* edited by D. Z. Chase and A. F. Chase, pp. 206–220. University of Oklahoma Press, Norman.

Cox, S. J., T. J. Sluckin, and J. Steele

1999 Group Size, Memory, and Interaction Rate in the Evolution of Cooperation. *Current Anthropology* 40(3):369–377.

Davidson, D. A.

1972 Terrain Adjustment and Prehistoric Communities. In *Man, Settlement and Urbanism,* ed-ited by P. J. Ucko, R. Tringham, and G. W. Dimbleby, pp. 17–22. Schenkman, Cam-bridge Mass.

DeCorse, C. R.

2001 *An Archaeology of Elmina: Africans and Europeans on the Gold Coast, 1400–1900.* Smith-sonian Institution Press, Washington D.C.

De Oliveira, O., and B. Roberts

1996 Urban Development and Social Inequality in Latin America. In *The Urban Transforma-tion of the Developing World,* edited by J. Gugler, pp. 253–314. Oxford University Press, Oxford.

Dike, A. A.

1979 Misconception of African Urbanism: Some Euro-American Notions. In *Development of Urban Systems in Africa,* edited by R. A. Obudho and S. El-Shakhs, pp. 19–30. Praeger, New York.

Di Segni, L.

1995 The Involvement of Local, Municipal and Provincial Authorities in Urban Building in Late Antique Palestine and Arabia. In *The Roman and Byzantine Near East: Some Re-*

cent *Archaeological Research,* edited by J. H. Humphrey, pp. 312–332. Journal of Roman
Archaeology Supplementary Series No. 14.

Dyos, H. J., and D. A. Reeder

1973　　　Slums and Suburbs. In *The Victorian City: Images and Realities,* edited by H. J. Dyos and
M. Wolff, pp. 359–386. Routledge and Kegan Paul, London.

El-Bushra, El-S.

1989　　　The Urban Crisis and Rural-Urban Migration in Sudan. In *The Geography of Urban-
Rural Interaction in Developing Countries,* edited by R. P. Potter and T. Unwin,
pp. 109–140. Routledge, London.

El-Shakhs, S.

1979　　　Urbanization in Egypt: National Imperatives and New Directions. In *Development of
Urban Systems in Africa,* edited by R. A. Obudho and S. El-Shakhs, pp. 116–131.
Praeger, New York.

Feinman, G. M., and L. M. Nicholas

1991　　　The Monte Alban State: A Diachronic Perspective on an Ancient Core and Its Periphery. In *Core-Periphery Relations in Precapitalist Worlds,* edited by C. Chase-Dunn
and T. D. Hall, pp. 240–276. Boulder, Colo., Westview Press.

Fine, B., and E. Leopold

1993　　　*The World of Consumption.* Routledge, London.

Fox, R. G.

1977　　　*Urban Anthropology: Cities in Their Cultural Settings.* Prentice-Hall, Englewood Cliffs, N.J.

Garnsey, P.

1983　　　Grain for Rome. In *Trade in the Ancient Economy,* edited by P. Garnsey, K. Hopkins,
and C. R. Whittaker, pp. 118–130. University of California Press, Berkeley.

Gottdiener, M.

1985　　　*The Social Production of Urban Space.* University of Texas, Austin.

1995　　　*Postmodern Semiotics: Material Culture and the Forms of Postmodern Life.* Blackwell, Oxford.

Granovetter, M.

1985　　　Economic Action and Social Structure: The Problem of Embeddedness. *American
Journal of Sociology* 91(3):481–510.

Grieco, M.

1995　　　Transported Lives: Urban Social Networks and Labour Circulation. In *The Urban
Context: Ethnicity, Social Networks and Situational Analysis,* edited by A. Rogers and S.
Vertovec, pp. 189–212. Berg, Oxford.

Hallman, H. W.

1984　　　*Neighborhoods: Their Place in Urban Life.* Sage Publications, Beverly Hills, Calif.

Hamilton, G. G., and C. Lai

1989　　　Consumerism without Capitalism: Consumption and Brand Names in Late Imperial
China. In *The Social Economy of Consumption,* edited by H. J. Rutz and B. S. Orlove,
pp. 253–279. University Press of America, Lanham, Mass.

Hansen, M. H. (editor)

2000　　　*A Comparative Study of Thirty City-State Cultures.* Royal Danish Academy of Sciences
and Letters, Copenhagen.

Harris, B.

1989   Commercialisation, Distribution and Consumption: Rural-Urban Grain and
            Resource Transfers in Peasant Society. In *The Geography of Urban-Rural Interaction in
            Developing Countries,* edited by R. P. Potter and T. Unwin, pp. 204–232. Routledge,
            London.

Haviland, W. A., and H. Moholy-Nagy

1992   Distinguishing the High and Mighty from the Hoi Polloi at Tikal, Guatemala. In
            Mesoamerican Elites: An Archaeological Assessment, edited by D. Z. Chase and A. F.
            Chase, pp. 50–60. University of Oklahoma Press, Norman.

Healan, D. M.

1993   Local versus Non-local Obsidian Exchange at Tula and Its implications for Post-
            Formative Mesoamerica. *World Archaeology* 24(3):449–466.

Heath, S.

1999   Urban Bishops and Rural Resources in Post-Roman Southern France. Paper presented
            at the 64th Annual Meeting of the Society for American Archaeology, Chicago.

Henig, J.

1982   *Neighborhood Mobilization: Redevelopment and Response.* Rutgers University Press, New
            Brunswick, N.J.

Herzog, Z.

1997   *Archaeology of the City: Urban Planning in Ancient Israel and Its Social Implications.* Insti-
            tute of Archaeology, Tel Aviv.

Hodge, M. G.

1994   Polities Composing the Aztec Empire's Core. In *Economies and Polities in the Aztec
            Realm,* edited by M. G. Hodge and M. E. Smith, pp. 43–71. Institute of Mesoamerian
            Studies, University at Albany, State University of New York, Albany.

Inoguchi, T., E. Newman, and G. Paoletto (editors)

1999   *Cities and the Environment: New Approaches for Eco-Societies.* United Nations University
            Press, Tokyo.

Jacobs, J.

1961   *The Death and Life of Great American Cities.* Random House, New York.

Joffe, A. H.

1998   Disembedded Capitals in West Asian Perspective. *Comparative Studies in Society and His-
            tory* 40(3):549–580.

Katten, M.

1999   Manufacturing Village Identity and Its Village: The View from Nineteenth-Century
            Andhra. *Modern Asian Studies* 33(1):87–120.

Keating, W. D., and N. Krumholzy (editors)

1999   *Rebuilding Urban Neighborhoods: Achievements, Opportunities, and Limits.* Sage Publica-
            tions, Thousand Oaks, Calif.

Khalat, S. and P. Kongstad

1973   *Hamra of Beirut: A Case of Rapid Urbanization.* E. J. Brill, Leiden.

Knox, P. L.

1995   World Cities in a World-System. In *World Cities in a World-System,* edited by P. L.
            Knox and P. J. Taylor, pp. 3–20. Cambridge University Press, Cambridge.

Kurin, R.

1997   The Hope Diamond: Gem, Jewel and Icon. In *Exhibiting Dilemmas: Issues of Representa-*
            tion at the Smithsonian, edited by A. Henderson and A. L. Kaeppler, pp. 47–69. Smith-
            sonian Institution, Washington.

Lefebvre, H.

1979   Space: Social Product and Use Value. Translated by J. W. Freiberg. In *Critical Sociology:*
            European Perspectives, edited by J. W. Freiberg, pp. 285–295. Irvington Publishers, N.Y.

Lewis, O.

1952   Urbanization without Breakdown: A Case Study. *Scientific Monthly* 75:31–41.

McCracken, G.

1988   *Culture and Consumption: New Approaches to the Symbolic Character of Consumer Goods and*
            Activities. Indiana University Press, Bloomington.

Marcus, J.

1998   The Peaks and Valleys of Ancient States: An Extension of the Dynamic Model. In
            Archaic States, edited by G. M. Feinman and J. Marcus, pp. 59–94. School of American
            Research, Santa Fe, N.M.

Marcus, J. and G. M. Feinman

1998   Introduction. In *Archaic States,* edited by G. M. Feinman and J. Marcus, pp. 3–13.
            School of American Research, Santa Fe, N.M.

Miles, S., and R. Paddison

1998   Urban Consumption: An Historiographical Note. *Urban Studies* 35(5/6):815–823.

Miller, D.

1987   *Material Culture and Mass Consumption.* Basil Blackwell, London.

Myers, G. A.

1996   Naming and Placing the Other: Power and the Urban Landscape in Zanzibar. *Journal*
            of Economic and Social Geography 87(3):237–246.

Netting, R. McC.

1993   *Smallholders, Householders.* Stanford University Press, Stanford.

O'Meara, M.

1999   *Reinventing Cities for People and the Planet.* Worldwatch Paper No. 147, Worldwatch In-
            stitute, Washington D.C.

Peiser, R. B., and A. C. Chang

1999   Is It Possible to Build Financially Successful New Towns? The Milton Keynes Expe-
            rience. *Urban Studies* 36(10):1679–1703.

Penvenne, J. M.

1997   Seeking the Factory for Women: Mozambican Urbanization in the Late Colonial Era.
            Journal of Urban History 23(3):342–379.

Perlman, J. E.

1976   *The Myth of Marginality. Urban Poverty and Politics in Rio de Janeiro.* University of Cali-
            fornia Press, Berkeley.

Possehl, G. L.

1998   Sociocultural Complexity without the State: The Indus Civilization. In *Archaic States,*
            edited by G. M. Feinman and J. Marcus, pp. 261–291. School of American Research,
            Santa Fe, N.M.

Potter, R. B.

1985   *Urbanisation and Planning in the 3rd World: Spatial Perception and Public Participation.* St. Martin's Press, N.Y.

Ray, H. P.

1996   Maritime Archaeology of the Indian Ocean: An Overview. In *Tradition and Archaeology: Early Maritime Contacts in the Indian Ocean,* edited by H. P. Ray and J.-F. Salles, pp. 1–10. Manohar, New Delhi.

Remus, H.

1996   Voluntary Association and Networks: Aelius Aristides at the Asclepieion on Pergamun. In *Voluntary Associations in the Graeco-Roman World,* edited by J. S. Koppenborg and S. G. Wilson, pp. 146–175. Routledge, London.

Renfrew, C.

1974   Beyond a Subsistence Economy: The Evolution of Social Organisation in Prehistoric Europe. In *Reconstructing Complex Societies,* edited by C. B. Moore, pp. 69–84. Supplement to the Bulletin of the American Schools of Oriental Research, Cambridge, Mass.

Robertson, J. F.

1995   The Social and Economic Organization of Ancient Mesopotamian Temples. In *Civilizations of the Ancient Near East,* edited by J. M. Sasson, pp. 443–454. Charles Scribner's Sons, New York.

Rubertone, P. E., and P. Thorbahn

1985   Urban Hinterlands as Frontiers of Colonization. In *The Archaeology of Frontiers and Boundaries,* edited by S. W. Green and S. M. Perlman, pp. 231–249. Academic Press, San Diego.

Schafer, E. H.

1963   *The Golden Peaches of Samarkand: A Study of T'ang Exotics.* University of California, Berkeley.

Schweizer, T., M. Schnegg, and S. Berzborn

1998   Personal Networks and Social Support in a Multiethnic Community of Southern California. *Social Networks* 20:1–21.

Sedov, A. V.

1996   Qana' (Yemen) and the Indian Ocean: The Archaeological Evidence. In *Tradition and Archaeology: Early Maritime Contacts in the Indian Ocean,* edited by H. P. Ray and J.-F. Salles, pp. 11–35. Manohar, New Delhi.

Shaffer, J. G.

1996   South Asian Archaeology 1995: New Data, Subdued Interpretations. *Antiquity* 70:995–998.

Shen, C.

1994   Early Urbanization in the Eastern Zhou in China (770–221 B.C.): An Archaeological View. *Antiquity* 68:724–744.

Smith, M. G.

1972   Complexity, Size and Urbanization. In *Man, Settlement and Urbanism,* edited by P. J. Ucko, R. Tringham, and G. W. Dimbleby, pp. 567–574. Schenkman, Cambridge, Mass.

Smith, M. E.

1987   Household Possessions and Wealth in Agrarian States: Implications for Archaeology. *Journal of Anthropological Archaeology* 6:297–335.

Smith, M. L.

1999   The Role of Ordinary Goods in Premodern Exchange. *Journal of Archaeological Method and Theory* 6(2):109–135.

Stein, G. J., R. Bernbeck, C. Coursey, A. McMahon, N. F. Miller, A. Misir, J. Nicola, H. Pittman, S. Pollock, and H. Wright

1996   Uruk Colonies and Anatolian Communities: An Interim Report on the 1992–93 Excavations at Hacinebi, Turkey. *American Journal of Archaeology* 100(2):205–260.

Stone, E.

1995   The Development of Cities in Ancient Mesopotamia. In *Civilizations of the Ancient Near East,* edited by J. M. Sasson, pp. 235–248. Charles Scribner's Sons, New York.

1997   City-States and Their Centers: The Mesopotamian Example. In *The Archaeology of City-States,* edited by D. L. Hichols and T. H. Charlton, pp. 15–26. Smithsonian Institution Press, Washington D.C.

Storey, R.

1992   *Life and Death in the Ancient City of Teotihuacan: A Modern Paleodemographic Synthesis.* University of Alabama, Tuscaloosa.

Streicker, J.

1997   Spatial Reconfigurations, Imagined Geographies, and Social Conflicts in Cartagena, Colombia. *Cultural Anthropology* 12(1):109–128.

Trigger, B.

1972   Determinants of Urban Growth in Pre-industrial Society. In *Man, Settlement and Urbanism,* edited by P. J. Ucko, R. Tringham, and G. W. Dimbleby, pp. 575–599. Schenkman, Cambridge Mass.

Trubitt, M. B. D.

2000   Mound Building and Prestige Goods Exchange: Changing Strategies in the Cahokia Chiefdom. *American Antiquity* 65(4):669–690.

Vagale, L. R.

1973   Local Government in Metropolitan Cities of India in Relation to Urban Planning and Development. In *Management Problems of Rapid Urbanization in Nigeria,* edited by A. Adedeji and L. Rowland, pp. 83–92. University of Ife Press, Ile Ife.

Walker-Ramisch, S.

1996   Graeco-Roman Voluntary Associations and the Damascus Document. In *Voluntary Associations in the Graeco-Roman World,* edited by J. S. Koppenborg and S. G. Wilson, pp. 128–145. Routledge, London.

Weber, M.

1958   *The City.* Translated and edited by D. Martindale and G. Neuwirth. The Free Press, Glencoe, Ill.

Webster, D.

1997   City-States of the Maya. In *The Archaeology of City-States,* edited by D. L. Hichols and T. H. Charlton, pp. 135–154. Smithsonian Institution Press, Washington D.C.

Williams, M. R.

   1985   *Neighborhood Organizations: Seeds of a New Urban Life.* Greenwood Press, Westport Conn.

Wirth, L.

   1938   Urbanism as a Way of Life. *American Journal of Sociology* 44(1):1–24.

Yoffee, N.

   1988   Aspects of Mesopotamian Land Sales. *American Anthropologist* 90(1):119–130.

   1995   Political Economy in Early Mesopotamian States. *Annual Review of Anthropology* 24:281–311.

Zeder, M. A.

   1991   *Feeding Cities.* Smithsonian Institution, Washington D.C.

T W O

Teotihuacan

Cosmic Glories and Mundane Needs

GEORGE L. COWGILL

Teotihuacan was a great prehistoric metropolis of the first millennium A.D. in the highland Basin of Mexico in central Mexico (figure 2.1). General summaries of our knowledge and beliefs about the city include Millon (1974, 1976, 1981, 1988, 1992) and Cowgill (1983, 1997, 2000a). In this chapter I focus especially on those aspects bearing on benefits and costs, satisfactions and dissatisfactions, of life in Teotihuacan as they may have been perceived by various elements among its inhabitants.

In the context of a well-established tradition of agricultural settlements and small polities in the Basin of Mexico, Teotihuacan began to grow very rapidly in the first or second century B.C. By around A.D. 200 it covered 20 square kilometers and had a population probably on the order of 100,000 or more. (For René Millon's map of the city at its height, see Cowgill 1983, 2000a; Cowgill et al. 1984; Millon 1973,

1974, 1976, 1981, 1988; or Sanders et al. 1979.[1]) The city's size seems to have changed little thereafter for several centuries, but by the 500s (or possibly as late as the 600s) population began to decline, and somewhere around A.D. 600 (though possibly as late as 750) the main civic-ceremonial buildings were destroyed by fire. Teotihuacan was probably briefly abandoned, but was soon partially reoccupied by people whose ceramics belonged to a markedly different pottery tradition, called Coyotlatelco.

The early period of rapid growth of Teotihuacan seems to have been accompanied by the near depopulation of the rest of the Basin of Mexico. About 80 to 90 percent of the population was, for a time, concentrated in the city (Sanders 1981:174; Sanders et al. 1979:107). Some moderately large regional centers within the basin, such as Azcapotzalco and Cerro Portezuelo, persisted or soon appeared, but Teotihuacan was a primate city, at least 10 times larger than any other settlement in the basin. The disparity between the size of Teotihuacan and the next largest settlements in its sustaining area is perhaps unusual among early urban societies. Any attempt to understand the perceived advantages and disadvantages of living in Teotihuacan must take into account the extreme degree of population concentration in the city.

Much of our knowledge of Teotihuacan comes from excavations, which have been especially extensive at major civic-ceremonial structures but also include studies in residential areas. A notable recent example of the latter is the work of Storey and others in a compound of lapidary workers and specialized potters called Tlajinga 33 (site 33:S3W1 in Millon's Teotihuacan map), in the "Tlajinga" district in the southern outskirts of the city (Sheehy 1992; Storey 1992; Widmer 1991; Widmer and Storey 1993). Also noteworthy are work by Manzanilla and others in the northwestern "Oztoyahualco" district, at a site labeled 15B:N6W3 (Manzanilla 1993, 1996; Manzanilla and Barba 1990), and excavations in the "Oaxaca" ethnic enclave near the western edge of the city (Rattray 1993; Spence 1992). Other important work on residences includes research by Rattray in an enclave with Gulf Lowlands and Maya affiliations on the eastern edge of the city (the so-called Merchants' barrio), and by Cabrera C. and others in a mix of high- and low-status compounds in the La Ventilla district, not far southwest of the Great Compound (Cabrera C. 1996).

A great deal of what we know of the extent and layout of the city and the characteristics of its various broad districts and smaller neighborhoods comes not from excavations, but from the intensive surface survey carried out by the Teotihuacan

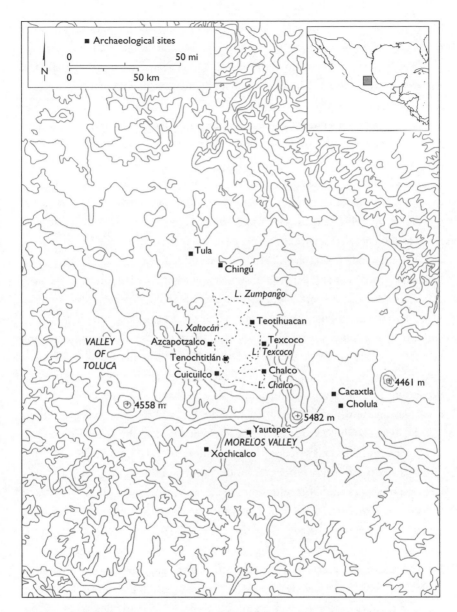

Figure 2.1. Teotihuacan in Mesoamerica (reprinted from R. E. W. Adams and M. J. MacLeod, eds., *The Cambridge History of the Native Peoples of the Americas*, vol. 2, with the permission of Cambridge University Press).

Mapping Project in the 1960s (Millon 1973; Millon et al. 1973). Discussions of what might be called the "anatomy" of the city, based on quantitative studies of Mapping Project data, include Cowgill (1974); Cowgill and colleagues (1984); and Robertson (1999, 2001). On the level of individual apartment compounds, Hopkins (1987) has carried out a network analysis.

Our knowledge of craft activities at Teotihuacan still depends mostly on surface survey. Spence has discussed the obsidian industry in a series of articles (e.g., Spence 1987). Except for the work at Tlajinga 33 noted above and a study of scale of production and product variability in cooking wares by Hopkins (1995), our knowledge of the ceramic industry is still largely based on surface survey and some incompletely published excavations. O. Cabrera C. (2001) has recently produced a study of the limited evidence for textile production at Teotihuacan, Turner (1987a, 1987b, 1992) and O. Cabrera C. (1995) have studied the lapidary industry, and Biskowski (1997) has studied ground stone implements. We still know little about craft specialization in Teotihuacan. Earlier estimates that there were 400 or more workshops in the city may be too high and need further evaluation.

Nevertheless, some general points are clear. At the center of the city, along the northern 2.5 kilometers of the Avenue of the Dead, there is a district of some 150–250 hectares, bordered for the most part by free-standing walls, that is comprised primarily of large civic-ceremonial structures and complexes. This includes the largest monuments in the city, such as the Sun and Moon Pyramids, the so-called Ciudadela, the "Avenue of the Dead Complex," and the Great Compound. There are also numerous smaller pyramids and residential complexes and room groups that were probably residences for the highest-ranking elites, and that likely included offices and other facilities for bureaucratic, ritual, and other activities of the Teotihuacan elite. A workshop specializing in making ceremonial ceramic censers and their symbol-laden ornaments is in a large enclosure attached to the north side of the Ciudadela, and the immense quantities of obsidian debris in the fill of structures and precincts near the Moon Pyramid suggest obsidian workshops in close proximity. The walls enclosing most of this central district were probably intended more to control the movement of people than to provide defense. These walls by no means imply that access to the central district was denied to those living outside, but they do suggest that there was a good deal of control over access.

This civic-ceremonial core is surrounded by other distinctive broad districts within the city on the order of 100 hectares in size. These districts were never very homogeneous and they contain mixes, in various proportions, of temples and other civic-ceremonial complexes, residences occupied by households of both high and low status, and varied kinds of craft workshops. Millon long ago (1976) noted this heterogeneity, which has been confirmed and amplified by more recent studies. Within these larger districts, distinct neighborhoods can sometimes be identified. In one particularly striking example furnished by the recent work by Rubén Cabrera C. and others in the La Ventilla district, apartments of "palatial" quality abut much more poorly built apartments that provide abundant evidence of lapidary and other craft specialization. This suggests that relations among occupants of these adjoining apartments may possibly have been those of patrons and clients. This is a topic for further study.

Of particular interest are the more than 2,000 distinctive "apartment compounds" in which nearly all the city's occupants lived after about A.D. 250. Nearly all were occupied during the city's height, although perhaps not all parts were simultaneously occupied in all cases. None appear to have more than one story. They are enclosed by thick concrete-faced walls with rubble cores and have only two or three entrances. In the higher-density parts of the city, compounds are separated from one another only by narrow streets, but in lower-density districts, fairly wide spaces often separate compounds. Some of these spaces could have been used for gardens, although most of the city's food must have come from outside. Many of the compounds are about 60 meters on a side, but there is great variation: many are smaller, a few are larger, and some are oblong in plan or have elbows or other extensions. Internal variation is also pronounced, although layouts imply occupation by two or more households in all but the smallest compounds. Typically, the rooms of an individual apartment are on low platforms arranged around a small, roughly square, central court or patio. These rooms are usually fronted by porticoes. Apartments may contain various additional rooms, passageways, and smaller patios or light-wells. Many have a larger patio with a central altar that may have served the compound as a whole (figure 2.2 shows examples of apartment compound plans).

Most significantly, the social units formed by households that shared occupancy of a multiapartment compound must have been larger than individual households but smaller than neighborhoods. Such units would have been important in the city's social organization and probably in its political administration. The composition of these units is uncertain, but most likely they included a fairly stable core of relatively close kin, together with a more fluctuating category of households or individuals bound by looser kin ties, or possibly in some cases by patron-client or

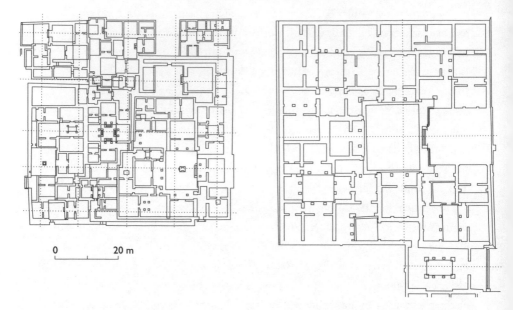

0   20 m

Figure 2.2. Plans of two Teotihuacan apartment compounds, Tetitla on the left and Zacuala on the right. The scale pertains to Tetitla; Zacuala is shown at a slightly larger scale. Both compounds are nearly the same size.

other relations. The fact that many burials are found under the floors of rooms and patios within apartment compounds suggests that at least many of the occupants expected that they and their descendants would continue to be closely associated with that compound in the future. Otherwise, it seems that the graves of ancestors would have been located in more accessible places outside the compounds.

At the same time, the relatively inflexible amount of living space in these walled compounds does not accord well with the developmental cycles of individual households or even extended families, as pointed out by Millon (1976). Households less tightly bound to the relatively stable core of compound residents may have shifted from one compound to another (especially at marriage) as various opportunities presented themselves (or in response to problems in their current compound). Such practices would also facilitate incorporation of newcomers to the city (see chapter 1). Localized enclaves of people with ties to Oaxaca, the Gulf Lowlands, the Maya area, and perhaps west Mexico are archaeologically very visible in elevated proportions of ceramics imported from those places (also found in small proportions everywhere in the city), in locally made imitations of foreign ceramics, and to some extent in distinctive styles of burials or architecture. Studies of ratios of stable isotopes of oxygen and strontium in bones and teeth are beginning to add to evidence about these ethnically different residents (e.g., White et al. 1998). One way of dealing with ethnic diversity appears to have been spatial segregation, a very common practice in other ancient and modern cities. However, since the death rate of the Teotihuacan urban population was probably too high for replacement, there was likely a constant inflow of persons from relatively nearby who were not ethnically very different from the majority of the city's occupants. These people may have found housing in scattered apartment compounds where they had some sort of preexisting tie, such as kinship or trade partnerships.

Another distinctive feature of Teotihuacan is the remarkably close adherence, throughout the city, to an orientation 15.5 degrees east of astronomic north, probably based on astronomical properties of a sacred calendar (Cowgill 2000b; Millon 1981). Major structures follow this very closely in their north-south walls, while east-west walls are often closer to 16.5 or 17 degrees south of true east. Less carefully built residences (e.g., Tlajinga 33) are laid out less exactly, but their orientations do not seem to differ in any systematic way. In contrast to many ancient cities, different districts do not have different orientations. It is possible that the canonical orientation was of unusual sacred significance, and this might be the reason for the uniformity of Teotihuacan, which is exceptional among Mesoamerican cities. However, this uniformity suggests a rather strong and effective centralized authority within the city. This may have some bearing on thought about the extent to which rulership at Teotihuacan, especially after about A.D. 300, may have had collective (or "corporate") aspects.

Headrick (1999) argues that at Teotihuacan there may have been large kin groups composed of multiple lineages, venerating mortuary bundles of revered ancestors. If such groups existed, they were probably internally ranked clans. Leading members of such groups might have formed an elite oligarchy from which heads of state were recruited, possibly by some elite election process. Such a system of headship circulating among elite families or "houses" might explain why so little evidence has been found that powerful individual rulers or specific dynastic lines were publicly celebrated. To be sure, during the interval when Teotihuacan was growing most rapidly and the overwhelmingly large principal civic-ceremonial structures and complexes were created, circa 100 B.C. to A.D. 250, it is difficult to imagine that there was not a series of extremely strong-willed and capable individual leaders. But these persons may have been something of an anomaly in a society whose political institutions were perhaps more oligarchic, both before and after this interval.

Any such oligarchic system would, of course, have lent itself to factionalism and would have had some divisive aspects. Were there crosscutting institutions, such as sodalities, that would have had more integrative effects? Iconography suggests there were military orders associated with fierce animals such as rattlesnakes, eagles, jaguars/pumas, and coyotes, foreshadowing the military orders of later Aztec times. Whether military orders would contribute much to cohesion in nonmilitary contexts is unclear. We can only speculate as to whether there were any guildlike organizations of merchants or artisans.

PERCEIVED ATTRACTIONS

No discussion of the perceived costs and benefits of living in Teotihuacan can ignore the grandeur of the central part of the city and its sacred aspects. Even today many visitors find the ruins awe-inspiring and overwhelming, although what we see now consists mainly of substructures for the temples, mansions, and other edifices, blazing with color and ornamentation, that once stood atop these low foundations. It is not just the scale of the largest structures that is impressive, though some are colossal, but also the vast and orderly panoramas afforded by the Avenue of the Dead and the central 2 or 3 square kilometers of the city. Perhaps all this satisfied the egos of early powerful leaders and their architects. Certainly it must have made most people feel insignificant by comparison. At the same time, it very likely made anyone who could identify with the grandeur feel proud and important to be a part of it all. The majority of Teotihuacanos may have felt small alongside the monuments and the sacred world the monuments represented, but nevertheless privileged compared with any humans who lived elsewhere. To judge by historic and present-day accounts of city-dwellers, such feelings would have gone a considerable distance in offsetting perceived disadvantages for many Teotihuacanos. This could have been a powerful means of creating sentiments of solidarity among elements of the population whose interests conflicted in many ways. The Gramscian concept of "hegemony" applies here.

The notion of Teotihuacan as a privileged place was reinforced by special sacred aspects. Teotihuacan, like many other ancient cities and even small municipalities (cf. Gossen 1974), was surely viewed by its inhabitants as the center of the universe, an *axis mundi*. One should not be seduced by the number games of "megalithic yard" devotees, but even a hard-headed look at standardized directional orientations and distances between key structures that are simple multiples of one another reveals much that cannot plausibly be attributed to chance (e.g., Cowgill 2000b; Sugiyama 1993). It would be too simple to say that the contemporary Maya people of Guatemala and the Yucatan peninsula to the southeast were preoccupied with counting and the Teotihuacanos with geometry, but I think this captures a broad contrast. Much remains to be learned and supported by convincing arguments about the geometry of Teotihuacan and its meanings. I strongly suspect that this knowledge will improve our understanding of Teotihuacan as a cosmic center. But that is a task for other occasions. For the present, the point is simply that by residing close to the center—the intersection of cosmic axes—one was close to exceedingly strong currents of cosmic energy. Today, we of a secular or scientific bent ridicule "pyramid power" enthusiasts. There is no reason to consider such ideas ridiculous in the context of Mesoamerican thought.

A city like Teotihuacan very likely evoked in its residents a duality in thinking and feeling. People must have viewed it as being sacred and laden with symbolism, yet they would have had to get on with the mundane activities, calculations, and negotiations of daily life. The civic-ceremonial core would have been sacred space par excellence, but probably also a place where routine government business was transacted. Many ordinary activities connected with daily living must have gone on in the apartment compounds, yet on ritual occasions their central patios and altars would have been transformed into sacred space.

A further possible reason to think that Teotihuacan was very likely seen as a supernaturally privileged place is provided by the volcanoes of central Mexico. I emphasize, however, that what follows is highly speculative and not central to my main theses. Much of Cuicuilco, Teotihuacan's early rival in the southern part of the Basin of Mexico, was overrun by a series of lava flows and falls of volcanic ash (for a recent review of the geological stratigraphy of Cuicuilco, see Pastrana 1997). This eliminated Cuicuilco as a serious rival to Teotihuacan and very possibly provided an influx of refugees. Plunket and Uruñuela (1998) report striking complementary evidence from the settlement of Tetimpa in the Valley of Puebla, just outside the Basin of Mexico and about 80 kilometers southeast of Teotihuacan, which was ruined by a heavy volcanic ash fall from Popocatépetl at about the time when Teotihuacan was developing most rapidly. Tetimpa is fascinating in its own right, as another example of rapid abandonment and excellent preservation, comparable to Cerén in El Salvador and to Roman Pompeii. It also provides further evidence of the spectacular effects of volcanic eruptions on early Teotihuacan's neighbors. There are extensive lava flows and layers of volcanic ash beneath parts of Teotihuacan and its environs, but these are from eruptions that occurred long before the beginning of Teotihuacan. Teotihuacanos would have asked themselves why they were spared the destruction wrought upon their neighbors. It is easy to imagine leaders attributing this to their special relationship with the Volcano God. They may have claimed that they could control the volcano power, both to protect their own city and to punish their enemies (as well as being able to invoke the lightning power of the Storm God). The devastation of Cuicuilco to the south and of Tetimpa and other sites to the east may have been perceived as something like that rained upon Biblical Sodom and Gomorrah.

There is abundant evidence of a widespread Mesoamerican view of sacred mountains as vessels full of the water so vital for agricultural fertility. Indeed, a distinctive kind of ceramic jar at Teotihuacan is in the form of the Storm God (a precursor of the Aztec Tlaloc), often carrying a wavy lightning bolt in one hand, and often with three tabs projecting upward from the rim. Langley (1986) shows that the three tabs are the "triple mountain" sign. I suggest that, just as the Storm God had dual aspects (the bringer of benevolent rain needed for food, but also of the terrible and destructive hail and lightning associated with war), so did sacred mountains, a source of the water that flows out of springs, but also of lava, a red-hot fiery liquid. This could explain, for example, why the diamond-shaped "fire" sign occurs in the headdress of a personified mountain in a Teotihuacan mural. Moreover, pyramids were generally regarded as sacred mountains in Mesoamerica. It is noteworthy, for example, that Cerro Gordo, a great extinct volcano, looms behind the Moon Pyramid, dominating the view along the Avenue of the Dead.

These observations lead into aspects of Teotihuacan iconography and thought that I will not pursue here, although I note that Pasztory (1997) expresses partially similar ideas. For present purposes, the point is that there is reason to suspect that people may have believed that by living at Teotihuacan they were protected from volcanic threats, at least as long as they enjoyed the goodwill of the rulers, and as long as the rulers enjoyed the goodwill of the Volcano God. This may have been another perceived advantage, offsetting perceived disadvantages, of life in the city. Whether or not these speculations about a Volcano God are supported by further studies, we can safely assume that Teotihuacan elites appealed to the sacred to help legitimize their status and authority.

Sacred caves, especially as places of ancestral emergence, are another prevalent concern in Mesoamerican thought (Heyden 1975). Caves abound today at Teotihuacan: many have been highly altered by humans, and some are perhaps entirely manmade (as argued by Barba et al. 1990). The earliest pyramid-temple complexes at Teotihuacan are scattered over a fairly wide area in the northwest part of the later city, and many are near cave entrances. The Sun Pyramid itself is built above a cave, which over time must have come to be accorded greater importance than the other caves. Sixteenth-century Aztec origin myths and migration stories refer to caves, but these caves seem to have been much farther away, well outside the Basin of Mexico and in keeping with the Aztec view of themselves as in-migrants. By contrast, dominant ethnic components of Teotihuacan society quite possibly believed they had lived in the Basin of Mexico since Creation. At any rate, the relative ceramic continuity in the Basin of Mexico from before 300 B.C. until about A.D. 600 lends some support to this conjecture. If so, the local caves would probably have added to the sacred significance of Teotihuacan as a place of origin and emergence.

A further kind of perceived advantage would have been that Teotihuacan is situated in a choice and lush area for agriculture. The Basin of Mexico as a whole poses challenges for agriculture—it is semiarid and the altitude (around 2,250 meters) creates a significant frost hazard. However, there is a swampy area of about 100 hectares just downstream from year-round springs on the southwestern fringe of the ancient city where intensive drained-field agriculture is practiced today. Downstream from that are several thousand hectares of normally dry land that can be irrigated by simple canals fed by the placid water that wells up steadily from the springs (or did, until the advent in the twentieth century of deep well drilling that has disastrously lowered the water table).

Although one might be tempted to consider military defense another incentive for living in Teotihuacan, the city lies on the flat valley floor rather than on high ground, and there is no evidence that it had an outer wall or other fortifications. Long walls within the city were more likely used for defining districts and controlling the movement of people. Nevertheless, the sheer size of the population would have provided safety in numbers. In any case, with so much of the basin's population in the city, not enough people would have remained elsewhere in the basin to pose much threat. By A.D. 200 or soon thereafter, even in regions that were not depopulated, there do not seem to have been any centers within a hundred kilometers, and probably much farther, that could have been very dangerous. Military defense has often been a reason for population aggregation in other times and places, but it does not seem likely to have been an important factor at Teotihuacan.

It has also been suggested that the excitement, bustle, and variety that many find inherent in city life would have been an additional attraction at Teotihuacan. It is hard for me to assess this. Country-bred, I count this a mixed blessing of urban settings. But perhaps I underestimate this attraction, and I leave it for others to judge. Was Teotihuacan a bustling place? The much later Aztec capital, Tenochtitlan, as described in sixteenth-century accounts, certainly seems to have been. Bustle seems conspicuously absent from surviving Teotihuacan scenes in mural and other art. Most scenes are rigidly formal; a few are what I would call bucolic. However, Teotihuacan art is notoriously selective in what it depicts, so this negative evidence counts for nothing. Any place with 100,000 people concentrated in 20 square kilometers cannot help but be busy and varied. I think that the extent to which Teotihuacanos perceived that busy-ness and variety as attractive is an open question.

PERCEIVED DISADVANTAGES

As for the perceived disadvantages of living in the city, the ones that come first to mind are crowding, provisioning, sanitation and health in general, and safety and public order. We still lack data on early residences at Teotihuacan, but they may have been quite similar to those at Tetimpa, the Late Preclassic site in the Valley of Puebla mentioned earlier. Residences at Tetimpa consisted typically of platforms with sloping aprons surmounted by vertical panels, so-called talud-tablero construction, arranged around three sides of a rectangular courtyard. Sometimes two of these units adjoin and seem related, but they do not appear to be surrounded by walls, and they are well separated from other such units or unit-clusters. Making *several* such courtyard-platform units more compact and enclosing them within a substantial outer wall would create an apartment compound of the sort well documented for Teotihuacan after about A.D. 200–250, in which the large open courtyards of Tetimpa are replaced by smaller unroofed patios. Such enclosing and modifying seems, in part, a simple response to greater crowding. Interestingly, however, it was not single courtyard-platform units, such as might have been occupied by a nuclear or small extended family, that were enclosed by a single wall, but clusters of several such units. These built environments would have created, if they did not already exist, sociopolitical units significantly larger than extended families but smaller than neighborhoods. Lineages based on real or fictive kinship may have formed the cores of these sociopolitical units, as discussed earlier.

Concerning provisioning of food staples, the apparently very scarce population in the countryside and the limited surpluses that can be produced by premodern agriculture imply that a high proportion of Teotihuacan's population must have been at least part-time specialists in the craft of farming, even though scarcely any artifacts identifiable as farming implements have been found in the city (or in the countryside). There is no question that total person-days required to get food from fields to mouths were significantly greater than would have been required if more of the population had lived outside the city and closer to many of the fields. However, the radius of the needed catchment area would have been well within the range of economically feasible overland foot transport (Drennan 1984). A different problem is faced by farmers who have to make frequent visits to fields for field preparation, sowing, tending growing crops, and harvesting. Daily round trips by foot of 20–30 kilometers are far beyond what is known ethnographically and would have left no time for fieldwork. I strongly suspect that city residents tending fields more than a few kilometers from the city had insubstantial field houses (as yet archaeologically undetected) in which they spent several days at a time. There may also have been a small number of full-time rural residents, perhaps too few and too dispersed to be easily recognized at the somewhat low intensity of the Basin of Mexico archaeological survey (Sanders et al. 1979).

One open question is how residents of the city gained rights to food and other provisions. To what extent, if at all, was the state involved? If the state was involved in the storage and redistribution of food, this could have been among the attractions of life in Teotihuacan. However, nothing suggestive of state storage facilities has yet been recognized, although some likely candidates, such as the structures atop the large north and south platforms of the Great Compound, have not yet been adequately investigated. For that matter, storage facilities are unexpectedly hard to recognize in apartment compounds, except for occasional very large ceramic jars. The extent to which provisioning was carried out through market institutions rather than administered by government institutions is highly unclear. One possibility (among many) is that most apartment compounds had rights to specified plots of land that were worked by some of their occupants, while other occupants pursued other craft activities.

Sanitation and health were probably not very good. Apartment compounds are well supplied with subfloor drains, but these must have been used mainly to carry off rainwater. Without drains, courtyards would have regularly flooded during the torrential storms of the rainy season. The drains lead to the streets just outside the compounds, in which the water seems to have flowed in open channels. Human excreta and food remains would not have been carried off to any extent by these drains, especially during the dry season. Presumably wastes would have been disposed of outside the apartment compounds, but the extent to which they were dumped nearby or carried outside the city is unclear. I suspect that it varied considerably, depending on the general state of the society. A little-known but important fact is that immense quantities of sherds have been found in the streets just outside the walls of some apartment compounds, such as Yayahuala (Séjourné 1966:21–24), in such amounts that they would have raised the street level considerably. This dumping may or may not be limited to the final decades of the Teotihuacan state. It is a matter that urgently needs further study, both as to its chronology and as to what other materials may have also been dumped in the streets. Presumably these dumps were not allowed to block drains.

Tlajinga 33 is a well-studied apartment compound in the southern part of the city, some of whose occupants engaged in fine stoneworking and, later, the specialized manufacture of utilitarian pottery. Judging by the quality of construction and other evidence, their socioeconomic status was quite low. Rebecca Storey's (1992) paleodemographic study indicates startlingly high mortality and low life expectancy, as well as a high proportion of episodes of stress survived before death, as indicated by skeletal and dental evidence. Such markers are not very informative about causes of stress, but presumably they reflect diseases, serious malnutrition, or both. I am not convinced that the Tlajinga 33 deaths represented by the recovered skeletal material are unbiased by age, and life expectancy may not have been quite as short as Storey calculates. Nevertheless, mortality must have been high and health and nutrition poor at Tlajinga 33.

Paleodemographic work comparable to Storey's has not yet been reported for other Teotihuacan residences. It is easy to imagine that health and nutrition were on average better and mortality rates lower in most other nonelite apartment compounds. Nevertheless, it looks as if Teotihuacan was not an especially healthful environment. But one should remember that, by present-day standards, mortality was probably high everywhere in ancient Mesoamerica, including rural as well as urban settings. Differences that look statistically significant to us may not have been very noticeable to Teotihuacanos and their neighbors. It is not at all clear that living in Teotihuacan would have been perceived as "hazardous to your health."

Safety and public order have become concerns in modern cities, whose middle classes generally consider suburban and rural contexts safer. It is not clear whether Teotihuacanos would have seen it that way. At any rate, the stout outer walls of apartment compounds, which usually had only two or three entrances, would have enabled the occupants to control access to them. Whether the Teotihuacan state provided anything like patrols or watchmen for areas outside the compounds is an open question.

COERCION

Up to now I have spoken as if, during Teotihuacan times, households or small groups of households in the Basin of Mexico were free to weigh perceived benefits and costs of living in Teotihuacan and make their decisions accordingly. Surely such calculations of perceived costs and benefits were important. But it is also certain that some degree of coercion was involved, which would have taken various forms. One form would have been tangible physical force or threat of its use. Another would have been the threat of exclusion from material benefits provided by the state, and a third the threat of supernatural displeasure, punishment, and withholding of good fortune. All this is familiar, but we should not lose sight of it. I know of no tangible evidence of means of coercion at Teotihuacan, such as prisons, instruments of punishment, or scenes of punishment. There is ample evidence of human sacrifice, but it is not clear whether victims were ever selected because of disobedience or violation of norms. Phrasing the matter as "carrot and stick" is a feeble metaphor that I hope has seen its day. Whether or not Teotihuacan coercion was at all sticklike, it should be abundantly clear that the manifold attractions of Teotihuacan are hardly suggested by the lowly carrot image.

Nevertheless, we still lack a reasonably accurate and nuanced concept of the mix of attraction, persuasion, danger, and duress that moved people to Teotihuacan and kept them there. It is likely that the mix changed considerably over time, but we still have only inklings of this.

ACKNOWLEDGMENTS

I thank Monica Smith for inviting and encouraging me to participate in the Society for American Archaeology session that led to this volume, and for helpful comments on the first draft of this chapter.

NOTE

1. My planned inclusion of the map in this volume could not be accommodated by the Press.

REFERENCES

Barba, L., L. Manzanilla, R. Chávez, L. Flores, and A. J. Arzate
  1990   Caves and Tunnels at Teotihuacan, Mexico: A Geological Phenomenon of Archaeo-
          logical Interest. In *Archaeological Geology of North America,* edited by N. P. Lasca and J.
          Donahue, pp. 431–438. Geological Society of America, Boulder, Colo.

Biskowski, M. F.
  1997   *The Adaptive Origins of Prehispanic Markets in Central Mexico: The Role of Maize-Grinding
          Tools and Related Staple Products in Early State Economies.* Unpublished Ph.D. dissertation,
          Department of Anthropology, University of California, Los Angeles.

Cabrera Castro, R.
  1996   Figuras glíficas de La Ventilla, Teotihuacan. *Arqueología* 15:27–40.

Cabrera Cortés, M. O.
  1995   *La lapidaria del proyecto Templo de Quetzalcoatl.* Thesis, Escuela Nacional de
          Antropología e Historia, México, D.F.
  2001   *Textile Production at Teotihuacan,* Mexico. Master's thesis, Department of Anthro-
          pology, Arizona State University, Tempe.

Cowgill, G. L.
  1974   Quantitative Studies of Urbanization at Teotihuacan. In *Mesoamerican Archaeology:
          New Approaches,* edited by N. Hammond, pp. 363–396. Duckworth, London.
  1983   Rulership and the Ciudadela: Political Inferences from Teotihuacan Architecture.
          In *Civilization in the Ancient Americas: Essays in Honor of Gordon R. Willey,* edited by
          R. M. Leventhal and A. L. Kolata, pp. 313–343. University of New Mexico Press and
          Peabody Museum of Archaeology and Ethnology, Harvard University, Cambridge,
          Mass.
  1997   State and Society at Teotihuacan, Mexico. *Annual Review of Anthropology* 26:129–161.
  2000a   The Central Mexican Highlands from the Rise of Teotihuacan to the Decline of
          Tula. In *Mesoamerica,* edited by R. E. W. Adams and M. J. MacLeod, pp. 250–317. The
          Cambridge History of the Native Peoples of the Americas, vol. 2, part 1. Cambridge
          University Press, Cambridge.
  2000b   Intentionality and Meaning in the Layout of Teotihuacan, Mexico. *Cambridge Archaeo-
          logical Journal* 10(2):358–365.

Cowgill, G. L., J. H. Altschul, and R. S. Sload
  1984   Spatial Analysis of Teotihuacan: A Mesoamerican Metropolis. In *Intrasite Spatial
          Analysis in Archaeology,* edited by H. J. Hietala, pp. 154–195. Cambridge University
          Press, Cambridge.

Drennan, R. D.
  1984   Long-Distance Transport Costs in Pre-Hispanic Mesoamerica. *American Anthropologist*
          86:105–112.

Gossen, G. H.

1974   *Chamulas in the World of the Sun.* Waveland Press, Prospect Heights, Ill.

Headrick, A.

1999   The Street of the Dead . . . It Really Was: Mortuary Bundles at Teotihuacan. *Ancient Mesoamerica* 10(1):69–85.

Heyden, D.

1975   An Interpretation of the Cave underneath the Pyramid of the Sun at Teotihuacan, Mexico. *American Antiquity* 40:131–147.

Hopkins, M. R.

1987   Network Analysis of the Plans of Some Teotihuacan Apartment Compounds. *Environment and Planning B: Planning and Design* 14:387–406.

1995   *Teotihuacan Cooking Pots: Scale of Production and Product Variability.* Unpublished Ph.D. dissertation, Department of Anthropology, Brandeis University, Waltham, Mass.

Langley, J. C.

1986   *Symbolic Notation of Teotihuacan.* British Archaeological Reports, International Series 313, Oxford.

Manzanilla, L. (coordinator)

1993   *Anatomía de un conjunto residencial Teotihuacano en Oztoyahualco.* Instituto de Investigaciones Antropológicas, Universidad Nacional Autónoma de México, México, D.F.

1996   Corporate Groups and Domestic Activities at Teotihuacan. *Latin American Antiquity* 7(3):228–246.

Manzanilla, L., and L. Barba

1990   The Study of Activities in Classic Households: Two Case Studies from Cobá and Teotihuacan. *Ancient Mesoamerica* 1:41–49.

Millon, R.

1973   *The Teotihuacan Map.* Part One: *Text.* University of Texas Press, Austin.

1974   The Study of Urbanism at Teotihuacan, Mexico. In *Mesoamerican Archaeology: New Approaches,* edited by N. Hammond, pp. 335–362. Duckworth, London.

1976   Social Relations in Ancient Teotihuacan. In *The Valley of Mexico: Studies in Pre-Hispanic Ecology and Society,* edited by E. R. Wolf, pp. 205–248. University of New Mexico Press, Albuquerque.

1981   Teotihuacan: City, State, and Civilization. In *Archaeology,* edited by V. R. Bricker and J. A. Sabloff, pp. 198–243. Supplement to the Handbook of Middle American Indians, vol. 1. University of Texas Press, Austin.

1988   The Last Years of Teotihuacan Dominance. In *The Collapse of Ancient States and Civilizations,* edited by N. Yoffee and G. L. Cowgill, pp. 102–164. University of Arizona Press, Tucson.

1992   Teotihuacan Studies: From 1950 to 1990 and Beyond. In *Art, Ideology, and the City of Teotihuacan,* edited by J. C. Berlo, pp. 339–429. Dumbarton Oaks, Washington, D.C.

Millon, R., R. B. Drewitt, and G. L. Cowgill

1973   *The Teotihuacan Map.* Part Two: *Maps.* University of Texas Press, Austin.

Pastrana, A.

1997   Nuevos datos acerca de la estratigrafía de Cuicuilco. *Arqueología* 18:3–16.

Pasztory, E.

1997   *Teotihuacan: An Experiment in Living.* University of Oklahoma Press, Norman.

Plunket, P., and G. Uruñuela

1998   Preclassic Household Patterns Preserved under Volcanic Ash at Tetimpa, Puebla, Mexico. *Latin American Antiquity* 9:287–309.

Rattray, E. C.

1993   *The Oaxaca Barrio at Teotihuacan.* Universidad de las Américas, Puebla.

Robertson, I. G.

1999   Spatial and Multivariate Analysis, Random Sampling Error, and Analytical Noise: Empirical Bayesian Methods at Teotihuacan, Mexico. *American Antiquity* 64(1):137–152.

2001   *Mapping the Social Landscape of an Early Urban Center: Socio-Spatial Variation at Teotihuacan.* Unpublished Ph.D. dissertation, Department of Anthropology, Arizona State University, Tempe.

Sanders, W. T.

1981   Ecological Adaptation in the Basin of Mexico: 23,000 B.C. to the Present. In *Archaeology,* edited by V. R. Bricker and J. A. Sabloff, pp. 147–197. Supplement to the Handbook of Middle American Indians, vol. 1. University of Texas Press, Austin.

Sanders, W. T., J. R. Parsons, and R. S. Santley

1979   *The Basin of Mexico: Ecological Processes in the Evolution of a Civilization.* Academic Press, New York.

Séjourné, L.

1966   *Arqueología de Teotihuacan: La cerámica.* Fondo de Cultura Económica, Mexico City.

Sheehy, J. J.

1992   *Ceramic Production in Ancient Teotihuacan, Mexico: A Case Study of Tlajinga 33.* Ph.D. dissertation, Department of Anthropology, Pennsylvania State University. University Microfilms International, Ann Arbor, Mich.

Spence, M. W.

1987   The Scale and Structure of Obsidian Production in Teotihuacan. In *Teotihuacan: Nuevos datos, nuevas síntesis, nuevos problemas,* edited by E. McClung de Tapia and E. C. Rattray, pp. 429–450. Instituto de Investigaciones Antropológicas, Universidad Nacional Autónoma de México, México, D.F.

1992   Tlailotlacan, A Zapotec Enclave in Teotihuacan. In *Art, Ideology, and the City of Teotihuacan,* edited by J. C. Berlo, pp. 59–88. Dumbarton Oaks, Washington, D.C.

Storey, R.

1992   *Life and Death in the Ancient City of Teotihuacan.* University of Alabama Press, Tuscaloosa.

Sugiyama, S.

1993   Worldview Materialized in Teotihuacan, Mexico. *Latin American Antiquity* 4:103–129.

Turner, M. H.

1987a   *The Lapidary Industry of Teotihuacan, Mexico.* Unpublished Ph.D. dissertation, Department of Anthropology, University of Rochester, Rochester, N.Y.

1987b   The Lapidaries of Teotihuacan, Mexico. In *Teotihuacan: Nuevos datos, nuevas síntesis, nuevos problemas,* edited by E. McClung de Tapia and E. C. Rattray, pp. 465–471. Instituto de Investigaciones Antropológicas, Universidad Nacional Autónoma de México, México, D.F.

1992   Style in Lapidary Technology: Identifying the Teotihuacan Lapidary Industry. In *Art, Ideology, and the City of Teotihuacan,* edited by J. C. Berlo, pp. 89–112. Dumbarton Oaks, Washington, D.C.

White, C. D., M. W. Spence, H. Le Q. Stuart-Williams, and H. P. Schwarcz

1998   Oxygen Isotopes and the Identification of Geographical Origins: The Valley of Oaxaca Versus the Valley of Mexico. *Journal of Archaeological Science* 25:643–655.

Widmer, R. J.

1991   Lapidary Craft Specialization at Teotihuacan: Implications for Community Structure at 33:S3W1 and Economic Organization in the City. *Ancient Mesoamerica* 2(1):131–147.

Widmer, R. J., and R. Storey

1993   Social Organization and Household Structure of a Teotihuacan Apartment Compound: S3W1:33 of the Tlajinga Barrio. In *Prehispanic Domestic Units in Western Mesoamerica,* edited by R. S. Santley and K. G. Hirth, pp. 87–104. CRC Press, Boca Raton, Fla.

THREE

The Spatial Patterns of Everyday Life in Old Babylonian Neighborhoods

KATHRYN KEITH

This chapter examines the neighborhood as a significant level of social and spatial patterning in ancient cities, specifically cities of Old Babylonian (second millennium B.C.) Mesopotamia (figure 3.1). It deals with three main issues: (1) the concept of the neighborhood, (2) the relationship between social and spatial organization, and (3) the sociospatial organization of Old Babylonian neighborhoods. Archaeological and textual data are explored to identify neighborhood facilities and patterns of activity that included them, their relationship to particular social roles, and their association with patterns of activity at both household and settlement levels.

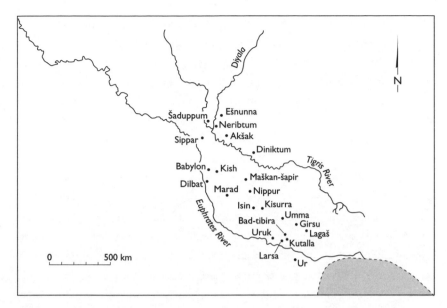

Figure 3.1. Map of southern Mesopotamia (W. Scavone, after Groneberg 1980).

THE NEIGHBORHOOD

The concept of neighborhood was introduced in sociology and urban planning in the early 1900s (Hester 1975:7; Keller 1968:125). Since then, various definitions of the neighborhood have been strongly debated. Some researchers have focused on the physical aspects (e.g., size, boundaries, aesthetics), others on the social (e.g., meaning, interaction, identity), and still others on a combination of both physical and social features (see Keller 1968). Generally, neighborhoods were considered places of limited extent (subdivisions of a larger community) whose inhabitants have distinct characteristics, and they were sometimes seen to have historical and political significance. Variation among neighborhoods was recognized, and dealt with through attempts at classification, such as the typology developed by Warren and Warren (1977). Controversy surrounded definitions of the neighborhood and its appropriate use in urban planning until sometime after World War II, when interest in the concept began to flag (Hester 1975:11).

As Keller (1968:126) points out, "From the start . . . the neighborhood unit was both a social and a planning concept." However, these analytical categories meant different things on the ground. One corrective to this early sociological work was the recognition that neighborhoods had significance for the inhabitants that often did not correspond to "the neighborhood" as defined by researchers on the basis of physical characteristics (e.g., Keller 1968; Morris 1975; Thursz and Vigilante 1978). Researcher-defined neighborhoods were often more like districts, with distinct physical boundaries and distinctive functions or character (such as socioeconomic level or ethnicity). The boundaries of neighborhoods as defined by their inhabitants, however, were often much narrower and were based on patterns of social interaction and a sense of common identity. Keller (1968:91) notes: "The sociological conception of neighborhood emphasizes the notion of shared activities, experiences, and values, common loyalties and perspectives, and human networks that give to an area a sense of continuity and persistence over time."

But a concept of neighborhood developed in industrial and postindustrial cities for the purposes of urban planning and revitalization is inappropriate for understanding the social dynamics and spatial organization of ancient neighborhoods, given differences in technology, transportation, economy, and social relations. What is needed is a definition that can be applied cross-culturally and that allows us to address archaeological questions. For the purposes of this discussion, the neighborhood is considered a level of sociospatial patterning and is defined as the area within which local residents conducted most of their daily activities. Such an area may or may not correspond to "the neighborhood" as identified by either the local inhabitants or the ancient administrative bureaucracy.

The neighborhood is intermediate between household and settlement levels of analysis. It is distinguished in part on the basis of the duplication of facilities and has both social and physical features related to the use of space. Physically, it is composed of buildings and spaces with residential areas that serve as settings for the various activities of neighborhood inhabitants. Neighborhood facilities may include shops and shrines, for example, in addition to houses. Socially, it involves people of various statuses and with various relationships to one another, both kin and nonkin, who regularly interact in this spatial context.

While it is tempting to see the household, neighborhood, and settlement levels of spatial patterning in a nested hierarchy, in practice this is not the case. Unlike the neighborhood, the household is an economic unit bound primarily by kinship and dependency. Physically, it is made up of structures and areas that belong to and are regularly used by individual families, including not only the house itself, but external activity areas and adjoining structures. The household is not necessarily a contiguous unit in space; a large, multiple-dwelling estate, for example, can include property both inside and outside the city walls (Keith 1999). The physical components of some households, then, can actually be dispersed over a wider area than that of the neighborhood. Activities at the household level are conducted by its members or dependents and may extend to any of the physical components of the estate; in contrast, the neighborhood is the level of local action and inter-action, conducted within a limited, contiguous area and involves people who are members of various households.

At the opposite end of the scale, the settlement level of spatial organization is associated with the city as a whole, including its agricultural hinterlands. It is the level most directly, but not exclusively, associated with the major institutions of temple and state. Features and facilities at the settlement level in Old Babylonian cities include the major temple complex, fortifications, quays, the city wall, and city gates. This level may also feature subdivisions such as administrative districts or city quarters that may encompass many neighborhoods.

The different levels of sociospatial organization are interdependent. Each level affects and is affected by the way in which activities are socially organized at the other levels. This further implies that any given level of spatial organization can-not be understood in isolation. Our understanding of the household level of or-ganization, for example, is informed by our knowledge of the types of facilities that existed within the neighborhood.

In the Old Babylonian period, the major institutions of palace and temple or-ganized the construction and maintenance of settlement-level features and facili-ties. Facilities at the neighborhood level, however, were maintained through a com-bination of private and institutional effort. Individual neighborhood residents, for example, constructed and maintained their own private workshops and commer-cial establishments; there is no evidence that such activity had to be approved by any local administrative body. Other facilities, such as neighborhood shrines or major streets and canals, may have relied on financing or labor organized by city institutions, although there is no specific evidence to that effect.

SPATIAL ORGANIZATION AND
SOCIAL ORGANIZATION

In order to interpret spatial patterns in terms of the social patterns that generated them, we first need to understand how social organization relates to spatial or-ganization. Do particular forms of social organization tend to generate certain spa-tial patterns? In fact, the relationship is less direct and more complex than that.

Material and spatial patterns of the city are generated as people act in accordance with cultural knowledge in the context of particular social roles. Most people act at a local (household and neighborhood) level. The cultural concepts that guide their actions are concerned with matters at that scale. It was not only the major institutions that determined the spatial patterns we as archaeologists study. They were also shaped by the common, pervasive, everyday activities—organized in space and time—through which ancient people practiced their culture.

Spatial organization is not simply the arrangement of districts and the placement of buildings and roads. Much more useful is Rapoport's (1969, 1990) compellingly dynamic conceptualization. Rather than seeing spaces as entities having one main, named purpose (for example, the kitchen), Rapoport sees spatial organization in terms of systems of activities that take place in systems of settings. The system of activities for food preparation, for example, includes procuring the raw materials (foodstuffs as well as objects to prepare them with), transport, storage (how, where, and how long), different steps in the preparation of certain ingredients or particular dishes, what is done with the inedible and uneaten portions, and the cleaning and storage of utensils after their use. Each of these activities may occur in different places, so the systems of activities take place in systems of settings.

The two systems are interdependent, since the activities in one setting affect what happens in other settings (Rapoport 1990:18). For example, the form in which foodstuffs are initially acquired, as well as how and when they are to be subsequently prepared for consumption, affects the degree and kinds of preparation that take place in the home. A change in the activity system would lead to changes in the settings; if, for example, flour were usually purchased rather than ground at home, we would expect to see mills or shops among the typical neighborhood facilities.

The setting itself includes not only fixed and semifixed features, but also nonfixed elements such as objects, people, and their activities (Rapoport 1990:13). The activities involved in a given task, though interrelated, may take place at different times, in different sequence, and be performed by different people. This can be summed up in a single question (paraphrasing Rapoport): Who does what when and where? In other words, to understand how spatial organization relates to social organization, we look at social roles (who), associated practices (does what), and settings (when and where).

In this chapter, I consider activities and settings at the neighborhood level of social organization, that is, systems of activities that involve the regular use of settings outside the household, but that do not encompass the city as a whole. To understand this level of spatial patterning, it is necessary to identify specific types of facilities within residential neighborhoods, and much of my discussion centers on this issue.

DATA AND METHODS

The ideal data for a study of spatial organization would include complete city plans with tight control on contemporaneity (for the study of circulation patterns), complete building plans, detailed records of artifact distributions and the locations of features, analyses of faunal and botanical materials, and texts that can be associated with particular buildings. What is actually available for Old Babylonian Mesopotamia, excavated mostly in the early decades of the twentieth century, are incomplete city plans, insecure contemporaneity (at a fine scale, at least), some building plans, little artifactual evidence, and texts. Some of these texts can be associated with particular buildings, some with particular cities, and some have no provenience whatsoever but were purchased from antiquities dealers. In spite of these limitations, however, several aspects of Old Babylonian spatial organization can be usefully investigated with the existing data.

The archaeological and textual data for Old Babylonian Mesopotamia are extremely uneven. I examined published archaeological materials on 16 Old Babylonian cities and found information on at least some major features of most of these cities; however, not many cities had exposed residential architecture and few had complete building plans. The cities with the best archaeological exposure were either excavated before the use of modern methods (e.g., Ur) or have not had their findings fully published (e.g., Šaduppum). There is very little archaeological information from Sippar, the city with the largest group of published texts giving property locations (an important source of information for this study). The texts most informative about what activities were carried out by whom (that is, Old Babylonian letters) can only occasionally be identified with a particular city, let alone with particular buildings. When taken together, however, the data provide a significant amount of information on urban spatial patterns.

One of the main questions of this study is how Old Babylonian people spatially organized their daily activities, especially those that involved neighborhood contexts. The most informative texts in this regard were composed for specific purposes in the course of daily life. They include sales, deeds, rental agreements, records of legal decisions, cultivation contracts, dowries, inheritance texts, merchant inventories, and letters.

In Old Babylonian neighborhoods, houses could be located next to or in close proximity to other houses, commercial property, storage facilities, ruins (buildings or rooms that were allowed to decay), temples or shrines, reed huts, or various types of empty lots (Keith 1999). Other features may have included gardens and animal pens, though no residential property is said to be located next to one of these features. We also know that streets in residential areas were of several types, including broad streets or plazas *(ribītum)* narrower streets *(sūqum)*, alleys *(suqāqum)*, and private exits *(mūṣûm)*.

No Old Babylonian city has been completely excavated, so our knowledge of the street patterns is based mostly on relatively small excavated areas. Most streets were winding and narrow, with blind alleys and smaller streets leading from them. Even major roads within cities did not extend very far from the gates (Schmidt 1964:138) and tended to lead to nearby temples or other public architecture. The range of street types in excavated residential areas (e.g., in Ur, Šaduppum, and Nippur) is similar to that attested in texts. Open areas, broad and narrow streets, alleys, and private entrances existed even within these limited areas of excavation. More interesting, however, are the transformations seen from one phase to the next, as alleys became rooms, and as open areas were built up and narrowed to form streets.

Thanks to Stone's (1987) work at Nippur, we can trace some changes in the circulation patterns of residential areas. In area TA (phase 12B), two narrow streets separated the houses. Though the buildings were destroyed in the following phase, leaving a large open space, by phase 11 they were rebuilt with much the same plan. The streets were in the same locations, but one was now a narrow alley and the other was broader than in the earlier phase. By phase 10A (floor 2), the addition of more buildings had further encroached on the open space, transforming the areas around house K into two narrow streets, and an extension on house I narrowed a third street. In the following phase, an alley next to house J was closed off and incorporated into the house. Stone's work supports Schmidt's (1964:135) observation that street lines in residential areas changed over time as houses were built, repaired, or fell into ruins.

Schmidt (1964) further noted that while small streets in residential areas of Ešnunna changed in size and location over time, the main streets remained much the same through several periods. The larger streets in Old Babylonian cities, those leading from the city gates to the main temple precinct, for example, are associated with the settlement level of spatial organization. Their maintenance over long periods of time and their association with public architecture suggest institutional involvement. The shifting patterns of smaller streets, seen in Nippur and Ešnunna, were associated with the neighborhood level of spatial organization. It is not known what controls may have existed to maintain circulation through residential areas, but the fluidity of the patterns seen here suggests that some form of local negotiation was involved.

Though private alleys could be inherited, streets were not. Even though they were sometimes named after individuals (who may have owned property in the area), those same individuals did not necessarily own or control the streets. Decisions about buildings that affected circulation patterns in a neighborhood may have been rendered by a neighborhood citizen association. However, I found no records of court decisions regarding, for example, conflicts between building construction and street boundaries, nor are such concerns expressed in letters. Schmidt (1964:144) further notes that the owner of property directly in front of a stretch of road would maintain it as his wishes and finances allowed, so that some stretches of a given street might be paved with material such as potsherds, while others may not be paved at all.

Canals are also attested in residential areas and were associated with built property, empty lots, and possibly storage facilities. The overall frequency of attestations of canals in residential areas is, as expected, lower than that of streets. Stone (1991:240) identifies an archaeological pattern in Maškan-šapir and Larsa in which streets run parallel and at right angles to the internal canals. This is supported in five texts (from Ašdubba and Sippar) in which residential property adjoins both a street and a canal. The street in every case was a broad street or plaza and was located at one end of the property, while the canal was located at the other end, suggesting that a broad street ran parallel to the canal. In a sixth example from Babylon, the property was on the bank of the canal, with the broad street on one end and residential property on three sides.

Though some houses were located along canals, I found no mentions of private docks or of boats within the city. Boats or rafts in private contexts were usually hired for shipment of goods or for travel between cities. The internal canals, then, may not have served as routes of transportation for private individuals within the city. The construction and maintenance of major waterways, presumably including those inside the city walls, were the responsibility of city institutions. The fact that broad streets ran parallel or perpendicular to the canals in residential areas suggests that both were part of the settlement level of spatial organization, not controlled or affected by changes at the neighborhood level.

So we see a combination of institutional and local forces influencing the location of streets and canals within residential areas. It is uncertain whether these forces involved formal mandates by official groups (such as the palace or a citizen association). Canals and broad streets could have been overseen informally when the administration called for dredging or other regular maintenance. The shifting patterns of smaller streets in residential areas could have been governed by commonly understood principles, with only disputes or actions beyond traditional practice being brought to the attention of local administrative bodies.

Neighborhood Facilities

Residential areas contained not only houses, but also chapels, bakeries, taverns, and shops. We know of some facilities from texts, and others have been identified archaeologically on the basis of features and finds. Archaeological survey at Maškan-šapir and at Larsa has shown that small-scale craft activities were present throughout residential areas (Stone 1991). Texts also refer to several occupations as well as to the purchase of particular goods and services.

The problem is identifying which buildings were houses, which were facilities, and which might have served some other function. Recorded information on features and finds in residential area buildings is uneven and rather sparse. Analysis must therefore rely largely on ground plans. These were compared using access graphs (a way of representing circulation patterns within a building) (see, e.g., Blanton 1994; Steadman 1983) and various measures derived from them (Keith 1999). As the following examples demonstrate, however, similar circulation patterns could have arisen for practical reasons (the relative location of rooms), social reasons (inheritance or sharing of the house by more than one family), or functional reasons (a workshop, bakery, or other commercial use of a room). Even within a particular society, there is no single way to interpret a given type of circulation pattern in social terms.

The evidence suggests that most facilities in residential areas were not in separate buildings but were physically part of houses. Most residential area buildings had features consistent with their identification as houses and their association with private domestic activities. The houses in residential areas varied in size and ground plan, with some generally common features (Keith 1999; Miglus 1996). Several houses, however, had a distinctive circulation pattern consisting of an isolated group of rooms with its own entrance, connected to one room of the main building. Beyond this one similar feature, the overall plans varied. This is expected, since the separated room groups were part of larger residences; the houses they were attached to would be expected to vary with the circumstances of the owners.

A few of these room groups have been identified as bakeries, primarily because of the presence of several ovens and quantities of ash. But the vast majority of the room groups had no preserved features or finds, and no domestic function can be definitely established for them on the basis of features, relative location within the building, or relative size. In other words, they were not courtyards, main rooms, chapels, stairways, or lavatories; they did not contain burials, and there is no evidence for household cooking activities occurring in them (with the exception of those identified as bakeries).

At house I in Nippur, studied by Stone (1981; 1987), similar circulation patterns resulted from the division of the house by inheritance. The main changes in circulation in house I consisted of the cutting of a second exterior doorway and the closing off of two rooms from use, after the house was inherited and two of the brothers bought out the shares of their siblings. The other rooms maintained the same links to each other. Though the circulation pattern is similar to that seen in the bakeries, in this case it was due to the sharing of the house by two of the brothers who inherited it.

House I was later connected to neighboring house H through purchase. Even when the two houses were joined, they each maintained their basic original circulation patterns. This was probably due, at least in part, to practical concerns. The end of house H abutted one side of house I, overlapping only slightly with house I's entrance room. There was, then, little choice in where connections between the two houses could be made. Privacy concerns may also have been a factor in maintaining essentially separate circulation patterns, particularly since the house continued to have two separate entrances. Like house I, house H was shared by two brothers. If both were in residence with their families, then the separate sections of house H/I may have been used by the two separate families.

Finally, several lines of evidence point to the existence of commercial and craft-related activities within residential neighborhoods. Textual data and surface remains indicate that larger cities had a variety of artisans working at small shops in neighborhood contexts. Since no separate workshop facilities have been identified among the buildings in Old Babylonian residential areas, this suggests that small-scale crafts and commercial establishments were typically located within private homes. We know that bakeries were located in some of the room groups identified here; perhaps neighborhood workshops were located in others.

The only distinctive buildings found within residential neighborhoods consisted of a few very large complexes of rooms, revealed through excavations at Šaduppum, Neribtum, and Ur. One such complex in the AH area at Ur consisted of structures identified by the excavators as Paternoster Row 4, 4A, 6, 8, and 12, and Bazaar Alley 1 (figure 3.2; as an aside, it should be noted that the streets of Ur were named after streets in Oxford, rather than on the basis of ancient texts). This area had been modified several times, sometimes with structures interconnected and others not. Different sections of the complex served residential or commercial functions for an extended family (Van De Mieroop 1992:149). A number of these rooms may at one time have formed a single unit, similar in scale to Paternoster Row 11 (a large complex across the street). It was divided through inheritance into several smaller buildings, but many continued to be occupied by family members. Paternoster Row 11 had at least 19 rooms on the ground level. Although initially convinced that it was a public facility of some sort, because of its size and complexity in comparison with other structures in AH, Woolley and Mallowan (1976:150) eventually decided it was more likely a large private home, given the presence of a private chapel and numerous burials in room 11. It is also possible that different parts of the complex served as a private residence or as a commercial or other neighborhood facility.

Old Babylonian neighborhoods, then, consisted of one or more very large buildings, probably owned by a prominent family, surrounded by small and medium-sized houses in which different types of workshops and commercial facilities might be located.

OLD BABYLONIAN FACILITIES:
THE EVIDENCE

The evidence suggests that Old Babylonian neighborhoods had several kinds of facilities: workshops, bakeries, mills, oil-pressing equipment, taverns, establishments for textile finishing (done by "fullers"), shops, and chapels, as well as some others.

Workshops

Most of the textual references to workshops and craft activities are associated with major institutions (e.g., Van De Mieroop 1983, 1986). Goldsmiths, leather workers,

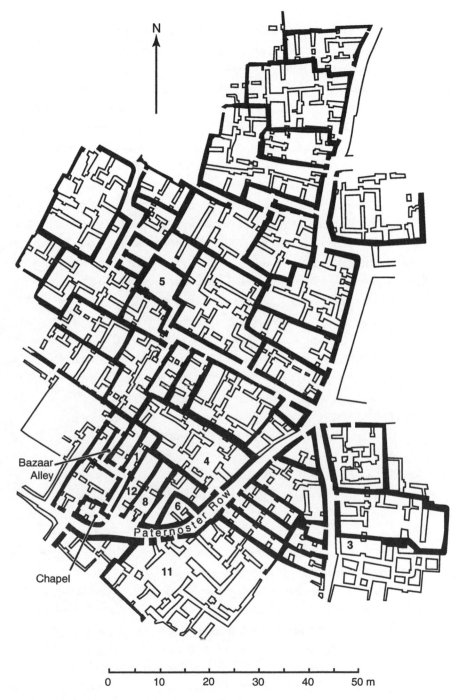

Figure 3.2. AH area of Ur (W. Scavone, after Woolley and Mallowan 1976, plate 124).

reedworkers, and carpenters, among others, produced work in different workshops for the palace or temples. In one case, a private workshop was rented (VAS 18, 29), but neither the occupation of the renter nor the location of the workshop were stated.

Residential areas at Maškan-šapir and Larsa showed a mix of craft debris, deriving from small-scale production (Stone 1991). If local artisans worked out of their homes rather than out of separate facilities, then the mixture of manufacturing debris throughout residential areas suggests that people with various occupations resided in a given neighborhood. It also suggests that inhabitants of local neighborhoods had access to a variety of goods within walking distance.

Most of the evidence for small-scale crafts is indirect and comes from the textual materials. Some texts refer to goods that were commissioned from particular artisans. In one case, reedworkers were commissioned to make a door for a gentleman's house (AbB 3, 34). Several texts refer to buying or sending copper so that a smith could make (usually agricultural) tools (e.g., AbB 9, 17; AbB 6, 89). The numbers of tools and the other concerns mentioned in these letters suggest that they were from private contexts. Occasional reference is also made to providing materials for woodworkers (AbB 3, 52; AbB 6, 167). In the case of the metal tools, the copper was taken to the smith and the tools later retrieved (AbB 6, 89). A woodworker, however, was sent to get the needed materials to make stools (AbB 6, 167).

Other evidence indicates that artisans also procured their own materials and made objects for sale. The fact that some goods, such as stools, were included in possible merchant inventories and sales documents (TCL X, 116; YOS 8, 174) suggests they were available for purchase rather than being specially commissioned. Letters refer to the purchase of baskets and nets (e.g., AbB 1, 60; YOS 5, 87). The various references to objects being available (or not) in other towns suggests that at least some goods were made and then offered for sale, perhaps to traveling merchants.

Specifically where local crafts trade took place is not clear. Did a servant go to the potter or reedworker's home and select a basket or vessel? Or did artisans regularly take their products to the city gates or to a large plaza where local residents could come to select what they needed? One letter bemoans that though the herald made an announcement, no one in the town came forward to buy the oil being offered for barley or silver (AbB 12, 95). That such mechanisms were in place suggests that this was not an unusual way for sellers and buyers to locate one another, and that local artisans might be expected to have some goods on hand for sale.

Bakeries

The writers of one Old Babylonian letter (AbB 6, 70) complain that they were forced to eat bought bread. This tells us that bread was available to private individuals for purchase, though bread made at home was apparently preferable, and that bakeries might be among neighborhood facilities. Several possible bakeries have been identified archaeologically at Ur and Nippur. They varied in scale from bakeries that supplied bread to the palace and temple, to smaller bakeries, perhaps associated with shops to serve local needs.

Niche Lane 3 in area AH at Ur was owned by Dumuzi-gamil who, among other things, organized and financed the provision of grain and supplies to several bakeries and the distribution of their products to the palace and temples (Van de Mieroop 1992:134). The facility in Baker's Square 1B may have been one of those bakeries. Woolley characterized 1B as a workshop and the three ovens as furnaces rather than bread ovens (Woolley and Mallowan 1976:158). Franke (1987:274), however, noted their similarity to bread ovens she observed in modern Iran. Another bread oven was located in the center of nearby Baker's Square.

House A in area WB at Nippur was also a larger-scale bakery, though it was located within a private home. It had "an enormous accumulation of ash and the occurrence of more bread ovens than would be necessary to supply the needs of a private household" (Franke 1987:278). Ovens were located inside the house as well as in an adjoining outdoor area. Two texts from the area, dated to the period in which breadmaking was taking place, deal with distributions of bread for potters, canal workers, and goldsmiths hired by or associated with the Ninurta temple (Franke 1987:278).

Smaller-scale bakeries may have been located in houses at TA and TB in Nippur. House P/J in area TA had a series of ovens, associated with shallow bowls typical in breadmaking contexts. No texts from the area deal with bread distribution, though we would not expect to find any unless the bakery had dealings with major institutions. The distribution of bread, as well as livestock, was noted in administrative texts from area TB (Stone 1987:81), where two possible bakeries may have existed. Two bread ovens associated with shallow bowls in a corner of house R definitely indicate that breadmaking took place, but it is uncertain whether this was a commercial bakery or simply the household bread ovens. House C had two bread ovens near the front entrance. In a later level, house C-1 had at least two bread ovens at the far end of the courtyard; a third was just inside the entrance to C-2. A large, probably beehive-shaped oven was located inside the northernmost of the two front exits (McCown and Haines 1967:59–60).

These examples emphasize the connection between institutional and private concerns within neighborhoods. Some of the products from the private, small-scale establishments scattered throughout residential areas could go to personnel associated with the major city institutions, while others could go to local households. Neighborhood shops could be linked economically to the temple or palace without being controlled by them. The neighborhood economy thus involved a combination of institutional and private ties. Finally, not all private homes relied on neighborhood bakeries for their bread supplies. Throughout all phases of areas TA and TB, for example, bread ovens were located in one or more private homes within the excavated area and presumably served household needs.

Mills

Flour mills were not among the facilities documented in Old Babylonian neighborhoods. Mills were mentioned only in connection with prisoners and were likely state facilities. Being a miller is attested as an occupation of some individuals (AbB 2, 6; AbB 6, 216; AbB 8, 43; AbB 9, 248, AbB 12, 17), but most of these also had institutional affiliations. All of them mentioned sending a miller someplace to work, but only one letter (AbB 6, 50) referred to hiring a miller to grind flour, possibly in a household context.

I found no references to private milling facilities, and the few property owners with listed occupations did not include millers. Households had their own millstones, which slaves, younger household members, or sometimes hired workers used to grind the household flour. I found only one reference to the purchase of flour (AbB 9, 144); it involved a high-quality flour, evidently for a special purpose, since the same text noted that flour for household use should be ground by the young women. Finally, in AbB 6, 50, there was no hired worker to grind the grain at home. However, the sender of the letter did not complain of having to buy commercially ground flour, but of having to eat bought bread. This supports the idea that small-scale mills where people could buy flour or take their grain to be ground were not among the facilities in Old Babylonian neighborhoods.

Oil-pressing Facilities

Oil preparers either went or sent someone to private homes to collect sesame for extraction (YOS 2, 11; YOS 2, 125). The tools of the oil preparer included several pieces of equipment (an oven, grinding tools, a sieve, jars, and an installation of some sort), and the process itself involved several steps (Stol 1985), so it is logical that the extraction would be carried out in his facility. No such facilities were identified archaeologically, however, and none of the listed finds for the excavated buildings included this particular group of tools. But textual references indicate that oil-pressing facilities must have existed.

Besides having private stores of sesame pressed, individuals could purchase oil (e.g., CT 29, 14). A letter involving a field dispute mentions an *ālik šamnim* (AbB 3, 86), translated as oil seller (Frankena 1968:65). But these references do not tell us how such trade was organized. As with the craft products, oil might have been sold at the presser's home, or in some public venue (as the letter about the herald and the oil implies).

Taverns

Taverns and cookshops were apparently common establishments in both cities and smaller settlements. They are attested near commercial property in Sippar and were rented in several cities. None, however, have been identified archaeologically. Goetze (1965) discusses a text from the Sippar region in which the tax obligations of innkeepers and cooks in the nearby villages were noted. A letter (AbB 12, 89) refers to an assembly of innkeepers; I found no other reference to other such occupational groups. Innkeepers were apparently called upon for various errands unrelated to serving drinks. In two texts (AbB 9, 240; AbB 6, 178), innkeepers are to be given money to bring barley to private individuals. Innkeepers were also entrusted with dry bran (AbB 7, 183) and captured slaves (AbB 1, 39; Riftin 46).

The relationship between brewers and innkeepers is unclear. Brewers were associated with temples and the palace; innkeepers ran private establishments. It is not clear, however, whether innkeepers got their beer from brewers or brewed it themselves. In either case, brewing beer was a multistep process requiring various tools (such as sieves, vats, jars, and ovens) and would have required standing facilities.

Fullers

Though usually noted in institutional contexts, fullers may also have been hired by private individuals to finish textiles. A woman writes (AbB 13, 192) that she has just finished a garment and given it to the fuller, and she requests wool so she can begin work on another garment. Another text (AbB 10, 112) similarly notes the delivery of garments to a fuller. While none have been identified archaeologically, the fuller may have had an establishment where garments from private households could be delivered for finishing or cleaning.

Shops

Thus far, the only shop that has been identified on archaeological grounds is Store Street 3 in Ur, which had two rooms preserved above ground and a series of below-ground chambers at the back, some of which contained remains of burnt grain, straw, and date pits (Woolley and Mallowan 1976). It is also possible that this was a private or shared storage facility. Small buildings at Šaduppum and Ur with one or two rooms were thought to be shops or possibly merchant stalls, but no finds or features were noted to support such an identification.

There were four references to commercial property among the property locations (Scheil Sippar 10; Scheil Sippar 100; BE 6/1, 13; TCL 1, 77); the latter two probably involve the same piece of property. In all four, the commercial property is associated with a tavern and is located near a broad street. Other commercial properties in Sippar (BE 6/1, 51; MHET 2/2, 169; MHET 2/3, 389), Neribtum (Greengus Studies 30), Kish (Genouillac Kich, C71), and Larsa (TCL XI, 219) were rented, usually for a year. None of the references, however, specify what activities were occurring within these facilities and none have been identified archaeologically so that features and finds could be analyzed.

Chapels

These are among the few archaeologically identified neighborhood facilities in Ur. Woolley and Mallowan (1976) identified four buildings as chapels on the basis of architectural and internal features and finds. These features included door-jambs with reveals at the exterior entrance and the entrance to the sanctuary, and an interior floor higher than the street level with steps leading up to it and reliefs flanking the entrance. The chapel interior had a courtyard with an altar and a sanctuary with a recess to hold the cult statue. Reiter (1991:56) further notes the use of reed wall paneling to mark special areas within chapels.

All of the chapels have different types of ground plans, and all of them have measures and plans within the known variation for Old Babylonian houses. On the basis of ground plan alone, neighborhood chapels were indistinguishable from other neighborhood buildings. Unlike larger city temples, chapels were not always built in the same place through time. The Bazaar Chapel in Ur's AH area, for example, was originally part of a house (14 Paternoster Row). Though their interior floors were sometimes raised above street level, the chapels did not rise on mounds above the surrounding buildings. The locations of neighborhood chapels were not apparently considered sacred places in the same way that the larger temples of the city were. Regardless of how they were maintained financially, they were part of the neighborhood fabric, and their location and specific layout were influenced by the existing neighborhood structure.

Other Features

Empty lots in Old Babylonian neighborhoods were regularly attested in residential sales and inheritance documents and are seen archaeologically (e.g., Ur AH Straight Street 5 and possibly areas associated with Church Street 9; behind New Street 5 in Ur's EM area; and areas in Nippur TA, TB, and WB). They were privately owned and were used for various purposes by area residents. For example, an oven was located in an alley associated with house B in Nippur's area TB, while trash dumping was noted in adjacent area Q. Detailed studies of outdoor activity areas, such as empty lots, streets, and alleys, however, are not available. The specific settings (rooms or outdoor areas) in which activities occurred are not usually specified in texts either, so our understanding of the uses of outdoor areas within cities is particularly limited.

A Kassite period map of Nippur (Franke 1987:17) shows an area of gardens at the south end of the site, associated with a temple. Texts also note a Dursagene garden gate (district) within Nippur, where payment is made (BE 6/2, 62) and oaths are sworn (e.g., PBS 7, 7). It is also possible that private individuals had small gardens in their courtyards or on empty lots they owned, but there are no direct attestations of private gardens within residential areas.

Animals were kept in agricultural areas outside the city walls, in the village property owned by a large estate or out in pasture areas (Keith 1999:271–272). There is little to no evidence bearing on animals kept within city walls. Faunal remains attest to the use of pig, goat, cow, and sheep as food items in private contexts at Nippur (Franke 1987) and at Maškan-šapir (Stone and Zimansky 1992). But there were no references to the purchase of meat, nor to a butcher as an occupation, and I found only one reference to slaughtering (CT 4, 13a). There were, however, numerous references to meat. Most of these were in rental or support agreements involving a devotee (*nadītum*) of Šamaš, in which the renter or heir would provide either beer or flour and a standard-sized meat portion. Though there are few references to having livestock sent from the village, there are none for meat to be sent to the city. It is likely that the animals were sent live to the city and slaughtered there. This may not, however, have required the presence of animal stalls or barns within residential neighborhoods.

The references to sending sheep usually involved wool (e.g., AbB 2, 82; AbB 10, 20). Sheep and possibly donkeys (AbB 12, 72) were taken to the city at least occasionally, but not apparently in large numbers. How long they stayed there, where they stayed, and whether the sheep were slaughtered or kept for wool was not noted, but there must have been at least temporary holding areas for them. Stone (1987:100) suggested that the open area P in Nippur TB could have been used for such a purpose. Waetzoldt (1996:150) similarly suggested that livestock could have been kept in empty lots or gardens. It is also possible that some of the isolated room groups (discussed above) were used to keep small numbers of livestock within residential areas, though none of them had related features (such as drinking troughs or food bins).

OCCUPATIONAL PATTERNING:
WHO DID WHAT

In both Ur and Nippur, there is evidence that some residential areas had stronger institutional affiliations than others. In Nippur, area TB was "apparently the residential quarter for landless employees of the state" (Stone 1987:76), while occupants of TA were small property owners (Stone 1987:71). Stone notes in particular the absence of administrative documents from area TA and a corresponding lack of property inheritance or sales documents from TB until quite late. The "neighborhoods" in question are relatively small, however, and larger excavations of these areas might reveal different patterns.

Both houses and occupations passed from father to son in area EM at Ur, which was occupied by priestly families associated with the Nanna and Ningal temples (Van de Mieroop 1992:123). Area AH was occupied by businessmen who financed trade expeditions as well as numerous other ventures, collected taxes and rents from fishermen, and delivered bread to the palace (Van de Mieroop 1992:163). The evidence from property locations is less clear, in part because various occupations can be, but are not necessarily, associated with the temple, the palace, or the military. A lamentation priest lived next door to a potter in Isin (BIN 7, 212). In Nippur, a priest of Ninlil and his brother had a cook and a carpenter as neighbors (BE 6/2, 10). These examples show seemingly disparate occupations within the same residential area. In YOS 8, 4, however, two wood or metal craftsmen lived next door to each other. This was only temporary, since one of them exchanged his property with a well-known Larsa businessman; the occupation of his new neighbor was not specified.

In some cases, the occupation of only one neighbor was listed. Such examples included a carpenter (BE 6/2, 14), a goldsmith (Scheil Sippar 87), a shepherd (CT 4, 41a), and a scribe (CT 4, 17b). Fishermen (sometimes a literal fisherman and sometimes a kind of soldier) (CBS 155; UET 5, 104), barbers (a kind of official) (AUAM 73, 3193; VAS 22, 28), bird catchers (BE 6/2, 44; VAS 22, 14), and physicians (CT 48, 14; Charpin Archives Familiales: 259, TS77; RA 73, pp. 74–75) were also noted as neighbors. It seems unlikely that noting the occupation of a neighbor would be useful as identification in a deed or inheritance text if the entire area were occupied by people of the same profession.

There were no occupationally defined residential districts in Old Babylonian cities. No districts, or even streets, were named for particular occupations; both appear to be named for either gods or individuals. But as Van de Mieroop (1992:166) points out, "The professional preferences of the inhabitants of various sites is clear and these areas must have been regarded as having a specific identity." That identity could have developed, however, as a result of family occupational and residential patterns, as sons followed in the occupations of their fathers and perhaps as family members took advantage of each other's professional connections. This is indicated in the southern part of Paternoster Row, where many of the residents shared both occupations and kinship. So while some texts show a tendency for people with similar occupational or institutional affiliations to live in the same area within a city, other texts demonstrate that this was not a hard-and-fast rule.

References to different categories of people and the activities in which they were engaged clearly indicate that most of the household work, including running various errands, was undertaken by either slaves *(wardum* or *amtum)* or younger household members *(ṣuhārum* or *ṣuhārtum).* The latter have been translated in the *Assyrian Dictionary of the Oriental Institute of the University of Chicago* as servants (in the case of males) or as young men and young women, respectively. Unlike slaves, they were not owned, sold, or inherited, but they did not receive wages, as did hired workers. They instead received regular food allotments, as did slaves and other household dependents. It is possible that these were younger members of the family, perhaps of the extended family, who ran errands and did much of the household work, particularly if the family owned no slaves.

Slaves and servants, both male and female, were most often attested (in letters) as bringing objects from the village to the city, or from one city to another (e.g., AbB 1, 134; AbB 2, 142; AbB 11, 51; AbB 11, 177; AbB 12, 59; AbB 13, 71). The goods they were entrusted with included letters, garments, wool, oil, and fodder. Household errands within the neighborhood would not be noted in letters or other texts, so we have no direct attestations regarding who was responsible for them. But given the fact that slaves and servants ran such errands in larger spatial contexts, it is likely that they were also responsible for going to various neighborhood facilities on household errands.

There is no information on patterns of visiting within neighborhoods, but letters do occasionally mention family members traveling to other cities or to village property to visit or for other purposes. Visiting among homes within neighborhoods probably occurred as well. Miglus (1996) notes a reception room among the typical rooms of an Old Babylonian house. It was usually the second largest room, located off the courtyard, with particularly well-built walls. It sometimes had an associated lavatory, and more than half had the unusual feature of a centrally located doorway (Keith 1999:258). Informal visiting may also have occurred in the courtyard of a house. As the central room, open to air and light, yet presumably shaded, the courtyard was the locus of many varied household activities, including food consumption and both general and specialized food preparation (Franke 1987). This would be compatible with informal visiting, where neighbors might have something to eat or drink, and perhaps even share a task, in the shaded "outdoor" part of the house.

So neighborhood-level social interaction may have included patterns of visiting among neighbors. Individuals traveled through their neighborhoods to meet with others over business dealings, to pursue a court action, to go to a tavern or cookshop, or to visit a chapel or temple for personal or professional reasons. Slaves and servants were also out running various household errands, and local artisans or their servants may have been out collecting materials or delivering goods. We see that people of different statuses and with various relationships to each other interacted in neighborhood contexts as they went about their daily activities.

CONCLUSION

This chapter has demonstrated that the neighborhood was a significant level of sociospatial patterning in Old Babylonian cities. Skilled artisans, bakers, and oil pressers were incorporated into the regular activities of some households as they engaged their services or procured household objects. People may also have called upon the services of tavern keepers, fullers, and cookshop owners. Such neighborhood facilities could have had economic ties with both major institutions and local households. Their number and location, however, were not controlled by city institutions but were determined by the individuals involved.

Most facilities in neighborhoods were located in private homes. The few archaeologically identified separate facilities include a possible bakery (at Ur) and several neighborhood chapels. The chapels were of various sizes and types and were not built in the same place over time. They were part of the neighborhood fabric, their form and location influenced by purely local concerns. Neighborhoods tended to consist of a large house surrounded by several smaller buildings. Houses could be located next to large and small houses, temples or shrines, commercial property, empty lots, or ruins. The specific locations of these neighborhood features changed over time as property was sold, inherited, or abandoned.

Circulation through neighborhoods was by way of large and small streets, alleys, dead-ends, and private exits, all attested both textually and archaeologically. The shifting patterns of small, winding neighborhood streets through time, as area houses were built, expanded, or destroyed, was indicative of local control, while the major city streets and the canals that tended to parallel them were the responsibility of city institutions. There is little evidence for separate occupational or commercial districts. What occupational patterning there was undoubtedly resulted from the tendency for the family house and the family trade to be passed down from father to son. There is evidence for some family patterning in residential areas, ranging from the division of a large complex (such as Paternoster Row 4 in Ur) with inheritance, to the coresidence of brothers who jointly owned a house (as at Nippur TA house H/I).

We have seen that we need to look at social patterning in order to understand spatial patterning. The same spatial pattern evident in residential area bakeries—that of an isolated room group with its own entrance attached to the house through one room—could have arisen for various social, practical, or functional reasons. As the discussion also demonstrates, the sociospatial organization of ancient neighborhoods cannot be studied in isolation. It affects and is affected by the ways in which activities are organized at household and settlement levels.

The particular features and functions of neighborhoods are expected to vary cross-culturally along several lines, depending on the overall social and economic organization of the city. The characteristics described here for Old Babylonian neighborhoods may not be the same for other ancient cities. The particular facilities used by local inhabitants, the relative involvement of major institutions or local decision-making bodies, patterns of formal and informal social interaction, and occupational or kinship patterning in residential areas are among some of the ways in which neighborhoods in different social and cultural contexts would be expected to vary. What is clear, however, is that the neighborhood is a potentially significant level of sociospatial patterning in ancient cities and should be included in studies of urban spatial organization.

TEXT ABBREVIATIONS

With the exception of AUAM, the abbreviations used in this paper follow those found in CAD. I have also listed them here for the convenience of nonspecialists.

AbB	Altbabylonische Briefe in Umschrift und Übersetzung
AUAM	Tablets in the collections of the Andrews University Archaeological Museum
BE	Babylonian Expedition of the University of Pennsylvania, Series A: Cuneiform Texts
BiMes	Bibliotheca Mesopotamica
BIN	Babylonian Inscriptions in the Collection of J. B. Nies
CAD	*The Assyrian Dictionary of the Oriental Institute of the University of Chicago*
CBS	Tablets in the collections of the University Museum of the University of Pennsylvania, Philadelphia
Charpin Archives Familiales	D. Charpin, Archives familiales et propriété privée . . . Tell Sifr

CT	Cuneiform Texts from Babylonian Tablets
Genouillac Kich	H. de Genouillac, Premières recherches archéologiques à Kich
Greengus Studies	S. Greengus, Studies in Ishchali Documents (= BiMes 19)
MHET	Mesopotamian History and Environment
RA	Revue d'assyriologie et d'archéologie orientale
Riftin	A. P. Riftin, Staro-Vavilonskie iuridicheskie i administrativnye dokumenty v sobraniiakh SSSR
Scheil Sippar	V. Scheil, Une saison de fouilles à Sippar
TCL	Textes cunéiformes du Louvre
UET	Ur Excavations, Texts
VAS	Vorderasiatische Schriftdenkmäler
YOS	Yale Oriental Series, Babylonian Texts

REFERENCES

Blanton, R.
   1994   *Houses and Households: A Comparative Study.* Plenum Press, New York.
Franke, J. A.
   1987   *Artifact Patterning and Functional Variability in the Urban Dwelling: Old Babylonian Nippur, Iraq.* Unpublished Ph.D. dissertation, University of Chicago, Chicago.
Frankena, R.
   1968   *Briefe aus der Leidener Sammlung (TLB IV).* Vol. 3. E. J. Brill, Leiden.
Goetze, A.
   1965   Tavern Keepers and the Like in Ancient Babylonia. *Assyriological Studies* 16:211ff.
Hester, R.
   1975   *Neighborhood Space.* Dowden, Hutchinson, and Ross, Stroudsburg, Pa.
Keith, K.
   1999   *Cities, Neighborhoods, and Houses: Urban Spatial Organization in Old Babylonian Mesopotamia.* Unpublished Ph.D. dissertation, University of Michigan, Ann Arbor.
Keller, S.
   1968   *The Urban Neighborhood: A Sociological Perspective.* Random House, New York.
McCown, D. E., and R. Haines
   1967   *Nippur I: Temple of Enlil, Scribal Quarter, and Soundings.* Vol. 78. University of Chicago Press, Chicago.
Miglus, P. A.
   1996   Die räumliche Organisation des altbabylonischen Hofhauses. In *Houses and Households in Ancient Mesopotamia: Papers read at the 40e Rencontre Assyriologique Internationale Leiden, July 5–8, 1993,* edited by K. R. Veenhof, pp. 211–220. Nederlands Historisch-Archaeologisch Intituut, Istanbul.
Morris, D.
   1975   *Neighborhood Power.* Institute for Policy Studies, Washington, D.C.
Rapoport, A.
   1969   *House Form and Culture.* Prentice-Hall, Englewood Cliffs, N.J.

1990   Systems of Activities and Systems of Settings. In *Domestic Architecture and Use of Space,* edited by S. Kent, pp. 9–20. Cambridge University Press, Cambridge.

Reiter, K.

1991   84) Kilkillu, archaeologisch. *Nouvelles Assyriologiques brèves et utilitaires* (3 September):55–57.

Schmidt, J.

1964   Strassen in Altorientalischen Wohngebieten: Eine Studie zur Geschichte des Städtebaues in Mesopotamien und Syrien. *Baghdader Mitteilungen* 3:125–147.

Steadman, J. P.

1983   *Architectural Morphology: An Introduction to the Geometry of Building Plans.* Pion, London.

Stol, M.

1985   Remarks on the Cultivation of Sesame and the Extraction of Its Oil. *Bulletin on Sumerian Agriculture* 2:119–126.

Stone, E.

1981   Texts, Architecture and Ethnographic Analogy: Patterns of Residence in Old Babylonian Nippur. *Iraq* 43(1):19–34.

1987   *Nippur Neighborhoods.* Vol. 44. Oriental Insitute of the University of Chicago, Chicago.

1991   The Spacial Organization of Mesopotamian Cities. *Aula Orientalis* 9:235–242.

Stone, E., and P. Zimansky

1992   Mashkan-shapir and the Anatomy of an Old Babylonian City. *Biblical Archaeologist* 55(4):212–218.

Thursz, D., and J. Vigilante

1978   *Reaching People: The Structure of Neighborhood Services.* Sage Publications, London.

Van De Mieroop, M.

1983   *The Early Isin Craft Archive.* Unpublished Ph.D. dissertation, Yale University, New Haven, Conn.

1986   The Administration of Crafts in the Early Isin Period. In *Cuneiform Archives and Tablets,* edited by K. R. Veenhof, pp. 87–95. Nederlands Historisch-Archaeologisch Intituut, Istanbul.

1992   *Society and Enterprise in Old Babylonian Ur.* Dietrich Reimer Verlag, Berlin.

Waetzoldt, H.

1996   Privathäuser: Ihre Größe, Einrichtung und die Zahl der Bewohner. In *Houses and Households in Ancient Mesopotamia: Papers read at the 40e Rencontre Assyriologique Internationale Leiden, July 5–8, 1993,* edited by K. R. Veenhof, pp. 145–152. Nederlands Historisch-Archaeologisch Intituut, Istanbul.

Warren, R., and D. Warren

1977   *The Neighborhood Organizer's Handbook.* University of Notre Dame Press, Notre Dame.

Woolley, Sir L., and Sir M. Mallowan

1976   *The Old Babylonian Period.* Vol. 7. British Museum Publications, London.

Life behind Walls

Patterns in the Urban Landscape on the
Prehistoric North Coast of Peru

JERRY D. MOORE

In the *Histories,* Herodotus (1972:81–83) describes the political rise of Deioces, "a man of great ability and ambitious for power," who emerged from the uncentralized village-level polities of Media as a leader famous for his skill at fairly adjudicating disputes. All the Medes turned to Deioces to resolve their conflicts, but eventually Deioces announced that "he had had enough of it—he would no longer sit in the chair of judgment. It was contrary to his own interest to spend all his time settling his neighbours' quarrels to the neglect of his own affairs," and he withdrew from public life. Conflict and chaos ensued until, finally, the assembly of the Medes decided to choose Deioces as king.

The new ruler's first act was to command that a palace be built and that a royal guard be established. Deioces then commanded that a royal city be built, "a single great city to which, as the capital of the country, all other towns were to be held of secondary importance." The city Ecbatana sat on a hill, "a place of great size and strength fortified by seven concentric walls," the innermost containing the royal palace and treasury. "These fortifications were to protect the king and his palace," Herodotus writes, and "the people had to build their houses outside the circuit of the walls."

At this point political wiles and defensive walls were complemented by ceremony. "When the work of building was complete," Herodotus writes, "Deioces introduced for the first time the ceremonial of royalty: admission to the king's presence was forbidden, and all communication had to be through messengers. Nobody was allowed to see the king, and it was an offence for anyone to laugh or spit in the royal presence. This solemn ceremonial was designed as a safeguard against his contemporaries . . . with whom he had been brought up in earlier years. There was a risk that if they saw him habitually, it might lead to jealousy and resentment, and plots would follow; but if nobody saw him, the legend would grow that he was a being of a different order from mere men."

The once-reluctant ruler evolved into a Machiavellian schemer, and Deioces consolidated his power with social distance and physical concealment. Just as in some societies display, pomp, and the common touch are important elements of political ceremony and the symbolic restatement of authority, an alternative path can emphasize the invisibility and difference of ruler from the ruled, an Oz-like authority hidden behind the curtain. And in some cases, this conception of social and political order may be reflected in architectural forms, as it is after circa A.D. 900 in urban centers on the North Coast of Peru (figure 4.1).

The North Coast of Peru has a long tradition of permanent communities with public residential structures dating to at least the Preceramic/Early Formative period (ca. 5000–2500 B.P.). For example, the coastal site of Huaynuná, located near the Casma Valley (figure 4.1), was a small but permanent community that terraced a hillside, fronted it with a central stairway and constructed a circular building on top of the hill at circa 4200–3450 B.P. (S. Pozorski and T. Pozorski 1987, 1992; T. Pozorski and S. Pozorski 1990). In the small Chao Valley, a more extensive settlement, Salinas de Chao, was a planned complex of platform compounds, open courtyards, terraces, residences, sunken circular plazas constructed by 3600–3400 B.P. (Alva Alva 1986). Contemporaneously, other enormous planned urban complexes were established in various North Coast valleys. For example, the site of Pampas de las Llamas-Moxeke, located in the Casma Valley and dating to about 3490–3700 B.P., was a planned community covering 2 square kilometers and con-

Figure 4.1. Location of Chan Chan and other sites discussed in text.

sisting of two gigantic mounds, linked by a chain of large plazas that were fronted by hundreds of small mound structures, all aligned at N 41° E (S. Pozorski and T. Pozorski 1986, 1987; T. Pozorski and S. Pozorski 1988, 1990).

Subsequent North Coast urbanism underwent significant transformations, including some in the late prehistoric urban societies of the Moche (A.D. 1–600) and Chimú (A.D. 900–1470). In spite of extensive knowledge about Moche ceramics (e.g., Donnan and McClelland 1999) and an increasing appreciation of Moche mural traditions (Franco et al. 1994; Uceda et al. 1994; Vásquez Sánchez 1997), archaeological data about Moche urban patterns are uneven. In part, this reflects an understandable fascination with Moche burials and monumental architecture, and less attention to more prosaic concerns such as domestic residences and urban plans. However, investigations at the site of Moche point to a well-planned urban center with established ceramic production areas, well-organized residential blocks, and cemeteries spread over an area of 1 square kilometer. Rather than being an "empty ceremonial center," as it once was characterized, the site of Moche was a major city framed by the extraordinary temple complexes of Huaca de la Luna and Huaca del Sol.

The apogee of North Coast urbanism occurred under the Chimú Empire (ca. A.D. 900–1470). The Chimú capital was Chan Chan, a city of 20–40,000 covering 20 square kilometers with an urban core of 6 square kilometers (figure 4.2; Moseley and Day 1982; Moseley and Cordy-Collins 1990). Chan Chan was a densely occupied urban landscape, with 10 large walled compounds *(ciudadelas)* built from adobe bricks and thought to be the residential, administrative, and funerary complexes of the Chimú kings (Conrad 1974, 1982, 1990; Day 1973, 1982). Chan Chan's constructed landscape also contained smaller adobe compounds associated with Chimú nobility (Klymyshyn 1976, 1982), large zones of cobblestone foundations and cane walls thought to be the dwellings and workshops of Chimú commoners (Topic 1977, 1982, 1990), four large platform mounds or huacas (Pillsbury 1993) and numerous cemeteries. Interestingly, Chan Chan's urban landscape lacked an obvious overarching plan (Conklin 1990). Unlike many of the cities discussed in this volume, Chan Chan has no central plazas, broad avenues, or central pyramids that unify the experience of place. Sitting on a flat terrace on the Pacific Coast, Chan Chan's walls would have blocked most vistas of distant mountains or the nearby sea, and the experience of place was a confined, visual purdah that enclosed different genders, ages, and classes (Moore et al. 2001).

A recurrent issue is whether the urban landscape of the later Chimú culture was a direct descendant of earlier, Moche patterns or rather represented an abrupt change in monumental architecture. Moche urban centers tend to emphasize large mound constructions; Chimú architecture emphasizes the construction of walled compounds. My previous analysis of access patterns in late Moche and Chimú

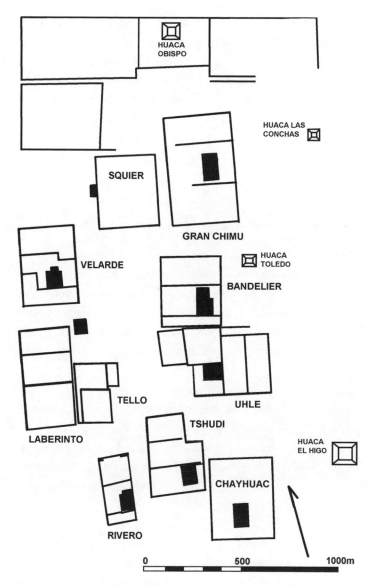

HUACA
OBISPO

HUACA LAS
CONCHAS

SQUIER

GRAN CHIMU

VELARDE

HUACA
TOLEDO

BANDELIER

TELLO

UHLE

LABERINTO

TSHUDI

HUACA
EL HIGO

CHAYHUAC

RIVERO

0   500   1000m

Figure 4.2. Schematic plan of Chan Chan.

monumental constructions indicates that Chimú architecture reflected a dramatic threshold of change marked by more complex control of access within structures whose deepest recesses were far from the entrance (Moore 1996a:191–192). I contend that this architectural tradition of a life behind walls is, in part, a material restatement of Chimú conceptions of social order. In the balance of this chapter, I outline a theoretical approach to architecture as an expression of social order, document the development of walled compound architecture in the North Coast, and suggest how architecture and cosmogonies restate a North Coast ideology of separation.

ARCHITECTURE AND THE EXPRESSION OF SOCIAL ORDER

Architecture never reflects a single set of concerns. Architecture is always a weighted manifestation of multiple dimensions: engineering limits, materials, costs, functions, style, and symbolic contents, among others (Moore 1996a; Rapoport 1969, 1990; Wilk 1990). By their very nature, constructions are always concrete compromises between different decision-domains. In outlining what he called "The Choice Model of Design," architect-anthropologist Amos Rapoport wrote:

> The organization of the [built] environment is, therefore, the result of the application of sets of rules that reflect differing concepts of environmental quality. Design can hence be seen as an attempt to give form of expression to some image of an ideal environment, to make actual and ideal environments congruent. *This involves ideas of environmental quality which are extremely complex and variable and cannot be assumed* a priori *but need to be discovered* (Rapoport 1982:15; emphasis added)

Rapoport (1982:15) further observed that constructed environments are "the result of a series of choices among various alternatives. All man-made environments are designed in the sense that they employ human decisions and choices and specific ways of resolving the many conflicts implicit in all decision-making." Rapoport (1982:15) concluded:

> What all this activity has in common is that it represents a choice among many alternatives. The specific nature of the choices made tend to be lawful, to reflect sets of rules, so that one way of looking at culture is in terms of the most common choices made. . . . This consistent set of choices also affects many aspects of human

behavior and symbolic meaning—the way people interact, their proxemic distances, how they structure space, whether they use streets for interaction and so on.

Thus, architecture is the product of a multidimensional and holistic process. As a practical matter, however, no archaeologist can examine simultaneously all its relevant domains. Rather, one can isolate a specific dimension for the purposes of brief analysis, and in this analysis I am concerned with the social meanings of the architecture and the built environment.

In thinking about the social meaning of architecture, I find Mary Douglas's ideas very useful (1966, 1970, 1973, 1982a, 1982b). To oversimplify, the built environment is just one manner in which humans make symbolic statements about social order. Different social experiences are symbolically restated in various media with varying material vocabularies. The culturally constructed material environment is encoded to different levels of ambiguity, multivocality, and symbolic condensation, and the meanings associated with the built environment may be generally held or bitterly contested as the social order is stable or factionalized. No society is perfectly stable, few are utterly chaotic for long, and thus there are significant differences between societies' experiences of social order. Douglas has proposed to examine these differences in terms of two concepts, *grid* and *group,* and has outlined expectations regarding the ways different experiences of grid and group will be symbolically expressed, say, in the built environment.

Douglas (1970, 1982a, 1982b) has explored how systems of classification and their symbolic representations are linked to various social experiences, and the concepts of group and grid are central to her analysis. "Group is obvious," Douglas (1970:viii) writes, "the experience of a bounded social unit. Grid refers to rules which relate one person to others on an ego centered basis." Group and grid are independent continuous variables—one could imagine a sliding scale of "group" between "no sense of a bounded social unit" to "a well-developed sense of bounded social unit"—but for this discussion, grid and group can be illustrated as nominal variables in a simple matrix (table 4.1).

Douglas (1982b:191) writes, "The group itself is defined in terms of the claims it makes over its constituent members, the boundary it draws around them, the rights it confers on them to use its name and other protections, and the levies and constraints it applies." In contrast, "The term grid suggests the cross-hatch of rules to which individuals are subject in the course of their interaction. As a dimension, it shows a progressive change in the mode of control. *At the strong end there are*

Table 4.1
Group/Grid Matrix

	Group	
	Low	High
Grid		
High	B	C
Low	A	D

Source: After Douglas (1982a).

visible rules about space and time related to social roles; at the other end, near zero, the formal classifications fade, and finally vanish" (Douglas 1982b:192; emphasis added).

Any brief summary is an injustice to Douglas's ideas, but the strength of this perspective is its stereoscopic focus on symbol *and* society, cultural meanings *and* social relations. Further, Douglas outlines testable hypotheses linking social order and symbolic statements, such as the economic and political expressions of differing social contexts, symbolic structures relating to the human body and society, and cosmological statements regarding nature, time, human nature, and social behavior (Douglas 1970, 1982a, 1982b; table 4.2). These ideas are relevant for understanding built environments such as the walled compound tradition on the North Coast of Peru.

WALLED COMPOUND ARCHITECTURE
ON THE NORTH COAST OF PERU

By A.D. 900, an architectural tradition had emerged on the North Coast marked by walled compounds that enclosed residential, storage, funerary, and other units. As already noted, this compound tradition was well developed in the large *ciudadelas* of Chan Chan. Ten *ciudadelas* exist, ranging from 6.73 to 21.2 hectares and containing from 113 to 907 rooms and interior spaces enclosed by adobe brick walls up to 9 meters tall (table 4.2). The *ciudadelas* combined multiple functions: they contained residential areas, plazas, royal burial platforms, walk-in wells, possible storerooms, and distinctive three-sided constructions called U-shaped rooms or *audiencias* (figure 4.3). Many *ciudadelas* have a single entrance and all have labyrinthine access patterns. Given their huge size, complexity, adornment, and their associated burial platforms, the *ciudadelas* are interpreted as the palaces of the Chimú kings: complexes that combined public, residential, storage, and burial functions.

Table 4.2
Expectations Regarding Spatial Order and Monuments

	Low Group	High Group
High grid		
Spatial order	Compartmentalism without special meanings	Develops complex spatial metaphors of symmetry, inequality, and hierarchy
Monuments	Respects burial places of private dead; few public monuments	Memorials to important group events
Low grid		
Spatial order	Spatial displays; strong division between public and private spaces with public areas decorated and maintained, private areas not	Recursive patterning of external boundaries at all levels; village, compound, and household boundaries demarcated
Monuments	Monuments, memorials to "famous" dead	Memorials to important group events

Source: After Douglas (1982b).

Walled compounds are known from other Chimú sites. At the southern frontier of the Chimú state, the site of Manchan contains a central zone of relatively open, agglutinated walled compounds that were flanked on the west by four isolated compounds (Mackey 1987; Mackey and Klymyshyn 1990; Moore 1981, 1985). These isolated adobe compounds, although much smaller than Chan Chan's *ciudadelas*, nonetheless contain similar architectural elements: baffled entries, bench and ramp combinations, niches, and so on. Similarly Farfán, the Chimú administrative center in the Jequetepeque Valley, contains six walled compounds including one with a burial platform, storerooms, and other features similar to the Chan Chan *ciudadelas*. In short, although Chan Chan's urban landscape contains a particularly developed set of walled compounds, the architectural tradition is found elsewhere in Chimú territory.

There is evidence that this walled compound tradition preceded the Chimú by several centuries, although the tradition represents a break with earlier Moche architecture and (as shown later in the chapter) is distinct from subsequent Inka urban patterns. At Moche sites, pyramids and temple complexes are the principal monumental constructions, although walled compounds appear with the final Moche V phase at sites such as Galindo (Bawden 1982) and Pampa Grande (Shimada 1994). The site of Pacatnamú, located in the Jequetepeque Valley, is marked by over 50 walled compounds enclosing truncated pyramids, plazas, kitchen areas, and other

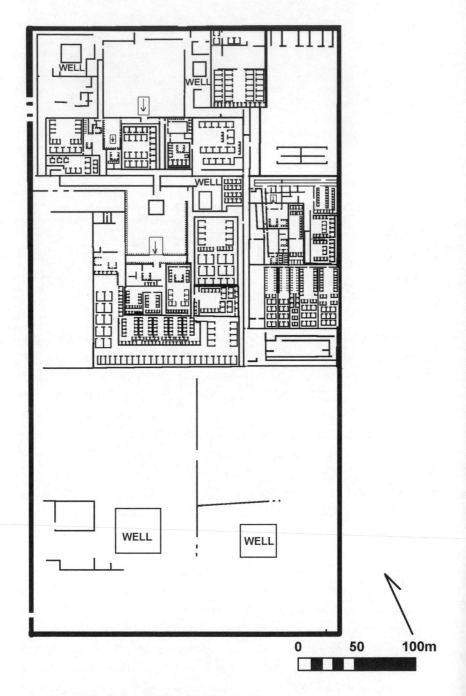

WELL

WELL

WELL

WELL

WELL

WELL

0   50   100m

Figure 4.3. Plan of Ciudadela Velarde, Chan Chan.

architectural units. Pacatnamú was occupied by the Moche beginning at circa A.D. 300 until a hypothesized El Niño event at A.D. 1050–1100 interrupted the occupation. At circa A.D. 1100–1150, Pacatnamú was reoccupied by the Lambayeque culture (Donnan and Cock 1986, Christopher Donnan, personal communication 1995). Like the Chimú compounds, the Pacatnamú compounds are surrounded by walls 5–7 meters tall that have restrictive access and enclose mortuary complexes. The largest and most impressive compound, the Huaca 1 Complex, contains a 70-by-70-meter ramped mound flanked by plazas and a tiered East Pyramid, and to the rear a walled compound ("The Major Quadrangle") 175 by 170 meters in area and enclosing multiple room complexes, some with niches that may have held ceremonial items (Donnan 1986:77–78), and a funerary mound. The Pacatnamú compounds differ from the Chan Chan *ciudadelas*—Pacatnamú compounds enclose pyramids, Chan Chan's *ciudadelas* do not—but there is an obvious continuity between Lambayeque and Chimú cultures in the emphasis on walled compounds. On the basis of current archaeological data, the earliest appearance for walled compounds probably dated to circa A.D. 600–750 and was well established by A.D. 900, when the Chimú began to construct their capital and empire.

LIFE BEHIND WALLS: SOCIAL ORDERS
AND ARCHITECTURE IN CHIMÚ SOCIETY

From current ethnohistoric and archaeological data, it appears that Chimú society was at the "high-grid" and "high-group" end of Douglas's scheme. The evidence for high grid is particularly good: clearly, class differences in Chimú society were marked and significant, with differential access to power, wealth, and prestige. Over 50 years ago John H. Rowe, the dean of American Andeanists, summarized the ethnohistoric information about the Chimú (Rowe 1948); his insights remain a starting point for inquiry. A handful of honorifics in Muchik mark the existence of a class-based society, terms for great lord *(çie quic)*, lord *(alæc)*, gentleman *(fixllca)*, vassal or subject *(paræng)*, and domestic servant *(yaná)* (Rowe 1948:47). "There was a rather remarkable preoccupation with stealing," Rowe (1948:49) observed, "and the punishment of thieves was a religious as well as civil matter as if property were a divine right—as the nobles quite possibly believed it was." Summarizing the ethnohistoric sources, Rowe (1948: 47) concluded: "Evidently differences between social classes were great and immutable on the north coast."

Architectural distinctions parallel these class differences. At Chan Chan the distinctions between *ciudadelas,* the smaller "intermediate" compounds, and the humble structures of cane and cobblestone called SIAR, obviously mirror differences between royalty, nobility, and commoners. This much is reasonably certain. But "group" is a bit more difficult: Was there a clear ethos of "being Chimú," and was it reflected in the built environment?

It is useful to recall Douglas's idea that group is in part the experience of being a member of a bounded social unit and that in high-group societies one would expect some physical expression of this, such as recursive patterning at the village, compound, and household levels. In this light, it is noteworthy that the largest spatial unit in the Chimú built environment was the compound. All Chimú residential architecture regardless of scale or building material was based on the compound. People lived and worked behind walled enclosures—whether a simple cane structure at a regional center like Manchan or the vast *ciudadelas* of Chan Chan. Compounds enclosed residential areas, storerooms, patios or plazas, and workshops. Domestic and production areas were spatially integrated. The division between domestic and workspace simply was not experienced in Chimú society, either within royal compounds or in commoners' houses.

A second point: although noble and commoner houses differ dramatically in construction, scale, and interior decoration, they appear very similar in internal access patterns. Access through the building—whether a relatively small cane-walled house with 5 to 12 rooms or an enormous royal compound—is chain-like, and movement is generally restricted. Access plans tend to be relatively deep, with several tiers of rooms separating the most isolated rooms from the outside. This modular compound architecture shaped the Chimú urban landscape, expressed in the absence of an overall plan or grid, the lack of major avenues, and the limited emphasis on plazas. As the architect and Andeanist Willliam Conklin (1990:64) observed:

> Nor does the detailed architectural planning seem to support the idea of Chan Chan as a unified empire capital. The largest-scale design unit seems to be the compound. Certainly, Chan Chan has the construction area of an empire capital, but it does not seem to have the city-scale patterns that would be expected of such a hypothesized capital.

Conklin (1990:71) concludes, "No single capital building or urban form at any site seems to have symbolized or summarized the whole empire." Conklin is clearly correct, but I add that this compound pattern includes not only the *ciudadelas* but also an array of Chimú residential architecture and is found not only at Chan Chan, but at other North Coast sites as well.

NORTH COAST COSMOGONY AND
THE IDEOLOGY OF SEPARATION

I suggest that this architectural tradition in part marks the emergence of a form of social order based on well-defined class divisions and an ideology of separation (Moore 1996a). Ethnohistoric documents from the North Coast contain relatively little information about indigenous worldview, as the oral traditions were filtered through the Inka and Spanish conquests (Netherly 1990; Rostworoski de Diez Canseco 1990). The violent Inka conquest of the Chimú—in which the last Chimú king was taken as a hostage to Cuzco where he died—was followed by significant reorganization of North Coast political institutions by the Inka (Zevallos Quiñones 1992:3–10; cf. Ramirez 1990). North Coast traditions were further disrupted by the postcontact demographic collapse (Cook 1981); Spanish political domination, which intensified with the administrative "reforms" implemented by Viceroy Francisco de Toledo y Figueroa during his 1569–1581 rule; and of course the imposition of Catholicism—a process replicated throughout the Andes (e.g., Silverblatt 1987:109–124).

Despite such disasters, a few scraps of North Coast cosmogony were preserved, and they suggest some of the cultural conceptions regarding social hierarchy—another point made 50 years ago by John Rowe (1948). The most explicit source is a creation myth recorded by Antonio Calancha (1977 [1638]:1244):

It was said in the treatise of Pachacamac that these Indians of the flatlands and sea-coasts were certain (and many believe it today) that their initial masses and founding fathers were not Adam and Eve, but four stars, that two gave birth to the Kings, Lords, and nobles, and the other two to the commoners, the poor, and the indentured, which—as the Faith we profess makes precise—are [actually the result of] the chances of this earth and not because it is thought that the rich and powerful are descendants of other beginnings than are the humble and poor, but they see the poor not as naturally equal but as the least valued of Fortune. (Translation mine)

Calancha recorded a second myth that describes the separate creations of different social classes from three eggs. The legend tells the story of the birth of the culture hero, Vichama, and of the struggles for divine supremacy between the Sun and Pachacamac (Calancha 1977 [1638]:930–935). It is a violent tale of murder and revenge set in a prehuman world, a detailed myth that concludes with the creation of human beings:

> Vichama seeing the world without men and the Sun and the huacas with none to worship them, prayed to his father the Sun to make new men, and the Sun sent three eggs, one gold, one silver, and one copper. From the golden egg came the Curacas, the Caciques, and the nobles they call *segunda personas* and *principales;* from the silver one came their women; and from the copper egg the common people, that today are called Mitayos, and their women and families. (Calancha 1977 [1638]:934–935)

In the North Coast cosmogonies, the celestial origins of social stratification are presented as inviolable as the movement of the moon and stars. North Coast cosmogonies are in marked contrast to the Inka creation myths, which describe the dynastic founders in kin terms (i.e., they are brothers and sisters; see Bauer 1191, 1992; Rostworowski de Diez Canseco 1983; Silverblatt 1987; Urton 1990; Zuidema 1964, 1990). In contrast, the divide between North Coast nobles and commoners is established at the beginning of time, potent justifications of unbridgeable social distinctions.

One myth linking this ideology of separation to architectural forms is the legend of Ñamlap, the culture hero of the Lambayeque Valley. Recorded by Miguel Cabello Balboa (1967) in 1551 and reiterated by Rubinos y Andrade (1936) in 1782, the legend has been glossed by Means (1931:51–53), Rowe (1948), and Donnan (1990:243–245), all of whom were primarily interested in the accuracy of the dynastic succession recorded in the tale (for an alternate interpretation, see Netherly 1990).

The tale begins in a mythic past "in very ancient, uncountable times" when Ñamlap, the "father of the Company, man of great valor and quality," led a flotilla of balsa wood rafts to northern Peru. Rubinos y Andrade (1936 [1782]:362) relates that Ñamlap had come from beyond Tumbes, the loser in a war between "some Kings or Caciques or Indian lords of certain states in some islands," a possible reference to the islands and coastal polities of southern Ecuador and far northern Peru. Accompanied by his principal wife, Ceterni, his concubines, 40 courtiers, and a great company, Ñamlap landed at the mouth of the Lambayeque Valley. With this retinue of noble courtiers who watched over Ñamlap's food, drink, face paints, and royal costume, Ñamlap's person and household were "adorned and authorized." Ñamlap and his retinue took land in the lower valley and a half league from the ocean established palaces at the place called Chot, where he enshrined the idol Yampallec, a green stone carved in the image of Ñamlap.

Ñamlap died after a long life of peaceful rule and numerous progeny, but so his vassals would not know that death had jurisdiction over him *(porque no entendiessen sus vassallos que tenia la muerte jurisdicion sobre el)*, Ñamlap was secretly buried in the palace where he had lived. It was announced throughout the land that because of his great virtue, Ñamlap had taken wing and disappeared, thus escaping death. Ñamlap's descendants multiplied and spread through the land, and his throne was inherited by his eldest son, Cium, who, in turn, begot 12 sons, each fathers of large families. Having lived and ruled many years, Cium was put in an underground crypt where he died, so that all took him for an immortal and a god.

According to Rubinos y Andrade (1936 [1782]:362), Ñamlap's name was given to the principal lineage in Lambayeque, "superior to the rest that were later established," which even until the late eighteenth century was known as the "parcialidad de Nam." Although he is a very late source, Andrade y Rubinos is interesting because his record suggests the elements of the myth that were repeated and maintained in Morrope, including a passage about the symbolic transformation of an architectural form. Rubinos y Andrade (1936 [1782]:363) writes:

> The oldest son and heir of this lord was called Suim [*sic* for Cium] and his wife Ciernuncacu; and these names were recorded for all time in two admirable registers [*se fixaron a la duración en otros dos recomendables padrones*]: the name of the inheriting prince was given to a palace, built in the same location, and as generations multiplied and he was the dominant lord over all, as they had descended from the great family of servants and officials that had loyally continued in his service [*siguieron su obediencia*]. And this palace they used to bury his [or their] successors.

Even in death, the difference between lords and subjects was maintained. Walled away in his house so that his vassals could not perceive his mortality, the lord's crypt became the burial place for his descendants and the descendants of his courtiers and servants. As the Indians of Lambayeque described and Ramirez (1996:147–148) has discussed, the houses of rulers were transformed into burial structures, and even later into temples or shrines: "A structure may have begun as a house or palace or a ceremonial structure and precinct with a burial platform in it. If a dead ruler was 'great' and he was remembered after several generations, his house and tomb may have become a temple or shrine, a monument to him where subsequent generations left offerings or were themselves buried."

A similar transformation occurred within the *ciudadelas* of Chan Chan. Geoffrey

Conrad (1982) has interpreted the burial platforms located inside the Chan Chan *ciudadelas* as the mortuary structures of the Chimú kings. After the burial platforms were constructed, annex structures were added to the platforms, which may have "housed heirs of the particularly prominent heirs of the ancestral mummy" (Moseley 1990:13). Conrad (1982:116) argues:

> As both a political leader and a demi-god, the king received the luxurious funerary treatment reflected in the burial platforms. Although he ceased to be the ruler of the empire upon his death, his divine status did not end at that time. The [annex structures] affixed to the burial platforms indicate that, as a member of the Chimú pantheon, the dead king continued to be a viable force in the world of the living.

Such annex structures and associated votive offerings suggest that the deceased Chimú king was remembered and honored at least by some portion of Chan Chan's populace, but this practice was only true for kings and nobles. Burial practice marked the division between dead commoners and lords as certainly as had their separate creations in the mythic past and just as the walls of Chan Chan had separated the living.

THE ARRIVAL OF THE INKA

The *ciudadelas* and other walled compounds dominated Chan Chan's urban landscape until the Chimú were conquered by the Inka at circa A.D. 1470, introducing an architectural tradition and ideology distinct from North Coast patterns (Gasparini and Margolies 1980; Hyslop 1990; Niles 1992; Protzen 1993). In Inka urban settlements, a basic unit is the *kancha,* a group of rectangular structures without internal divisions arranged symmetrically around an open patio and enclosed within a wall. Inka residential architecture tends to be shallow: access to *kancha* is often through a single door, but once inside, access patterns are very open, "ringy," and symmetrical, sometimes with paired doors leading to a single room (Hillier and Hanson 1984:149). In turn, *kancha* were building blocks in Inka urban planning, replicated to form larger architectural units. Many Inka settlements obviously were planned, organized by a cross-hatch of streets into roughly orthogonal plans (e.g., central Cuzco, Ollantaytambo, Chucuito, etc: see Hyslop 1990:192–202) or in radial plans in which roads splay out from a central plaza (e.g., Huanuco Pampa, Pumpu; see Hyslop 1990:202–220.) Finally, Inka sites have extremely large, central plazas that are often the dominant element in the built environment. Unlike Chan Chan where plazas are hidden behind *ciudadela* walls, Inka plazas are enormous areas designed to be experienced by thousands of people (Moore 1996b, 1997). Interestingly, an integral element of several major Inka ceremonies in the main plazas of Cuzco was the display of the mummies of dead rulers, former rulers who were brought out, consulted, feted, and revered as ancestors. Unlike the North Coast kings, the Inka rulers were manifestly mortal.

CONCLUSION

This brief comparison of Inka and Chimú built environments suggests that we are not only looking at different architectural traditions but also are examining different social schemata. In his thought-provoking book *Mummies and Mortuary Monuments,* William Isbell argues that ancestor worship and the *ayllu*—a kin-based social group with shared resources and associated with a common founder or ancestor (Isbell 1997:99)—are also associated with the "open sepulcher," a tomb form that allowed descendants to have "nearly constant access to the [ancestral] mummy" (Isbell 1997:139). Interestingly, there are no such tombs on the North Coast. From the Late Intermediate Period on, North Coast societies buried their dead in two manners: commoners were buried in cemeteries in graves without openings, while elites often were interred within their compounds. In neither case was there "nearly constant access" to the dead.

At the risk of oversimplification, I suggest the Inka and Chimú had very different conceptions of social order. The Inka employed ancestor worship and the trope of kinship in their ideologies of kingship and empire; they created built environments that conceptually unified their empire and marked the landscape with their presence. A variety of public ceremonies emphasized the importance of display, in which the king was presented as a special being of a select dynasty but was indisputably mortal. The Chimú apparently emphasized class in describing social order, but perhaps never articulated an ethos of "Chimú-ness" that could overarch the boundaries of compound walls. Rather, the special nature of the Chimú social order simultaneously was expressed by concealment and the constructed labyrinths that hid the apotheosis of kings.

Though this discussion has been limited to selected Andean societies, some of these ideas may be relevant for other urban societies. Minimally, if prehistoric urban environments lack massive public monuments, large public plazas, or wide straight boulevards, we should not assume that those societies lacked the where-withal for public works, the love of order, or the gumption to build. It may be that alternative conceptions of social order are being expressed—a gridlike hierarchy of social divisions, an undeveloped overarching sense of group, or the mystery of power and difference—similar to those of the late pre-Hispanic societies of the North Coast or the political and architectural innovations of Deioces the Mede.

REFERENCES

Alva Alva, W.
    1986   *Las salinas de Chao: Asentamiento temprano en el norte del Perú.* Verlag C. H. Beck, Munich.
Bauer, B.
    1991   Pacariqtambo and the Mythical Origins of the Inka. *Latin American Antiquity* 2(1):7–26.
    1992   *The Development of the Inka State.* University of Texas Press, Austin.
Bawden, G.
    1982   Galindo: A Study in Cultural Transition during the Middle Horizon. In *Chan Chan: Andean Desert City,* edited by M. Moseley and K. Day, pp. 285–320. University of New Mexico Press, Albuquerque.
Cabello Balboa, M.
    1967   *Miscelánea Antártica.* Instituto de Ethnología, Universidad Mayor de San Marcos, Lima.
    [1551]
Calancha, A.
    1977   *Crónica moralizada.* 4 vols. Ignacio Prado Pastor, Lima.
    [1638]
Conklin, W.
    1990   Architecture of the Chimú: Memory, Function, and Image. In *The Northern Dynasties: Kingship and Statecraft in Chimor,* edited by M. Moseley and A. Cordy-Collins, pp. 43–74. Dumbarton Oaks Research Library and Collection, Washington, D.C.
Conrad, G.
    1974   *Burial Platforms and Related Structures on the North Coast of Peru: Some Social and Political Implications.* Unpublished Ph.D. dissertation, Department of Anthropology, Harvard University.
    1982   The Burial Platforms of Chan Chan. In *Chan Chan: Andean Desert City,* edited by M. Moseley and K. Day, pp. 87–117. University of New Mexico Press, Albuquerque.
    1990   Farfán, General Pacatnamú and the Dynastic History of Chimor. In *The Northern Dynasties: Kingship and Statecraft in Chimor,* edited by M. Moseley and A. Cordy-Collins, pp. 227–242. Dumbarton Oaks Research Library and Collection, Washington, D.C.
Cook, N. D.
    1981   *Demographic Collapse, Indian Peru, 1420–1620.* Cambridge University Press, Cambridge.
Day, K.
    1973   *The Architecture of Ciudadela Rivero.* Unpublished Ph.D. dissertation, Department of Anthropology, Harvard University.

1982   Ciudadelas: Their Form and Function. In *Chan Chan: Andean Desert City,* edited by M. Moseley and K. Day. pp. 55–66. University of New Mexico Press, Albuquerque.

Donnan, C.

1986   The Huaca 1 Complex. In *The Pacatnamu Papers.* Vol. 1, edited by C. Donnan and G. Cock, pp. 63–84. Fowler Museum of Culture History, University of California, Los Angeles.

1990   An Assessment of the Validity of the Naymlap Dynasty. In *The Northern Dynasties: Kingship and Statecraft in Chimor,* edited by M. Moseley and A. Cordy-Collins, pp. 243–274. Dumbarton Oaks Research Library and Collection, Washington D.C.

Donnan, C., and G. Cock (editors)

1986   *The Pacatnamu Papers.* Vol. 1. Fowler Museum of Culture History, University of California, Los Angeles.

Donnan, C., and D. McClelland

1999   *Moche Fineline Painting: Its Evolution and Artists.* UCLA Fowler Museum of Cultural History, Los Angeles.

Douglas, M.

1966   *Purity and Danger: An Analysis of Concepts of Pollution and Taboo.* Praeger Publishers, New York.

1970   *Natural Symbols: Explorations in Cosmology.* Pantheon Books, New York.

1973   *Rules and Meanings: The Anthropology of Everyday Knowledge—Selected Readings.* Penguin Books, Harmondsworth, England.

1982a   Introduction to Group/Grid Analysis. In *Essays in the Sociology of Perception,* edited by M. Douglas, pp. 1–18. Routledge and Keegan Paul, London.

1982b   *In the Active Voice.* Routledge & Kegan Paul, London.

Franco, R., C. Gálvez, and S. Vásquez

1994   Arquitectura y decoración Mochica en la huaca cao viejo, complejo el brujo: Resultados preliminarios. In *Moche propuestas y perspectivas,* edited by S. Uceda and E. Mujica, pp. 147–180. Universidad Nacional de la Libertad Trujillo/ L'Institut Francais D'etudes Andines.

Gasparini, G., and L. Margolies

1980   *Inca Architecture.* Translated by Patricia Lyon. Indiana University Press, Bloomington.

Herodotus

1972   *The Histories.* Book I, 96–103. translated by A. Sélicourt. Penguin Books, Harmondsworth.

Hillier, B., and J. Hanson

1984   *The Social Logic of Space.* Cambridge University Press, Cambridge.

Hyslop, J.

1990   *Inka Settlement Planning.* University of Texas Press, Austin.

Isbell, W. J.

1997   *Mummies and Mortuary Monuments: A Postprocessual Prehistory of Central Andean Social Organization.* University of Texas Press, Austin.

Klymyshyn, A. M. U.

1976   *The Intermediate Compounds at Chan Chan, Peru.* Unpublished Ph.D. dissertation, Department of Anthropology, Harvard University.

1982   Elite Compounds in Chan Chan. In *Chan Chan: Andean Desert City,* edited by M. Moseley and K. Day, pp. 119–143. University of New Mexico Press, Albuquerque.

Mackey, C.

1987   Chimú Administration in the Provinces. In *The Origins and Development of the Andean State,* edited by J. Haas, S. Pozorski, and T. Pozorski, pp.121–129. Cambridge University Press, Cambridge.

Mackey, C., and A. Klymyshn

1990   The Southern Frontier of the Chimú Empire. In *The Northern Dynasties: Kingship and Statecraft in Chimor,* edited by M. Moseley and A. Cordy-Collins, pp.195–226. Dumbarton Oaks Research Library and Collection, Washington, D.C.

Means, P.

1931   *Ancient Civilizations of the Andes.* Charles Scribner's Sons, New York.

Moore, J.

1981   Chimú Socio-Economic Organization: Preliminary Data from Manchan, Casma Valley, Peru. *Ñawpa Pacha* 19:115–128.

1985   *Household Economics and Political Integration: the Lower Class of the Chimú Empire.* Ph.D. dissertation, University of California, Santa Barbara. University Microfilms International, Ann Arbor.

1996a   *Architecture and Power in the Prehispanic Andes: The Architecture of Public Buildings.* Cambridge University Press, Cambridge.

1996b   The Archaeology of Plazas and the Proxemics of Ritual: Three Andean Traditions. *American Anthropologist* 98:789–802.

1997   Le place dans les Andes anciennes: Le controle des espaces ouverts dans les villes Précolumbiennes. In *La Ville et le Pouvoir en Amérique,* edited by J. Monnet, pp. 228–239. Edition Karthala, Paris.

Moore, J., R. Christel, and E. Hudson.

2001   The Illusion of Plans: Understanding the Built Landscape of Chimú Urbanism. Paper presented at the Society for American Archaeology Annual Meeting, April 2001, New Orleans, La.

Moseley, M.

1990   Structure and History in the Dynastic Lore of Chimor. In *The Northern Dynasties: Kingship and Statecraft in Chimor,* edited by M. Moseley and A. Cordy-Collins, pp. 1–41. Dumbarton Oaks Research Library and Collection, Washington D.C.

Moseley, M., and A. Cordy-Collins (editors)

1990   *The Northern Dynasties: Kingship and Statecraft in Chimor.* Dumbarton Oaks Research Library and Collection, Washington D.C.

Moseley, M., and K. Day (editors)

1982   *Chan Chan: Andean Desert City.* University of New Mexico Press, Albuquerque.

Netherly, P.

1990   Out of Many, One: The Organization of Rule in the North Coast Polities. In *The Northern Dynasties: Kingship and Statecraft in Chimor,* edited by M. Moseley and A. Cordy-Collins, pp. 461–487. Dumbarton Oaks Research Library and Collection, Washington D.C.

Niles, S.

1992   Inka Architecture and the Sacred Landscape. In *The Ancient Americas: Art from Sacred Landscapes,* edited by R. Townsend, pp. 347–357. The Art Institute, Chicago.

Pillsbury, J.

1993   *Sculptural Friezes of Chimor.* Unpublished Ph.D. dissertation, Columbia University.

Pozorski, S., and T. Pozorski

1986   Recent Excavations at Pampa de las Llamas-Moxeke, a Complex Initial Period Site in Peru. *Journal of Field Archaeology* 13:381–401.

1987   *Early Settlement and Subsistence in the Casma Valley, Peru.* University of Iowa Press, Iowa City.

1992   Early Civilization in the Casma Valley, Peru. *Antiquity* 66:845–870.

Pozorski, T., and S. Pozorski

1988   An Early Stone Carving from Pampa de las Llamas-Moxeke, Casma Valley, Peru. *Journal of Field Archaeology* 15:114–119.

1990   Huaynuná, a Late Cotton Preceramic site on the North Coast of Peru. *Journal of Field Archaeology* 17:17–26.

Protzen, J.-P.

1993   *Inca Architecture and Construction at Ollantaytambo.* Oxford University Press, New York.

Ramirez, S.

1990   The Inca Conquest of the North Coast: A Historian's View. In *The Northern Dynasties: Kingship and Statecraft in Chimor,* edited by M. Moseley and A. Cordy-Collins, pp. 507–537. Dumbarton Oaks Research Library and Collection, Washington D.C.

1996   *The World Turned Upside Down: Cross-Cultural Contact and Conflict in Sixteenth-Century Peru.* Stanford University Press, Stanford.

Rapoport, A.

1969   *House Form and Culture.* Prentice-Hall, Englewood Cliffs, N.J.

1982   *Human Aspects of Urban Form: Towards a Man-Environment Approach to Urban Form and Design.* Pergamon Press, Oxford.

1990   *History and Precedent in Environmental Design.* Plenum Press, New York.

Rostworowski de Diez Canseco, M.

1983   *Estructuras Andinas del poder.* Instituto de Estudios Andinos, Lima.

1990   Ethnohistorical Considerations about the Chimor. In *The Northern Dynasties: Kingship and Statecraft in Chimor,* edited by M. Moseley and A. Cordy-Collins, pp. 447–460. Dumbarton Oaks Research Library and Collection, Washington D.C.

Rowe, J.

1948   The Kingdom of Chimor. *Acta Americana* 6:26–59.

Rubinos y Andrade, J. M. de

1936   Un manuscrito interesante. Succesión cronológica de los Curas de Mórrope y Pacora.

[1782] *Revista Histórica,* 10(3):291–363.

Shimada, I.

1994   *Pampa Grande and the Mochica Culture.* University of Texas Press, Austin.

Silverblatt, I.

1987   *Moon, Sun, and Witches: Gender Ideologies and Class in Inka and Colonial Peru.* Princeton University Press, Princeton, N.J.

Topic, J.

1977   *The Lower Class at Chan Chan: A Qualitative Approach.* Unpublished Ph.D. dissertation, Department of Anthropology, Harvard University.

1982   Lower-Class Social and Economic Organization at Chan Chan. In *Chan Chan: Andean Desert City,* edited by M. Moseley and K. Day, pp. 145–175. University of New Mexico Press, Albuquerque.

1990   Craft and Production in the Kingdom of Chimor. In *The Northern Dynasties: Kingship and Statecraft in Chimor,* edited by M. Moseley and A. Cordy-Collins, pp. 145–176. Dumbarton Oaks Research Library and Collection, Washington, D.C.

Uceda, S., R. Morales C., José Canziani A., and M. Montaya V.

1991   Investigaciones sobre la arquitectura y relieves polícromos en la Huaca de la Luna, Valle de Moche. In *Moche propuestas y perspectivas,* edited by S. Uceda and E. Mujica, pp. 251–303. Universidad Nacional de la Libertad Trujillo/ L'Institut Francais D'etudes Andines.

Urton, G.

1990   *The History of a Myth: Pacariqtambo and the Origin of the Inkas.* University of Texas Press, Austin.

Vásquez Sánchez, S.

1997   Iconografía del paramento inferior de Huaca Cao Viejo, Valle de Chicama: Un estudio preliminar. *Revista del Museo de Arqueología, Antropología e Historia,* 7: 157–172. Universidad Nacional de Trujillo, Peru.

Wilk, R.

1990   The Built Environment and Consumer Decisions. In *Domestic Architecture and the Use of Space: An Interdisciplinary Cross-Cultural Study,* edited by S. Kent, pp. 34–42. Cambridge University Press, Cambridge.

Zevallos Quiñones, J.

1992   *Los Cacicazgos de Trujillo.* Fundación Alfredo Pinillos Goicochea, Trujillo.

Zuidema, R. T.

1964   *The Ceque System of Cuzco: The Social Organization of the Capital of the Inca.* E. J. Brill, Leiden.

1990   *Inka Civilization in Cuzco.* University of Texas Press, Austin.

F I V E

Early Urban Configurations on the Middle Niger

Clustered Cities and Landscapes of Power

RODERICK J. McINTOSH
AND SUSAN KEECH
McINTOSH

The investigation of early cities has historically focused on the most visible, monumental, exemplars of ancient urbanism.[1] Urban elites—whose activities, agendas, and strategies the monuments are presumed to reflect—have accordingly received primary attention. In recent years, archaeologists have shown growing interest in a wider range of urban forms, such that a study from West Africa of large-scale, densely populated settlement complexes that appear to lack both monuments and an elite class may now be considered relevant to an understanding of urban development in comparative perspective. This chapter turns to the clustered cities of the Middle Niger region (figure 5.1), where population aggregation in a number of locales in the first millennium A.D., and perhaps earlier, characteristically comprised a large, central settlement mound of up to 10 meters in height and 20 to 80 hectares in area, surrounded by intermediate and smaller size mounds at dis-

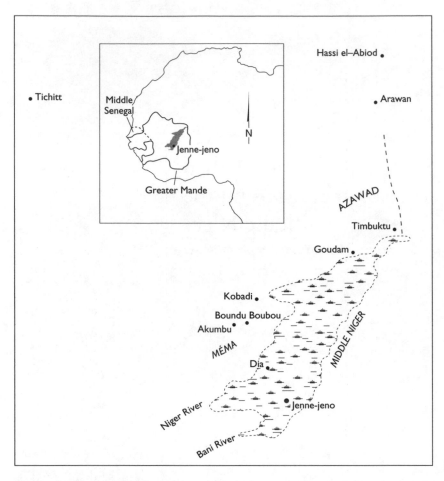

Figure 5.1. Location of sites and regions, Middle Niger, West Africa.

tances of 200 meters or less. For over 20 years, we have been involved in discovering, investigating, and attempting to interpret this pattern, which has some of the familiar attributes of urbanization (aggregation, population growth, increasing scale, and specialization) but not others (subsistence intensification, highly visible ranking or stratification, imposing public monuments).

This early form of urbanism appears to be both a functional response to a highly variable and unpredictable flood and climate regime and a distinctive distribution of urban space that grew out of a deep-time conception of authority that sustained a lengthy resistance to centralization on the part of the populations occupying the various mounds within a cluster. We suggest that this pattern reflects a highly complex configuration of horizontally aligned power relations. These clustered cities not only existed in the absence of the state but were organized largely without a centralized hierarchy of any kind.

Our struggle to devise appropriate conceptual frameworks for Middle Niger clustered cities is part of the long history of Western difficulties with understanding, or even recognizing, urbanism in sub-Saharan Africa. The idea that urbanism was an indigenous and recurrent phenomenon in the West African savanna and sahel dates largely to the postcolonial period. In the colonial imagination, Africa was predominantly rural in character, composed of small, undifferentiated villages of mud and thatch huts. Consequently, the walled cities and towns of the sahel (Kano province alone had 170 in 1900) were a colossal surprise to Europeans. Frederick Lugard commented in 1902, before his assault on Kano, that "I have never seen, nor even imagined, anything like it in Africa" (cited in Connah 2000:43). Colonial era historians and archaeologists accommodated this urban anomaly by "medievalizing" the sahel and conceptualizing it as an economic and cultural dependent of the Islamic world (S. K. McIntosh 2001). Cultural and political achievements in the sahel were attributed to influences from the north, and a diffusionist paradigm formalized the belief that urbanism was not native to Africa.

Further south, European administrators and anthropologists did not even recognize the large, densely populated, nucleated Yoruba settlements as urban in character (Mabogunje 1968). Why was this? One of the main reasons was that all the conceptual tools available for investigating this topic were dependent on Western sequences of historical development tracking European urban transformations from classical antiquity through the Middle Ages and the Industrial Revolution. Thus, many nineteenth- and early-twentieth-century attempts to define "urban" proceeded by constructing ideal types that identified essential features differentiating Western urban society from pre- or nonurban society.

V. G. Childe (1950) compiled a list of essential features of urban civilization, including writing and monumental architecture, thereby excluding much of black Africa from consideration. The West has long associated cities, as centers of despotic power, with impressive architecture reflecting that power. It is now recognized that monumentality, while a common strategy employed by rulers of early city-states in Mesoamerica and Mesopotamia (among others) was not an inevitable accompaniment of early urbanism. The early Bronze Age cities of China, for example, had no monumental architecture. Among the reasons for the lack of investment in monuments in much of sub-Saharan Africa are lack of suitable building materials (such as stone) in some areas and the prevalence of extensive, slash-and-burn agricultural systems that required settlement relocation after several decades. This worked against permanent installation of populations at one location for long periods. In many areas, the location of the capital city shifted with every accession of a new ruler. Ecological constraints linked to a value system that conceived of space as a social construction (rooted in kin groups and genealogical proximity), rather than as a particular physical place, produced African urban configurations that looked quite different from the cities of the West.

To reiterate, early European observers failed to recognize African towns and cities because they did not conform to concepts of urbanism derived from Western historical sequences. In the postcolonial period, research has exposed the ethnographic assumptions and ideological underpinnings of these theories of urbanism and shifted emphasis from what a city *is* (widely agreed to be a futile pursuit in view of the tremendous range of urban forms) to what a city *does*. Both human geographers and early anthropologically oriented archaeologists realized that urban centers never exist in isolation; they are always articulated with a regional hinterland. Whatever else a city may be, it is a unit of settlement that performs specialized functions in relation to a broader hinterland (Trigger 1972). The specialized functions may be of an economic nature, such as the production and export of goods and services, or they may have a more social aspect, such as the elaboration of power and new social institutions or the exchange of information. Urbanism thus represents a novel kind of relationship among sites in a region involving the emergence of specialization and functional interdependence. The symbiosis characteristic of the urban system emerges out of the circulation of goods and services essential to subsistence within it. In the Middle Niger area, as in many regions, these included food, iron used to produce food, and ritual knowledge required to produce iron and rain.

We have considerable evidence to suggest that the clustered cities of the Middle Niger exhibited specialization and functional interdependence. The anchoring sequence for understanding urban development in the Middle Niger comes from the Upper Inland Delta (southern Middle Niger) site of Jenne-jeno. Results of the excavations at the principal site and at 10 satellites in the Urban Complex, and of survey in its hinterland are available in several publications (Clark 1997; R. J. McIntosh and S. K. McIntosh 1987; R. J. McIntosh et al. 1996; S. K. and R. J. McIntosh 1980; S. K. McIntosh 1995; Togola 1996), so only the key elements will be highlighted here (figure 5.2).

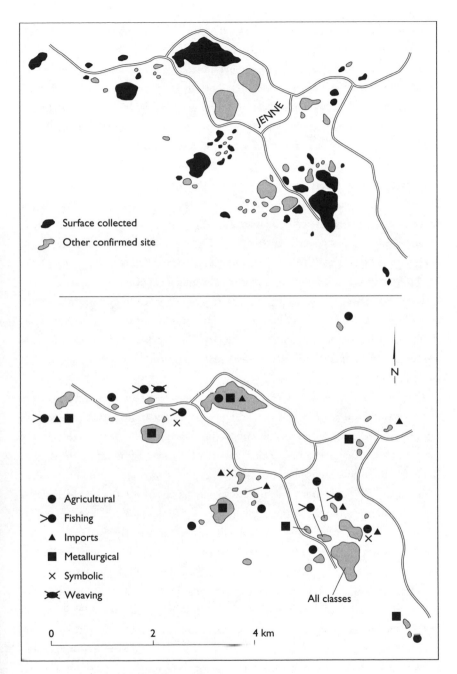

Figure 5.2. The Jenne-jeno urban complex.

Surface collected
Other confirmed site

JENNE

N

Agricultural
Fishing
Imports
Metallurgical
Symbolic
Weaving

All classes

0   2   4 km

As recently as the middle of the last millennium B.C., this sector of the Middle Niger was uninhabited, or frequented only by nomadic pastoralists, hunters, or fisherfolk. Ambiguous debris of their ephemeral presence is found encased within the upper alluvium beneath a very few sites. This and the independent geomorphological assessment of the region lead us to believe that the Jenne area was a paludial (more-or-less permanent swamp), if not long-seasonal lake environment until the great pan-tropical dry episode of circa 300 B.C. to A.D. 300 (Jacobberger 1987; R. J. McIntosh 1983; 2000:155).

Permanent occupation began shortly after the onset of that dry episode, when annual floods diminished and the swamps decreased in size. We know little of the first colonists, besides their physical kinship to earlier groups in the Malian Sahara (Hassi el-Abiod) and Méma (Kobadi) and their Saharan ceramic affinities (S. K. McIntosh 1995;356, 362). In the first centuries of the settlement's existence, in the final centuries B.C., the community pioneered a mixed economy that apparently remained remarkably stable during the 1,600-year sequence: rice, sorghum, millet, and a high volume of wild grains; domesticated cattle and sheep/goat and a significant hunted component; and, of course, fish and aquatic reptiles and mammals. Exchange for stone and iron tied earliest Jenne-jeno to communities in the adjacent regions.

The Jenne vicinity is a wonder of highland and floodplain soils at the different elevations and bathymetric progressions necessary for high-volume recessional farming of millet and sorghum and floodwater farming of rice (which remains the main staple in the area today). The diversity of farmland provides a measure of food security in this environment of high-interannual variation in rain (which fluctuates in annual total, monthly distribution, date of onset) and flood (which affects the date and speed of evacuation, annual crop of rizophagous fish, and so on). The Jenne vicinity is close to dune highlands necessary for keeping cattle in an active floodplain. And Jenne's merchants could exploit the maze of streams and major rivers (Niger and Bani) giving access to the towns and villages within the traditional hinterland as well as to distant commercial partners, such as Dia and Timbuktu. All the foregoing were sufficient conditions but do not, of course, explain why this area was selected over many hundreds of other advantageous locales.

S. K. McIntosh's (1999) functionalist approach has suggested that pioneering settlement targeted narrow zones of maximum productivity. For the mixed agriculturalists colonizing the Inland Niger Delta (IND), this meant zones with the following characteristics: good rice-growing soils (not too shallowly or too deeply inundated); noninundated areas (primarily levees or areas beyond the floodplain) for pasturing livestock in flood season; and deep basins for dry-season pasture. Given the extremely patchy distribution within the Inland Delta of levees and deep basins, only a few areas have all these resources relatively close to one another. If colonists in fact preferentially sought such maximally productive areas, population could have increased quickly. In fact, this is precisely what happened at Jenne-jeno, where the total occupied mound surface in the Urban Complex exceeded 100 hectares within a millennium of the initial pioneering settlement circa 250 B.C. Oral traditions support the idea of founding communities saltating across the virgin floodplain to a few locales (Dia and Jenne most prominently mentioned), from which daughter communities later arose through fissioning and migration (S. K. McIntosh 1981).

Moving beyond functionalist explanations, R. J. McIntosh (2000) has considered the effects of powerful belief systems including magic and blacksmithing. He offers an alternative explanation for the siting of IND population centers based on the Mande (large language family in West Africa to which the original Soninke inhabitants of Jenne belong) attraction to locations steeped in occult power, in this case the *nyama,* the life-energy of the earth, harnessed by the blacksmiths who were smelting iron at Jenne-jeno in the earliest occupation levels despite the necessity of importing iron ore from outside the floodplain. If the current belief that concentrations of water spirits are particularly high in the distributaries around Jenne is of any antiquity, this source of *nyama* may have attracted blacksmiths to the Jenne vicinity initially. Later in the first millennium, ironworking took place at several of the satellite mounds.

The *tells* (deeply stratified mounds entirely of anthropogenic origin) that comprise the component sites of the Jenne-jeno Urban Complex are enormously expensive to excavate, and efforts have been concentrated on the principal site of Jenne-jeno (a total of 17 units have been excavated to sterile at depths of 4 to 6 meters). However, we now have limited excavations at 10 satellites (Clark 1997), auger coring at several others (R. J. McIntosh et al. 1996), and four campaigns of recording surface ceramics, small finds, and features at all satellites within a 4-kilometer radius of Jenne. It is clear from this research that some degree of clustering was a feature of the very earliest settlement expansion here. Further, specialists appear to have occupied and conducted their business on many and perhaps most of the satellites. The 1997 research conducted by Mary Clark on surface features in the Jenne-jeno Urban Complex suggests, however, that temporal variability is characteristic of surface features, owing to both differential use in time and postdepositional erosion (Clark and Hietala 2002). Thus, considerable additional research will be required to understand the dynamics of the region's clustered settlement organization and the role of the specialist producer. And until many more units are sunk into the lowest levels of a large sample of satellites, it will be impossible to know if occupational specialization characterized the initial emergence of clustering.

Without house foundation counts, estimates are a risky business (S. K. McIntosh and R. J. McIntosh 1993; S. K. McIntosh 1999). Nonetheless, we can offer some parameters of population size. At its apogee, circa A.D. 800, Jenne-jeno reached 33 hectares in extent and was home to, conservatively, at least 4,000 and perhaps as many as 10,000 people. The Jenne-jeno Urban Complex of 40 mounds within a 4-kilometer radius at this time totaled almost 137 hectares of mound surface, occupied by, at a most conservative estimate, 11,000 and possibly as many as 40,000 to 50,000 people.

Such a large population distributed in such a peculiar manner over the landscape might be explained away as an exception were urban clustering not so widely distributed across the vast 120,000-square-kilometer Middle Niger. Other instances are not as well documented as the Jenne-jeno Urban Complex, but we have only begun to inventory the clustered towns that functioned within the extensive commercial network of the first millennium A.D. that predated trans-Saharan trade. Northwest from Jenne-jeno and across the Niger is Dia, where two large sites have extensive basal deposits of the last centuries B.C. These focus sites are surrounded by over 100 satellites, distributed in long curvilinear bands along present or senescent distributaries. Could all these have been occupied at the same time? The surface material studied and recorded in 1986–1987 suggests that many of the abandonment assemblages are indeed approximately contemporaneous (R. J. McIntosh and S. K. McIntosh 1987).

Further afield, the Malian archaeologist Téréba Togola (1996) has investigated urban clusters in the Middle Niger's "dead delta." The Méma is the now-senescent northeast alluvial basin that was possibly the first magnet to Saharan communities migrating out of their increasingly distressed homelands during the last two millennia B.C. Togola's urban complexes of Akumbu (8 tells) and Boundu Boubou (31 tells) are particularly important because of their supporting evidence of specialist occupation at some of the mounds. Togola's most recent work at the former shows that the Méma, and not the Jenne region, is the place to investigate the continuity of this settlement pattern from stone- to iron-using communities.

Indeed, the 1989-1990 Méma survey by Togola and Kevin MacDonald carefully documented 28 second- and first-millennium Late Stone Age sites (MacDonald 1994). These show patterns in lithics and ceramics as well as in the remains of animals and fish that suggest some degree of contemporaneous occupation of separate but adjacent sites by specialist hunters, fishers, and pastoralists. All apparently exchanged with one another. However articulated, these are still tiny communities without urban pretensions, although they do show the antecedent conditions of corporate distinctness, exchange, and reciprocity.

What is going on at these clustered towns? During 20 years of research in the Middle Niger we have tended to favor functional and ecological explanations. For the moment, this is our working definition of urban clustering: segmented communities of specialists or distinct corporate groups that voluntarily come together to take advantage of the services of others and a larger market for their products, but that make a demonstrable effort to preserve their separate identity by strategies of physical distinctiveness. The clustered city was a stable solution to the complementary ecological problems of the Middle Niger. The unavoidable reality was of life within a rich environment, but one marked by rain and flood regimes of high interannual variability. We suggest that the solution hit upon by the inhabitants to combat unpredictability was to develop increasingly specialized artisan and subsistence producers linked into a generalized economy.

If this thesis is correct, the clusters needed mechanisms of integration. To model this, we have, in the past, relied frankly upon direct historical canons of cooperation and ethnic reciprocity among various Mande groups that maintain the modern ethnic mosaic of the Middle Niger. Extrapolated back into later prehistory, the occupation of separate mounds would be a strategy of physical segregation to complement foundation myths and ritual practices of integration (R. J. McIntosh 1993). These might include

1. Privileges of "first arrivals": certain decisions vital to the subsistence or ritual life of one group can be made only by another, linking everyone in a network of reciprocity (see also Yaeger chapter 6).
2. Bonds of fictive kinship: myths and legends of common origin and rules of obligatory common labor.
3. Undischargeable debt: lore of extraordinary sacrifice by one group for others, under conditions of ecological stress—linking everyone in a fabric of expectations for future behavior.

This functional-ecological explanation leads to a prediction of cultural innovations that give rise to true urban clustering. In this model, late Stone Age communities would be encouraged to specialize (including those new practices that led to domestication of African rice, sorghums, millets, and fonio, among others) if they have a season of joint occupancy of a shared locale with other (emerging) specialist groups (R. J. McIntosh 1993). If peaceful, predictable reciprocity succeeded among these groups, further specialization might be encouraged. So, too, would a progressive lengthening of the period of joint occupancy. In time, seasonality withered away for some economic specialists (especially for agricultural producers), while it may have increased for others, such as herders and fishers (S. K. McIntosh 1999). The security of the generalized economy encouraged further in-migration. Under salubrious conditions, there would be normal population increases associated with sedentism. Eventually, the tiny seasonal, componential hamlets of the second and first millennium B.C. in the Méma would evolve into Akumbu (80 hectares) and Boundou Boubou. Further migrations of Mande-speakers into the live alluvial basins to the east brought the development of Jenne-jeno and Dia undisputed urban status.

The functional-ecological explanation of componential, specialists producers linked into a generalized economy has had some successes. It helped predict the Méma results for earlier periods and allows us to compare similar urban clusters from far distant parts of the globe. For example, compare the map of presumed specialist components at the Jenne-jeno Urban Complex with K. C. Chang's (1971:130) model of components at Shang capitals, such as An-yang or Cheng-chou. At these northern Chinese sites, plenty of specialist producers are distributed over an extensive landscape. But there are clear differences too. Those Middle Bronze Age state capitals have evidence of coercive, centralized mechanisms dedicated to political control, including walled royal precinct, chariot burials, and noble and elite hamlets. These celebrations of despotic power and extreme social ranking throw their absence in the Middle Niger into greater relief. The comparison with Jenne-jeno becomes more pertinent, we believe, when we compare plans of Middle Niger settlement complexes with earlier, yet still large and complex Chinese "Neolithic" sites lacking enclosure walls and monumental structures, such as Erh-li-t'ou, Hsing-T'ai, and Lo-yang (R. J. McIntosh 1991).

Despite these successes, the essential problem for archaeologists interested in the long-term transition to urbanism is that these explanations and models of componential networks of subcommunities are fundamentally synchronic. They describe an

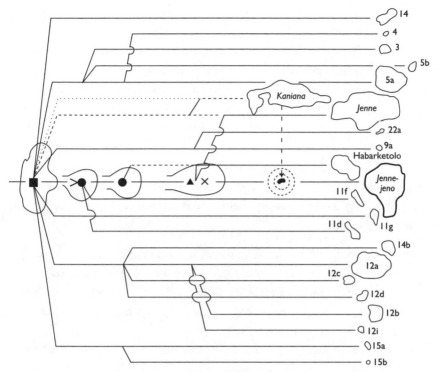

Figure 5.3. Alternate routes to clustering at the Jenne-jeno complex shown as a cladogram (branching diagram of shared derived characteristics).

integrative state at discrete points in time. They do not provide a diachronic mechanism of change and evolution, with continuity, over the long periods of time. It may be more helpful to move away from a representation of the dynamic urban clustering phenomenon as a static network diagram, as in the "structural model" of figure 5.3. Figure 5.3 presents an adaptation of cladistics, the science of systematics. The sites in this figure are those from which we have the best data from surface features and small finds relating to occupational specialization. Cladistics and, specifically, cladograms such as these that show ever-elaborating branching of related but differentiating organisms from common stems, are a tool to help us comprehend urban clusters as temporal sequences of branching relationships among component specialist communities. Cladistics are frequently used in ethnogenetic studies (Moore 1994), where language and cultural borrowings provide (often highly contested) windows on processes of historical contacts, borrowings, and coevolution.

On the positive side, cladograms do not presume a prestige or power ranking among the components. They allow us to depict stable heterarchy over the long term. Vertically oriented hierarchy diagrams will not do this (Butzer 1982:281–94). In heterarchy, the relations between subgroups are those not of coercion and control, but of separate but linked, overlapping yet competing, spheres of authority (Crumley 1987, 1995). It is a reasonable working hypothesis that these clustered Middle Niger cities are a physical expression of persistent, highly successful resistance to power and monopolized authority represented within a highly complex society. The branching diagrams of cladism may be the best way to represent the temporal elaboration of alternative routes to authority as these cities evolved.

But what was the core dynamic behind the systematics? Figure 5.3 illustrated three probable alternatives:

1. Single core priority: a large and dominant central settlement (Jenne-jeno) spawns multiple daughter communities that specialize subsequently;
2. Multiple founding communities: several early specialized communities (parts of an eponymous cluster) give birth to daughter communities as all interact liberally in a rhizotic mode.
3. Metallurgical antecedents in which blacksmiths, with their industrial and occult powers, drive the settlement pattern.

These are just three alternatives among the several imaginable. Little in the functionalist explanations would direct an empirical test of one pathway over another. However, if we are willing to credit the idea of a perceived environment (Butzer 1982:252–257; Gregory 1994), in which the group makes decisions about where to place their communities and how to use the land on the basis of values and symbolic abstractions, then several venerable Mande notions of the grid of occult power and authority are laid over the landscape and can take excavation and survey into novel data fields. Here we tread upon the sacred landscape in deep time, though we first have to confront the debates about an archaeology of mind.[2]

CLUSTERED CITIES ON THE MANDE
SACRED LANDSCAPE

To understand the rise and interaction of the various corporate groups comprising the clustered city, one must appreciate an alternative route to authority among the Mande: how those groups harvest occult knowledge and, hence, power (R. J. McIntosh 1995). Authority is harvested by *nyamakalaw,* professional classes of artists and occupational specialists from a sacred landscape, a spatial blueprint of power in three dimensions. It is entirely reasonable that there is a very long pedigree to related notions of landscape, occult access to knowledge, and the translation of that knowledge into authority within the community. Possessing just cast-aside settlements and the garbage of the ages, how can the archaeologist test the impact of (antecedent) Mande beliefs and values upon behavior at the founding of cities such as Jenne-jeno? Put a different way, the prehistorian's problem is to verify motivations and intentionality in the remote past. The test must be done *empirically.* In any hypothesis of deep-time intentionality, of persistent notions of authority or sacrality we must, of course, guard against a reinvention of essentialism and the historicist's conceits: immanent change, privileging an "inner rules" metaphysic, and history ruled by contingent forces.

All this suggests a future strategy for urban research, not just along the Middle Niger, but in Greater Mande generally, because of two fundamental inadequacies of the functional-ecological explanation. First, where are the elites, the chiefs, the kings, the early state bureaucracies? In other words, who keeps the peace? The Middle Niger towns do not appear to conform to the traditional "hierarchy as adaptive solution" approach to emerging complex society (S. K. McIntosh 2000). To date, excavation at sites such as Jenne-jeno reveals no obvious signs of social stratification, as opposed to abundant evidence of (horizontal) social complexity. Where are the public buildings, the monuments, the shrines to state ideologies that classic preindustrial city theory tells us should be present (R. J. McIntosh 1999)? Many archaeologists retain a traditional view of authority and power in complex society as always vested in a charismatic leader or in elite monopoly of decision making. But in the Jenne-jeno urban cluster, one has the strong impression of a highly complex society, with multiple overlapping and competing agencies of authority, decision making, and of resistance to centralization. The dispersed-cluster city layout was an instrument of that resistance.

This assertion that heterarchy, rather than hierarchy, is the better description of authority at these cities recalls persistent Mande notions of who has decision-making roles in society. This construction of social interaction is very familiar to historians, social anthropologists, and art historians. Authority is shared among many corporate groups rather than being the monopoly of a charismatic individual (in the sense of Weber 1956) or of one bureaucratic lineage. Contrast the Middle Niger situation with Weber's interpretation of early Mesopotamian urbanism as being conditional upon the prior monopolization of authority by the prince ("patrimonial kingship"), and as being a situation where no "municipal associations" can develop.

This notion from the Urban Clusters of alternative, multiple paths to authority calls up the second fundamental complaint with functional or strictly ecological explanations. Such explanations ignore the persistent Mande view of sacred geography and power places in the landscape. This forces upon us a very different view of "urban cladistics." The long-term systematics of urban space are shared by environmental concerns and by competition among subgroups within the community for advantageous siting upon the power grid. In Mande thought, one can gain occult knowledge and harvest power either by taking a knowledge quest (*dalimasigi*) to visit distant masters or power-invested points of the wilderness (R. J. McIntosh 2000:157–173). Or, one can locate at and extract occult power (preeminently for smiths, by the act of the smelt) from locations loaded with occult power. In local tradition, the marigots (floodplain distributaries) encircling both Jenne and Dia are particularly noteworthy for their concentration of *faaro* (water spirits with whom Mande heroes entered into contracts [S. Haidera, Institut des Sciences Humaines, Bamako, personal communication 1994]; oral tradition collected in Jenne in 1977, 1981, 1994 by R. J. and S. K. McIntosh). In order to understand the rise and sustained interaction of the various corporate groups, one needs to appreciate how they differentially harvest occult power and, hence, authority from the power grid of the Mande landscape.

In ethnographic time, the ancient cities of Mande (including, but not limited to ancient Middle Niger cities such as modern Jenne or Dia) occupy a prominent position, in three dimensions, on the sacred landscape. That landscape may be thought of as a local power grid and a map for navigation for occult knowledge. Thus far, we are entirely in the realm of speculation when we extrapolate earlier versions of these notions back even to the time of the Mali empire (at its apogee in the thirteenth and fourteenth centuries A.D.). However, there should be ways empirically to test the proposition that some recognizable (although greatly altered) conception of landscape as a spatial blueprint of power has a very long pedigree in the Middle Niger. If so, corporate groups, through their mythic founders and heroes, or through the agency of the knowledge-traveler well known among Mande smiths, sculptors, and bards (McNaughton 1991), would conceivably have been involved in the acquisition and maintenance of occult and political authority by harvesting that authority from a symbol-charged and dangerous landscape.

In Mande, authority derives not just from economic monopolies, but from multiple (and danger-filled) sources differentially accessible to various groups. Weber's quasi-theocratic, charismatic prince would have a rough time of it. This is a roadmap to successful municipal associations—heterarchy as resistance to non-consultative power. This implies that we must expand our analytic repertoire to include an archaeology of mind and a prehistory of deep-time intentionality that would throw light on the motivations for the foundation of urban clusters. This is certainly not an isolated call for an exercise in cognitive archaeology to supplement (never entirely to replace) functional, or economic, or ecological analyses. Chinese archaeologists, for example, are exploring the transformation by Middle Shang times of deep-time (late Neolithic) notions of shamanism. Shamans were repositories for local and lineage authority. Such notions were eventually transformed into the monopolized High Shamanism, with sumptuary ritual implements, that were the signature of the king's ideological right to power (Chang 1983:44–48, 56–63, 114; 1986:365–367).

Of course, all of these explorations of deep-time transformations and reinventions of ideologies and cross-cultural symbols share the risk of falling into the same logical traps as have discreditied historicism (Sanderson 1992). Ultimately, if these traps are to be avoided, we must find ways to test empirically the proposition that some, perhaps many, Middle Niger cities were founded and flourished because of the position they occupied on the perceived landscape of occult power. If we are to give any credence to the possibility of alternate routes to authority at the foundation of clustered cities, we must be prepared to experiment, with all caution and skepticism, with research that might open a window upon ancient motivations. The earliest cities would appear to be among our best proxy evidence for those novel transformations of a landscape of power and authority.

NOTES

1. Portions of this chapter are excerpted with permission from R. J. McIntosh,"Clustered Cities of the Middle Niger: Alternative Routes to Authority in Prehistory" in *Africa's Urban Past,* edited by D. M. Anderson and R. Rathbone (James Currey, Oxford), pp. 19–35.

2. As used here, an "archaeology of mind," also sometimes called cognitive archaeology, emphatically does not imply adherence to the postprocessual arguments of the 1980s and 1990s that the essential motivations of behavior in the past are forever hidden and obscured to archaeologists (reviewed in R. J. McIntosh 1996). Renfrew (1994) persuasively argues that an examination of prehistoric intentionality can be pursued within a hypothesis-testing framework.

REFERENCES

Butzer, K. W.

1982   *Archaeology as Human Ecology: Method and Theory for a Contextual Approach.* Cambridge University Press, Cambridge.

Chang, K. C.

1971   *Shang Civilization.* Yale University Press, New Haven, Conn.

1983   *Art, Myth and Ritual: The Path to Political Authority in Ancient China.* Harvard University Press, Cambridge, Mass.

1986   *The Archaeology of Ancient China.* 4th ed. Yale University Press, New Haven, Conn.

Childe, V. G.

1950   The Urban Revolution. *Town Planning Review* 21:3–17.

Clark, M.

1997   Site Structural Research at the Jenne-jeno Settlement Complex, Mali. Report to the Institut des Sciences Humaines, Bamako, Mali.

Clark, M., and H. Hietala

2002   Complexity at the Periphery: A Spatial Analytic Approach to Understanding Settlement Organization in Nucleated Site Clusters, Inland Niger Delta, Mali. Paper presented at the 16th Biennial Meeting of the Society of Africanist Archaeologists, May 18–21, Tucson.

Connah, Graham

2000   African City Walls: A Neglected Source? In *Africa's Urban Past,* edited by D. M. Anderson and R. Rathbone, pp. 36–51. James Currey, Oxford.

Crumley, C.

1987   A Dialectical Critique of Hierarchy. In *Power Relations and State Formation,* edited by T. Patterson and C. Gailey, pp. 144–169. American Anthropological Association, Washington, D.C.

1995   Heterarchy and the Analysis of Complex Societies. In *Heterarchy and the Analysis of Complex Societies,* edited by R. Ehrenreich, C. Crumley, and J. Levy, pp. 1–6. Archaeological Papers of the American Anthropological Association, No. 6, Washington, D.C.

Gregory, D.

1994   *Geographical Imaginations.* Oxford University Press, Oxford.

Jacobberger, P.

1987   Geomorphology of the Upper Inland Niger Delta. *Journal of Arid Environments* 13:95–112.

Mabogunje, A. L.

1968   *Urbanization in Nigeria.* University of London, London.

MacDonald, K.

1994   *Socio-Economic Diversity and the Origin of Cultural Complexity along the Middle Niger (2000 B.C. to A.D. 300).* Unpublished Ph.D. dissertation, Cambridge University.

McIntosh, R. J.

1983   Floodplain Geomorphology and Human Occupation of the Upper Inland Delta of the Niger. *Geographical Journal* 149(2):182–201.

1991   Early Urban Clusters in China and Africa: The Arbitration of Social Ambiguity. *Journal of Field Archaeology* 18:199–212.

1993   The Pulse Theory: Genesis and Accommodation of Specialization in the Middle Niger. *Journal of African History* 34:181–220.

1995   Jenne and the Mande Scred Landscape. Paper presented at the 1995 annual meeting of the Mande Studies Association, Leiden.

1996   Intellectual History of Archaeology. In *The Oxford Companion to Archaeology,* edited by B. M. Fagan, pp. 280–285. Oxford University Press, Oxford.

1999   Western Representations of Urbanism and Invisible African Towns. In *Beyond Chiefdoms: Pathways to Complexity in Africa,* edited by S. K. McIntosh, pp. 56–65. Cambridge University Press.

2000   Social Memory in Mande. In *The Way the Wind Blows: Climate, History, and Human Action,* edited by R. J. McIntosh, J. Tainter, and S. K. McIntosh, pp. 141–180. Columbia University Press, New York.

McIntosh, R. J., and S. K. McIntosh

1987   Prospection archéologique aux alentours de Dia, Mali: 1986–1987. *Nyame Akuma* 29:4245.

McIntosh, R. J., P. Sinclair, T. Togola, M. Petrén, and S. K. McIntosh

1996   Exploratory Archaeology at Jenné and Jenné-jeno, Mali. *Sahara* 8:19–28.

McIntosh, S. K.

1981   A Reconsideration of Wangara/Palolus, Island of Gold. *Journal of African History* 22:145–158.

1995   *Excavations at Jenné-jeno, Hambarketolo, and Kaniana: The 1981 Season.* University of California Monographs in Anthropology. University of California Press, Berkeley.

1999   Modeling Political Organization in Large-Scale Settlement Clusters: A Case Study from the Inland Niger Delta. In *Beyond Chiefdoms: Pathways to Complexity in Africa,* edited by S. K. McIntosh, pp. 66–79. Cambridge University Press, Cambridge.

2000   Floodplains and the Development of Complex Society: Comparative Perspectives from the West African Semi-Arid Tropics. In *Complex Polities in the Ancient Tropical World,* edited by E. Bacus, pp. 151–165. Archaeological Papers of the American Anthropological Association, no. 9.

2001   Africa, Sudanic Kingdoms. In *Encyclopedia of the History of Archaeology, History and Discoveries,* vol. 1, edited by T. Murray, pp. 71–78. ABC CLIO, Santa Barbara, Calif.

McIntosh, S. K., and R. J. McIntosh

1980   *Prehistoric Investigations at Jenné, Mali.* 2 vols. BAR, Oxford.

1993   Cities without Citadels: Understanding Urban Origins along the Middle Niger. In *The Archaeology of Africa: Food, Metals and Towns,* edited by C. T. Shaw, P. Sinclair, B. Andah, and A. Okpoko. Routledge, London.

McNaughton, P. R.

1991   Is There History in Horizontal Masks? *African Arts* 24:40–53, 88–90.

Moore, J. H.

1994   Ethnogenetic Theory. *National Geographic Research* 10(1):10–23.

Renfrew, C.

  1994   Towards a Cognitive Archaeology. In *The Ancient Mind,* edited by C. Renfrew and E.
                Zubrow, pp. 3–12. Cambridge University Press, Cambridge.

Sanderson, S. K.

  1992   *Social Evolutionism: A Critical History.* Oxford University Press, Oxford.

Togola, T.

  1996   Iron Age Occupation in the Méma Region, Mali. *African Archaeological Review*
                13(2):91–110.

Trigger, B.

  1972   Determinants of Growth in Pre-industrial Societies. In *Man, Settlement, and Urbanism,*
                edited by P. J. Ucko, R. Tringham, and D. E. Dimbleby, p. 577. Duckworth, London.

Weber, M.

  1956   *Economy and Society.* 4th ed. Bedminster Press, New York.

S I X

Untangling the Ties That Bind

JASON YAEGER

The City, the Countryside, and the Nature of Maya Urbanism at Xunantunich, Belize

Scholars have recognized the central role of the city in the organization and development of complex societies and have adopted an array of perspectives for understanding the city. For many, the city forms the social and cultural heart of a civilization, embodying the core social and cultural concepts of its members (Hall 1998; Weber 1958). Some stress the city's place as home to the greatest diversity of a society's members, a dense nexus of social relationships and a key locus of cultural innovation and change (Hannerz 1980; Redfield and Singer 1954). Still others see the city as a paradoxical juxtaposition of a civilization's artistic, intellectual, and architectural splendors with the stark economic inequalities that make such achievements possible (Childe 1950; Southall 1998). And a number are interested in the ways in which the city materializes the sacred world, making numinous principles visible and reifying them in stone and mortar (Fritz 1986; Wheatley 1971).

Those advocating a comparative, cross-cultural perspective have sought to establish a set of criteria to distinguish cities from other settlements along the continuum from ephemeral campsite to megalopolis. One of the best-known examples is Louis Wirth's (1938) definition of the city as a large number of people living in a densely nucleated settlement with a high degree of social and economic heterogeneity. Recognizing that Wirth's definition obscures important differences between cities, others have developed formal and functional urban typologies (e.g., Fox 1977; Redfield and Singer 1954; Sjoberg 1960; Wheatley 1983). Of these, Richard Fox's (1977) distinction between regal-ritual, administrative, mercantile, colonial, and industrial cities has been most widely used in the study of ancient Mesoamerica (see applications by Ball and Taschek 1991; Marcus 1983; Sanders and Webster 1988; Webster 1997).

These cross-cultural definitions of the city and its various subtypes are generally based on characteristics of the city itself, and only secondarily on the relationship between a city and its hinterland (Fox 1977 is an important exception). Many archaeologists have criticized this city-centered perspective, calling for more emphasis on the complex network of social, political, and economic relationships that connect city and hinterland (Adams 1966; Hayden 1994; Marcus 1983; Sanders and Santley 1983; Schwarz and Falconer 1994; Smith 1994; Trigger 1972). These relationships structure many of the basic formal properties of the city, such as its size and degree of population nucleation, as well as the historical processes of the development, maintenance, and decline of the city and the larger society of which it forms the heart.

This broader frame of reference allows models of the city to be more comprehensive and often more congruent with the emic concepts of the cultures we study. Joyce Marcus (1983:208) convincingly argues that distinguishing the Mesoamerican city from its politically controlled territory creates a division that would have seemed artificial to the people we seek to understand: "What was most important to [the ancient Mesoamerican] was the fact that he belonged to a particular region controlled by a specific native ruler, to whom he owed allegiance and tribute and from whom he received protection and civic-ceremonial leadership." Clearly, we cannot ignore the countryside in Mesoamerica if we are to understand ancient urbanism there, or the social and political relationships that linked city and hinterland.

Accepting the intimate link between city and hinterland, I consider the city a nexus of social and political relationships (Hannerz 1980) that forms the heart of larger social and political networks (also Fox 1977:24). These networks are continually reconstituted through the social practices of its members, including those resident in the city and those living in the surrounding hinterland. This definition emphasizes the social aspects of the city over its formal properties of population size and nucleation. It also recognizes the city as a physical place, the venue for socially generative practices such as regional market exchanges, polity-wide judicial hearings, and politically charged ritual performances that either implicitly recognize or explicitly advocate the existence and legitimacy of the larger political entity focused on the city (discussed in the next section; see also Moore this volume). Nor does it ignore the city as a potent unifying symbol, as the core of an identity that unites residents of the city and hinterland alike into a single "imagined community" (Anderson 1991).

These three aspects of the city—the center of larger social networks, a physical place, and a symbol of identity—cannot be meaningfully separated, because they all interrelate to structure social practice and thus affect urban development. Urbanism entails the formation of a larger social group, which I call an imagined community (Anderson 1991) when referring to its unifying horizontal aspect, and a polity (Ferguson and Mansbach 1996) when alluding to its hierarchical political aspect. The symbolic nexus of such a group is an overarching identity that is ultimately founded on socially generative practices, often interactive in nature, of both urban and hinterland residents. A shared identity is based in part on shared experiences in a common environment, the consequent shared understandings of the nature of the world and common expectations, and practices by which people work to achieve goals perceived as held in common. Especially important are politically charged practices that explicitly recognize and foster participants' membership in larger groups. Such practices often employ symbols that acknowledge and maintain status distinctions within that group, and while this identity creation need not have its origins among the urban elite, the latter group often has much to gain from the crafting of a powerful imagined community centered on the city. Note, however, that because such practices make membership explicit, they expose the criteria of group membership and the rights and responsibilities of membership to negotiation and contestation.

The emergent urban identity stresses the unity of the imagined community and, if strong enough, can undermine and weaken the competing ethnic, factional, and local community loyalties that crosscut any complex society (Adams 1992; Brumfiel 1994; McAnany 1993). This imagined community often forms the foundation of a polity based in the city but encompassing the hinterland. However, the urban identity rarely supplants or entirely replaces the other identities to which individuals have recourse (Schortman 1989; Schortman and Nakamura 1991); it serves instead as but one additional identity entailing actions, expectations, and premises that can be deployed as the "salient identity" in a given social and political context. Furthermore, the city can serve as a place for the emergence of new identities. While some of these identities may be officially sanctioned, interaction in the city often occurs in situationally anonymous contexts in which individuals act outside the authoritative gaze of local leaders and polity rulers alike. This latter fact makes the city a place for the potential creation of alternative identities and competing factions and polities that can subvert the dominant social and political structures (Hannerz 1980).

Although this discussion focuses on the role of practice and identity in the creation of a larger urban polity, I recognize that a wide range of factors condition the organization and development of each city. These factors include the organization of agricultural production that allows an accessible surplus (Drennan 1988; Sanders and Webster 1988), the beliefs and institutions (including coercive institutions) that secure and legitimate the place of the elite at the apex of the sociopolitical order (Baines and Yoffee 2000; Freidel and Schele 1988; Kolata 1997), and effective institutions of tribute collection (Stanish 1992). Processes of identity formation are neither secondary nor epiphenomenal to the diverse ecological and economic changes that mark urbanism, however. They are integral to them, and the study of the social practices that constitute the urban polity should complement investigations of these other topics, thereby allowing us to build more complex models of urbanism. The teasing apart of these complex processes represents an analytical endeavor beyond the scope of a single chapter, however. Accordingly, I concentrate on the formation of a political identity that united the members of the polity centered at Xunantunich, a Classic Maya city in western Belize.

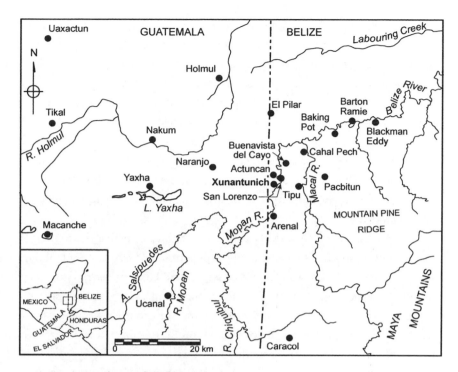

Figure 6.1. Regional map of the Maya region.

Urban Form: Xunantunich as City

Xunantunich is located near the west bank of the Mopan River in a region known generally as the upper Belize River Valley (figure 6.1). Between 1991 and 1997, Richard M. Leventhal and Wendy Ashmore directed the Xunantunich Archaeological Project (XAP), two principal goals of which were to explain the relatively late founding and florescence of Xunantunich and to understand the links between the city's rulers and their hinterland subjects (Ashmore and Leventhal 1993). The project combined mapping and extensive excavation of buildings at Xunantunich with a comprehensive settlement survey and hinterland excavation program. The following description of Xunantunich draws heavily on data produced by many of my colleagues on XAP as presented in the project's annual reports (Leventhal 1992, 1993; Leventhal and Ashmore 1994, 1995, 1996, 1997), and I acknowledge my debt to their collective efforts.

The core of Xunantunich consists of four adjacent architectural groups built on a large ridge overlooking the Mopan River floodplain (figure 6.2). The city's architectural heart is Group A, organized around three large plazas demarcated by tall platforms faced with limestone blocks, most of which are surmounted by masonry buildings. At the very center of the city is the Castillo, a 43-meter-high platform that is the cumulative product of several centuries of construction, crowned by a large, multiroom building adorned with stucco friezes depicting the ruling family in cosmologically significant locales (Fields 1994; Satterthwaite 1950). Three stelae arrayed along the south side of Str A-1—Stelae 8, 10, and 11—bear depictions of nobles dressed in elaborate warrior costumes and, in one case, standing in front of a bound captive (Graham 1978). These visually rich images are accompanied by hieroglyphic texts, most of which are unfortunately illegible because of their eroded condition.

Arrayed around Group A are three more modest groups. These include Group B, a residential complex of two adjoining patios surrounded by masonry buildings on low platforms (Thompson 1940; Pendergast and Graham 1981); Group C, a poorly understood aggregation of platforms including a residential group, large nonresidential range structures, and a sweatbath; and Group D, a complex occupied by a powerful elite family group (Braswell 1998). Together, these groups cover an area of 14 hectares and comprise the city's core.

There is evidence of only sparse occupation at Xunantunich prior to the seventh century A.D. The earliest monumental architecture in the core of the site is an early phase of the Castillo that probably dates to the Samal ceramic phase (A.D. 600–670; figure 6.3). Most of the other large structures in Group A were probably built early in the Hats' Chaak phase (A.D. 670–780), however, and were conceived of as a group to achieve the city's cruciform plan. The amount of Hats' Chaak–phase architecture at Xunantunich is much greater than that of its contemporaries elsewhere in the upper Belize River Valley, which suggests that Xunantunich came to dominate the valley during this period (LeCount et al. 2002). But it did not replace older cities there since noble families continued to add monumental buildings, collect tribute, and, in some cases, sponsor artisans (e.g., Awe 1992; Ball 1993; Ball and Taschek 2001; Healy 1990; Reents-Budet et al. 2000; Taschek and Ball 1999).

Xunantunich was subject to substantial modifications throughout the Hats' Chaak phase, but by the early facet of the Tsak' phase (A.D. 780–890), the site began a decline, marked by the successive abandonment of important spaces in the ancient city, including the Plaza A-III palace compound and the Str A-11 royal residence, the formal Northeast Complex, and Group C and the patios immediately

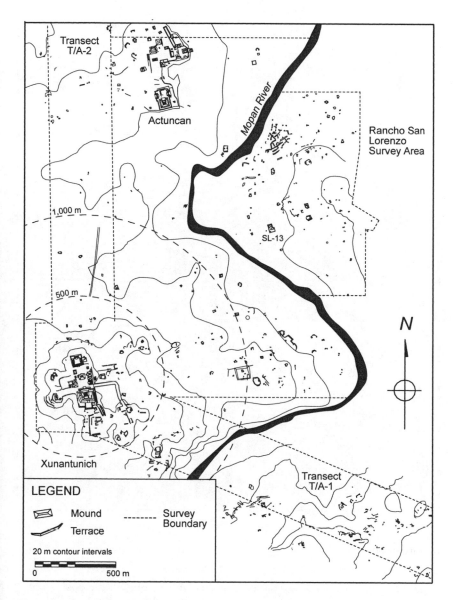

Figure 6.2. Regional map of Xunantunich.

south of the Castillo (LeCount et al. 2002). By the Tsak' phase, most of the activity in Group A was restricted to Plaza A-I and its surrounding buildings and, perhaps, Plaza A-II. Intriguingly, this marked contraction of the city corresponds with the erection of the three carved stelae between A.D. 820 and A.D. 849.

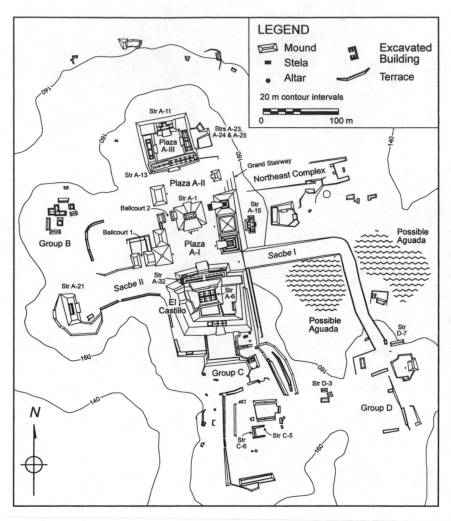

Figure 6.3. Map of Xunantunich.

It was during the Hats' Chaak phase, the period of interest here, that the city was at its greatest extent (LeCount et al. 2002) and the polity's regional population reached its peak (Neff 1998; Neff et al. 1995). Despite the impressive size of the monumental buildings at Xunantunich, many scholars would hesitate to call it a city because the site's monumental core lacked a substantial nucleated population. Some (e.g., Ball and Taschek 1991; Webster 1997) prefer to use terms like "center" to refer to politically important settlements with low population densities, such as those common in Mesoamerica (Smith 1994; Webster 1997), the Andes

(Kolata 1997), and Southeast Asia (Miksic 2000). Nevertheless, I believe it is important to consider larger Maya centers like Xunantunich cities for three reasons.

First and foremost, although the population of Xunantunich was not densely nucleated as was the case at other ancient cities like Chan Chan or Uruk, it was nonetheless quite large. Extrapolations from the survey data discussed in this chapter suggest that over 35,000 people lived within 5 kilometers of Xunantunich in the later Late Classic period, and Xunantunich occupied a key place in those people's political and religious experiences. Although nonnucleated, a population of this size living in such close proximity does entail the high frequency of interaction, social diversity, and degree of relative anonymity that distinguish the city's social environment from that of smaller settlements. It also constitutes the large pool of consumers and producers that give a city its great potential as a base of political and economic power for aspiring leaders.

Second, a relatively broad use of the term "city" facilitates comparative analyses that can yield important insights (e.g., Fox 1977; Marcus 1983; Sanders and Santley 1983; Sanders and Webster 1988). Finally, this usage avoids the implicit logic that politically important settlements with nonnucleated populations or with a low level of centrally located economic production "lack" some key characteristic that would take them over the threshold to city-ness, or that they ran out of evolutionary steam before becoming a city (Chase et al. 1990). Regardless of one's choice of labels, those who would study the city within its larger social context generally agree that terminological issues should not overshadow larger issues, such as the role of cities—or centers—in social evolution (also, Sanders and Webster 1988; Wilson 1997).

Xunantunich was not a densely nucleated city like some others described in this volume. Figure 6.2 shows the distribution of mounds—the general term for the piles of earth, rock, and refuse created by the Maya, the majority of which are the remains of residential platforms—around Xunantunich and the limits of 500-meter and 1,000-meter radii drawn from the site center. In the 140.4 hectares surveyed within 1,000 meters of Str A-6, excluding Group A but including Groups B, C, and D, the density of mounds of a size and shape typical of residential mounds in the Xunantunich region is 88 mounds per square kilometer (table 6.1). Within 500 meters of the site, mound density increases slightly to 140 mounds per square kilometer. It is instructive to compare these population densities with those of other areas in the Xunantunich polity, shown in table 6.1. The figure of 140 mounds per square kilometer within 500 meters of Xunantunich is clearly greater

Table 6.1

Mound Densities in the Xunantunich Polity

Zone	Area Surveyed (ha)	Number of Mounds	Mound Density (per km²)
Within 500-m radius of Xunantunich, excluding Group A	47.1	79	168
Within 500-m radius of Xunantunich, excluding Group A and atypical mounds[a]	47.1	66	140
Within 1,000-m radius of Xunantunich, excluding Group A and atypical mounds[a]	140.4	123	88
Transect T/A1	313	407	130
Transect T/A2	153	151	99
Transect T/A3	124	31	25
Aggregate of all transects	590	598	101
Rancho San Lorenzo survey area	86	110	128

[a]Many of the mounds in the immediate vicinity of Xunantunich are piles of stone detritus associated with the hillside quarries that surround the site (Keller 1993). Furthermore, the smallest mounded features (< 25 square meters in area) are unlikely to have been residences, nor are the very long mounds in Groups C and D.

Source: Transect figures from Neff et al. (1995).

than the overall average of 101 mounds per square kilometer in the 590 hectares of hinterland area mapped in the three transects of the Xunantunich Settlement Survey (Neff et al. 1995), a figure that provides the best approximation of the overall population density in the Xunantunich polity. Portions of the Xunantunich hinterland, however, are nearly as densely occupied as the zone within 500 meters of the Castillo. The Rancho San Lorenzo Survey Area, a zone of settlement 1.5 kilometers northeast of Xunantunich on the opposite side of the Mopan River, has a density of 128 mounds per square kilometer, and survey transect T/A1, which traverses 8 kilometers of interfluvial hills marked by agricultural terraces between Xunantunich and the Macal River, has a density of 130 mounds per square kilometer. Although mound density—and, by implication, population density—within the 500 meters immediately surrounding Xunantunich is somewhat higher than that in the polity's hinterland, the degree of nucleation is slight when compared with that of Maya cities such as Copan (Webster 1997) and Tikal (Puleston 1983).

Xunantunich also had a low resident population. Extrapolating from the density figures in table 6.1 and applying a standard algorithm for converting mound counts to population estimates, I calculate that 553 people lived within 500 meters of the site center, and 1,384 people within 1,000 meters of the site center.[1] To these figures, one must add the occupants of Group A, a total that is unlikely to be greater than 200 people (see Webster 1997:140). Thus fewer than 1,600 people probably lived within 1,000 meters of Xunantunich. In this way, Xunantunich is again quite similar to other cities in the upper Belize River Valley, such as Baking Pot, which had a population of about 1,061 people living in the 1.54 square kilometers surveyed around the site (Conlon and Moore 2002).[2]

Although Groups A, B, C, and D of Xunantunich covered only 14 hectares and housed a relatively small population, variability in the amount of labor invested in residential architecture suggests that the residents of those central architectural groups ranged from those with a high degree of access to the polity's resources to those with quite limited economic opportunities. Four categories of residential architecture plausibly correspond with differences in the wealth of their occupants. The most elaborate are corbel-vaulted, masonry structures that sit atop high masonry substructures, such as the royal residence, Str A-11, which was further embellished with stucco sculpture (MacKie 1985). This category is followed by somewhat smaller buildings of fine masonry—some with vaulted roofs—such as Str A-15 (MacKie 1985), many of the structures in Group B (Thompson 1940), and some in Group D, like Str D-7 (Braswell 1998); buildings that sit on sizable substructures but that likely lack substantial masonry walls, such as Str D-3 and Strs C-5 and C-6; and finally the many small wattle-and-daub buildings sitting on low, stone platforms. Although more systematic investigation of the residential architecture at Xunantunich, using energetics, for example (e.g., Abrams 1994), might refine the heuristic typology offered in this chapter, the city's residential architecture demonstrates that Xunantunich was a heterogeneous settlement with marked wealth differences.

Although the population of Xunantunich included the rich and the relatively poor, it was not a significant center of economic production. The quarries that are ubiquitous on slopes around Xunantunich provided limestone blocks for the city's buildings, but there was apparently little production of utilitarian tools or prestige goods. Production debris and some finished products suggest that a slate-carving workshop existed in Group D (Braswell 1998), and distribution of lithic debitage hints at limited stone tool production west of Ballcourt #1 (Keller 1997) In this respect, Xunantunich differs somewhat from other cities in the region, where excavations have yielded greater evidence of craft production. At Buenavista, for example, artisans in the palace compound painted polychrome ceramic vessels (Ball 1993; Reents-Budet et al. 2000), and at El Pilar a stone tool workshop was found immediately adjacent to the city (Michaels 1993). In neither of these cases, however, does the city seem to have been the primary focus of craft production within the larger polity.

At Xunantunich, the strongest evidence of craft production comes from the hinterland. The best example is a lithic production site on the opposite side of the Mopan River where people made chert bifaces at a scale that suggests full-time craft production (VandenBosch 1997). I identified a smaller chert tool production locale at San Lorenzo (Yaeger 2000a). These production locales are located approximately 1.5 kilometers from the city center in zones with plentiful chert nodules. Although their hinterland location does not necessarily indicate a low level of elite control over their production, Jon VandenBosch (1999; cf. Michaels 1993) found little evidence for top-down control of lithic production or distribution in his study of hinterland lithic assemblages. Despite this lack of craft production, Xunantunich might have been a locus for economic distribution. The low mounds flanking broad, plastered surfaces in the site's northeast entryway and along the plastered entryway between Plaza A-I and Str A-21 plausibly supported ephemeral shelters used during periodic markets, although we lack direct evidence to that effect (Keller 1997; also Jones 1996).

Although architectural and artifactual evidence of craft production and economic distribution may be limited at Xunantunich, there is ample evidence that ritual activity was very important at the city. The kinds of buildings that its rulers commissioned, their decoration, and spatial patterning all indicate that the primary concern structuring the built environment at Xunantunich was the same as that at most Maya cities: to provide a cosmologically meaningful venue for celebratory and ritual practices (Miller 1998; Schele and Mathews 1998; Tate 1992). Many of these involved the spatial segregation of participants, explicitly manifesting their social differences (Houston 1998; Schele and Freidel 1990:chap. 3; Webster 1998a). The heart of Xunantunich consists of two large, open plazas surrounded by steep-sided pyramids, topped by small masonry structures thought to be temples, a layout that is ideal for large public rituals and private religious celebrations (Jamison and Leventhal 1997).

The buildings and plazas of Xunantunich also represent a cosmogram, as is often the case in precapitalist cities (e.g., Ashmore 1991; Fritz 1986; Matos Moctezuma 1987; also Cowgill this volume). The site's distinct cruciform pattern formed by the intersection of two formal east-west causeways, *Sacbe* I and *Sacbe* II, and the north-south axis of the city demarcated by the three main plazas and their adjacent buildings recreates the quadripartite Maya cosmos (Ashmore 1998; Keller 1997). At the center of the cruciform template, and thus conceptually at the center of the cosmos, is the Castillo. The presence of World Tree symbolism on the stucco friezes of Str A-6-2nd, at the apex of the Castillo, suggests that the Castillo may represent the World Tree, which stood in the center of the Maya cosmos and formed the *axis mundi* (Fields 1994; cf. Schele 1998:491–492).

Although the celebrations that occurred in the symbolically charged public and semipublic spaces of Xunantunich may never be completely understood, one of their most important concerns was the legitimation of Maya kingship. The most prominent features of the city's built environment were pyramidal structures presumed to contain the remains of deified royal ancestors, and the city's public sculpture glorified the rulers and their ancestors, both as spiritually powerful maintainers of celestial and cosmic order and as militarily successful protectors of terrestrial political order. These three interrelated roles of the king—as war leader (Schele and Miller 1986; Webster 1998b), as primary intercessor with the spiritual realm (Houston and Stuart 1996), and as the semidivine descendant of divine ancestors (Houston and Stuart 1996; Schele and Miller 1986)—were all essential to the ideology that justified a Maya ruler's place at the apex of the sociopolitical structure of the polity.

The argument that Xunantunich was a locus of important administrative functions is drawn largely from observations of the site's built environment, particularly Plaza A-III and the adjacent structures. This complex is widely interpreted as the residential complex for the Hats' Chaak rulers of Xunantunich (MacKie 1985), and its location and internal spatial divisions suggest it was where the royal family and its representatives interacted with their subjects. Xunantunich could be entered from the Mopan Valley via the Northeast Complex, a broad, paved causeway that ended in a monumental stairway leading into Plaza A-II (Keller 1997). The entire northern side of Plaza A-II was dominated by the elevated platform of Str A-13, the southernmost building on Plaza A-III. To the arriving visitor, this structure would have been visually prominent, and the stairway leading up to it would have been easily accessible. This suggests that at least some of the activities in Str A-13 and the architectural spaces reached through Str A-13 were meant for the visiting public.

Roughly half of the rooms of Str A-13 have been excavated, and they all contain high benches that faced outward. In the absence of reported in situ assemblages, the function of these rooms is difficult to identify, but their high benches, proximity to the city's main entrance, and lack of privacy suggest a public, administrative function. It is plausible that hinterland residents would have come here to consult with the representatives of the polity's rulers about matters such as tribute payments, village disputes, and ritual concerns. The principal entrance to Plaza A-III was a large doorway at the midpoint of Str A-13, flanked by small rooms that would have permitted control of access into the plaza.

The northern gallery of rooms in Str A-13 faces into Plaza A-III. These rooms are nearly identical to those on the south side, which suggests they were venues for broadly similar activities but plausibly were reserved for higher-status petitioners who were permitted to enter the plaza. A third level of access to those who ruled Xunantunich is indicated by the broad frontal terrace and lower rooms of the northernmost Str A-11, which also face Plaza A-III and were accessible by a broad stairway. Directly under the ruler's residential suite (MacKie 1985) but not directly accessible from the ruler's chambers (Yaeger 1997), this terrace and the three rooms behind provide yet two more spatially discrete spaces for interaction and consultation, perhaps with the ruler himself. The stagelike masonry block that extended the terrace surface out over the middle of the stairway suggests that some of this interaction was publicly displayed, while activities in the adjacent rooms would have been secluded from public view. Among the latter practices, the ruler or other religious specialists may have consulted the spiritual realm, as suggested by registers of incised "graffiti" that probably represent visions achieved during ritual trances (Haviland and Haviland 1995) and a *patolli* board, a cruciform matrix of squares often used in divination.

In sum, the archaeological data allow us to confidently reconstruct Xunantunich as a city with a relatively small resident population and a high degree of wealth differences. The city was not a venue for intensive craft production but instead was structured primarily by concerns revolving around politically important celebrations and, to a lesser degree, administrative activities. This description fits well Fox's expectations for a regal-ritual city, as Joseph Ball and Jennifer Taschek (1991) originally proposed on the basis of the site's architecture and layout. This characterization, while a useful shorthand describing the activities that occurred at Xunantunich and, indirectly, the nature of Maya political legitimacy, does not directly address the practices through which the rulers and residents of Xunantunich and the inhabitants of the settlements created a larger polity focused at Xunantunich.

THE SOCIAL CONSTITUTION OF AN
URBAN POLITY: XUNANTUNICH AND
ITS HINTERLAND SETTLEMENTS

The late establishment of Xunantunich in a region characterized by competing, powerful cities with deep historical roots on the landscape—such as Buenavista (Ball and Taschek 2001), Cahal Pech (Awe 1992; Ball and Taschek 2001), and Pacbitun (Healy 1990)—and its rapid transformation into a major political center lead one to ask how the rulers legitimated their place at the controlling apex of an emerging urban polity (Ashmore and Leventhal 1993). The amount of labor required for the Hats' Chaak building programs and the pace of construction demonstrate that the rulers of Xunantunich controlled labor from a relatively large region in the upper Belize River Valley, plausibly including areas once ruled by other cities in the valley. Several lines of evidence indicate that the rise of Xunantunich was linked intimately to the powerful kingdom of Naranjo, just 15 kilometers to the west, which had inserted itself into the political affairs of the Mopan River Valley by at least the seventh century (Ashmore 1998; Ashmore and Leventhal 1993; Ashmore and Sabloff 1997; Ball and Taschek 1991; Houston et al. 1992; Taschek and Ball 1992). Regardless of Naranjo's role, the rulers at Xunantunich still had to establish and legitimate their place in the local sociopolitical context of the upper Belize River Valley.

Direct economic control and military coercion appear to have played relatively limited roles in the rise of Xunantunich. As already mentioned, there is little evidence of strong involvement of the Xunantunich rulers in economic production or distribution, and the only obvious representations of military themes are found on carved stelae dating to the ninth century, during Xunantunich's decline. Ashmore (1998) has suggested that the rulers spatially and visually referenced the nearby Preclassic center of Actuncan as a way of claiming historical legitimacy as the conceptual successors of the rulers of that polity. In my view, another process that was also crucial to the creation of a relatively centralized Xunantunich polity was the emergence of an imagined community predicated on the existence of a "Xunantunich identity" shared by residents of the city and the hinterland. This identity was overtly and implicitly fostered and reinforced in political and religious celebrations at Xunantunich, but its creation was not a top-down process. Politically charged practices in hinterland settlements helped define the criteria of membership in this community and the rights and responsibilities of its members, and the community's existence was implicitly accepted and reinforced through daily practices throughout the Xunantunich hinterland.

Constituting the Xunantunich Identity in the City

Our best evidence for practices by which a larger Xunantunich identity or imagined community was constituted is the city's built environment (Lawrence and Low 1990; Rapoport 1990). As in many Maya cities (Fash 1998; Houston 1998; Miller 1998), architectural spaces at Xunantunich were designed for celebrations on a grand scale. The monumental center of the city, with ample space in the plazas for thousands of participant-spectators, provided an ideal venue for socially integrative activities. Judging from the Maya textual record, many celebrations bolstered the place of the ruling family of the Xunantunich polity by emphasizing its central role in maintaining cosmic and sociopolitical order. Yet at a more fundamental level, participation in those celebrations was integral to the very existence of the polity itself, as the rituals united large numbers of its members in a collective enterprise that transcended local communities (Braswell et al. 1994). High frequencies of very large cooking pots in Strs A-23, A-24, and A-25, a small complex just off Plaza A-II, suggest that at least some of those celebrations involved feasting, a very potent way to build social bonds (LeCount 1996, 2001).

The polity was far from egalitarian, however, and rituals took place in a spatial venue designed in part to reinforce the polity's inequalities. At the plaza level, movement within the city was relatively restricted, as people had to pass through narrow gaps between buildings to move between plazas. Furthermore, most of the primary access points were ceremonially charged, requiring the visitor to walk past stela-altar pairs, powerful religious monuments erected by and intimately linked to the royal family, or through ballcourts, spaces that represented the entrance to the underworld (Schele and Freidel 1991).

While most participants in public rituals probably remained at ground level in the plazas, the terraces and buildings on the surrounding platforms provided architecturally differentiated, visually distinct stages for components of complex ritual performances. These spaces, especially the small masonry buildings on the tops of the pyramidal platforms, could not hold many people and could only be reached via steep stairways, often marked by stela-altar pairs. The small size and restricted access of these spaces arguably created a movement flow that manifested the hierarchical social differences within the Xunantunich polity (Jamison and Leventhal 1997), perhaps indexing those differences by the level of access that a person was permitted.

This would have been most true of the Castillo, which incorporated several levels of increasingly restricted architectural spaces, from the long gallery (Str A-32) that ran along its first terrace and was reached by a broad frontal staircase, to the medial terraces on the east and west sides of the complex, reached by smaller staircases accessible only through Str A-32. This ascent culminated in Str A-6, the highly decorated building on a tall substructure, which was reached from the medial terraces by very narrow side steps. Celebratory activities at the Castillo, as elsewhere at Xunantunich, would have recognized the unity of the polity by bringing together most of its members in one place for a common celebratory purpose, while simultaneously reinforcing the social differences inherent in the polity (also Fash 1998; Moore 1996 and this volume).

Constituting the Xunantunich Identity in the Hinterland

Many of the participants in Xunantunich's identity-building events were presumably residents of hinterland settlements, and it is thus logical to examine the practices there that may have helped create the new polity. Note that I use the term "hinterland" settlements instead of "rural" settlements, because the latter term implies a dichotomous settlement organization, with a densely populated urban center surrounded by a sparsely populated countryside. That is a questionable pattern in the Maya lowlands (Marcus 1983; Sanders and Webster 1988), with a few exceptions (Chase et al. 1990). Data from San Lorenzo, a small hinterland settlement, clearly show not only the impact that the founding of Xunantunich had on the region's hinterland communities, but also the important role of those communities in creating and maintaining the larger Xunantunich polity. In the San Lorenzo settlement cluster, families who had privileged access to extra-household labor and items of exotic raw materials also made the strongest claims of affiliation to the city's elite residents. I argue that SL-13, an adjacent ritual complex, was commissioned by the rulers of Xunantunich as part of a deliberate strategy to integrate settlements like San Lorenzo into the new polity centered on Xunantunich.

San Lorenzo is a spatially discrete settlement cluster of 17 residential mound groups, located 1.5 kilometer northeast of Xunantunich (figure 6.1). These mound groups include 7 multiple-mound groups organized around rectangular patios, 9 individual mounds, and 1 multiple-mound group lacking a formal patio (figure 6.4).

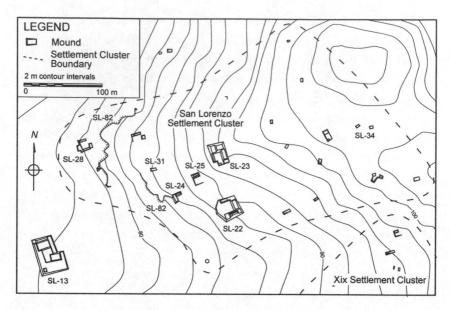

Figure 6.4. Map of San Lorenzo.

Also located within the boundaries of the settlement cluster are a chert quarry and associated debitage mounds (SL-82 collectively) and three small mounds that, given their size, are not likely to be residential in nature. Excavations first by Sabrina M. Chase and later by this author (both summarized in Yaeger 2000a) between 1992 and 1996 cleared large portions of five of the settlement's domestic groups: one single-mound group (SL-31), the only informal multimound group (SL-34), and three multimound patio groups, including a small three-structure group (SL-28), a large two-structure group (SL-24), and a large three-structure group (SL-22). I also supervised extensive excavations at SL-13, a locally unique multipatio group that sits just beyond the settlement's boundaries. A complementary program placed test units adjacent to almost every other structure in San Lorenzo, two of its three debitage mounds, and the chert quarry.

San Lorenzo appears to have been founded as early as the Ak'ab phase (A.D. 300–600), although the locale saw some earlier, intermittent occupations. The settlement grew rapidly during the Samal phase and expanded to its maximum size during the Hats' Chaak phase, when all 17 domestic groups were occupied. Population dropped during the early facet of the Tsak' phase, and the inhabitants of San Lorenzo abandoned the site completely sometime during the late facet of the Tsak' phase. The fact that San Lorenzo was founded prior to Xunantunich underscores the importance of understanding the practices that created links of affiliation between hinterland residents and the emergent Hats' Chaak rulers of Xunantunich, who had to craft their strategies in light of firmly established local sociopolitical institutions and practices (Yaeger 2000a, 2002; cf. the case of Mocollope discussed by Attarian this volume). The effectiveness of these strategies is indicated by the striking parallel trajectories of Samal growth, Hats' Chaak peak, and Tsak' contraction at Xunantunich and San Lorenzo. This suggests that the fortunes of the San Lorenzo residents were closely linked to those of the polity's rulers, as were most settlements in the Xunantunich hinterland (Ashmore et al. n.d.), a point to which I will return after discussing Hats' Chaak practices at San Lorenzo.

I have argued elsewhere that there was a local sense of community at San Lorenzo (Yaeger 2000b). This local identity was built in part on shared quotidian experiences and was reinforced actively through celebratory feasts in household contexts, perhaps related to ancestor veneration (see also McAnany 1995). Despite this local, shared identity and the small size of the settlement, San Lorenzo demonstrates a remarkable degree of socioeconomic inequality. For example, the aforementioned feasts, indicated by the presence of high frequencies of serving vessels, were hosted only by the families living in the three largest patio groups (SL-22, SL-23, SL-24). The distribution of faunal remains indicates that these feasts constituted the only local opportunity for the settlement's residents to eat meat (Yaeger 2000a), although bone chemistry analysis from contemporary, nearby Barton Ramie suggests all hinterland residents ate similar amounts of meat (Gerry 1993). Hosting feasts and providing meat were arguably important markers of social difference at San Lorenzo, and the residents of the hosting patio groups also consistently possessed more material markers of wealth than their neighbors and more material symbols that represented their political connections to the rulers of Xunantunich.

Economic differences at San Lorenzo are most clearly and durably expressed in the amount of labor that households invested in domestic architecture. Most mound groups consisted of low substructural platforms less than 1 meter in height, faced with cobblestones and, in a few cases, limestone blocks. These platforms were topped by perishable wattle-and-daub buildings. Four groups (SL-22, SL-23, SL-24, SL-25) stand out, however, because their much larger substructure platforms were made of limestone blocks, and they often supported buildings with masonry walls. Some of these structures required over 1,000 person-days to build, including the labor of specialized masons (Yaeger 2000a). Elliot Abrams (1994) has argued that this scale of labor investment requires mobilizing significant extra-household labor, which suggests that the four families living in these groups had a notable degree of authority over their neighbors.

One likely foundation of authority at San Lorenzo was differential access to local productive resources. According to Patricia McAnany (1995:96–97), the founders of Maya settlements and their descendants controlled the best local resources, as legitimated through a "principle of first occupancy." Given that two of the hosting groups (SL-22, SL-23) were among the first established at San Lorenzo, it seems plausible that a principle of first occupancy gave the Hats' Chaak descendants of these households a privileged claim to the best land and other local resources through their ancestors, whose veneration was arguably the focus of many local rituals and feasts (Gillespie 2000; McAnany 1995). Access to the most productive land would have become increasingly important during the course of the Classic period, as the landscape of the upper Belize River Valley became densely occupied (Ford 1990; Neff 1998; Willey et al. 1965). In that sociopolitical context, we should expect increasing contention and contestation over the legitimacy of land claims. Thus it is not surprising to find that the same families that hosted feasts actively represented an affiliation with the newly established Xunantunich rulers through their domestic architecture and the ornaments of exotic raw materials that they wore.

The families that lived in the four largest compounds and hosted feasts chose to incorporate in their houses architectural elements such as basal moldings (SL-22, SL-24) and high interior benches (SL-22, SL-24). Although lacking in the other houses in San Lorenzo, these features are common in Maya elite architecture, the nearest examples of which were at Xunantunich. Thus these four households not only conspicuously consumed the labor of others, but they used that labor to create domestic settings that resembled elite residences at Xunantunich more than they did the wattle-and-daub houses of the surrounding community members.

The distribution of important material symbols, specifically items of adornment made of exotic raw materials, also reflects internal social differences at San Lorenzo. Although most families had access to marine shell ornaments, the residents of the more modest houses possessed fewer such ornaments, most of which were *Oliva* shell "tinkler" pendants, while the inhabitants of larger houses had more elaborate shell pendants and beads. More striking is the distribution of greenstone, including jadeite. Of the five groups that we excavated extensively, we found greenstone only in those groups that had the largest houses (SL-22, SL-24). The distribution of these ornaments of exotic materials was probably controlled tightly by Maya rulers (Hirth 1992; Rice 1987), and I suspect that the connection between these materials and the elite was relatively transparent to members of Classic Maya society. If so, the residents of San Lorenzo who wore those items clearly and purposefully represented their political and economic ties to the Xunantunich rulers, thus further differentiating themselves from their neighbors. Although practices of social differentiation predate the establishment of Xunantunich (Yaeger 2002), the rapid growth of that city during the Hats' Chaak phase provided new symbolic and material resources that local leaders like those of San Lorenzo strategically deployed to bolster their local authority, actively representing affiliations to the polity elite (Yaeger 2000b). They reinforced this affiliation through periodic interactions in venues beyond the settlement, such as SL-13.

The multipatio group SL-13 is a locally unique architectural complex, much greater in volume than any of the residential groups in San Lorenzo and the only group with two connected patios. Excavation of portions of the northern patio of SL-13 revealed buildings of an unusual morphology, unlike any houses excavated at San Lorenzo. The architectural data, coupled with an artifact assemblage with a high frequency of incensarios, serving vessels, and ornaments, a bone flute, and a high frequency of faunal remains, suggest that the group was a ritual venue and not a residence (Yaeger 2000b).

Three facts suggest that SL-13 formed an intimate part of strategies to integrate this section of the Mopan River Valley into the Xunantunich polity: it is located between several adjacent settlement clusters on the Mopan floodplain, the amount of labor involved in its construction suggests that it was not built by the inhabitants of any single settlement, and the construction of its North Patio—and probably the entire complex—early in the Hats' Chaak phase coincides with the height of Xunantunich power. Further supporting this reconstruction is the fact that SL-13 Str 3 is the only platform in the local area known to have two stairways, one facing the patio and the other looking toward Xunantunich, possibly providing an entryway for visitors from Xunantunich.

As is the case at Xunantunich, the data from SL-13 do not permit us to identify the exact nature of the rituals celebrated in the complex. It seems likely, though, that the complex served as the venue for a variety of celebrations and events that would have united different combinations of participants, both from local settlements and from Xunantunich. Some arguably brought together an entire local settlement with representatives of Xunantunich, negotiating that local community's place within the newly emerging Xunantunich polity, but others probably contributed to internal divisions within those settlements like those described earlier for San Lorenzo.

The layout of SL-13 provided spaces for inclusive practices, such as the enclosed and plastered North Patio, and spaces for exclusive, differentiating activities. The latter include the buildings that surround the North Patio and the distinction between an exterior plastered space along SL-13's northern side and the North Patio. Accepting that the built environment structures social practice, celebrations at SL-13 had the potential to differentiate those participants who could enter the patio from those who could not. Although the criteria by which people were differentiated probably varied contextually, rituals that made use of those two spaces would have made these criteria manifest, thus reflecting and reproducing social distinctions. It seems very likely that at least some of the celebrations at SL-13 involved Xunantunich representatives and forged links between the rulers of Xunantunich and the local leaders of San Lorenzo and other nearby settlements, a crucial task if the new rulers were to routinize and institutionalize the flow of tribute and corvée labor from the hinterland to their capital. Simultaneously, such celebrations would have created horizontal affiliations among those included and those excluded from the interior patio or the buildings adjacent to the North Patio, thus forming identities that crosscut local settlements and may have competed with local loyalties.

The data from SL-13 and San Lorenzo demonstrate that the establishment of Xunantunich stimulated important social changes in the adjacent Mopan River Valley, as its rulers, leaders of hinterland settlements such as San Lorenzo, and the nonleadership hinterland populace attempted to negotiate more advantageous places within the emerging social system. Note, however, that San Lorenzo should not be taken to represent all of the hinterland communities in the Xunantunich polity. XAP excavations have demonstrated a remarkable number of differences among hinterland settlements (Connell 2000; Robin 1999; Yaeger 2000a). Although this diversity is too complicated to outline here, it does seem that the residents of the different hinterland settlements—themselves internally heterogeneous social groups (Yaeger and Robin n.d.)—negotiated different roles within the Xunantunich polity (also LeCount 1999). As a result, a larger urban polity emerged that encompassed the hinterland, although this polity ultimately dissolved during the Tsak' phase (Ashmore et al. n.d.; LeCount et al. 2002).

The data from Xunantunich and its hinterlands strongly support the argument that an overarching identity linking city and hinterland into an imagined community is central to the establishment of a city. The rulers of Xunantunich designed their new city to create a space where thousands of people could come together, thus reinforcing and recognizing the common bonds that linked hinterland and urban residents. They extended this strategy into the hinterland, where they were involved in the construction of SL-13, the ritual complex that brought the inhabitants of hinterland settlements together, plausibly to interact with representatives from Xunantunich in some contexts. The detailed data from hinterland communities such as San Lorenzo, however, remind us that elite strategies were but one factor in the creation of a polity-wide identity, which is better understood as an emergent, negotiated product of the interaction between the polity rulers, the leaders of local communities, and other hinterland community residents.

At San Lorenzo, the Hats' Chaak residents shared a community identity that was made explicit and reinforced in practices such as feasts. As at Xunantunich, however, these feasts and other common events such as the building of a house provided contexts for the reproduction of inequalities within the community. Local leaders who hosted feasts sought to maintain or increase their local status by using material symbols to represent their connections and affinities, whether real or not, to the rulers and other elite of Xunantunich.

The founding of Xunantunich and the ambitious Hats' Chaak building program there must have required new levels of corvée labor and tribute from the local populace, a change that undoubtedly transformed the social and political dynamics of local settlements. For hinterland leaders, like the founding families of San Lorenzo, these changes presented opportunities to enhance their local positions by serving as intermediaries between local settlements and the political and economic networks of the emerging polity. However, the nonleadership residents of hinterland communities, like those who lived in the simpler houses at San Lorenzo, also had reasons for participating in practices that helped create the polity, even though these practices also legitimated local inequalities. Although one should not ignore the fact that they may have had little power to resist participation, their participation also presumably ensured their access to land and other resources and satisfied familial obligations. Furthermore, it is not unlikely that the rulers of the

Xunantunich polity represented a powerful authority, independent of the local community, which less powerful hinterland residents could employ to strategically oppose their local leaders. For their part, the rulers of Xunantunich had to accommodate their strategies to the social and political structures presented by pre-existing settlements such as San Lorenzo and to the demands and desires of hinterland residents, especially those in leadership positions.

The case study presented here raises several important larger points. First, the data from San Lorenzo belie the existence of a simple opposition between a rural identity and a city identity, or between a peasant culture and an elite culture or "high culture" (Baines and Yoffee 2000). The Hats' Chaak social strategies and practices at San Lorenzo and SL-13 sometimes reinforced local identities, but they also had the potential to create affiliations that horizontally crosscut settlements and factions that vertically linked some members of local communities with polity elite (Brumfiel 1994). Another identity that was reinforced through activities in SL-13 and in the ceremonial spaces of Xunantunich was a polity-wide identity, centered on Xunantunich and its rulers. There would have been a constant tension between these different identities and affiliations, as individuals evaluated them and deployed them in different interactions across the polity. From this perspective, the processes of urban development are quite dynamic, contingent upon the strategic choices of the urban polity's members and constrained by the material and cultural contexts within which they make those choices.

Social differences at San Lorenzo were made materially manifest in several ways: in the labor families could call upon when building their homes, in the architectural choices they made, in their ability to host feasts and to obtain meat for those feasts, and in their access to greenstone and marine shell ornaments. The differences marked by these various material domains were overlapping rather than coterminous, which further indicates that social differentiation was not a simple structural difference between local leaders and followers, but rather was a complicated, emergent product that was negotiated and continually re-created in daily practice.

A second important conclusion to draw from this work is that the constitution of Maya urban polities varied from place to place, even within the upper Belize River Valley (Yaeger 2002). Individuals in different places and at different times employed distinct strategies to create the political networks that constituted the societies in which they lived. Furthermore, the economic, social, and symbolic resources that they could employ in these efforts varied. Such differences therefore strongly conditioned the structure of hinterland settlements and polities alike, and they provide a potentially fruitful direction for future comparative analyses of the diversity inherent in Maya urban form and process.

Finally, urban polities cannot be fully understood from a top-down perspective that focuses on the city or the elite, nor by a bottom-up perspective that treats societies as the aggregate of its member households. Instead, social and political institutions like city and polity are best understood by employing a middle-level approach (de Montmollin 1988; Iannone 2002; Yaeger 2000b; Yaeger and Canuto 2000). Although household-level excavations provide detailed data regarding a society's past members, a middle-level perspective provides the analytical framework needed to understand the complex relationships between larger political and material structures that influenced a given settlement, the settlement-level political and social institutions, and the strategies of individuals within the settlement and beyond its boundaries.

ACKNOWLEDGMENTS

I would like to thank the Belize Department of Archaeology and its commissioners, Harriot Topsey, John Morris, Alan Moore, and Brian Woodeye, for their consistent support of the Xunantunich Archaeological Project. Rudy Juan, Dorrell Biddle, and Mel Xix kindly allowed me to work on their properties, and the Juan and Penados families were gracious and cordial hosts in Belize. My colleagues on the Xunantunich Archaeological Project created an intellectually stimulating and supportive environment, and I especially thank Richard M. Leventhal, Wendy Ashmore, Sabrina Chase, Sam Connell, Jennifer Ehret, Virginia Fields, Tom Jamison, Angela Keller, Lisa LeCount, Julie Miller, Ted Neff, Aimee Preziosi, Cynthia Robin, Jon VandenBosch, and Laura Villamil. I also would like to acknowledge the crew members from San José Succotz and Benque Viejo del Carmen, whose work at San Lorenzo laid the empirical foundation for my study. Finally, my understanding of the upper Belize River Valley has benefited greatly from the exchange of data and ideas with other scholars working in the area, notably Jaime Awe, Joseph Ball, James Conlon, Anabel Ford, James Garber, Gyles Iannone, and Terry Powis. The analysis presented here owes much to these individuals, although I bear full responsibility for the synthesis I have presented. The comments of Monica Smith and two anonymous reviewers helped me clarify several key aspects of the discussion, and I thank Monica Smith for the invitation to contribute to this volume and for her feedback during the revisions. Generous funds supporting the San Lorenzo fieldwork and analysis came from the National Science Foundation (SBR9321503, SBR9530949), the Fulbright / II-E Program, Dumbarton Oaks, the Graduate School of Arts and Sciences and the Department of Anthropology at the University of Pennsylvania, and Sigma-Xi.

NOTES

1. Using a standard algorithm that draws upon household excavation data in the Maya lowlands (following Rice and Culbert 1990), I estimate that 16 percent of the mounds are nonresidential, consisting of shrines, kitchens, and other ancillary structures. I assume that the remaining 84 percent of the mounds are the remains of houses inhabited by minimally extended families, with an average of 5.4 people per house. Note that this procedure assumes that all mounds that were occupied during a given ceramic phase were occupied contemporaneously, an assumption that is open to question but unfortunately cannot be resolved with current dating methods (Tourtellot 1993).

2. The population figure I give differs slightly from their figure of 1,170 because we use different algorithms to calculate populations estimates.

REFERENCES

Abrams, E. M.

1994   *How the Maya Built Their World: Energetics and Ancient Architecture.* University of Texas Press, Austin.

Adams, R. McC.

1966   *The Evolution of Urban Society.* Aldine, Chicago.

1992   Ideologies: Unity and Disunity. In *Ideology and Pre-Columbian Civilizations,* edited by A. A. Demarest and G. W. Conrad, pp. 205–222. School of American Research, Santa Fe, N.M.

Anderson, B.

1991   *Imagined Communities: Reflections on the Origins and Spread of Nationalism.* 2d ed. Verso, London.

Ashmore, W.

1991   Site-Planning Principles and Concepts of Directionality among the Ancient Maya. *Latin American Antiquity* 2:199–226.

1998   Monumentos políticos: sitio, asentamiento, y paisaje alrededor de Xunantunich, Belice. In *Anatomía de una civilización: aproximaciones interdisciplinarias a la cultura maya,* edited by A. Ciudad Ruiz, Y. Fernández Marquínez, J. M. García Campo, M. J. Iglesias Ponce de León, A. Lacadena García-Gallo, and L. T. Sanz Castro, pp. 161–183. Sociedad Española de Estudios Mayas Publicación 4. Madrid.

Ashmore, W., and R. M. Leventhal

1993   Xunantunich Reconsidered. Paper presented at the Belize Conference, University of North Florida, Jacksonville.

Ashmore, W., and J. A. Sabloff

1997   On Spatial Order in Maya Civic Plans. Paper presented at the Segunda Palenque Mesa Redonda, Palenque, Chiapas, Mexico.

Ashmore, W., J. Yaeger, and C. Robin

n.d.   Commoner Sense: Late and Terminal Classic Social Strategies in the Xunantunich Area. In *Collapse, Transition, and Transformation: New Views of the End of the Classic Period in the Maya Lowlands,* edited by D. S. Rice, P. M. Rice, and A. A. Demarest. Westview Press, Boulder, Colo.

Awe, J. J.

1992   *Dawn in the Land between the Rivers: Formative Occupation at Cahal Pech, Belize, and Its Implications for Preclassic Development in the Maya Lowlands.* Unpublished Ph.D. dissertation, Institute of Archaeology, University College of London, London.

Baines, J., and N. Yoffee

2000   Order, Legitimacy, and Wealth in Ancient Egypt and Mesopotamia. In *Order, Legitimacy, and Wealth in Ancient States,* edited by J. Richards and M. V. Buren, pp. 13–17. Cambridge University Press, Cambridge.

Ball, J. W.

1993   Pottery, Potters, Palaces, and Polities: Some Socioeconomic and Political Implications of Late Classic Maya Ceramic Industries. In *Lowland Maya Civilization in the Eighth Century A.D.,* edited by J. A. Sabloff and J. S. Henderson, pp. 243–272. Dumbarton Oaks, Washington, D.C.

Ball, J. W., and J. T. Taschek

1991   Late Classic Lowland Maya Political Organization and Central-Place Analysis. *Ancient Mesoamerica* 2:149–165.

2001   The Buenavista-Cahal Pech Royal Court: Multi-Palace Court Mobility and Usage in a Petty Lowland Maya Kingdom. In *Royal Courts of the Ancient Maya,* vol. 2: *Data and Case Studies,* edited by T. Inomata and S. D. Houston, pp. 165–200. Westview Press, Boulder, Colo.

Braswell, J. B.

1998   *Archaeological Investigations at Group D, Xunantunich, Belize.* Ph.D. dissertation, Department of Anthropology, Tulane University. University Microfilms International, Ann Arbor.

Braswell, J. B., A. H. Keller, and J. Yaeger

1994   Community Integration at Terminal Classic Xunantunich, Belize. Paper presented at the 93d Annual Meeting of the American Anthropological Association, Atlanta, Ga.

Brumfiel, E. M.

1994   Factional Competition and Political Development in the New World: An Introduction. In *Factional Competition and Political Development in the New World,* edited by E. M. Brumfiel and J. W. Fox, pp. 3–13. Cambridge University Press, Cambridge.

Chase, D. Z., A. F. Chase, and W. A. Haviland

1990   The Classic Maya City: Rethinking "The Mesoamerican Urban Tradition." *American Anthropologist* 92:499–506.

Childe, V. G.

1950   The Urban Revolution. *Town Planning Review* 21:3–17.

Conlon, J. M., and A. F. Moore

2002   Plazuela Groups of the Late Classic Period: A Comparison and Contrast of Community Interaction and Integration at Baking Pot, Belize. In *Perspectives on Ancient Maya
Rural Complexity,* edited by G. Iannone and S. V. Connell. Monograph 49. Cotsen Institute of Archaeology, Los Angeles.

Connell, S. V.

2000   *Were They Well Connected? An Exploration of Ancient Maya Regional Integration from the
Middle-Level Perspective of Chaa Creek, Belize.* Ph.D. dissertation, Department of Anthropology, University of California, Los Angeles. University Microfilms International, Ann Arbor.

de Montmollin, O.

1988   Settlement Scale and Theory in Maya Archaeology. In *Recent Studies in Pre-Columbian
Archaeology,* edited by N. J. Saunders and O. de Montmollin, pp. 63–104. British Archaeological Reports, International Series 431. Oxford.

Drennan, R. D.

1988   Household Location and Compact versus Dispersed Settlement in Prehispanic
Mesoamerica. In *Household and Community in the Mesoamerican Past,* edited by R. R.
Wilk and W. Ashmore, pp. 273–293. University of New Mexico Press, Albuquerque.

Fash, W. L.

1998   Dynastic Architectural Programs: Intention and Design in Classic Maya Buildings at
Copan and Other Sites. In *Function and Meaning in Classic Maya Architecture,* edited by
S. D. Houston, pp. 223–270. Dumbarton Oaks, Washington, D.C.

Ferguson, Y. H., and R. W. Mansbach

1996   *Polities: Authority, Identities, and Change.* University of South Carolina Press, Columbia.

Fields, V. M.

1994   The Royal Charter at Xunantunich. In Xunantunich Archaeological Project: 1994
Field Season, edited by R. M. Leventhal and W. Ashmore, pp. 65–74. Unpublished
report on file at the Belize Department of Archaeology, Belmopan, and the Cotsen
Institute of Archaeology, Los Angeles.

Ford, A.

1990   Maya Settlement in the Belize River Area: Variations in Residence Patterns of the
Central Maya Lowlands. In *Precolumbian Population History in the Maya Lowlands,* ed-
ited by T. P. Culbert and D. S. Rice, pp. 167–181. University of New Mexico Press,
Albuquerque.

Fox, R. G.

1977   *Urban Anthropology: Cities in Their Cultural Setting.* Prentice-Hall, Englewood Cliffs, N.J.

Freidel, D. A., and L. Schele

1988   Symbol and Power: A History of the Lowland Maya Cosmogram. In *Maya Iconography,* edited by E. P. Benson and G. G. Griffin, pp. 44–93. Princeton University Press,
Princeton, N.J.

Fritz, J. M.

1986   Vijayanagara: Authority and Meaning of a South Indian Imperial Capital. *American
Anthropologist* 88:44–55.

Gerry, J. P.

1993   *Diet and Status among the Classic Maya: An Isotopic Perspective.* Ph.D. dissertation, Department of Anthropology, Harvard University. University Microfilms Interntional, Ann Arbor.

Gillespie, S. D.

2000   Rethinking Ancient Maya Social Organization: Replacing "Lineage" with "House." *American Anthropologist* 102:467–484.

Graham, I.

1978   *Corpus of Maya Hieroglyphic Inscriptions,* vol. 2, pt. 2: *Naranjo, Chunhuitz, Xunantunich.* Peabody Museum of Archaeology and Ethnology, Harvard University, Cambridge, Mass.

Hall, P.

1998   *Cities in Civilization.* Weidenfeld & Nicolson, London.

Hannerz, U.

1980   *Exploring the City.* Columbia University Press, New York.

Haviland, W. A., and A. de Laguna Haviland

1995   Glimpses of the Supernatural: Altered States of Consciousness and the Graffiti of Tikal, Guatemala. *Latin American Antiquity* 6:295–309.

Hayden, B. D.

1994   Village Approaches to Complex Societies. In *Archaeological Views from the Countryside,* edited by G. M. Schwartz and S. E. Falconer, pp. 198–206. Smithsonian Institution Press, Washington, D.C.

Healy, P. F.

1990   Excavations at Pacbitun, Belize: Preliminary Report on the 1986 and 1987 Excavations. *Journal of Field Archaeology* 17:247–262.

Hirth, K. G.

1992   Interregional Exchange as Elite Behavior: An Evolutionary Perspective. In *Mesoamerican Elites: An Archaeological Assessment,* edited by A. F. Chase and D. Z. Chase, pp. 18–29. University of Oklahoma Press, Norman.

Houston, S. D.

1998   Classic Maya Depictions of the Built Environment. In *Function and Meaning in Classic Maya Architecture,* edited by S. D. Houston, pp. 333–372. Dumbarton Oaks, Washington, D.C.

Houston, S. D., and D. Stuart

1996   Of Gods, Glyphs, and Kings: Divine Rulership among the Classic Maya. *Antiquity* 70:289–312.

Houston, S. D., D. Stuart, and K. Taube

1992   Image and Text on the "Jauncy Vase." In *The Maya Vase Book,* vol. 3, edited by J. Kerr, pp. 498–512. Kerr Associates, New York.

Iannone, G.

2002   A Multiplicity of Integrative Strategies: Toward an Understanding of Middle-Level Settlement Variability in the Vicinity of Cahal Pech, Belize. In *Perspectives on Ancient Maya Rural Complexity,* edited by G. Iannone and S. V. Connell. Monograph 49. Cotsen Institute of Archaeology, Los Angeles.

Jamison, T. R., and R. M. Leventhal

    1997   Creating and Holding a Political Center: Architecture and Space at Xunantunich. Paper presented at the 92d Annual Meeting of the Society for American Archaeology, Nashville.

Jones, C.

    1996   *Excavations in the East Plaza of Tikal.* Tikal Report 16. University Museum, University of Pennsylvania, Philadelphia.

Keller, A. H.

    1993   Vision and Revision: The Remapping of Xunantunich. In Xunantunich Archaeological Project: 1993 Field Season, edited by R. M. Leventhal, pp. 86–99. Unpublished report on file at the Belize Department of Archaeology, Belmopan, and the Cotsen Institute of Archaeology, Los Angeles.

    1997   Testing and Excavation around *Sacbe* II and Group C. In Xunantunich Archaeological Project: 1997, the Final Field Season, edited by R. M. Leventhal and W. Ashmore, pp. 96–115. Unpublished report on file at the Belize Department of Archaeology, Belmopan, and the Cotsen Institute of Archaeology, Los Angeles.

Kolata, A. L.

    1997   Of Kings and Capitals: Principles of Authority and the Nature of Cities in the Native Andean State. In *The Archaeology of City-States: Cross-Cultural Approaches,* edited by D. L. Nichols and T. H. Charlton, pp. 245–254. Smithsonian Institution Press, Washington, D.C.

Lawrence, D. L., and S. M. Low

    1990   The Built Environment and Spatial Form. *Annual Review of Anthropology* 19:453–505.

LeCount, L. J.

    1996   *Pottery and Power: Feasting, Gift-Giving and Ceramics in Xunantunich, Belize.* Ph.D. dissertation, Department of Anthropology, University of California, Los Angeles. University Microfilms International, Ann Arbor.

    1999   Polychrome Pottery and Political Strategies in Late and Terminal Classic Lowland Maya Society. *Latin American Antiquity* 10:239–258.

    2001   Like Water for Chocolate: Feasting and Political Ritual among the Late Classic Maya at Xunantunich, Belize. *American Anthropologist* 103:935–953.

LeCount, L. J., J. Yaeger, R. M. Leventhal, and W. Ashmore

    2002   Dating the Rise and Fall of Xunantunich, Belize, A Late and Terminal Classic Lowland Maya Regional Center. *Ancient Mesoamerica* (13)1:41–63.

Leventhal, R. M. (editor)

    1992   Xunantunich Archaeological Project: 1992 Field Season. Unpublished report on file at the Belize Department of Archaeology, Belmopan, and the Cotsen Institute of Archaeology, Los Angeles.

    1993   Xunantunich Archaeological Project: 1993 Field Season. Unpublished report on file at the Belize Department of Archaeology, Belmopan, and the Cotsen Institute of Archaeology, Los Angeles.

Leventhal, R. M., and W. Ashmore (editors)

    1994   Xunantunich Archaeological Project: 1994 Field Season. Unpublished report on file at the Belize Department of Archaeology, Belmopan, and the Cotsen Institute of Archaeology, Los Angeles.

1995   Xunantunich Archaeological Project: 1995 Field Season. Unpublished report on file at the Belize Department of Archaeology, Belmopan, and the Cotsen Institute of Archaeology, Los Angeles.

1996   Xunantunich Archaeological Project: 1996 Field Season. Unpublished report on file at the Belize Department of Archaeology, Belmopan, and the Cotsen Institute of Archaeology, Los Angeles.

1997   Xunantunich Archaeological Project: 1997, the Final Field Season. Unpublished report on file at the Belize Department of Archaeology, Belmopan, and the Cotsen Institute of Archaeology, Los Angeles.

McAnany, P. A.

1993   The Economics of Social Power and Wealth among Eighth-Century Maya Households. In *Lowland Maya Civilization in the Eighth Century A.D.,* edited by J. A. Sabloff and J. Henderson, pp. 65–89. Dumbarton Oaks, Washington, D.C.

1995   *Living with the Ancestors: Kinship and Kingship in Ancient Maya Society.* University of Texas Press, Austin.

MacKie, E. W.

1985   *Excavations at Xunantunich and Pomona, Belize, in 1959–60.* British Archaeological Reports, International Series 251. Oxford.

Marcus, J.

1983   On the Nature of the Mesoamerican City. In *Prehistoric Settlement Patterns: Essays in Honor of Gordon R. Willey,* edited by E. Z. Vogt and R. M. Leventhal, pp. 195–242. University of New Mexico Press, Albuquerque.

Matos Moctezuma, E.

1987   Symbolism of the Templo Mayor. In *The Aztec Templo Mayor,* edited by E. H. Boone, pp. 185–210. Dumbarton Oaks, Washington, D.C.

Michaels, G. H.

1993   *Evidence for Lithic Craft Specialization by the Classic Period Maya of the Upper Belize River Valley, Belize.* Ph.D. dissertation, Department of Anthropology, University of California, Santa Barbara. University Microfilms International, Ann Arbor.

Miksic, J. N.

2000   Heterogenetic Cities in Premodern Southeast Asia. *World Archaeology* 32:106–120.

Miller, M.

1998   A Design for Meaning in Maya Architecture. In *Function and Meaning in Classic Maya Architecture,* edited by S. D. Houston, pp. 187–222. Dumbarton Oaks, Washington, D.C.

Moore, J. D.

1996   The Archaeology of Plazas and the Proxemics of Ritual: Three Andean Traditions. *American Anthropologist* 98:789–802.

Neff, L. T.

1998   Precolumbian Lowland Maya Population Dynamics and Intensive Terrace Agriculture in the Xunantunich Area, Belize, Central America. Paper presented at the 97th Annual Meeting of the American Anthropological Association, Philadelphia.

Neff, L. T., C. Robin, K. Schwarz, and M. K. Morrison

    1995   The Xunantunich Settlement Survey. In *Xunantunich Archaeological Project: 1995 Field Season*, edited by R. M. Leventhal and W. Ashmore, pp. 139–166. Unpublished report on file at the Belize Department of Archaeology, Belmopan, and the Cotsen Institute of Archaeology, Los Angeles.

Pendergast, D. M., and E. Graham

    1981   Fighting a Looting Battle: Xunantunich, Belize. *Archaeology* 34(4):12–19.

Puleston, D. E.

    1983   *The Settlement Survey of Tikal*. Tikal Report 13. University Museum, University of Pennsylvania, Philadelphia.

Rapoport, A.

    1990   *The Meaning of the Built Environment: A Nonverbal Communication Approach*. University of Arizona Press, Tucson.

Redfield, R., and M. Singer

    1954   The Cultural Roles of Cities. *Economic Development and Social Change* 3:53–73.

Reents-Budet, D., R. L. Bishop, J. T. Taschek, and J. W. Ball

    2000   Out of the Palace Dumps: Ceramic Production and Use at Buenavista del Cayo. *Ancient Mesoamerica* 11:99–121.

Rice, D. S., and T. P. Culbert

    1990   Historical Context for Population Reconstruction in the Maya Lowlands. In *Precolumbian Population History in the Maya Lowlands*, edited by T. P. Culbert and D. S. Rice, pp. 1–36. University of New Mexico Press, Albuquerque.

Rice, P. M.

    1987   Economic Change in the Lowland Maya Late Classic Period. In *Specialization, Exchange, and Complex Societies*, edited by E. M. Brumfiel and T. K. Earle, pp. 76–85. Cambridge University Press, Cambridge.

Robin, C.

    1999   *Towards an Archaeology of Everyday Life: Maya Farmers of Chan Nòohol and Dos Chombitos Cik'in, Belize*. Ph.D. dissertation, Department of Anthropology, University of Pennsylvania. Ann Arbor: University Microfilms

Sanders, W. T., and R. S. Santley

    1983   Tale of Three Cities: Energetics and Urbanization in Pre-Hispanic Central Mexico. In *Prehistoric Settlement Patterns: Essays in Honor of Gordon R. Willey*, edited by E. Z. Vogt and R. M. Leventhal, pp. 243–291. University of New Mexico Press, Albuquerque.

Sanders, W. T., and D. L. Webster

    1988   The Mesoamerican Urban Tradition. *American Anthropologist* 90:521–546.

Satterthwaite, L.

    1950   Plastic Art on a Maya Palace. *Archaeology* 3(4):215–222.

Schele, L.

    1998   The Iconography of Maya Architectural Façades during the Late Classic Period. In *Function and Meaning in Classic Maya Architecture*, edited by S. D. Houston, pp. 479–517. Dumbarton Oaks, Washington, D.C.

Schele, L., and D. Freidel

1990   *A Forest of Kings: The Untold Story of the Ancient Maya*. William Morrow, New York.

1991   The Courts of Creation: Ballcourts, Ballgames, and Portals to the Maya Otherworld. In *The Mesoamerican Ballgame*, edited by D. Wilcox and V. Scarborough, pp. 289–317. University of Arizona Press, Tucson.

Schele, L., and P. Mathews

1998   *The Code of Kings: The Language of Seven Sacred Maya Temples and Tombs*. Scribner, New York.

Schele, L., and M. E. Miller

1986   *The Blood of Kings: Dynasty and Ritual in Maya Art*. Kimbell Art Museum, Fort Worth, Tex.

Schortman, E. M.

1989   Interregional Interaction in Prehistory: The Need for a New Perspective. *American Antiquity* 54:52–65.

Schortman, E. M., and S. Nakamura

1991   A Crisis of Identity: Late Classic Competition and Interaction on the Southeast Maya Periphery. *Latin American Antiquity* 2:311–336.

Schwartz, G. M., and S. E. Falconer

1994   Rural Approaches to Social Complexity. In *Archaeological Views from the Countryside*, edited by G. M. Schwartz and S. E. Falconer, pp. 1–9. Smithsonian Institution Press, Washington, D.C.

Sjoberg, G.

1960   *The Preindustrial City: Past and Present*. The Free Press, New York.

Smith, M. E.

1994   Social Complexity in the Aztec Countryside. In *Archaeological Views from the Countryside*, edited by G. M. Schwartz and S. E. Falconer, pp. 143–159. Smithsonian Institution Press, Washington, D.C.

Southall, A.

1998   *The City in Time and Space*. Cambridge University Press, Cambridge.

Stanish, C.

1992   *Ancient Andean Political Economy*. University of Texas Press, Austin.

Taschek, J. T., and J. W. Ball

1992   Lord Smoke-Squirrel's Cacao Cup: The Archaeological Context and Socio-Historical Significance of the Buenavista "Jauncy Vase." In *The Maya Vase Book:* vol. 3, edited by J. Kerr, pp. 490–497. Kerr Associates, New York.

1999   Las Ruinas de Arenal: Preliminary Report on a Subregional Major Center in the Western Belize Valley (1991–1992 Excavations). *Ancient Mesoamerica* 10:215–236.

Tate, C. E.

1992   *Yaxchilan: The Design of a Maya Ceremonial City*. University of Texas Press, Austin.

Thompson, J. E. S.

1940   *Late Ceramic Horizons at Benque Viejo, British Honduras*. Contributions to American Anthropology and History, vol. 7, no. 35. Carnegie Institution of Washington Publication 528. Washington, D.C.

Tourtellot, G. III

    1993   A View of Ancient Maya Settlement in the Eighth Century. In *Lowland Maya Civilization in the Eighth Century A.D.,* edited by J. A. Sabloff and J. Henderson, pp. 219–241. Dumbarton Oaks, Washington, D.C.

Trigger, B. G.

    1972   Determinants of Urban Growth in Pre-Industrial Cities. In *Man, Settlement and Urbanism,* edited by P. J. Ucko, R. Tringham, and G. W. Dimbleby, pp. 575–599. Schenkman Publishing, Cambridge, Mass.

VandenBosch, J. C.

    1997   Specialized Lithic Production in the Suburbs of a Late to Terminal Classic Center in Western Belize. Paper presented at the 20th Annual Midwest Conference on Mesoamerican Archaeology and Ethnohistory, Ann Arbor.

    1999   *Lithic Economy and Household Interdependence among the Late Classic Maya of Belize.* Ph.D. dissertation, Department of Anthropology, University of Pittsburgh. University Microfilms International, Ann Arbor.

Weber, M.

    1958   *The City,* translated by D. Martindale and G. Neuwirth. Free Press, Glencoe, Ill.

Webster, D.

    1997   City-States of the Maya. In *The Archaeology of City-States: Cross-Cultural Approaches,* edited by D. L Nichols and T. H. Charlton, pp. 135–154. Smithsonian Institution Press, Washington, D.C.

    1998a   Classic Maya Architecture: Implications and Comparisons. In *Function and Meaning in Classic Maya Architecture,* edited by S. D. Houston, pp. 5–48. Dumbarton Oaks, Washington, D.C..

    1998b   Warfare and Status Rivalry: Lowland Maya and Polynesian Comparisons. In *Archaic States,* edited by G. M. Feinman and J. Marcus, pp. 311–351. School of American Research, Santa Fe, N.M.

Wheatley, P.

    1971   *The Pivot of the Four Quarters.* Aldine, Chicago.

    1983   *Nagara and Commandery: Origins of the Southeast Asian Urban Traditions.* Department of Geography Research Papers, Nos. 207–208. University of Chicago Press, Chicago.

Willey, G. R., W. R. Bullard Jr., J. B. Glass, and J. C. Gifford

    1965   *Prehistoric Maya Settlement in the Belize Valley.* Papers of the Peabody Museum of Archaeology and Ethnology, vol. 54. Harvard University, Cambridge, Mass.

Wilson, D. J.

    1997   Early State Formation on the North Coast of Peru: A Critique of the City-State Model. In *The Archaeology of City-States: Cross-Cultural Approaches,* edited by D. L. Nichols and T. H. Charlton, pp. 229–244. Smithsonian Institution Press, Washington, D.C.

Wirth, L.

    1938   Urbanism as a Way of Life. *American Journal of Sociology* 44:1–24.

Yaeger, J.

    1997   The 1997 Excavations of Plaza A-III and Miscellaneous Excavation and Architectural

Clearing in Group A. In Xunantunich Archaeological Project: 1997, the Final Field Season, edited by R. M. Leventhal and W. Ashmore, pp. 24–55. Unpublished report on file at the Belize Department of Archaeology, Belmopan, and the Cotsen Institute of Archaeology, Los Angeles.

2000a   *Changing Patterns of Social Organization: The Late and Terminal Classic Communities at San Lorenzo, Cayo District, Belize.* Ph.D. dissertation, Department of Anthropology, University of Pennsylvania. University Microfilms International, Ann Arbor.

2000b   The Social Construction of Communities in the Classic Maya Countryside: Strategies of Affiliation in Western Belize. In *The Archaeology of Communities: A New World Perspective,* edited by M. A. Canuto and J. Yaeger, pp. 123–142. Routledge, London.

2002   Internal Complexity, Household Strategies of Affiliation, and the Changing Organization of Rural Communities in the Upper Belize River Valley. In *Perspectives on Ancient Maya Rural Complexity,* edited by G. Iannone and S. V. Connell, pp. 45–60. Monograph 49. Cotsen Institute of Archaeology, Los Angeles.

Yaeger, J., and M. A. Canuto

2000   Introducing an Archaeology of Communities. In *The Archaeology of Communities: A New World Perspective,* edited by M. A. Canuto and J. Yaeger, pp. 1–15. Routledge, London.

Yaeger, J., and C. Robin

n.d.   Heterogeneous Hinterlands: The Social and Political Organization of Commoner Settlements near Xunantunich, Belize. In *Ancient Maya Commoners,* edited by J. Lohse and F. Valdez. Manuscript submitted to the University of Texas Press, Austin.

SEVEN

Food Provisioning in Urban Societies

A View from Northern Mesopotamia

MELINDA A. ZEDER

Specialized relationships that structure urban economies provide perhaps the most tangible expression of the urban form. The exploding out of productive activities from the bounds of household and community, the disarticulation of production from the distribution of products, the creation of surplus above the needs of the producer, the mobilization of that surplus to serve the needs of a burgeoning elite—all these aspects of urban economy leave an indelible stamp on the distribution of goods and people across a landscape, a stamp detectable even many millennia after the urban society has faded from memory. It is not surprising, then, that urban economic relations have, until recently, been the primary focus of archaeological studies of the initial contexts and consequences of the emergence of urbanism in premodern societies around the globe.

There are, of course, other potent manifestations of urbanism: the hierarchical social relations, the co-option of power into the hands of a ruling elite, the manipulation of symbols of religious and corporate identity to create an urban ethos of cohesion and membership, the free-wheeling and at times quite fluid negotiation of status within cities and between cities and their hinterlands. And it is entirely appropriate, if not overdue, that these aspects of the urban phenomenon are receiving increased notice by archaeologists interested in the study of early premodern urban societies. But as our attention turns to these social and political aspects of urbanism, it is important to keep in mind that at its core urbanism represents the disaggregation of a wide range of social, political, and economic relations that were once embedded in kinship and community into a more fragmented matrix of progressively segregated and impersonalized actions and actors. It is also important to remember that the developments in each of these spheres take direction from, and in turn help to direct, the trajectory of the others. Throughout this process, economic relations serve as a major engine both driving and supporting the reconfiguration of social and political spheres into uniquely urban forms. Continued attention to economic relations in early urban society, then, still holds considerable potential for understanding the genesis of urbanism, both as a direct marker of one of its key characteristics, and as a means of monitoring the progressive restructuring of other key components of urban society.

Studies of ancient urban economy have tended to concentrate on tracing the emergence of specialized craft production and the development of mechanisms that co-opt and channel the products of these activities within and outside the system (Earle and Brumfiel 1987; Johnson 1973; Smith 1976). While craft production is a highly visible marker of the specialized relationships that underlie the urban economy, other economic relations may be equally illuminating as to how urban economies arose and functioned. In particular, food provisioning in early urban societies has increasingly been recognized as a highly profitable area of study (Hastorff 1993; Zeder 1991). Indeed, one of the most remarkable transformations of the urban economy is the way in which basic activities related to the production of food, its distribution, and consumption become increasingly separated from household units and transformed into distinct sets of activities conducted by segregated groups of specialists, provisioning a network of people engaged in the production of goods and provision of services totally unrelated to subsistence. The degree to which urban households can afford to abandon direct involvement in food production may, in fact, be a marker of the ability of the system to ensure that the basic needs of the specialist producers will be provided for. By the same token, the extent to which households remain involved in food production for their own consumption might also be taken as a measure of independence from, or perhaps even resistence to, incorporation into the larger urban economy. The differential control of production and distribution of foodstuffs and the increasing differentiation in access to food resources along the lines of social and economic status is a powerful agent in the development of social hierarchy.

This chapter considers food provisioning in early premodern urban societies, particularly their handling of animal resources. A study of pastoral economy in the Khabur Basin of Northern Mesopotamia is used as a case study. The development of specialized pastoralism in this region in the third millennium B.C. provides unique insights into the realignment of economic relations between hinterland settlements and an emergent urban center, Tell Leilan. By looking at provisioning pathways within the center, this study also has bearing on the social structuring of resource access and the role on animal production within the city in maintaining economic autonomy. In addition, this chapter serves as an example of how these processes can be monitored through the zooarchaeological analysis of animal remains.

CHARACTERISTICS OF
URBAN ECONOMY

Though universally characterized as highly specialized, urban-based economies are not unique in this regard. Indeed, varying scales of specialized economic relations can be found within nonurban contexts as well. What distinguishes the urban economy from other economic forms is the degree to which different stages of production and product distribution become increasingly specialized and segregated (Zeder 1988, 1991:12–22). Under such a system, various sets of activities related to the production and distribution of goods may be conducted by unrelated groups of people who bring different skill sets to bear on different components of the productive process, working in separate locales, over extended periods of time. Of course the success of such an economy rests of the ability of the system to bring together these disparate activities in a way that ensures a smooth progression from production to consumption. These mechanisms may be centrally coordinated by urban elites, or by more diffuse market principles through a web of entrepreneurial activities. More likely, a complex interplay of both more centralized and more broadly based forces are responsible for bringing coherence to economic relations even in the earliest urban societies. Clearly, the ability of these mechanisms to coordinate disparate sets of activities related to the production, movement, and distribution of goods has a major impact on the complexity, degree of integration, and the scale of the urban economy (Blanton 1976).

But not all components of the economy are equally susceptible to specialization and higher-order coordination, especially in early urban economies. Certain sets of economic activities may become highly specialized and regulated, while others may not change appreciably from unspecialized forms of operation. Moreover, this segmentation of economic activities may be introduced at the different stages in the production, movement, and distribution of a single good. Finishing stages in the production of finely crafted objects may be conducted by skilled artisans working in workshops attached to elite residential areas within an urban center, for example, but the initial processing of materials used to make the object may remain diffusely organized within domestic households in hinterland settlements. Moreover, the movement of partly processed materials from household to workshop and the distribution of the finished good might be directed by distinct groups of individuals answering to separate overseers.

Certain factors may make various economic activities more susceptible to specialization and control than others. Certainly, the level of knowledge, skill, or artistry needed to produce an item plays a significant role in the level of specialization practiced in its manufacture. The rarity of raw materials and limited access to the technology required for production are also important in the propensity of an activity for specialization. The likelihood that higher-order control will be imposed becomes greater if unspecialized modes of production cannot meet an emerging larger demand. Higher-order coordination of diverse sets of productive activities might be required if there are scheduling conflicts over the resources, personnel, and location needed to produce high-demand items. The proximity of producers to those responsible for mobilizing and channeling the goods they produce also plays a role in the likelihood that a productive activity will come under higher-order control.

At the same time, the movement and distribution of a good are likely to be more specialized and highly regulated the more removed producers of a high-demand item are from its consumers. In fact, it seems likely that the most cost effective way for central authorities to co-opt and control economic activity is to focus more on the channeling of goods to consumers, than on the productive process. In particular, the tightly controlled distribution of finely crafted objects or rare raw materials used in the display of status is often a way of cementing allegiances and signaling power relationships.

FOOD PROVISIONING IN EARLY
URBAN ECONOMIES

It is easy to see how the manufacture of craft goods becomes incorporated into an urban system. The procurement of raw materials, the various stages of manufacture that transform these materials into finished goods, and the coordination of the movement of materials and products from the site of initial procurement into the hands of the consumer could all undergo differential degrees of specialization and control in an urban economy. But the same is also true for food resources. Indeed, given the central and universal importance of food to all members of a society, and the likelihood that specialist producers of goods and services require food provisioning from outside sources, this sector of the urban economy holds tremendous promise for exploring the complex factors that shape economic relations in emergent urban contexts.

Food resources also have their own special requirements that shape the roles they play in urban economies. The first is the degree to which production levels can be predicted and controlled, a factor evident in the domestic/wild divide. Wild resources may provide as nutritious and, in some circumstances, as abundant a subsistence base as domestic resources. However, the yield of hunting and collecting activities cannot be as reliably predicted or controlled as the yield of plant and animal resources produced through agricultural activities. There are always good years and bad years for farmers and herders, and there is always the threat that catastrophic droughts or diseases might result in widespread crop failures or wipe out whole herds of animals. Yet domestic crops and livestock provide producers a much surer return for investment, and a much greater opportunity to both project and manipulate levels of production.

The second key factor shaping the role of food resources in an urban economy is the degree to which these resources are amenable to movement, stock-piling, and delayed distribution. Here the perishability of food resources plays a special role, circumscribing the ways in which plant resources like fleshy vegetables and greens, or animal products like uncured meat and unprocessed dairy products, enter into the specialized economic relationships in urban societies that lack advanced storage technologies.

It is not surprising, then, that throughout history the world's urban systems have been based on intensive agricultural systems focused on domesticated cereals and other cultivated crops. Wheat, barley, rice, and pulses in the Old World, and corn, quinoa, potatoes, squash, and beans in the New were all resources that could be produced in quantity to meet burgeoning need. Moreover, these crops could all be stored for extended periods of time and used in delayed, directed distribution, or as investments in future harvests. While the carbohydrates that fueled urban societies in the ancient world were uniformly supplied by cultivated crops produced through increasingly intensive agricultural practices, the protein base of the diet in early urban societies came from more diverse sources.

Domesticated animals played only a limited role in the provisioning of urban societies in the New World. Although people raised llamas and guinea pigs in South America, and dogs and turkeys in Mesoamerica, much of the protein intake in the urban societies that arose in these areas came from wild species. In most cases, the primary large mammal utilized was some species of deer. Deer are generally solitary animals whose capture requires skill and patience. And while they may be more easily captured in certain seasons of the year, the yield and predictability of the success of the hunt of these animals cannot be compared to that of domesticated animals. In addition, fish, birds, and a variety of small mammals such as rabbits and hares were also primary sources of protein in these societies. Although in certain instances fish may have attained a semimanaged status, all of these game species represent fairly small meat packages obtained only through considerable effort, with a high probability of failure in capture. Moreover, without smoking or curing, wild game could not be moved over substantial distances or stored for delayed distribution. Despite these limitations, wild animal resources played distinctive roles in the complex economies of New World urban societies (Hamblin 1985; Pohl, 1985a, 1985b; Wing 1981; see also Jackson and Scott 1995; Welch and Scarry 1995). Access to prestige or exotic wild game or to prime cuts of wild animals seems to have been used as a mark of status in these societies. Moreover, the large-scale mobilization of wild game for sponsored feasts helped reinforce positions of secular and religious authority and important allegiances.

In the Old World, domesticated animals were more common, and the production and distribution of animal resources assumed a much more prominent and pervasive role in the development of specialized urban economies. The production of resources could be more directly manipulated with domestic livestock, and problems of perishability could be solved by using live animals as their own transport systems. Yet even with domesticates, the ways in which animals and animal products were incorporated into these economies varied depending on the management requirements of the species and the number and types of products they produced.

In particular, the primary livestock species of sheep and goats, cattle and pigs all offered different challenges and opportunities to emergent urban economies in the Near East (Zeder 1991).

SHEEP AND GOATS

Sheep and goats have been the primary livestock species in the Near East to the present day. Even young children in rural settings, today and in the past, have knowledge of the behavioral and biological requirements of these animals and the herding practices needed to manage them. While sheep and goats provide a variety of resources, both regenerative (milk, wool, hair, and dung) and nonregenerative products (meat and skins), the same generalized management strategies will produce enough of these animals to service the needs of a herding household or a community (Redding 1981).

However, even in the earliest agricultural communities in the Near East, more than 8,000 years ago, the need to keep herds away from areas under cultivation and the damaging impact of overgrazing seem to have led to a progressive separation of farming and herding activities (Köhler-Rollefson 1988, 1989). Sheep and goats are tractable herd animals whose natural tendency to follow a dominant animal can easily be transferred to humans. They also naturally migrate between seasonally ripening pasturelands. It would have been fairly easy, then, for a segment of these early communities to herd these animals to more distant pasturelands removed from the area around settlements while crops matured, and then bring them back after harvest to feed on field stubble and fallow fields, where they supplied resident populations with meat, milk, and other resources.

Over time, increased segregation of caprine herding from farming activities would have been encouraged by the need to dedicate more land to agricultural production to feed growing populations, and the ease with which sheep and goats can be moved over considerable distances to utilize more marginal, poorly watered pasturage. But perhaps the primary factor contributing to the increasing specialization of sheep and goat pastoralism in the region was the growing importance of wool in the Mesopotamian economy during the late fourth and third millennia B.C. (Jacobsen 1953; Adams 1981; McCorriston 1997). Wool is a regenerative product that can be moved over considerable distances, stored for indefinite periods of time, and transformed into a range of finished products targeted for multiple consumer markets. Indeed, finely woven woolen textiles proved the ideal way to transform the agricultural bounty of the Mesopotamian alluvium into lightweight luxury items used in long-distance exchange with neighbors in resource-rich mountainous regions to the north and east (Adams 1981:149–150).

The importance of the textile industries seems to have resulted in an explosive growth of pastoral production during the third millennium. From the high volume of sheep and goats and the impressive tonnage of wool accounted for in early second millennium Ur III economic texts, Adams (1981:149) estimates that the ratio of sheep and goats to humans in Southern Mesopotamia during the late third millennium was about four times greater than it is today. These large herds of animals would surely have had to be pastured for at least some portion of the year in steppelands some distance away from primary areas of settlement and cultivation. Changes in crop preferences from wheat to barley attested to in both texts and the archaeobotanical record suggest that there was also some reordering of agricultural practices to supply fodder for these expanded flocks. A heightened demand for wool might also have resulted in the development of more specialized herd management practices designed to augment wool production, and perhaps even in the development of new breeds of high-wool-producing animals (Zeder 1994b).

In addition to drawing on large, state-sponsored herds, however, Ur III administrators also obtained wool and other pastoral products from independent pastoral specialists. Small farmers kept sheep and goats for their own use, and urban entrepreneurs owned herds managed for them by hired shepherds (Postgate 1992:158). As is the case today, it is also likely that people moved fairly fluidly between mobile pastoralism and settled agricultural ways of life. Thus, there were multiple production systems for sheep and goats, operating on different levels of specialization and targeted at supplying different products to different groups of consumers.

The general removal of pastoral activities from centers of urban power, however, effectively limited the degree to which their activities could be centrally regulated, even in state-sponsored herds (Adams 1981:151; Postgate 1992:160). Urban administrators could control access to certain pasturage, fallow fields, and harvested field stubble near populated areas. And they had some control over the flow of pastoral products, especially into urban markets. But they likely had little involvement in the management of herds. The Ur III archives from the ancient site of Puzrish Dagan (modern Tell Drehem), for example, provide detailed accounts of the movement of animals from producers through an elaborate multitiered processing hierarchy (Jones and Synder 1961; Kang 1972). For all their specificity, however, these texts are by and large mute when it comes to the breeding, feeding, or herding of the animals accounted for in these records. Instead the facility at Drehem was more concerned with the collection of a fairly restricted range of species (primarily sheep and goats) from a variety of different producers, and their disbursement to a relatively limited set of different consumer groups following fairly standardized proportions of species, ages, and sexes of animals (Zeder 1994b). Large groups of consumers (craftsmen, farmers, and even the herders themselves) are nowhere mentioned in these texts and likely received these resources through entirely different, undocumented, and possibly unregulated channels of production and exchange.

Urban emergence not only encouraged the growth of a highly productive subset of the population that both fed urban consumers and fueled a burgeoning textile industry, but in so doing it also created an independent, mobile, and potentially quite powerful element of society that, during periods of weakened central control, was capable of causing considerable social friction and even political collapse (Adams 1981:151; Rowton 1973). The influence of pastoral specialists became even more strongly felt in the late third and second millennia with the widespread adoption of horses by pastoralists in steppelands that bracketed the northern margins of Mesopotamia and of camels by pastoral groups in the arid deserts of the Arabian peninsula to the south (Zarins 1989). The addition of these domesticates, which could be both ridden and loaded with goods and belongings, greatly increased the mobility and speed of travel of these pastoral groups, making them major players in far-flung silk and spice trade networks and vastly enhancing their ability to threaten the stability of settled urban areas in the Mesopotamian heartland.

CATTLE

Like sheep and goats, cattle provide multiple high-demand resources that were intricately involved in the early urban economies of the ancient Near East. These large animals yielded considerably greater output in both meat and milk per animal than their smaller caprine cousins. And although cattle did not produce usable fiber for textile production, they did provide another invaluable service that became an integral part of the agricultural economy of early urban societies in the region—their ability to serve as beasts of burden in agricultural production.

At the same time, cattle have higher water requirements than sheep and goats and more selective pasturing preferences (Dahl and Hjort 1976), both factors that kept cattle more tightly tethered to well-watered alluvial areas also extensively used for agriculture. Satisfying the demands of large cattle herds for quality pasturage near water sources when the same land was needed for agricultural production required careful scheduling. Extensive foddering may have been needed to maintain cattle within areas under intensive cultivation (Postgate 1992:164). The important role that cattle play in agricultural production, however, would have more than compensated for the increased difficulties of meeting cattle pasture needs in these areas (Zeder 1991:28–30).

Keeping cattle for draft animals requires that a high proportion of castrate males be allowed to live a good deal longer than would be the case in herds managed for meat and milk. By contrast, when animal products are eaten, there is a premium on prolonged female survivorship and early slaughter of all but a few males kept for breeding purposes. The conflicting management strategies needed to produce these different resources may have contributed to greater specialization, and perhaps even breed differentiation, in the management of cattle for the different resources of traction, meat, and milk. Textual references document an elaborate hierarchy of individuals involved in raising cattle, using different management techniques depending on the intended use of the animals (Keintz and Lambert 1963). Linguistically, the texts also clearly distinguish cattle on the basis of their different uses for beef, draft, or dairy (Keintz and Lambert 1963:98).

Furthermore, the varied resources cattle produced may have been channeled in very different ways. The use of cattle as draft animals tied them tightly to the agricultural sector of the economy. The care and use of cattle as draft animals were likely managed by individual farming households that kept a limited number of cattle for draft and dairy products (Postgate 1992:163–164). However, the ability of cattle to produce large quantities of meat per individual animal would have made them an attractive source for urban provisioning. Drehem texts document the channeling of older cattle, perhaps those no longer useful for draft or dairying, to state-sponsored kitchens, ultimately designated for "the troops" (Zeder 1994b). Excess cattle were also channeled to tanneries engaged in large-scale leather production (Postgate 1992:164).

Although cattle also produce large quantities of high butterfat milk, the perishability of milk products may shape the channels and mechanisms by which dairy products enter the diets of urban dwellers. In fact, the general absence of dairy products in the accounts of Ur III merchants (Curtis and Hallo 1959) suggests that perishable products did not play a prominent role in regulated delayed distribution systems (Gelb 1967). The few texts that do refer to dairy products almost always mention cow's milk, probably because cows were kept closer to settled areas than sheep and goats (Adams 1981:142). Ur III records tracing the growth and productivity of a herd of dairy cattle over a 10-year period (Gelb 1967) reflect the care with which this segment of the pastoral economy may have been monitored. However, the low volume of milk and cheese production of this carefully managed dairy herd suggests that the bulk of its dairy products did not enter into regulated distribution systems but were handled through more direct exchanges between producers and consumers.

PIGS

Pigs provide yet a different set of opportunities and obstacles for provisioning in early urban contexts (Zeder 1991:30–32, 1996, 1998a). Pigs have higher reproductive rates and a greater per capita yield of fat-rich meat than any other Near Eastern livestock species, yet they are usually never more than a minor contributor to most post-Neolithic assemblages in the region. Indeed, swine consumption was eventually proscribed by the two dominant religions there. As with caprines and cattle, the biology and behavior of pigs played an important role in shaping their place in urban economies of the ancient Near East.

Pigs require more water and are less heat resistant than domesticated bovids, they have different forage requirements from other livestock, and they provide essentially only one nonrenewable resource: meat. They are also not temperamentally suited to being driven over long distances (Krader 1955), and large herds of free-foraging swine raised around sedentary settlements can wreak havoc with agricultural production (Redding 1991). All of these factors mitigated against pigs becoming a large-scale enterprise either directly controlled by urban authorities or as part of a specialized interaction between independent, mobile pastoralists and sedentary agriculturalists. In fact, textual evidence for the management and disposal of pigs is almost entirely lacking (Postgate 1992:166). This strongly implies that swine production did not play a major role in the regulated urban economies of the ancient Near East.

Within the confines of small household-based sty management, however, pigs provide a low-cost, low-labor-intensive, highly reliable, and highly productive resource (Van Loon 1978) that can give the urban household considerable autonomy in an otherwise highly specialized interdependent economy (Diener and Robkin 1978; Hesse 1990, 1994). And we know from zooarchaeological evidence that pigs were a common staple in the diet in poor urban residential areas in early Near Eastern cities (Mudar 1982; Bökönyi 1978). Thus, the failure of pigs to play a greater role in the economies of complex societies in the Near East may have less to do with ecological parameters that dictate the conditions of swine management in arid regions than with the tension that small-scale pig rearing by the urban poor creates within a society that puts a premium on the control of both social and economic relations. The possibility that household-based swine management in urban contexts was the domain of women may present some worthwhile avenues of investigation for those interested in the role of gender in emergent complexity. Certainly pigs would have been a more likely candidate for eventual proscription than an animal more tightly linked to large-scale urban provisioning systems. Moreover, since pigs offer a more limited range of resources than other major livestock species in the region, their classification as unclean would have a more narrowly focused economic impact. In addition, the identification of pigs with sedentary village or lower-class urban dwellers might have contributed to the dietary exclusion of pork by Jews and Muslims, both groups whose social identity relies heavily on their nomadic heritage.

Interestingly, sometime in the first millennium B.C., around the period of the Israelite expansion in the Levant, chickens begin to play a role in Near Eastern subsistence. A new domestic arrival from the east, chickens, like pigs, make an ideal supplementary meat crop that can be easily raised on a small scale by individual households. Also, the smaller package of meat per chicken and the added benefit of egg production may have made chickens an ideal replacement for pigs as the preferred animal "garden crop" that provided urban households a measure of economic autonomy in an otherwise highly controlled economy (see Redding 2000).

PASTORAL ECONOMIES OF THE
KHABUR BASIN

For all the remarkable evidence that Mesopotamian accountants supply on early urban pastoral economy, many major segments of that economy clearly never made it into their record books. That is why archaeologists have increasingly turned to animal bones as the primary data set for monitoring this key component of the economy of early Near Eastern urban societies. For example, Mudar's (1982) early work at ancient Lagash documented status-based differences in the diets of elite and nonelite urban dwellers, and she was the first to detect the pattern of higher pork consumption in poor urban residential areas. My own research in highland Iran traced the development of indirect distribution systems that channeled meat to urban residents of the Elamite capital of ancient Anshan over periods of urban emergence, florescence, and decline (Zeder 1988, 1991). Stein and Wattenmaker tracked the flow of animals from a rural production center to a midlevel town site in the Upper Euphrates region of southeastern Turkey (Stein 1986, 1987; Wattenmaker 1987a, 1987b). Wattenmaker has used the animal remains from this town to examine the economic impact of changing degrees of integration within a larger urban economy (Wattenmaker 1994). All of these studies have helped underscore the value of animal remains in examining core processes of urban emergence, growth, and collapse.

For the past decade I have been engaged in a regional-scale project aimed at tracking the development of pastoral economy in the Khabur River Basin in northeastern Syria over a 5,000- year period, from the first introduction of domestic animals in the region in the mid-eighth millennium up through the rise of the first urban society in the region in the mid-third millennium B.C. (figure 7.1; Zeder 1994a, 1995, 1998a, 1998b, 1998c, 2000). Over 200,000 animal remains from 33 phases of occupation at 15 sites within this region have been processed at least to an initial level of analysis. This research has provided an unparalleled opportunity to monitor the ecological impact of agricultural intensification over a deep time transect. This study has also yielded new insights into the role of pastoral economy in the emergence of urbanism in Northern Mesopotamia, and thus serves as an ideal case example of some of the processes highlighted here. On the regional scale, the study allows us to examine the incorporation of hinterland areas into a region-wide specialized urban economy. It also sheds new light on the ways in which provisioning within urban centers became socially structured, and how city-based animal production can provide both nonelite and elite residents a buffer against provisioning uncertainties.

PRE-URBAN ANIMAL ECONOMY IN
THE KHABUR BASIN

Over the course of the first four millennia of occupation in the region (from the eighth through the fourth millennium B.C.) people in different parts of the region followed a number of highly localized subsistence strategies. Small village communities in the better-watered northern part of the region concentrated primarily on domesticated livestock and crops, with wild resources playing a relatively minor supporting role (figure 7.2). However, several occupational layers at one of these

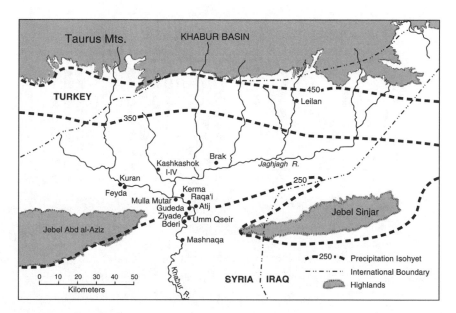

Figure 7.1. Map of Khabur Basin.

northern communities contain an extraordinarily high proportion of a variety of wild game species—gazelle, auroch, and onager, suggesting that game was still available in the northern steppe in some quantity. In contrast, wild species were much more heavily utilized by settlements established in the more arid and more sparsely occupied southern portion of the region prior to the third millennium (figure 7.2). In fact, wild animals were often the predominant meat supplier in southern settlements, with each site having its own distinctive signature mixture of wild and domestic resources (Zeder 1994a, 1998b).

While it might be tempting to link these highly localized subsistence patterns to the expression of ethnicity or other forms of cultural identity through food preference, I think that these patterns more likely stem from the payoffs and risks of animal exploitation within the different ecological parameters of the northern and southern steppe. In the northern steppe, where rainfed agriculture provided a reliable resource base, domestic plants and animals gave more assured returns to small farming communities. Moreover, in this more densely settled region, domestic animals could be used in social and economic commerce with neighbors. These conditions favored a concentration on domesticated species, even though wild game was still available in this part of the Khabur Basin. On the other hand, reliance

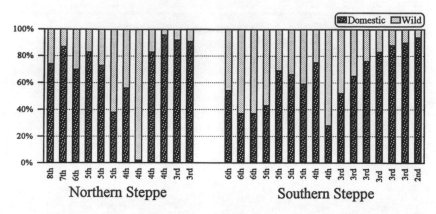

Figure 7.2. Proportions of domestic and wild fauna.

on domesticated plants and animals was riskier in the more arid southern steppe. Also given the low density of settlements in this region prior to the third millennium, there was little purpose in building ties to neighbors to serve as a hedge against provisioning uncertainties. Thus the strategy adopted by residents of these small outpost settlements was to broaden their resource base to include a mix of both domesticated and wild resources. Each small community seemed to tailor its subsistence economy in extremely individualistic ways to meet its own highly localized needs, whether it was a pioneer settlement, the encampment of mobile pastoralists, or a small river bank farming settlement that served as a home base for pastoralists utilizing the rich and relatively untouched steppic grasses.

REGIONAL ECONOMIC
RESTRUCTURING IN THE
THIRD MILLENNIUM B.C.

During the third millennium there was a substantial increase in settlement throughout the Khabur Basin, culminating in the mid-third millennium with the establishment of large urban centers on the northern steppe that were sustained by highly structured supporting settlement systems (Stein and Wattenmaker 1990; Weiss 1986). The florescence of indigenous urban society in the Khabur during the mid-third millennium was preceded by a remarkable explosion of sites in the southern part of the region. During the initial third millennium more than 20 small (2- to 4-hectare) sites were established along the banks of the Khabur River, in a linear area of less than 50 kilometers, at or below the present-day 250-millimeter

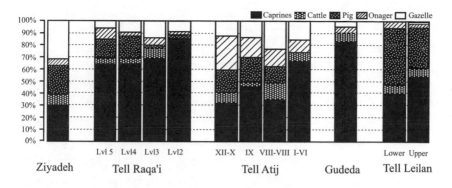

Figure 7.3. Proportions of fauna, by type, in third millennium sites.

rainfall isoheyet—the effective boundary for dependable rainfed agriculture. This same area had supported only three or four small sites during the late fourth millennium. Many of these third-millennium settlements contained silos or other special function features that excavators have linked to grain or other commodity storage (Fortin 1991, 1993; Fortin and Cooper 1994; Fortin and Routledge 1994; Margueron 1991; Schwartz 1993, 1994a). In addition, a recent archaeological survey in the Khabur has discovered a contemporary expansion into the steppe by the Jebel Abd al-Aziz directly west of this river-bound boom area (Hole 1997, 1999; Hole and Kouchoukos in press; Kouchoukos 1998). At its peak, more than 36 sites were encountered in this now largely vacant area.

Some researchers have proposed that these riverside sites were established as part of a colonization of the middle Khabur by powers outside the immediate region. Schwartz, Margueron, and Fortin, for example, have argued that these granaries served as temporary storage depots for grain grown either through intensive irrigation agriculture on the southern steppe or transported from rainfed farming areas to the north (Fortin 1991, 1993; Fortin and Cooper 1994; Margueron 1991; Schwartz 1994a, 1994b). Grain collected in these riverside depots was later transshipped by boat down the Khabur to the large urban center of Mari, situated below the junction of the Khabur and the Euphrates more than 200 kilometers to the south (Fortin 1991, 1993; Fortin and Cooper 1994; Margueron 1991; Schwartz 1994a, 1994b). McCorriston (1997) also sees an outside impetus to the establishment of these depots but looks to the pastoral rather than the agricultural economy as the primary draw of the southern steppe for external urban powers, which, like Mari, were heavily invested in booming textile industries. Despite the distance from these centers, the relatively untouched grasslands of the southern steppe may have been an irresistible lure to specialized pastoralists whose flocks supplied the wool and hair that drove these industries.

In contrast, Hole (1991) maintains that these sites arose as a result of local processes and not because of economic pressures from outside the region. Rather than being a sharp departure from earlier patterns thrust on the region by external powers, he argues, developments in the southern steppe during the early third millennium represent an expansion and elaboration of a long-standing pattern of exploitation made possible by a shift to more favorable climatic conditions. In this marginal high-risk zone it only takes a slight change in rainfall patterns to make the area either highly profitable or inhospitable. Since the sixth millennium, when pioneer families first came to this more arid part of the Khabur Basin, people had followed a diversified resource strategy in which they built small villages on the alluvium where they raised crops and herded pigs and then used the steppe to procure game and graze sheep and goats. A shift toward wetter conditions at the beginning of the third millennium allowed people to venture farther from their river tether and make greater use of the relatively untouched grasslands of the open steppe.

Faunal remains from four of these small riverside sites provide important new insights into third-millennium developments in the southern steppe that have direct bearing on the contrasting models offered to explain the proliferation of sites in the area during this time. Remains from four of these sites—Ziyadeh, Raq'ai, Atij, and Gudeda—document a profound transformation in which the localized subsistence economies that drew animal resources from a mix of wild and domestic species (characteristic of the southern steppe for more than three millennia) were replaced by a pastoral economy focused almost exclusively on sheep and goats (see figure 7.3) (Zeder 1998a, 1998c). However, this transformation did not occur suddenly, as might be expected if the major impetus of change came from outside the region as postulated under either the grain transhipment model of Fortin, Margueron, and Schwartz or the long-distance pastoral exploitation model offered by McCorriston. Instead, it was a more gradual transition, taking place over 200 to 300 years, as might be expected if, as Hole suggests, the impetus for change came from internal sources. Yet this was not a simple expansion of a long-standing indigenous pattern of exploitation. Instead, the changes indicated in the faunal record are part and parcel of a fundamental shift in the nature of economic relations in the Khabur Basin as a whole.

Several shifting patterns of faunal exploitation are evident in the assemblages from these riverside settlements. The first is a steady decline in the importance of hunted game at these sites, from nearly 36 percent of the faunal assemblage at the site of Ziyadeh, established at the beginning of the third millennium, to only 6 percent at the Gudeda site, occupied at about 2600 B.C. The increased emphasis on domestic species might be interpreted as an indication of the eradication of wild game due to overhunting by an expanded population. It might also be seen as the adoption of the more northern pattern of animal use as a response to more felicitous climatic conditions. However, a corresponding shift in the range of domestic species utilized argues against these more environmentally driven explanations.

If the once plentiful herds of gazelle and onager on the southern steppe had been substantially reduced, it is unlikely that people would have responded to this threat to their livelihood by narrowing their diet breadth even further and concentrating on only one element of the domestic pastoral economy. Indeed, it is more likely that people would have replaced the former broadly based animal resource base (that had consisted of a mix of domesticated and wild animals) with a similarly diversified economy made up of an array of domesticated animals. In particular, pigs as high meat producers that could be easily raised at riverside sites would be expected to show a significant increase to take up the slack left by the decimation of wild game. If, on the other hand, the shift to domestic resources was prompted by enhanced potential for domestic production due to ameliorating climatic conditions, one would expect both pigs and cattle to increase. Wetter conditions would not only favor cattle rearing but also stimulate agricultural production, which in turn would increase the demand for cattle used as draft animals.

And yet instead of diversifying in the exploitation of domestic species, as might be expected under these environmentally driven scenarios, the pastoral economy of the southern steppe narrows to concentrate almost exclusively on sheep and goats. In particular, pigs, once 20 percent of the assemblages from initial third-millennium sites in the region, almost disappear from assemblages dating to the mid-third millennium. And cattle remain relatively constant at about 5–8 percent. In contrast, sheep and goats steadily increase, from less than 30 percent of assemblages at the beginning of the third millennium to more than 80 percent of assemblages among identifiable bones from sites dating to the mid-third millennium

This pattern strongly suggests that while environmental factors may have played a supporting, but perhaps not starring, role in these developments, the restructuring of the pastoral economy in the southern steppe was largely driven by economic forces. The relationship of these riverside sites to the newly discovered settlements on the steppe to the west is not yet clear. However, it is likely that early on in the sequence both riverside and steppe settlements were occupied by shifting elements of the same corporate groups. Through time, as people moved further out into the steppe and their utilization of this region intensified, it is possible that these two elements of the economy of the southern steppe became increasingly disarticulated. Once part of a single corporate group engaged in generalized strategies of mixed resource exploitation, the increasingly disparate river-focused and steppe-focused peoples became linked through more formalized economic exchange of pastoral and agricultural goods. The tokens and numerical tablets found at one of these sites (Fortin 1998a; Hole 1999) imply that some level of accounting may have been needed to coordinate these relations. The defensible granaries at some of the riverside sites and their location on the opposite side of the riverbank from the western steppe have been taken as possible evidence of the threat of incursions from steppe-dwelling pastoralists (Kouchoukos 1998). This in all likelihood reflects the transformation of the more fluid movement of peoples between riverside and steppe into a more formalized, focused exploitation of these different ecozones under a more highly specialized agropastoral system.

The final crystallization of this pattern of pastoral specialization in the southern steppe (when sheep and goat increase to more than 80 percent of faunal assemblages in this region and pigs drop out of the economy altogether) comes about at about 2600 B.C. and coincides with the expansion of Tell Leilan, on the well-watered northern steppe, from a small 15-hectare town into a major 90-hectare walled city (Weiss 1986). This period of urban emergence in the north seems to coincide with a dramatic elaboration in the settlement hierarchy of sites in the western steppe, which now include both small camps and villages and at least one large town about 30 hectares in size (Hole 1997, 1999; Kouchoukos 1998).

During the apogee of urbanism in the second half of the third millennium, the numerous, possibly competing, small riverside sites seem to coalesce into a few settlements. Analysis of the animal remains from one of these sites indicates that the emphasis on specialized pastoral production in the region increased during this time (Loyet n.d.). Both the marked increase in the proportion of sheep over goats and a delayed kill-off strategy suggest increased emphasis on wool production. This zooarchaeological evidence for an emphasis on wool production is accompanied by the recovery of a large number of artifacts associated with spinning and weaving, and possibly those associated with accounting for wool or textiles as well. Evidence of weaving in the lower town areas of Tell Leilan suggests that production and initial processing of wool may have taken place in settlements on the southern steppe, with the final production of textiles undertaken by households within the city.

The second half of the third millennium also saw the abandonment of the settlements established less than 200 years earlier on the western steppe—a response, Hole postulates, to a return to more arid conditions. And indeed a regional (if not global) drought is held by some to have caused the eventual abandonment of Tell Leilan and the collapse of the urban system centered on the city at the close of the third millennium (Weiss et al. 1993). It is also likely, however, that the shifting settlement pattern in the southern steppe during this period of urban florescence was part of a consolidation of urban power in the agricultural sector of the north steppe and a corresponding reorientation of pastoral economy in the south toward servicing northern centers and their hinterlands.

Thus against this background of environmental change, in which shifts in rainfall patterns serve as both catalytic and cataclysmic forces of change, powerful social and economic forces were also reshaping formerly localized, diversified socioeconomic systems tied to specific ecozones into a highly structured region-wide urban society. Faunal evidence from the Khabur gives us special insight into the process through which a localized system of diversified exploitation of riverside and steppe environments was transformed into a set of highly specialized economic relations that became incorporated into the larger developing urban economy centered in the northern steppe. Rather than being passively drawn into the vortex of emergent urbanism centered in the northern Khabur, the development of specialized pastoralism in this region may have actually been an active force in the restructuring of regional economic relations that ultimately led to the emergence and expansion of urban society in the Khabur Basin.

SOCIAL DIMENSIONS OF ANIMAL ECONOMY WITHIN TELL LEILAN

Animal remains from the northern steppe city of Tell Leilan shed new light on socially dictated distinctions based on access to food within cities and the economic practicalities of urban provisioning (Zeder 1998a, 1998c). Animal remains have been examined from two distinct sectors: the upper town, dominated by large public buildings presumably occupied by elite power brokers, and the lower town, where more humble residences and shops were encountered (figure 7.3). Faunal remains from lower-town contexts are dominated by pig, which accounts for nearly 50 percent of the identifiable animal remains from the area. The presence of both young and fully adult swine in the assemblage from this sector of the city suggests that pigs were being both eaten and produced there. Thus Leilan joins a growing number of urban sites in which lower-status residents seem to have been directly involved in raising pigs for their own consumption, a profile that neatly fits expectations for pig production in urban contexts in the Near East. Whether raised to make up for provisioning deficiencies in the channeling of meat to poorer urban residential areas or, as is currently fashionable to suppose, as an overt symbol of resistance to elite control, locally produced swine would have given these households a reliable, low-labor-intensive, highly productive source of meat.

In contrast, caprines comprise 54 percent of the assemblage from the upper-town public/elite area. Sheep, generally considered the higher-prestige caprine resource, are significantly better represented here than in lower-town contexts. And while it is not a major contributor to the diet, gazelle, another animal often associated with high status, is four times more common here than in lower-town deposits. Wild fowl are also better represented here. All of these patterns might be taken as markers of preferential access to higher-status foods in elite areas. Multiple channels of urban provisioning are implied, both external to the city (caprines and game) and internal (pigs), with clear indications of differential access to food resources based on the socieconomic status of urban residents.

Though less well represented than they are in the lower town, at 34 percent of the assemblage of identifiable animal bones, pig consumption still seems unexpectedly high in this elite sector of the city. Initial inspection suggests, however, that upper-town pig remains are almost exclusively from very young piglets. It is possible that these animals represent off-take from the small-scale swine production of lower-town residents. If so, it seems that this household-level activity was taxed in some way to provide urban elites a steady diet of suckling pig. Thus, city-bound pig production not only provided lower-status residents a measure of economic autonomy and independence from elite provisioners, it also provided urban elites a buffer against the possible vicissitudes of an externally oriented provisioning system dependent on the steady extraction of pastoral resources from mobile pastoral specialists, who themselves maintained some degree of independence from urban control.

CONCLUSIONS

This example of provisioning in urban economies of Northern Mesopotamia underscores the point that studies of ancient urban economies must recognize the great diversity of operational alternatives around which these economies might be organized. In any given urban system, many levels of specialization and control may be operating at once, even within single economic spheres. There is no single model of specialization; nor does control apply in the same way to all urban economies, or even to all components of single urban systems.

This case example also demonstrates that a focus on urban economy does not deny the powerful social and political relationships that are also central to the urban phenomenon. Instead an emphasis on economy provides a tangible way to monitor the increasing segregation and specialization of actors and activities found in all of these arenas in urban contexts, by demonstrating some of the ways in which an economy serves both to create and to buttress conditions of social inequalities and power imbalances found in urban societies.

It also clearly establishes that all aspects of the urban economy experience varying degrees of specialization and control, and that we should not confine ourselves to only the production and distribution of craft goods if we want to learn how these specialized economies operated in early urban contexts. The production and distribution of both agricultural and pastoral staples clearly provide another highly rewarding way of monitoring the origin and operation of Near Eastern urban economies. Not only is it possible to use our understanding of the biology and behavior of these resources (and the methods used today to produce them) to model how plant and animal resources might have been incorporated into emergent urban economies in the ancient world, but we can also assess the strengths of these models more or less directly through careful study of the hardy remains they leave behind in archaeological sites.

The study of pastoral economy in the Khabur Basin has provided a concrete example of how urban provisioning can be examined on both a regional and a site-focused scale. Animal remains from this region not only give testimony to long-term trends in pastoral economy across a broad geographic area, but they also allow us to pinpoint the crystallization of specialized pastoral economy and to relate this process to the broader context of urban emergence in the Khabur Basin. We have also been able to examine provisioning within a large urban center and get some sense of the ways in which urban provisioning added to the social dynamics that separated elites from nonelite urban dwellers. In addition, we were able to uncover the multiple channels of resource provisioning that fed large urban centers such as Tell Leilan, including one internal to the city itself that has important implications for understanding the social dynamics of city life, as well as the relations between the city as a whole and outside specialist provisioners.

I hope that this contribution has helped demonstrate the utility of archaeology in urban studies. Concentrating on the earliest expressions of urbanism, we can perhaps better see some of the primary forces responsible for shaping the complex web of relations characteristic of urban society today. With the luxury of deep time and the ability to watch these systems emerge, grow, and decline on both a regional and site-specific scale, we have a unique vantage point from which to watch the urban process unfold. We can also compare independent examples of urbanism as they manifested themselves in many places and at different times around the world. Certainly there is a huge amount of the essence of urbanism that is lost to us over the ages, as many interactions central to the functioning of urban society leave no trace in the archaeological record. But a lot still remains behind, even in the least impressive and least appealing of the archaeological remnants of these interactions. Our study of these remnants has a lot to offer to a broader understanding of how urban societies around the world came to be and how they prevailed over many thousands of years to become to the pervasive form of social organization in the world today.

REFERENCES

Adams, R. McC.
    1981   *Heartland of Cities: Surveys of Ancient Settlement and Land Use on the Central Floodplain of the Euphrates.* University of Chicago Press, Chicago.

Blanton, R. E.
    1976   Anthropological Studies of Cities. *Annual Reviews in Anthropology* 5:249–264.

Bökönyi, S.
    1978   The Animal Remains of the 1970–1972 Excavation Seasons at Tell el-Der: A Preliminary Report. In *Tell II: Progress Reports* (First Series), edited by L. De Meyer, pp. 185–189. Editions Peeters, Leuven.

Curtis, J. B., and W. W. Hallo
    1959   Money and Merchant in Ur III. *Hebrew Union College, Annual* 30:103–139.

Dahl, G., and A. Hjort
    1976   *Having Herds: Pastoral Herd Growth and Household Economy.* Stockholm Studies in Social Anthropology, 2.

Diener, P., and E. E. Robkin

1978   Ecology and Evolution and the Search for Cultural Origins: The Question of Islamic Pig Prohibition. *Current Anthropology* 19:493–540.

Earle, T. K., and E. Brumfiel

1987   *Specialization, Exchange, and Complex Societies.* Cambridge University Press, Cambridge.

Fortin, M.

1991   Récentes recherches archéologiques dans le Moyenne Vallée du Khabour (Syrie). *Bulletin of the Canadian Society for Mesopotamian Studies* 21:5–16.

1993   Résutats de la 4ème Campagne de Fouilles à Tell 'Atij et de la 3ème à Tell Gudeda, Syrie. *Echos du Monde Classique/Classical Views* 37:97–121.

Fortin, M., and L. Cooper

1994   Canadian Excavations at Tell 'Atij (Syria) 1992–1993. *Bulletin of the Canadian Society for Mesopotamian Studies* 27:33–50.

Fortin, M., B. Routledge, and C. Routledge

1994   Canadian Excavations at Tell Gudeda (Syria) 1992–1993. *Bulletin of the Canadian Society for Mesopotamian Studies* 27:51–64.

Gelb, I.

1967   Growth of a Herd of Cattle in Ten Years. *Journal of Cuneiform Studies,* 21:64–69.

Hamblin, N.

1985   The Role of Marine Resources in the Maya Economy: A Case Study from Cozumel, Mexico. In *Prehistoric Lowland Maya Environment and Subsistence Economy,* edited by M. Pohl, pp. 159–176. Papers of the Peabody Museum of Archaeology and Ethnology, No. 77.

Hastorff, C.

1993   *Agriculture and the Onset of Political Inequality before the Inka.* Cambridge University Press, Cambridge.

Hesse, B.

1990   Pig Lovers and Pig Haters: Patterns of Palestinian Pork Production. *Journal of Ethnobiology* 10:195–225.

1994   Husbandry, Dietary Taboos, and the Bones of the Ancient Near East: Zooarchaeology in the Post-Processual World. In *Methods in the Mediterranean,* edited by D. B. Small, pp. 197–232. E. J. Brill, Leiden.

Hole, F. A.

1991   Middle Khabur Settlement and Agriculture in the Ninevite 5 Period. *Bulletin of the Canadian Society for Mesopotamian Studies* 21:17–30.

1997   Evidence for Mid-Holocene Environmental Change in the Western Khabur Drainage, Northeastern Syria. In *Third Millennium* B.C. *Climate Change and Old World Collapse,* edited by H. N. Dalfes, G. Kukla, and H. Weiss, pp. 39–66. NATO ASI Series, vol. 129. Springer-Verlag, Berlin-Heidelberg.

1999   Economic Implications of Possible Storage Structures at Tell Ziyadeh, N.E. Syria. *Journal of Field Archaeology* 26: 267–283.

Hole, F. A., and N. Kouchoukos

In press   *Preliminary Report on an Archaeological Survey in the Western Khabur Basin, 1994.* Annales Archéologique Arabes Syriennes.

Jackson, H. E., and S. L. Scott

1995   The Faunal Record of the Southeastern Elite: The Implications of Economy, Social Relations, and Ideology. *Southeastern Archaeology* 14:103–119.

Jacobsen, T. K.

1953   On the Textile Industry at Ur under Ibbi-Sin. In *Studia Orientalia,* edited by I. Pedersen, pp. 172–187. Hauniae, Helsinki.

Johnson, G. A.

1973   *Local Exchange and Early State Development in Southwestern Iran.* Museum of Anthropology, University of Michigan, Anthropological Papers, 51.

Jones, T. B., and J. W. Snyder

1961   *Sumerian Economic Texts from the Third Ur Dynasty: A Catalogue and Discussion of Documents from Various Collections.* University of Minnesota Press, Minneapolis.

Kang, S. T.

1972   *Sumerian Economic Texts from the Drehem Archive: Sumerian and Akadian Texts in the Collection of the World Heritage Museum of the University of Illinois,* vol. 1. University of Illinois Press, Urbana.

Kientz, J.-M., and M. Lambert

1963   L'élevage du gros betail a Lagash au temps de Lugalanda et d'Urukagina. *Revista degli Studi Orientalia* 38:93–138.

Köhler-Rollefson, I.

1988   The Aftermath of the Levantine Neolithic Revolution in the Light of Ecological and Ethnographic Evidence. *Paléorient* 14: 97–93.

1989   Resolving the Revolution: Late Neolithic Refinements of Economic Strategies in the Eastern Levant. *Archaeozoologia* I: 202–208.

Kouchoukos, N.

1998   *Landscape and Social Change in Late Prehistoric Mesopotamia.* Unpublished Ph.D. dissertation, Yale Univesity, New Haven.

Krader, L.

1955   Ecology of Central Asian Pastoralism. *Southwestern Journal of Anthropology* 11:301–326.

Loyet, M.

n.d.   Tell Tuneinir and Its Place in the Development of Animal Economy in the Middle Khabur Valley. Unpublished manuscript.

McCorriston, J.

1997   The Fiber Revolution: Textile Extensification, Alienation, and Social Stratification in Ancient Mesopotamia. *Current Anthropology* 38:517–549.

Margueron, J.-C.

1991   Mari, L'Ephrate, et le Khabur au milieu du IIIe millénaire. *Bulletin of the Canadian Society for Mesopotamian Studies* 21:79–100.

Mudar, K.

1982   Early Dynastic III Animal Utilization in Lagash: A Report on the Fauna from Tell Al-Hibba. *Journal of Near Eastern Studies* 4:23–34.

Pohl, M.

1985a   Osteological Evidence for Subsistence and Status. In *Prehistoric Lowland Maya Environ-*

ment and Subsistence Economy, edited by M. Pohl, pp. 107–114. Papers of the Peabody Museum of Archaeology and Ethnology, No. 77.

1985b The Privileges of Maya Elites: Prehistoric Vertebrate Fauna from Seibal. In *Prehistoric Lowland Maya Environment and Subsistence Economy,* edited by M. Pohl, pp. 133–146. Papers of the Peabody Museum of Archaeology and Ethnology, No. 77.

Postgate, J. N.

1992 *Early Mesopotamia: Society and Economy at the Dawn of History.* Routledge, London.

Redding, R. W.

1981 *Decision Making in Subsistence Herding of Sheep and Goats in the Middle East.* Ph.D. dissertation, University of Michigan. University Microfilms International, Ann Arbor.

1991 The Role of Pig in the Subsistence System of Ancient Egypt: A Parable on the Potential of Faunal Data. In *Animal Use and Culture Change,* edited by P. J. Crabtree and K. Ryan, pp. 20–30. University of Pennsylvania, MASCA Research Papers in Science and Archaeology, Supplement 8.

2000 The Pig and the Chicken: A Parable on Modeling Human Subsistence Behavior. Paper presented at the Annual Meetings of the Society of Ethnobiology, Ann Arbor, Mich., March.

Rowtan, M. B.

1973 Urban Autonomy in a Nomadic Environment. *Journal of Near Eastern Studies* 32:201–214.

Schwartz, G. M.

1993 Rural Archaeology in Early Urban Mesopotamia. *National Geographic Research and Exploration* 9:120–131.

1994a Rural Economic Specialization and Early Urbanization in the Khabur Valley, Syria. In *Archaeological Views from the Countryside: Village Communities in Early Complex Societies,* edited by G. M. Schwartz and S. E. Falconer, pp. 19–36. Smithsonian Institution Press, Washington, D.C..

1994b Before Ebla: Models of Pre-State Political Organization in Syria and Northern Mesopotamia. In *Chiefdoms and Early States in the Near East: The Organizational Dynamics of Complexity,* edited by G. Stein and M. Rothman, pp. 153–174. Prehistory Press, Madison, Wis.

Smith, C. A.

1976 Exchange Systems and the Spatial Distribution of Elites: The Organization of Stratification in Agrarian Societies. In *Regional Analysis,* vol. 2: *Social Systems,* edited by C. A. Smith, pp. 309–374. Academic Press, New York.

Stein, G. J.

1986 The Use of Animal Bone Remains to Reconstruct Ancient Economic Systems. *Expedition* 28:37–42.

1987 Regional Economic Integration in Early State Societies: Third Millennium B.C. Pastoral Production at Gritille, Southeast Turkey. *Paléorient* 13:101–111.

Stein, G. J., and P. Wattenmaker

1990 The 1987 Tell Leilan Regional Survey: Preliminary Report. In *Economy and Settlement in the Near East: Analysis of Ancient Sites and Materials,* edited by N. Miller, pp. 8–18.

University of Pennsylvania, MASCA Research Papers in Science and Archaeology, Supplement 7.

Van Loon, D.

1978   *Small-Scale Pig Raising.* Storey Communications, Vermont.

Wattenmaker, P.

1987a   The Organization of Production and Consumption in a Complex Society: A Study of a Village Site in Southeastern Turkey. *MASCA Journal* 4:191–203.

1987b   Town and Village Economies in an Early State Society. *Paléorient* 13:117–126.

1994   *Household Economies in Northern Mesopotamia.* Smithsonian Institution Press, Washington, D.C.

Weiss, H.

1986   The Origins of Tell Leilan and the Conquest of Space in Third Millennium Mesopotamia. In *The Origins of Cities in Dry Farming Syria and Mesopotamia in the Third Millennium B.C.,* edited by H. Weiss, pp. 71–108. Four Quarters, Guilford, Conn.

Weiss, H., M.-A. Courty, W. Wetterstrom, F. Guichard, L. Senior, R. M. Meadow, and A. Curnow

1993   The Genesis and Collapse of Third Millennium North Mesopotamian Civilization, *Science* 26:195–1008.

Welch, P. D., and M. M. Scarry

1995   Foodways Variation in the Moundville Chiefdom. *American Antiquity* 60:397–419.

Wing, E. S.

1981   A Comparison of Olmec and Maya Foodways. In *The Olmec and Their Neighbors. Essays in the Memory of Matthew W. Stirling,* organized by M. D. Coe and D. Grove, edited by E. O. Benson, pp. 21–28. Dumbarton Oaks, Washington, D.C.

Zarins, J.

1989   Pastoralism in Southwest Asia: The Second Millennium B.C. In *The Walking Larder,* edited by J. Clutton-Brock, pp. 127–155. Unwin Hyman, London.

Zeder, M. A.

1988   Understanding Urban Process through the Study of Specialized Subsistence Economy in the Near East. *Journal of Anthropological Archaeology* 7:1–55.

1991   *Feeding Cities: Specialized Animal Economy in the Ancient Near East.* Smithsonian Series in Archaeological Inquiry, Washington, D.C.

1994a   After the Revolution: Post-Neolithic Subsistence Strategies in Northern Mesopotamia. *American Anthropologist* 1:97–126.

1994b   Of Kings and Shepherds: Specialized Animal Economy in Ur III Mesopotamia. In *Chiefdoms and Early States in the Near East: The Organizational Dynamics of Complexity,* edited by G. Stein and M. Rothman, pp. 175–191. Prehistory Press, Madison, Wis.

1995   The Archaeobiology of the Khabur Basin. *Bulletin of the Canadian Society for Mesopotamian Studies* 29:21–32.

1996   The Role of Pigs in Near Eastern Subsistence from the Vantage Point of the Southern Levant. In *Retrieving the Past: Essays on Archaeological Research and Methodology in Honor of Gus Van Beek,* edited by J. D. Seger, pp. 297–312. Eisenbrauns/Cobb Institute of Archaeology.

1998a   Pigs and Emergent Complexity in the Ancient Near East. In *Ancestors for the Pigs,* edited by S. Nelson, pp. 109–122. University of Pennsylvania, MASCA Research Papers in Science and Archaeology.

1998b   Regional Patterns of Animal Exploitation in the Khabur Basin, 7000 to 1500 B.C. In *Man and the Animal World: Studies in Archaeozoology, Archaeology, Anthropology, and Palae-olinguistics in Memoriam Sándor Bökönyi,* edited by P. Anreiter, L. Bartosiewicz, E. Jerem, and W. Meid, pp. 569–582. Archaeolingua vol. 8, Budapest.

1998c   Environment, Economy, and Subsistence on the Threshold of Urban Emergence in Northern Mesopotamia. In *Espace naturel, espace habité en Syrie Nord (10e-2e millénaire av. J.-C.),* edited by M. Fortin and O. Aurenche, pp. 55–67. Bulletin of the Canadian Society for Mesopotamian Studies 33 and Travaux de la Maison de l'Orient 28. Québec.

2000   Archaeological Perspectives on Human Impact on Steppe Environments: A View from Ancient Mesopotamia. *Open Country* 2:5–17.

Cities as a Place of Ethnogenesis

Urban Growth and Centralization in the Chicama Valley, Peru

CHRISTOPHER J. ATTARIAN

As has long been recognized, urbanism plays a crucial role in increasing social complexity as human groups develop from small village or tribal-level groups to states and empires (Blanton et al. 1993; Carneiro 1967; Childe 1950; Claessen 1984; Flannery 1972; Johnson and Earle 1987; Service 1977; Spencer 1990; Wright 1977, 1986). In addition, the process of urbanism is a cause of cultural change. Urban sites form the context in which increased social complexity, craft specialization, and population migration combine to effect the trajectory of culture change and development. This chapter investigates a component of both economic stratification and increasing social complexity in emerging urban environments, with the emphasis on community identity and material expression, and how both change during the shift from rural to urban settlement. Decorative elements on pottery as well as settlement data from the Chicama Valley, Peru, are used to test whether cultural change occurred in an early urban center dating to the latter part of the Early Intermediate period (EIP) (A.D. 1–200). The dynamic settlement and social changes that led up to the appearance of the Moche state began at this time. The Gallinazo Ceramic phase is ideal for the study of this emerging urbanism, migration, and the spatial and social centralization of authority.

The central question addressed in this chapter is: how does urbanism cause changes in social identity? Urbanism arises with population resettlement in emerging cities, in which migrants are faced with a new economy, new neighbors, and new rules and laws. If we accept the premise that culture is a product of human interaction with social and physical surroundings, we can predict that culture will change in response to new environmental stimuli (Downs and Bleibtreu 1969; Harris 1977; Hill 1977; Netting 1968, 1977; Rappaport 1967). To explore these changes I apply the theory of ethnogenesis (defined in the next section). I do not wish to imply, however, that the differences between Gallinazo villages are *ethnic* in the sense of formally defined linguistic ethnic groups. The vast majority of the material culture among all Gallinazo period sites is generally the same (Bennett 1950; Collier 1955; Strong and Evans 1952). I investigate both variation in material expression as a manifestation of community notions of identity, and how identity is challenged during the shift from rural to urban settlement.

During the latter part of the Early Intermediate Period (EIP) (A.D. 1–200), the demographic changes that led up to the appearance of the Moche state began. Because of dynamic settlement changes and social changes that occurred during this time, the Gallinazo Ceramic phase is ideal for the study of emerging urbanisms, migration, and cultural change.

ETHNOGENESIS AND
SOCIAL COMPLEXITY

Fredrik Barth (1969) predicted that ethnic group distinctions would become less pronounced in areas of interaction because the two groups would tend to become economically interdependent and thus wish to deemphasize differences that could potentially become divisive. While this is often the case, the cause-and-effect relationship also works in reverse; in instances of interaction and conflicting interest, groups may tend to emphasize their identity in opposition to others (Hodder 1979). Ethnogenesis encompasses both of these two processes and the tension between them. Ethnogenesis (Brumfiel 1994; Gailey 1987; Grant et al. 1996; Gregory

1992; Wolf 1982) describes the processes by which new social identities are created that reflect new and shared conditions. As groups of people enter a new environment, their previous sense of identity will be challenged and reshaped by the new conditions that they must confront in order to survive.

The theoretical literature on ethnic groups and ethnicity can be applied to subethnic-level interaction as well. Fredrik Barth (1969) summarizes that ethnic groups are defined on the basis of (1) biological self-perpetuation, (2) shared cultural values that can be observed in cultural forms, (3) a field of shared communication and interaction, and (4) membership that is both self-identified and identified by others. For Abner Cohen (1974a), ethnicity is situation dependent, and an ethnic group is a collection of people who have shared behaviors and are a component of a larger population. Eugene E. Roosens (1989:19) also relies on the contextual component of ethnicity. Ethnic identity, he writes, is defined only within a system of "cultural forms that give the impression that they are inherent to a particular category or group of individuals." All three of these authors conceive of ethnicity as operating on the individual level, as well as on the small-community and linguistic-group level. All three also state that socially defined interaction is another important criterion in the functioning of ethnic groups within a society. Scholars therefore need to understand patterns of interaction within whole populations in order to define meaningful ethnic or social gorups. Archaeology, through regional analysis, has the capacity to discern probable examples of both group isolation and interaction.

Group interaction can also be studied as interactions across group boundaries, as is well documented in the literature (for a summary, see Lightfoot and Martinez 1995). Traditional models describing group interaction boundaries have stressed the effect on group identity and material expression in situations involving two cohesive groups. In these models, the mixing of cultural traits is attributed to diffusion and emulation. While this model is useful, as Lightfoot and Martinez point out, it minimizes the potential for new groups to arise out of the multitude of interactions that occur where preexisting groups interact. Although the authors do not use the term, the process that they are describing is essentially that of ethnogenesis.

Emerging craft specialization may also cause changes in community identity. This is clearly evident in the transition from a rural agrarian economy to one with an urban specialist component. Two other relevant factors appear to be production aspects of the economy (craft specialization) and social complexity (Brumfiel and Earle 1987; Costin 1991; Sinopoli 1988). Specialized economic activities often take place in urban centers where labor is plentiful, exchange partners are nearby, and supervision by elites is inexpensive.

Urban populations almost always exceed the carrying capacity of the immediate area, a factor that necessitates flexible strategies of provisioning (see Zeder this volume). The importation of food suggests that at some level, there is surplus wealth; migration also suggests that there is surplus labor. Both surplus labor and wealth are necessary conditions for craft specialization to be a viable mode of production. As individuals or groups take on different professions, society becomes more varied. Although the participants must then become more reliant on other professions to supply necessary goods and services, the fortunes of each profession may, though not always, be at odds with each other. In other words, what is good for the merchant is not always good for the manufacturer.

A specialist-based economy will tend to fragment society into subgroups that perform specific functions. This process of fragmentation and specialization has been recorded ethnographically in contact and precontact state societies in Peru. For example, the Inka state used a variety of methods during its expansion and absorption of other peoples. The Inka alternated between intentionally disrupting the community solidarity within a region by forced resettlement, and incorporating indigenous populations peacefully (D'Altroy 1992; Stanish 1997). There is also evidence to show that the Inka conscripted laborers and relocated them, often on a permanent basis, to special compounds. A famous example of this is the *aclla,* the young women recruited to produce fine cloth and brew maize beer *(chicha)* for the Inka state (Rowe 1946). Two other Inka labor institutions that had a similar impact were the *mitmaq* (or *mitmae,* Stanish 1997:200) and *yana.* The *mitmaq* were ethnic populations removed from their indigenous areas by the state for the purpose of providing specialized labor for state projects. The *yana* were individuals who were attached to elite patrons and served as domestic servants and agricultural laborers (Murra 1980 [1956]).

While there is no direct evidence of these labor institutions existing on the North Coast of Peru during the Early Moche period, 1,500 years before the Inka, they do illustrate likely possibilities for the shifting relations of production that could have been occurring as the Moche state developed. There are well-documented cases of attached ceramic specialization in the late Moche phase at Mocollope (Russell et al. 1994) and from other Middle and Late Moche centers, including Pampa Grande (Shimada 1994b) and the pyramids at Moche (Uceda et al. 1997).

With the creation of such institutions, communities must inevitably be defined by their shared place in the economy and be isolated from their indigenous networks (i.e., kinship or village of origin). The degree of the imposed fragmentation, specialization, and relocation will influence the form of the generated resistance (Gailey 1987). For example, if some kinship bonds remain, or, if village or regional populations are assigned as a group to the same specialization, individuals will have more in common with their new neighbors as they begin the process of redefining themselves in resistance to their new situation.

URBAN ETHNOGENESIS

What constitutes an urban center (for more on this subject, see Blanton 1976; Childe 1950; Fox 1977; Silverman 1988; Smith's introduction to this volume) is not as important to this discussion as the primary events that occur during urbanization. The first process is the act of migration itself as people move from villages and small towns to larger settlements. Communities are uprooted and transplanted, either in part or in entirety. The alienation or outright loss of family homes, ancestral fields, and familiar landmarks necessarily affect the spatial foundations of community cohesion (Bradley 1998; Kuper 1972; Tilley 1994). Second, the urban economy is often fundamentally different from the rural economy since people are now dependent on each other for at least some of their daily needs. Finally, this specialized and interlocking economy brings about social changes. Economic specialization removes people from their traditional means of production and creates new groups and networks constructed around new economic roles (Childe 1950).

The Chicago School of the 1920s and 1930s characterized the modern urban community as a series of niches that together comprise a larger urban environment. This kind of environment may be defined by class, occupation, and ethnic group (Low 1996). Robert E. Park (1974[1925]), part of the Chicago movement, anayltically subdivided the urban population into demographic categories of overt to hidden interpersonal relationships. Park's model is one way, if somewhat long, to describe the composition of urban society. The strength of his method is that it starts with obvious demographic divisions and progressively emphasizes more hidden and small-scale associations between families and individuals. However, it has little to offer in the way of elucidating processes.

In a more recent study of the effects of differing economic situations, Steven Gregory (1992) has examined a once-coherent African American community in New York City where families with rising incomes were able to buy homes while lower-income residents tended to rent. The differences in economic status influenced social identity between the two groups: eventually, the homeowners petitioned the city, asking to be recognized as a different neighborhood with a different name and residents' association. Also departing from the traditional view of cities as corporate, integrated wholes, Cohen (1974a, 1974b) has considered cities to be a collection of smaller, usually kin-based networks. We can agree that cities are collections of previously separate peoples who come together, usually in a relatively short period of time, for economic or political survival. The ethnography and sociology of modern cities describe networks that, although rooted in ancestral communities, develop a complexity that could only exist in the dense milieu of urban life. Therefore archaeologists may find it useful to look for similar processes in ancient cities.

EVALUATING ETHNICITY
THROUGH STYLE

For my purposes, ethnic groups are considered in terms of their material culture. As Elizabeth Brumfiel (1994:96) states:

> Individuals assert their ethnic membership by joining in group rituals or by displaying symbols of ethnic identity, usually items of dress or personal adornment. Whether behavioral or material, ethnic group markers tend to be both unique to the ethnic group and part of a set of contrasting markers of other ethnic groups.

An illustration of the coherence of ethnic style may be found in Margaret Hardin's (1991) survey of modern Native American Zuni potters who were shown photos of Zuni pottery that had been collected by the Smithsonian Institution in the nineteenth century and asked to rank the "Zuniness" of the various pieces. All the artisans gave very similar rankings, which showed that they shared a sense of "proper" Zuni ceramics. This is also consistent with James Sackett's (1990, 1985) work on the notion of isochrestic style, a shared sense of the form that an object should have regardless of its functional attributes.

Other studies in the American Southwest (Plog 1980) and Midwest (Braun 1991) have linked ceramic decorations to particular communities. The work of Stephen Plog (1980) shows that Southwestern pottery style is correlated to community interaction at a level smaller than linguistic ethnic groups. Plog found that, as interaction increased, individual villages accentuated the uniqueness of their material culture in contrast to their neighbors. It is likely that domestic pottery in the Chicama

Valley would show similar patterns to that described by Braun and Plog. In these instances, increased stylistic difference between communities is correlated with evidence of population pressure and increased interaction between communities.

Pottery style, along with all media of style, is a rich field of intentional and unintentional social symbolism. Style has been shown to be a manifestation of identity: particular decorations and styles function as devices for communicating group identity and distinction. It is well documented that intentional decoration on ceramics, in particular, is a way of communicating identity to members of other groups (Braun 1991; Hodder 1979, 1982; Plog 1980; Sterner 1989; Washburn 1977, n.d.; Wheat et al. 1958; Wiessner 1983, 1984, 1990; Wobst 1977). The unintentional use of decoration and form are just as significant. As Sackett (1982, 1985, 1990) has explained (see also Ericson and Meighan 1984; Hardin 1991; and van der Leeuw 1991), an artist's or craftsperson's unconscious sense about the proper look for an object is just as reflective of unique norms and codes. Changes in style do, therefore, reflect larger shifts—not necessarily changes in physical persons, but changes in the intentional and unintentional expressions that people produce.

Under conditions of urban migration and economic specialization, ethnogenesis occurs when the social networks of rural immigrants are no longer useful in the urban environment. I explore these changes using the stylistic expression in ceramic vessels of a particular type: Castillo Incised, which spans the transition between the Late Gallinazo culture and the Early Moche culture in the Chicama Valley of Peru.

EARLY URBANISM ON THE
NORTH COAST

The North Coast region of Peru is well suited to archaeological investigation because of its cultural history and excellent conditions of preservation. Most of the information collected from Moche urban centers is from the latter Moche V period (A.D. 550–700). At this time, Moche society was characterized by full-time specialization, intensive agriculture, and shared storage (Attarian 1996; Anders 1977; Bawden 1995; Shimada 1994b). Excavations at the Moche V sites of Galindo (Bawden 1982) and Pampa Grande (Shimada 1994b) reveal distinct *barrios,* or neighborhoods. These areas are defined by differences in the size and development of domestic architecture and by the type and abundance of certain wealth-related artifacts, such as textiles and metal objects. At the Galindo site in the Moche Valley, massive stone walls with formal gates separate the *barrios.* The evidence from both

Galindo and Pampa suggests that social groups were segregated in terms of settlement. This social division seems to be associated with economic differences. The stone walls at Galindo suggest that this segregation was related to social conflict possibly related to economic stress caused by environmental catastrophe (Bawden 1982).

Little has been learned about earlier periods (with the notable exceptions of Billman 1996; and Brennen 1980, 1982). Survey data suggest that from the beginning of the Salinar phase (500–200 B.C.) settlement clustered in areas with access to river water and defensible positions (Billman 1996; Leonard and Russell 1996; Wilson 1988). In the Moche and Chicama valleys, these settlement clusters actually decreased in size during the Early Gallinazo, possibly because of settlement nucleation in the Virú Valley (Billman 1996). Sometime during the later Gallinazo period, however, large settlements were formed in the central valleys and the fortified sites were abandoned. These large settlements became the Moche urban centers of the next four centuries.

The settlement data describe a very dynamic transition at numerous locations along the north coast (for the Moche Valley, see Billman 1996; for the Chicama Valley, Leonard and Russell 1996; and for the Santa Valley, Wilson 1988). The general pattern includes abandonment of up-valley fortified sites that were founded 200 years earlier, during the Salinar ceramic phase. Settlement shifted to midvalley, nonfortified sites. Elite architecture, begun during the late Gallinazo phase, increased dramatically during the early Moche phase. At that point, the distinctive Moche fine-line vessel forms were introduced (Donnan and McClelland 1999), but restricted to elite contexts (Leonard and Russell 1996). Yet some of the changes in the material culture were not so dramatic; there is continuity from Early Gallinazo to Early Moche of many artifact types, including types of domestic pottery (Bawden 1996; Shimada 1994a, 1994b; Shimada and Maguiña 1994).

RESEARCH PARAMETERS AT MOCOLLOPE:
PREVIOUS WORK AT MOCOLLOPE
AND THE CHICAMA VALLEY

Survey observations and excavations show no trace of an early Moche occupation at the Gallinazo sites that have been identified. Continuity of occupation is evident at only two sites: the El Brujo complex, near the coast, and Mocollope. Hence it can be assumed that these six villages were abandoned and that the population nucleated around Mocollope, which explains its sudden size increase (figure 8.1).

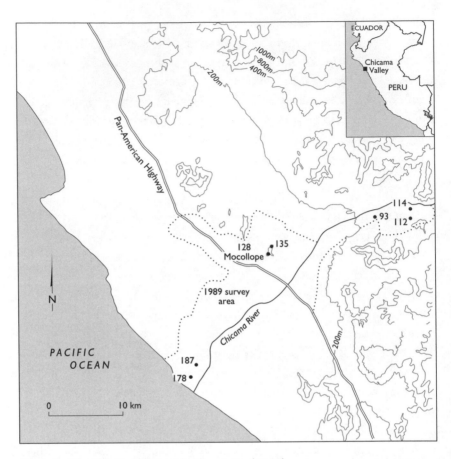

Figure 8.1. The Chicama Valley with relevant sites located.

Between 1997 and 2000, our team of researchers from Peru and the University of California at Los Angeles recovered a large amount of Gallinazo phase ceramic material from areas just north of the monumental architecture (figure 8.2). We also found that the Gallinazo occupation in this area was the first occupation, attesting to the expansion of the site and arrival of new people during this period.

Research Design and Hypotheses

Previous research has confirmed that the settlement structure and community compositions changed during the Gallinazo-Moche transition (Leonard and Russell 1996). Therefore it is logical to look for changing community expression during

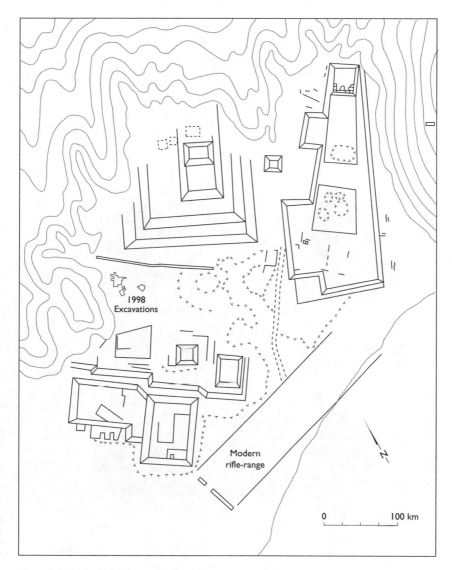

Figure 8.2. Schematic of Site 128, Mocollope, showing the location of major architecture and the 1998 excavation units.

this period as well. This process of ethnogenesis would be instigated by two conditions: (1) the migration of peoples into urban centers, and (2) the increased role of specialization in the economy of these urban centers. This change may be evident in the archaeological record by a gradual differentiation of the material

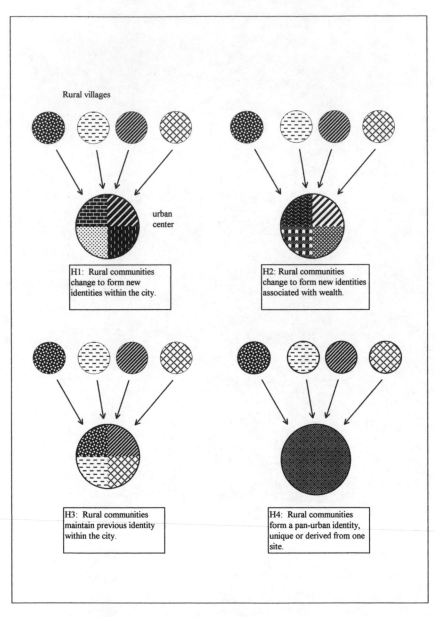

Figure 8.3. Four hypotheses of urban migration and cultural change. Small circles represent rural sites; large circle represents urban center. Fill pattern represents community style.

culture between the groups that are engaged in distinct specialties and living in discrete areas of the site. Migration and increased specialization must both be evident in order to interpret either new or maintained material expression through the use of this model.

Migration can be inferred from previous survey data, which show signs of numerous small, single-component sites across the floodplain near Mocollope during the pre-Moche, Gallinazo, period (Leonard and Russell 1996). During the late Gallinazo and early Moche periods, Mocollope expanded and the small sites were abandoned. Migration of rural populations into the emerging center best explains the site size increase at Mocollope during this period. In numerous cases around the world, site nucleation has been associated with the rise of one or a few major urban centers. Particularly well-known examples in the New World are Teotihuacan in the Basin of Mexico (Sanders 1965; Sanders et al. 1979; see also Cowgill chapter 2) and Tiwanaku in the Bolivian highlands (Albarracin-Jordan 1996; Kolata 1986, 1993).

Across the Peruvian North Coast region, increased specialization is indicated by the increased output and standardization of manufactured goods, particularly pottery (Russell et al. 1994; Shimada 1994b; Uceda et al. 1997) and adobe bricks (Shimada 1997). It should be noted that no workshops have been identified from the late Gallinazo or early Moche periods. The massive ceramic workshop associated with Mocollope, Cerro Mayal, dates to the Moche IV and Moche V phases (A.D. 450–700) (Russell et al. 1994). It can be assumed, however, that specialized and attached forms of production were emerging during the period of urbanization, as they are well developed during the following ceramic phases.

DATA MODELS

This section presents four possible models for community identity and expression. As a first step, however, it is necessary to isolate community expression from economic-class distinctions through an independent assessment of relative wealth. The theory of ethnogenesis includes the caveat that social identity is fluid and situational; for this reason, the ideal patterns described here must be considered guides in interpreting a more complex pattern reflected in the data.

Pottery Style

Ceramic vessels are particularly useful in studying identity because both form and surface decoration can be independently measured. Intensive survey of the Lower Chicama Valley detected only one Early Intermediate Period ceramic workshop, a Late Moche site found at Cerro Mayal, near Mocollope (Attarian 1996; Russell et al. 1994). The evidence from Cerro Mayal suggests that it was an elite-controlled workshop that produced many decorated and mold-made forms. Neither undecorated utilitarian nor fine-line stirrup-spout ceramics were found. The implication is that most, if not all, domestic ceramics were manufactured elsewhere, presumably by the households or the communities that used them (for a comparative case, see Feinman 1999). Ceramic design elements reflect the preferences of the local group. In the Titicaca Basin, Charles Stanish (1989) reported dramatic differences in the ratio of local to nonlocal pottery in domestic versus nondomestic contexts. Excavations focused on residential areas can capture local pottery traditions, in contrast to excavations of tombs and ceremonial structures that produce a high proportion of traded or exotic wares.

Wealth

In order to determine how material goods show evidence of changing group identity and expression, we also need to account for emerging differences in wealth that may affect the form, decoration, and substance of such items. Previous research on the coast of Peru has identified artifact types that seem to co-occur and require high amounts of labor investment. These items include metal artifacts such as ornaments, tools, and beads. Copper, silver, and gold were all used by the peoples of the North Coast. Silver and gold tend to be very rare. However, excavations at the Chimú site of Pacatnamu (Donnan 1997; Donnan and Cock 1986; Gumerman 1991; Lechtman 1997) recovered copper tools and ornaments in a variety of domestic contexts. Stone and shell beads were common items of adornment and exchange. According to Patricia Netherly (1977), production specialists of the contact period were paid with beads for the goods produced. Textiles have long been identified with wealth in the Andes (Murra 1975; Rowe 1946). Excavations at Pacatnamu also revealed a higher association of metal, beads, and textiles in areas of large elite architecture. Another measurement of relative wealth is the volume

Table 8.1

Summary of Material Correlates of Four Hypotheses

Hypothesis	H₁: change due to new and unique social networks and communities	H₂: change due to differences in wealth and power	H₃: no new communities form; indigenous communities maintain their identity within the urban environment	H₄: a new but uniform social identity forms
Pottery style	New/different styles in distinct areas of the city	New/different styles, correlated to traditional wealth items	Same as earlier rural sites; styles may or may not be spatially segregated	New/different style, uniform throughout the city

and investment in architecture. These measurements of relative wealth need to be considered since differences in style may often precipitate changes in community identity.

Four Hypotheses

Four possible hypotheses can be generated from the preceding discussion to explain group interaction with the urban environment. They provide a guide for the interpretation of data in a way that is meaningful to the issues of community integration, conservancy, and ethnogenesis discussed here (figure 8.3, table 8.1).

Hypothesis 1 (H₁). The processes of urbanization will encourage the differentiation of new communities within the new urban environment. New communities will arise from the new social and economic networks formed in a specialist urban economy. The material correlates of H₁ would be a new combination of stylistic forms in material artifacts that are used to signal self-identity to both the included and the excluded audience. Ceramic vessel style and design elements used on utilitarian ceramics will be different and more spatially segregated in the urban domestic areas. Pottery style elements will be clustered in different areas of the site.

Hypothesis 2 (H₂). The process of urbanization will encourage the differentiation of new communities, and the division criteria will be correlated directly with differences in wealth. Such results would obscure community expressions independent of wealth. The material correlates of H₂ include an emergence of new styles as assumed under H_1, but these changes will be associated with relative differences in wealth items, including imported ceramics, labor-intensive artifacts, and domestic architecture with different amounts of labor investment. Ceramic vessel style will change, but this change will correlate with the traditional measures of wealth and status reflected in such data sets as imported ceramics, elite forms, metal ornaments, textiles, and high-labor domestic architecture. Clusters of different styles will exist as with H_1, but these clusters will be distinct and correlated with meaningful differences on wealth items.

Hypothesis 3 (H_3). The process of urbanization will not cause differentiation into new communities; rather, communities will be unchanged between the early, rural settlements and the latter, urban settlement. This would support the idea of deeper, more resilient community identification forged in the original rural communities. This situation implies a more loosely aggregated, as opposed to a more fully integrated, urbanism. The material correlates of H_3 would include urban ceramic styles similar to those found in the pre-urban settlements, which would suggest that group identifying styles are determined by the original community and are not significantly influenced by the new urban environment. H_3 predicts that the rural communities will remain intact within the city. Clusters will be evident, but they will correspond to style populations identified in the rural settlements.

Hypothesis 4 (H_4). The process of urbanization will cause group homogeneity so that a new social identity that encompasses all members of the urban community will replace rural identity, and stylistic variation will decrease. This could be due to either an emerging shared identity forged in the new settlement or the increasing influence of the emerging Moche elite. In the case of material correlates, ceramic vessel style will change from those forms found in the rural communities, but the new styles will be common throughout the city. H_4 predicts that social identity will become more uniform in the new city. No spatial clusters or distinct group patterns will be detected.

Quite possibly a combination of the above four hypotheses will be evident in the data. A mathematical evaluation such as chi-square analysis should be used to test whether differences between both villages and sectors of the urban site are statistically meaningful. At this point, the samples are not large enough to make chi-square analyses worthwhile. However, preliminary data from surface-collected ceramics suggest (with no statistical significance) that one rural community does maintain itself but two others lose their unique stylistic forms.

Castillo Incised pottery, first described by Strong and Evans (1952:316–325), was selected for study because it is highly decorated and because it spans the time period of concern. Castillo Incised is a domestic pottery type common to the North Coast of Peru during the Early Intermediate Period. It is particularly well suited to this analysis because it was in use during both the pre-urban phase and the period of urbanism at Mocollope. An attribute analysis was performed to separate the components of the particular design elements on the vessels in question. Attribute analysis is a means of studying variation within a predefined type class. By focusing on particular design elements or physical characteristics of a vessel or sherd, comparisons can be made independent of previous typological schemes (Rice 1987:275–276).

The ceramic type in general is characterized by the incision of various small repeated elements, including small triangles, dots, small circles, dashes, and squares (figure 8.4). Also, appliqué stripes are sometimes attached to the vessel and these are incised with the same shapes in addition to diagonal dashes, divots, or dashes that penetrate the entire appliqué band. In total, 18 distinct shape elements were identified on the observed sherds (tables 8.2 and 8.4). Variations may also occur in the particular pattern of the incised shape elements on the vessel. The patterns include continuous rows of incisions that travel around the vessel, discontinuous rows, florets, nonlinear discontinuous patterns of incisions, multiple rows, multiple rows that are offset, and a few variants. In total, 14 particular patterns were definable (tables 8.3 and 8.4). The location of the decoration varied as well and could be found on the upper shoulder, neck, spout (if applicable), or upper, middle, and lower rim of neckless ollas.

For three of the eleven late Gallinazo sites that are abandoned, enough surface collection data are available to perform a tentative analysis based on the hypotheses presented earlier. The assemblage is discussed in terms of the variation in shape elements and patterns.

Element Variation

Shape element variation is evident between the rural and urban communities. Elements 3, 6, 13, 15, 16, 17, and 18 are only present at Mocollope (Site 128) (table 8.2).

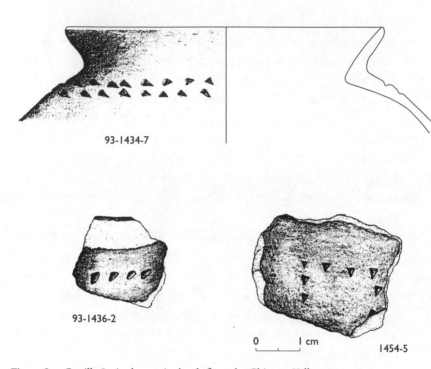

Figure 8.4. Castillo Incised ceramic sherds from the Chicama Valley.

Table 8.2
Percentages of Shape-Element Types

Site	0	1	2	3	4	5	6	7	8
128-surf	11.76	19.61	0	1.96	25.49	1.96	0	11.76	0
128-exc.	4.76	19.05	1.59	0	25.4	0	1.59	38.1	1.59
112	0	12.5	12.5	0	75	0	0	0	0
114	0	16.67	25	0	41.66	16.67	0	0	0
93	0	22.5	18.75	0	17.5	16.25	0	13.75	1.25

Site	9	10	11	12	13	14	15	16	17	18
128-surf	3.96	0	0	1.96	0	0	0	1.96	9.8	9.8
128-exc.	1.59	1.59	0	1.59	1.59	0	1.59	0	0	0
112	0	0	0	0	0	0	0	0	0	0
114	0	0	0	0	0	0	0	0	0	0
93	0	1.25	2.5	6.25	0	0	0	0	0	0

Table 8.3

Percentages of Pattern Types

Site	0	1	2	3	4	5	6	7	8	9	10	11	12	13	14
128-surf	11.76	17.65	11.76	7.84	15.69	7.84	3.92	7.84	7.84	0	7.84	0	0	0	0
128-exc.	1.59	15.87	6.35	3.17	4.76	1.59	3.17	12.7	7.94	0	31.75	4.76	3.17	0	3.17
112	0	62.5	0	0	0	0	0	25	12.5	0	0	0	0	0	0
114	0	41.67	16.67	16.67	0	0	0	8.33	8.33	8.33	0	0	0	0	0
93	0	21.25	15	7.5	8.75	0	0	16.25	11.25	2.50	10	0	2.5	5	0

Table 8.4

Attributes Used in Ceramic Analysis of Castillo Incised Pottery

Location
0 = none
1 = body
2 = lower rim
3 = upper rim
4 = middle rim
5 = spout
6 = neck
7 = shoulder joint

Continuous
0 = no
1 = yes

Rows
= number

Shape
0 = none
1 = dots
2 = triangles
3 = circles
4 = dashes
5 = divits
6 = pushed-up triangles
7 = dashes that penetrate (appliqué)
8 = straight continuous line
9 = squares
10 = pinched finger marks
11 = triangles with tails
12 = short lines
13 = impressed cord
14 = n.a.
15 = n.a.
16 = shallow parallel impressions
17 = thin hatching

Pattern
0 = none
1 = continuous row
2 = discontinuous row
3 = single shape element
4 = flourette
5 = no rows but continuous
6 = no rows, discontinuous
7 = rows, unknown if continuous and number of rows is unknown

8 = rows, unknown if continuous or grouped and number or rows is known
9 = offset rows, continuous
10 = single row per appliqué, multiple appliqué rows
11 = either 5 and 6, unknown which
12 = offset rows discontinuous
13 = geometric pattern
14 = as 10, but number of rows unknown

Banded
0 = none
1 = horizontal
2 = vertical
3 = diagonal
4 = unknown
5 = circular
6 = both horizontal and vertical

Zone
0 = none
1 = inclusive
2 = exclusive
3 = separating
4 = unknown
5 = both inclusive and exclusive

Space between elements
0 = n.a.
1 = <1 cm
2 = approx. 1 cm
3 = >1 cm
4 = touching

Application
0 = none
1 = straight band
2 = nub
3 = curved band
4 = thick-end rim
5 = wing
6 = multiple appliqué bands
7 = unknown

Space between groups
Centimeters

Number of elements per group or row
Number

n.a. Not available.

Note: In the case of pottery fragments, a minimum of six elements on a single sherd was required for a "row" or "cluster" to be considered continuous. Any other sherd with less than six elements or with a visible margin next to incised elements was considered to be either of unknown continuity or a discontinuous group, respectively.

Elements 7, 8, and 11 are only present at site 93. Site 93 and Mocollope have more variation of element forms overall (9 are present at site 93 and 16 are present at Mocollope). Seven of the 9 elements present at site 93 are also present at Mocollope. However, all elements found at sites 112 and 114 are present at Mocollope. There are no elements exclusive to sites 112 and 114. Only 4 of the 18 possible elements are found at these two sites, but this may be because the sample size is very small.

Sites 112 and 114 are dominated by element 4 (incised triangles without tails). At site 112, element 4 accounts for 75 percent of the assemblage; at site 114, it accounts for 41.66 percent of the assemblage. Element 4 is present at Mocollope also but is less dominant (25.49 percent of surface and 25.4 percent of excavated). No one element form dominates the assemblage at Mocollope, as is the case at sites 112 and 114; elements 1 and 7 are well represented at Mocollope and absent at sites 112 and 114. Likewise, site 93 is not dominated by one particular form. Five of the 9 elements present have percentage values above 13 percent. Elements 8 through 18 are present at Mocollope but either absent or sparse at the three rural sites. This analysis indicates that individual rural communities do not necessarily mimic the element ditribution present at Mocollope. However, it cannot be said that element styles are wholy unique at Mocollope.

Pattern Variation

Pattern types found at the rural sites vary greatly from those at the city of Mocollope (table 8.3). For example, patterns 5, 6, 11, and 14 are only found at Mocollope. As with shape elements, the site 93 assemblage has more variability than either 112 or 114. Here, too, sample size is a factor.

At Mocollope, a greater percentage (7.84 percent surface-collected and 31.75 percent excavated) of pattern 10 (single row per appliqué band with multiple appliqué bands) is found. In the rural sites, pattern 10 is only found at site 93 and accounts for 10 percent of the variation as opposed to over 30 percent at Mocollope.

Patterns 10, 11, 12, 13, 14 are absent at sites 112 and 114, but are present at site 93. Finally, pattern type 1 (continuous rows of shapes) is much more dominant at the rural sites. It accounts for 62.5 percent of the assemblage at site 112, 41.67 percent at site 114, and 21.25 percent at site 93. It is somewhat less frequent at Mocollope, where it accounts for only 17.65 percent of the surface material and 15.87 percent of the excavated samples.

The foregoing data strongly suggest the presence of a distinct stylistic repertoire at the different sites. Two of the sites, 112 and 114, seem to share more stylistic attributes than either shares with site 93 or with the urban center of Mocollope (site 128). It should be noted that sites 112 and 114 are relatively close to each other and perhaps share a common ancestry from pre-Gallinazo times.

CONCLUSION

The preliminary data strongly suggest that individual rural communities in the Chicama Valley of Peru had their own particular pottery styles, and that when the population concentrated at Mocollope, new styles were created. This conclusion supports hypotheses 1 or 2, which postulate that urbanization encouraged the formation of new communities and networks within the city. H_1 suggests that new communities are promoted by new residential pattern and new economic specialization, as well as the process of estrangement from old systems of social integration and the loss of familiar surroundings. H_2 differs in that the above situation correlates with emerging differences in wealth. At this time there are no data to test this idea. Considering what is known of later Moche civilization, however, H_2 is a possibility that cannot be discounted. Further data collection and better stratigraphic control will be needed to differentiate H_1 from H_2. Nonetheless, the current data strongly suggest that individual styles were associated with the pre-urban communities.

Perhaps the community at site 93 was dominant in the part of Mocollope that has been investigated so far. There appears to be more continuity between the urban inhabitants at Mocollope and the rural community at site 93 than there is betweenthe communities at sites 112 and 114.

These results indicate that stylistic features do vary among the Gallinazo communities of the Chicama Valley. Also, it appears that when individuals migrated to the emerging urban center of Mocollope, stylistic behavior changed as well. The substantial literature linking style with group identity suggests that these changes relate to new social networks and new communities forming in the emerging urban environment. Furthermore, the observed similarities between the rural population at site 93 and the urban community at Mocollope suggest that some rural communities retained more of their indigenous structure than others.

Recently, archaeologists have begun to examine the phenomenon of ethnicity in the archaeological record. More important, we have begun to look critically at what material identities reflect of the living people who created them (Jones 1997). The study described here is an attempt to show how archaeological data can be brought to bear on the issue of group identity as a dynamic process, rather than a static process limited to space and time systematics. Likewise, urbanism is a process of dramatic importance as it created an environment wholly unique to the human experience.

ACKNOWLEDGMENTS

This research was funded by the Department of Anthropology at the University of California, Los Angeles, the UCLA Friends of Archaeology, and University Research Expeditions Program (UREP). My fieldwork has been greatly assisted by Thomas A. Wake, John H. Schroeder, Adella Valdez, and Flor Diaz. I thank Glenn Russell and Charles Stanish for introducing me to Peruvian archaeology. Wake, Schroeder, Stanish, Scott Pletka, Elizabeth Brumfiel, Amanda Cohen, Monica Smith, and the editorial staff at Smithsonian Books provided many useful suggestions on this chapter. I am grateful for all their help. I retain responsibility, however, for any shortcomings.

REFERENCES

Albarracin-Jordan, J.
1996   *Tiwanaku: Arqueología regional y dinámica segmentaria.* Editores Plural, La Paz.
Anders, M. B.
1977   Sistema de depositos en Pampa Grande, Lambayeque. *Revista el Museo Nacional* 43:243–280.
Attarian, C. J.
1996   *Plant Foods and Ceramic Production: What Can One Tell Us about the Other?* Master's thesis, Department of Anthropology, University of California, Los Angeles.
Barth, F., ed.
1969   *Ethnic Groups and Boundaries: The Social Organization of Culture Difference.* Little, Brown, Boston.
Bawden, G.
1982   Community Organization Reflected by the Household: A Study of Pre-Columbian Social Dynamics. *Journal of Field Archaeology* 9:165–181.
1995   The Structural Paradox: Moche Culture as Political Ideology. *Latin American Antiquity,* 6:255–273.
1996   *The Moche.* Blackwell, Cornwall.
Bennett, W. C.
1950   *The Gallinazo Group, Virú Valley, Peru.* Yale University Publications in Anthropology 43.

Billman, B. R.

1996   *The Evolution of Prehistoric Political Centralization in the Moche Valley, Peru.* Unpublished
        Ph.D. dissertation, University of California, Santa Barbara.

Blanton, R. E.

1976   Anthropological Studies of Cities. *Annual Review of Anthropology* 5:249–264.

Blanton, R. E., S. A. Kowalewski, G. M. Feinman, and L. M. Finsten

1993   *Ancient Mesoamerica: A Comparison of Change in Three Regions.* Cambridge University
        Press, New York.

Bonnier, E., and H. Bischof (editors)

1997   *Archaeologica Peruana 2,* pp. 63–89. Sociedad Arqueologica Peruano-Alemana, Mannheim.

Bradley, R.

1998   *The Significance of Monuments: On the Shaping of Human Experience in Neolithic and Bronze
        Age Europe.* Routledge, London.

Braun, D. P.

1991   Why Decorate a Pot? Midwestern Household Pottery, 200 B.C.–A.D. 600. *Journal of
        Anthropological Archaeology* 10:360–397.

Brennan, C. T.

1980   Cerro Arena: Early Cultural Complexity and Nucleation in North Coastal Peru. *Jour-
        nal of Field Archaeology* 7:1–22.

1982   Cerro Arena: Origins of the Urban Tradition on the Peruvian North Coast. *Current
        Anthropology* 23:247–254.

Brumfiel, E. M.

1994   Ethnic Groups and Political Development in Ancient Mexico. In *Factional Competition
        and Political Development in the New World,* edited by E. M. Brumfiel and J. W. Fox,
        pp. 89–102. Cambridge University Press, Cambridge.

Brumfiel, E. M., and T. K. Earle (editors)

1987   *Specialization, Exchange, and Complex Societies.* Cambridge University Press, Cambridge.

Carneiro, R.

1967   On the Relationship between Size of Population and Complexity of Social Organiza-
        tion. *Southwestern Journal of Archaeology* 23:234–243.

Childe, V. G.

1950   The Urban Revolution. *Town Planning Review* 21:3–17.

Claessen, H. J. M.

1984   The Internal Dynamics of the Early State. *Current Anthropology* 25:365–379.

Cohen, A.

1974a   *Urban Ethnicity.* Tavistock, New York.

1974b   Two-Dimensional Man; An Essay on the Anthropology of Power and Symbolism in
        Complex Society. University of California, Berkeley.

Collier, D.

1955   *Cultural Chronology and Change as Reflected in the Ceramics of the Virú Valley, Peru.* Natural
        History Museum Publication 779, Chicago.

Costin, C. L.

1991   Craft Specialization: Issues in Defining, Documenting, and Explaining the Organiza-
        tion of Production. *Archaeological Method and Theory* 3:1–56.

D'Altroy, T. N.

1992   *Provincial Power in the Inka Empire.* Smithsonian Institution Press, Washington.

Donnan, C. B.

1997   A Chimu-Inka Ceramic-Manufacturing Center from the North Coast of Peru. *Latin American Antiquity* 8:30–54.

Donnan, C. B., and G. A. Cock

1986   *The Pacatnamu Papers,* vol. 1. Museum of Cultural History, University of California, Los Angeles.

Donnan, C. B., and D. McClelland

1999   *Moche Fineline Painting, Its Evolution and Its Artists.* University of Southern California Fowler Museum of Cultural History, Los Angeles.

Downs, J. F., and H. K. Bleibtreu

1969   *Human Variation: An Introduction to Physical Anthropology.* Glenoe Press, New York.

Ericson, J. E., and C. W. Meighan

1984   Boundaries, Alliance and Exchange in California. In *Exploring the Limits: Frontiers and Boundaries in Prehistory,* edited by S. P. De Atley and F. J. Findlow, pp. 143–152. B.A.R., Oxford.

Feinman, G. M.

1999   Rethinking our Assumptions: Economic Specialization at the Household Scale in Ancient Ejutla, Oaxaca, Mexico. In *Pottery and People: A Dynamic Interaction,* edited by J. M. Skibo and G. M. Feinman, pp. 81–88. University of Utah Press, Salt Lake City.

Flannery, K. V.

1972   The Cultural Evolution of Civilization. *Annual Review of Ecological Systematics* 3:399–426.

Fox, R.

1977   *Urban Anthropology.* Prentice-Hall, Englewood Cliffs, N.J.

Gailey, C. W.

1987   Culture Wars: Resistance to State Formation. In *Power Relations and State Formation,* edited by C. W. Gailey and T. C. Patterson, pp. 35–56. American Anthropological Association, Washington D.C.

Grant, D. M., M. L. Oliver, and A. D. James

1996   African American: Social and Economic Bifurcation. In *Ethnic Los Angeles,* edited by R. Waldinger and M. Bozorgmehr, pp. 379–412. Russell Sage Foundation, New York.

Gregory, S.

1992   The Changing Significance of Race and Class in an African American Community. *American Ethnologist* 19:255–274.

Gumerman, G. J.

1991   *Subsistence and Complex Societies: Diet between Diverse Socio-Economic Groups at Pacatnamu, Peru.* Unpublished Ph.D. dissertation, University of California, Los Angeles.

Hardin, M. A.

1991   Sources of Ceramic Variability at Zuni Pueblo. In *Ceramic Ethnoarchaeology,* edited by W. A. Longacre, pp. 40–70. University of Arizona Press, Tucson.

Harris, M.

1977   *Cannibals and Kings: The Origins of Cultures.* Random House/Vintage, New York.

Hill, J. N.

1977   Systems Theory and the Explanation of Change. In *Explanation of Prehistoric Change*, edited by J. N. Hill, pp. 59–103. University of New Mexico Press, Albuquerque.

Hodder, I.

1979   Economic and Social Stress and Material Culture Patterning. *American Antiquity* 44:446–455.

1982   *Symbols in Action*. Cambridge University Press, Cambridge.

Johnson, A. W., and T. Earle

1987   *The Evolution of Human Societies: From Foraging Group to Agrarian State*. Stanford University Press, Stanford.

Jones, S.

1997   *The Archaeology of Ethnicity*. Routledge, London.

Kolata, A.

1986   The Agricultural Foundations of the Tiwanaku State: A View from the Heartland. *American Antiquity* 51:748–762.

1993   *Tiwanaku: Portrait of an Andean Civilization*. Blackwell, Cambridge.

Kuper, H.

1972   The Language of Sites in the Politics of Space. *American Anthropologist* 74:411–425.

Lechtman, H.

1997   Copper Artifacts from Moche Burials at Pacatnamu. In *The Pacatnamu Papers,* vol. 2, edited by C. B. Donnan and G. A. Cock, pp. 251–254. University of California Fowler Museum of Cultural History, Los Angeles.

Leonard, B., and G. S. Russell

1996   The Politics of Settlement in the Lower Chicama Valley, North Coast of Peru. Paper presented at the 61st Meeting of the Society for American Archaeology, New Orleans, La.

Lightfoot, K. G., and A. Martinez

1995   Frontiers and Boundaries in Archaeological Perspective. *Annual Review of Anthropology* 24:471–492.

Low, S. M.

1996   The Anthropology of Cities: Imagining and Theorizing the City. *Annual Review of Anthropology* 25:383–409.

Murra, J.

1975   *Formaciones economicas y politicas del mundo andino*. Instituto de Estudios Peruanos, Lima.

1980 [1956] *The Economic Organization of the Inka State*. JAI Press, Greenwich, Conn.

Netherly, P.

1977   *Local Level Lords on the North Coast of Peru*. Ph.D. dissertation, Department of Anthropology, Cornell University. University Microfilms International, Ann Arbor.

Netting, R.

1968   *Hill Farmers of Nigeria: Cultural Ecology of the Kofyar of the Jos Plateau*. University of Washington Press, Seattle.

1977   *Cultural Ecology*. Cummings, Menlo Park.

Park, R. B.

1974 [1925]   *The City.* Chicago University Press, Chicago.

Plog, S.

1980   *Stylistic Variation in Prehistoric Ceramics: Design Analysis in the American Southwest.* Cambridge University Press, Cambridge.

Rappaport, R.

1967   *Pigs for the Ancestors.* Yale University Press, New Haven.

Rice, P. M.

1987   *Pottery Analysis: A Sourcebook.* University of Chicago Press, Chicago.

Roosens, E. E.

1989   *Creating Ethnicity: The Process of Ethnogenesis.* Sage, London.

Rowe, J.

1946   Inca Culture at the Time of the Spanish Conquest. In *Handbook of South American Indians,* 2, edited by J. Steward, pp. 183–330. Smithsonian Institution, Washington, D.C.

Russell, G. S., B. L. Leonard, and J. B. Rosario

1994   Producción alfarera en gran escala en el valle Chicama, Peru: El taller de cerro mayal. In *Producción prehispánica céramica en los Andes,* edited by I. Shimada, pp. 201–227. La Catolica University, Lima.

Sackett, J. R.

1982   Approaches to Style in Lithic Archaeology. *Journal of Anthropological Archaeology* 1:59–112.

1985   Style and Ethnicity in the Kalahari: A Reply to Wiessner. *American Antiquity* 50:154–166.

1990   Style and Ethnicity in Archaeology: The Case for Isocrestism. In *The Uses of Style Archaeology,* edited M. Conkey and C. Hastorf, pp. 32–43. Cambridge University Press, Cambridge.

Sanders, W. T.

1965   *The Cultural Ecology of the Teotihuacan Valley.* Department of Sociology and Anthropology, Pennsylvania State University, Pittsburgh.

Sanders, W. T., J. R. Parsons, and R. S. Santley

1979   *The Basin of Mexico: Ecological Processes in the Evolution of a Civilization.* Academic Press, New York.

Service, E.

1977   Classical and Modern Theories of the Origin of Government. In *Origins of the State,* edited by R. Cohen and E. Service, pp. 21–34. ISHI, Philadelphia.

Shimada, I.

1994a   Los modelos de la organizacion sociopolitica de la cultura Moche. In *Moche: Propuestas y perspectivas,* 79, edited by S. Uceda and E. Mujica, pp. 359–387. Travaux de l'nstitut d'Etudes Andines, Lima.

1994b   *Pampa Grande and the Mochica Culture.* University of Texas Press, Austin.

1997   Organizational Significance of Marked Bricks and Associated Construction Features on the North Peruvian Coast. In *Archaeologica Peruana 2,* edited by E. Bonnier and H. Bischof, pp. 63–89. Sociedad Arqueologica Peruano-Alemana, Mannheim.

Shimada, I., and A. Maguina

1994   Nueva vision sobre la cultura Gallinazo y su relacion con la cultura Moche. In *Moche: Propuestas y perspectivas,* 79, edited by S. Uceda and E. Mujica, pp. 31–58. Travaux de L'Institut Français d'Etudes Andines, Lima.

Silverman, H.

1988   Cahuachi: Non-Urban Cultural Complexity on the South Coast of Peru. *Journal of Field Archaeology* 15:403–430.

Sinopoli, C. M.

1988   The Organization of Craft Production at Vijayanagara, South India. *American Anthropologist* 90:580–597.

Spencer, C. S.

1990   On the Tempo and Mode of State Formation: Neoevolutionism Reconsidered. *Journal of Anthropological Archaeology* 9:1–30.

Stanish, C.

1989   Household Archaeology: Testing Models of Zonal Complementarity in the South Central Andes. *American Anthropologist* 91:7–24.

1997   Nonmarket Imperialism in the Prehispanic Americas: The Inka Occupation of the Titicaca Basin. *Latin American Antiquity* 8:195–216.

Sterner, J.

1989   Who Is Signaling Whom? Ceramic Style, Ethnicity and Taphonomy among the Sirak Bulahay. *Antiquity* 63:451–459.

Strong, W. D., and C. Evans Jr.

1952   *Cultural Stratigraphy in the Virú Valley, Northern Peru.* Columbia University Press, New York.

Tilley, C.

1994   *Phenomenology of Landscapes: Places, Paths, and Monuments.* Oxford University Press, Oxford.

Uceda, S., E. Mujica, and R. Morales (editors)

1997   *Investigaciones en la Huaca de la Luna 1995.* Universidad Nacional de la Libertat, Trujillo.

van der Leeuw, S. E.

1991   Variation, Variability, and Explanation in Pottery Studies. In *Ceramic Ethnoarchaeology,* edited by W. A. Longacre, pp. 11–39. University of Arizona Press, Tucson.

Washburn, D. K.

1977   *A Symmetry Analysis of Upper Gila Area Ceramic Design.* Peabody Museum of Archaeology and Ethnology, Harvard University, Cambridge.

n.d.   Symmetry Analysis of Ica Valley Ceramics: Insights into Ica-Inca Interactions. MS on file with the author.

Wheat, J. B., J. C. Gifford, and W. W. Wasley

1958   Ceramic Variety, Type Cluster, and Ceramic System in Southwestern Pottery Analysis. *American Antiquity* 24:34–47.

Wiessner, P.

1983   Style and Social Information in Kalahari San Projectile Points. *American Antiquity* 48:253–276.

1984   Reconsidering the Behavioral Basis for Style: A Case Study among the Kalahari San. *Journal of Anthropological Archaeology* 3:190–234.

1990   Is There Unity in Style? In *The Uses of Style Archaeology*, edited by M. Conkey and C. Hastorf, pp. 105–112. Cambridge University Press, Cambridge.

Wilson, D. J.

1988   *Prehispanic Settlement Patterns in the Lower Santa Valley, North Coast of Peru: A Regional Perspective on the Origins and Development of Complex Society.* Smithsonian Institution Press, Washington D.C.

Wobst, H. M.

1977   Stylistic Behavior and Information Exchange. In *For the Director: Research Essays in Honor of James B. Griffen,* edited by C. E. Cleland, pp. 317–342. Museum of Anthropology, University of Michigan Anthropological Papers No. 61, Ann Arbor.

Wolf, E. R.

1982   *Europe and the People without History.* University of California Press, Los Angeles.

Wright, H. T.

1977   Recent Research on the Origin of the State. *Annual Review of Anthropology* 6:379–397.

1986   The Evolution of Civilizations. In *American Archaeology Past and Future,* edited by D. J. Meltzer, D. D. Fowler, and J. A. Sabloff, pp. 323–365. Society for American Archaeology, Washington D.C.

NINE

The Moral Community

Maya Settlement Transformation at Piedras Negras, Guatemala

At some level, city-making always entails an act of will on the part of a leader or collectivity.

(KOSTOFF 1991:33)

STEPHEN D. HOUSTON,
HÉCTOR ESCOBEDO,
MARK CHILD,
CHARLES GOLDEN,
AND RENÉ MUÑOZ

The life span of a city encompasses three modes of change. The first is *pace of change,* which refers to whether a city expanded or contracted at a fast, slow, or steady clip in relation to other settlements of the time. The second is *scale of change,* meaning the nature of jumps from village to city, or, in periods of societal collapse, from city to almost no settlement. And the third is *direction of change,* which might range from robust growth to deterioration, or even the maintenance of some balance or cyclic equilibrium between the two. From an understanding of these dimensions comes a cogent portrait of a city in flux.

But these are not the only dimensions worth considering. Equally important are *quantity,* the absolute numbers attached to pace, scale, and direction (how much area is involved, how many buildings, how much time?), and *palaeodemography,* the

Figure 9.1. Map of region around Piedras Negras (courtesy Department of Geography, Brigham Young University).

connection, still somewhat tenuous, between the settlements studied by archaeologists and the actual people who created and lived in such cities. At present, few archaeologists would rely on settlement evidence to determine anything more than general tendencies in population growth or decline. No one doubts, for example, the prodigious growth of Maya cities during the Late Classic period (A.D. 600–800), but the total number of people estimated for this time and place fluctuates by the millions, depending on the researcher (Turner 1990:table 15.1). Moreover, pace, scale, direction, quantity, and demography are only the beginning. Even if they can be measured with confidence, what do such changes mean, and what is their separate or collective explanation?

A useful place to evaluate these questions is the Classic Maya city of Piedras Negras, a city on the banks of the Usumacinta River, about halfway between the Guatemalan highlands and the Gulf coast (figure 9.1). Between 1997 and 2000, a joint archaeological project of the Brigham Young University and the Universidad del Valle examined the chronology, character, and history of this city, building in no small part on extensive work by the University of Pennsylvania in the 1930s (Holley 1983; Houston, Escobedo, Child et al. 1998; Houston, Escobedo, Forsyth et al. 1998; Houston, Escobedo, Hardin et al. 1999; Houston, Escobedo, Terry et al. 2000; Houston et al. 2000; Satterthwaite 1943). This project included special-ists of diverse expertise, who brought to it a richness of viewpoint that offers un-usual opportunities for synthesis and, on occasion, divergent interpretation. In this essay we grapple with new data from this site as a preliminary step in explaining urban process at an important pre-Columbian city.

Piedras Negras offers unusual richness in another sense, through the fine-grained historical chronology worked out some 30 years ago by Tatiana Proskouriakoff (1960), who used evidence from Piedras Negras to pioneer a historical approach to Maya archaeology. Surprisingly, the historical content of inscriptions at Piedras Negras has proved a mixed blessing. How, for example, are we to distinguish be-tween the role of specific rulers as decisive agents of urban change and the pres-ence of broad, almost unconscious processes? The tendency in many Maya stud-ies has been to focus on a historical narrative of city development and on the role of kings, especially in accounts of growth in monumental urban cores (Sharer, Fash et al. 1999:table 10.1). Structures and building programs are correlated, often quite persuasively, with particular rulers, and an account crafted of monumental growth that follows the imperatives and decisions of a royal court. It is likely that schol-ars of Marxist bent would find such explanations irrelevant or misleading in their disregard for modes of production or economic forces, the "real" shapers of cities and ambient landscapes (Southall 1998:12–13). One does not need to be an ardent Marxian—as the majority of those studying the city from a theoretical perspective appear to be (e.g., Castells 1977; Gottdeiner 1985; Southall 1998)—to see that a balance must be sought, in the same way that anthropology as a whole grapples continually with the interplay of individual and society. In this essay we attempt to balance history, in the sense of decisions and actions made by known or sus-pected agents, with settlement transformation, as registered in pace, scale, direc-tion, quantity, and demography, and as linked ultimately to larger causes.

In our opinion, the beginnings of Piedras Negras and many other Maya cities can be interpreted as a historical act. Individuals of unusual charisma, persuasion, and authority caused some cities to come into existence through the sponsorship and promotion of migration and new settlement, a process that seems common throughout Mesoamerica, and probably elsewhere as well (e.g., Fowler 1989:49). For example, Igor Kopytoff (1987, 1999:88), working with African materials, has described the birth of new polities along "internal frontiers," as the political offspring of "more complex polities" that contributed models for political practice and the principal actors who harnessed and steered such systems. This model is fully consistent with our provisional view of the data. It also accords with what is now known of Maya kingship and its reliance on rituals of place, including fire ceremonies and acts of dedication, and the housing and maintenance of tutelary deities (Houston and Stuart 1996; Stuart 1998). On arrival at its new seat, a dynasty constructed monumental architecture not only as a symbolic projection of authority, but as a key means of organizing society around a royal court and of entrenching such beliefs and practices in fixed spaces. At Piedras Negras, complex social arrangements—in the sense of a preexisting dynasty, royal court, and their political economy—were a necessary condition for population movement from a source location, and massive and extensive buildings projects served to confirm and consolidate social hierarchies within new settlement. Without them, the city and its organizational premises could not survive.

This process might be termed a "royal strategy," a deliberate set of linked policies, culturally conditioned and historically variable, that were systematically applied by monarchs to their subjects, allies, and enemies.[1] Such strategies involved many inducements, shaped into an instrumentality that weighed and expressed all the tools at a ruler's disposal, including the exertion of coercive force (Smith and Berdan 1996:8). We detect a royal strategy in the origins of Piedras Negras and its subsequent functioning as a dynastic center. In contrast, the collapse of Piedras Negras represents a dramatic unraveling of strategy and the rapid decentralization of decision making. Whatever strategies were in place could not contain or ameliorate the disaster. We assert that the moral authority of the Maya "holy lord" operated initially as the stabilizing element and, later, through its attenuation, as an actively expulsive force. For the Classic Maya of Piedras Negras, moral authority functioned as a form of social "enchantment" that, when broken, could not heal or reconstitute itself; the lord as mediator of factions could no longer persuade and cajole. In such a potentially anarchic milieu, a political economy would neither flourish nor find sufficient stability to operate. For Mesoamerica and the Maya region, the widespread definition of "cities" as "place(s) of residences for the native lord" (Marcus 1983:226, 239), regardless of population, suggests that it is the central figure of the king that makes cities understandable in growth and decline. At present, there is not a single, attested term in Maya hieroglyphic inscriptions for cities per se or for the polities that heavily concern Mayanists. The ruler and his titles predominate instead.[2]

PIEDRAS NEGRAS AS PRIMATE
CENTER AND AS PROBLEM

Piedras Negras is a city of at least 80 hectares in its epicenter and close to 300 hectares in its supporting zone, with a ratio of approximately 1:3 between built-up areas (including platforms) in dense settlement at the core and the more amply spaced mound groups of the periphery (Webster and Kirker 1997:figs. 1–2).[3] If roofed area were the basis of comparison, then the ratio between center and periphery would be closer to 1:1, suggesting, perhaps, some degree of functional complementarity between these two broad sectors of settlement. Conceivably, there existed twin seats of occupation for particular families, households, or other collective units of production and consumption, although, as David Webster (personal communication 1999) has pointed out to us, it may be that the close proximity of such settlements to the center would make such twin residences unlikely. Most peripheral sites lie well within the distances (ca. 2–4 kilometers) covered daily by modern peasants in Guatemala.

The peripheral area is also notable in that it appears to contain two kinds of settlement cluster (Webster et al. 1998; Webster and Kovak 1998). One is more or less regularly spaced along the river, probably as part of a pattern determined by year-round access to water and by control over circa 32 hectares of surrounding land. The other kind occupies ravines that contain pockets of deeper soil. These groups skirt routes that lead into Piedras Negras but are so far from water sources as to seem impractical as year-round settlements. Possibly they were intermittently occupied during parts of the planting cycle or when water flowed locally for impoundment or collection during the rainy season (David Webster, personal communication 1999). The presence of a possible drain in outlying settlements strongly hints at wet-season occupation (e.g., Webster and Kirker 1997:fig. 90).

The city itself holds, for the Usumacinta River drainage, an unusually large and massive collection of platforms, terraces, pyramids, ballcourts, sweatbaths, house mounds, and palaces. There seems little doubt that it was a primate center for the zone. Its historical subsidiaries, such as El Porvenir and El Cayo (Mathews and Aliphat Fernández 1998:fig. 2), the seat of a subordinate noble known as a *sajal,* were smaller than Piedras Negras, especially in the case of El Porvenir, with none of the same density of settlement or complexity and variety of building type. In essence, they are little more than enlarged patio groups.[4] Accordingly, Piedras Negras fulfilled unique functions that do not seem have been duplicated at nonroyal centers nearby. Vaulted space, the areas covered by masonry roofs, differs dramati-

Stephen Houston, Héctor Escobedo, Mark Child, Charles Golden, and René Muñoz

cally: at El Cayo such areas amount to about 200 square meters (this is a rough estimate and likely to be generous, at least to judge from plans in the excavation report of the site); at Piedras Negras at least 2,125 square meters out of a total of 13,129 square meters of usable, covered floor, with the majority (about 65 percent) in the visible architecture of the "Acropolis" or royal palace (table 9.1).

In our view, the population of the city is almost impossible to reconstruct with any degree of accuracy. Nonetheless, there are some clues that indicate general patterns. The free-standing buildings at the site core (about 386, of all types) are mostly small house mounds, and we infer from extensive test-pitting that Piedras Negras did not possess many "hidden house mounds" that inflate demographic estimates at other sites (Johnston 1994; however, visible mound groups without doubt had subsurface extensions that are no longer evident in ground survey). From this, even a generous estimate of five persons per building would place the number of occupants during the height of occupation (late Yaxche, early Chacalhaaz periods) at considerably less than 3,000 people and probably closer to 2,000. Another approach would target the dead and then move to the living. This can be done by examining a neighborhood that has been thoroughly excavated, the "U-sector." An estimate of 60 burials for this area of three mound groups is not unreasonable (Houston et al. 2000). Multiplied by the total number of mound groups within the epicenter—so defined as the area of dense settlement between a southern complex known as "Yax Nit" and the peripheries of the Northwest Group Court—we reach a total of about 5,000 bodies (20 burials per mound group × 250 groups; note that the sum of known burials would comprehend only 2.4 percent of this statistical universe). These burials would issue from a span of roughly A.D. 400–800, with most deriving from the final two centuries, since early burials at Piedras Negras are rare. In our opinion, this number cannot possibly represent the full number of individuals who lived at Piedras Negras, although we recognize the extreme difficulty of establishing the ratio of burials to total population. Nonetheless, the numbers do seem consistent with relatively low numbers of people in the city. Although undependable in any exact sense, these demographic figures are unlikely to be off by any great order of magnitude.[5]

Where did these people come from? During the full Late Classic period, the demographic peak in most zones of the Maya lowlands (Turner 1990:fig. 15.1), the population might have resulted from natural, internal increase but for one characteristic of pre-industrial settlements: these cities kill, albeit selectively. Comparative studies (Storey 1992:35–42) demonstrate that urban zones in pre-industrial so-

Table 9.1
Covered Floor Space at Piedras Negras

Structure Type	Stone Vault Usable Floor (m²)	Stone Vault (%)	Thatch Vault Usable Floor (m²)	Thatch Vault (%)	Total Usable Floor (m²)	Total Vault (%)	Total Number of Buildings	Total Number of Mound Groups
Ball court	0.00	0.0	238.00	2.0	238.00	1.5	4	0
Palace	1,590.75	75.0	96.00	1.0	1,686.75	11	17	4
Sweatbath	121.25	6.0	726.25	5.0	847.50	5.5	8	2
Temple	294.25	14.0	104.00	1.0	398.25	2.5	13	4
Unclassified	118.75	5.0	11,964.75	91.0	12,083.50	79.5	344	25
Totals	2,125.00	100	13,129.00	100	15,254.00	100	386	35
Quadrant number								
B	0.00	0.0	53.75	0.5	53.75	0.5	3	0
C	0.00	0.0	1,086.75	8.0	1,086.75	7.0	39	3
D	0.00	0.0	133.75	1.0	133.75	1.0	6	0
E	0.00	0.0	79.50	0.5	79.50	0.5	2	0
F	32.00	1.5	487.25	4.0	519.25	3.5	13	2
G	0.00	0.0	560.75	4.0	560.75	3.5	19	1
H	0.00	0.0	228.75	2.0	228.75	1.5	8	1
J	1,373.25	65.0	435.75	3.0	1,809.00	12.0	25	4
K	29.00	1.0	1,551.75	12.0	1,580.75	10.0	43	4
L	0.00	0.0	82.75	0.5	82.75	0.5	2	0
N	16.75	1.0	605.00	5.0	621.75	4.0	18	1
O	172.25	8.0	1,218.50	9.0	1,390.75	9.0	30	3
P	7.25	0.5	874.75	7.0	882.00	6.0	25	2
Q	0.00	0.0	93.75	0.5	93.75	0.5	5	1
R	299.25	14.0	1,293.00	10.0	1,592.25	10.5	34	4
S	153.75	7.0	2,109.00	16.0	2,262.75	15.0	45	2
T	0.00	0.0	232.00	2.0	232.00	1.5	3	1
U	41.50	2.0	796.75	6.0	838.25	5.5	27	2
V	0.00	0.0	950.75	7.0	950.75	6.0	29	3
W	0.00	0.0	127.75	1.0	127.75	1.0	3	0
Z	0.00	0.0	127.00	1.0	127.00	1.0	7	1
Total	2,125.00	100	13,129.00	100	15,254.00	100	386	35

cieties are not so much demographic nurseries as greedy consumers of human life, especially of new migrants in unsteady urban footholds (David Webster, personal communication 1999; Sharlin 1978).[6] For net growth, they rely heavily on immigration from rural zones. In no small part, this feature of urban existence stems from poor sanitation, indifferent access to food, inadequate medicine, contaminated water supplies, and the simple fact that crowding spreads disease. Piedras Negras is no exception. According to preliminary research (Andrew Scherer, personal communication 1999), most skeletal remains at the site (67 examined thus far) show persistent levels of stress, including evidence of periostitis and linear enamel hypoplasias, both conceivably the result of infections or disease, although other factors may have contributed as well. These stresses hit children with special force (Andrew Scherer, personal communication 2000). Even today, the waters of the Usumacinta are highly polluted and, as our own unpleasant experience attests, can lead rapidly to giardiasis and other intestinal diseases. In two cases, cellulitis, a severe infection afflicting the legs of bathers, could only be combated with intravenous antibiotics. During the Classic period, the epidemiological condition of the zone could scarcely have been much better, since the effluent of the entire Pasión, Salinas, and Usumacinta drainages washed by dense settlement on its way toward Piedras Negras and beyond. In short, the city was not a healthy place, and explanations must be sought for its expansion and for why people found it attractive to begin with.[7]

EARLY PIEDRAS NEGRAS

During the Preclassic and Protoclassic periods, Piedras Negras was, on present evidence, a small village or set of sequent villages, with the beginnings of monumental architecture but of an unprepossessing sort. People probably came to the area for practical reasons. A large outcrop of chert attracted settlement (Hruby 1998:375), along with other appealing features, including a beach of thick sand for parking canoes during the dry season and, most important, a seasonally flooded valley (the Spanish word *arroyo* captures its modest size) with exceptionally rich soil (Hardin et al. 1998:385); in the rainy season of 2000, the valley was inundated for most of its length, to a depth of 50 centimeters to a meter. Ceramics of Middle Preclassic date (ca. 600–400 B.C.) have been found in a few locations, but mostly in lenses directly on bedrock in the South Group Court and adjacent areas. These are just above the beach and valley, equidistant from both. Ceramic types of this period include Guitarra Incised, Pital Cream, and Juventud Red, material also found at the center of El Cayo, a Late Classic political subsidiary of Piedras Negras (Lee and Hayden 1988:27–31). Samples of this material at other sites, such as Nakbe, are vastly larger, but there already appear to be some local emphases, including unusually thick ceramics and the absence of certain forms that are common in the northern Petén, where Nakbe and other great sites of this period lie (Forsyth 1993:34–35; Forsyth, personal communication 1999; Forsyth and Hruby 1997; Hansen 1998:56). Excavations in 2000 revealed the first public architecture from this time, consisting of a platform leveled from bedrock (R-32) and faced with squarish stones, along with a 1-meter-high building with finely polished stucco floors (R-3-3rd). The descriptive "public," rather than "monumental," precisely fits the structure, for the amount of labor involved would have been relatively small. It seems likely that most of the site resembled small settlements found throughout northern Guatemala today, with perishable buildings made of thatch and pole, focused on one or two public structures. Constant sweeping down to bedrock reduced muddiness during the rainy season. At some point there may have been an attempt to produce a broader, more level area, hence the layer of Middle Preclassic material directly above bedrock and the Middle Preclassic building, R-3-3rd. For the first time, the people of Piedras Negras began the process of physically elevating their community, a process that would culminate a millennium later in the great mass of the Acropolis.

The Late Preclassic is more of a puzzle. In a few deposits, such as those in the South Group Court (Operation 4), there may be slight evidence of ceramics at the transition between Middle and Late Preclassic periods (Donald Forsyth, personal communication, 1999). The other material, again clustering in the South Group Court, with a single sherd of Laguna Verde Incised from the Acropolis, is not easily dated within the chronological parameters of this period (ca. 400 B.C. to A.D. 100). The presence of Protoclassic ceramics mixed with Late Preclassic shows an occupation toward the end of this period, as it approaches what has been described by some scholars as Protoclassic 1 (Brady et al. 1998:33); two sherds, one under Pyramid O-13, the other from Pyramid R-3, have Preclassic, waxy finishes but Early Classic forms. Two impressions come to mind so far: that the Late Preclassic occupation is comparable in size to the small Middle Preclassic presence; and that the chronology accords not with a continuous population at Piedras Negras, but with episodic occupation, one clustering temporally at the end of the Middle Preclassic period, the other at the end of the Late Preclassic. However, the combination

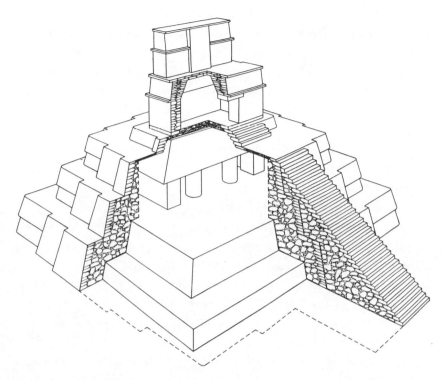

Figure 9.2. Cross section through Early Classic and Preclassic buildings and platforms, Pyramid R-3 and Platform R-32 (drawing: Mark Child).

of uncertain and deeply buried samples and the inherently small size of Piedras Negras at this time may point to the alternative of continuous, low-level settlement. Survey information shows feeble-to-absent occupation throughout the zone. El Porvenir, a peripheral site near another seasonally flooded ravine to the north, contains a small quantity of Late Preclassic ceramics (Webster and Kirker 1997:190), although none seem to occur at El Cayo (Lee and Hayden 1988:71). Reconnaissance in 1998 also recovered a few Late Preclassic ceramics from the site of La Pasadita, some 25 kilometers to the south of Piedras Negras.

The Preclassic occupants of Piedras Negras continued the patterns established during the Middle Preclassic (figure 9.2). Excavations by Mark Child and Jessica Child under Pyramid R-3 and Platform R-32 showed two earlier phases of construction, R-3-2nd and R-3-3rd. The earlier building and platform have been described above. The second, Late Preclassic structure was raised another 2 meters, for a height of 3 meters in total. Probings within the structure failed to reveal a tomb or other special deposit; hence it appears unlikely that this elevated building was a mortuary feature. The uses of these buildings are still unclear, but they unquestionably show the need at Middle and Late Preclassic Piedras Negras for public spaces, as well as evidence of the organizational wherewithal to plan and build them. To judge from the ceramics, the structures seem also to have been built in fairly close sequence, in a burst of activity unparalleled in other parts of the middle Usumacinta. It is telling that the Early Classic building on top is separated by centuries from the Preclassic structures underneath.

Thus the Preclassic shows two related patterns. The Middle Preclassic exhibits the following: *pace,* slow and episodic, with fitful purchase on the landscape; *scale,* small; *direction,* maintenance at best; *quantity,* low but generally uncertain; *palaeodemography,* village society, likely consisting of several related families. The Maya of Piedras Negras had begun to undertake modest, public building programs, exemplified by the open space of South Group Court. The court doubtless served as a focus for community activities, showing a formality that bespeaks a more centrally organized society. Nonetheless, it seems unlikely that this community was ruled by anyone like the kings of the Classic period. The Late Preclassic displays essentially the same configuration.

The Early Classic period (ca. A.D. 250–550) is different. Table 9.2 lists a minimum of find-spots around the site, pending further ceramic evaluation of results from the 2000 (and final) field season. The so-called Tzakol 2 period (ca. A.D. 350–450) is weakly represented in two operations, Structure S-11 (PN15A-3-5) and the R-13 sweatbath (PN18A-11-4).[8] These finds consist of deep, orange-painted polychromes with interior and exterior decoration. They present a great paradox for the archaeologist, in that, despite what appear to be population shifts, Piedras Negras emerges from the Preclassic with a distinctively local style, including dishes with moderate angles and basal flanges. These later develop into what had been termed Dos Arroyos polychrome, a type of the central Petén and sites such as Tikal and Uaxactun, into a local variant, Virgilio polychrome. But the fact remains that Piedras Negras continues its earlier pattern of a small village, only to change radically by the end of the Early Classic, over a time that we estimate to be no more than 100 years in length and probably rather less than that, embracing a phase that began about A.D. 400–450. Rather than a pattern of gradual growth—the dominant model in Maya studies, in our instance the "Lubaantun"/"Palenque" pattern with largely Late Classic occupation as adumbrated by Hammond (e.g., Hammond 1991:fig. 11.3)—we see far more sudden shifts.

Table 9.2
Lots with Early Classic Material: A Minimal List

Lot	Material	Lot	Material
5B-6-3 [P-7 Sweatbath]	Eroded fragmentary Naba	11F-3-4 [Court 3, Acropolis]	Naba
5B-9-9 [P-7 Sweatbath]	Possible Naba or Balche	12G-2B-5 [under West Group Plaza]	Naba
5B-12-9 [P-7 Sweatbath]	Naba	15A-3-4 [S-11]	Naba
11A-2-4 [Court 3, Acropolis]	Naba	15A-3-5 [S-11]	Naba
11A-3-4 [Court 3, Acropolis]	Naba	5D-5-4 [S-8]	Undatable? (1 possible Balanza fragment)
11A-4-4 [Court 3, Acropolis]	Naba		
11A-5-3 [Court 3, Acropolis]	Naba	18A-1-4 [R-13 Sweatbath]	Naba
11A-5-4 [Court 3, Acropolis]	Naba	18A-6-4 [R-13 Sweatbath]	Naba or Balche
11A-5-5 [Court 3, Acropolis]	Naba	18A-11-4 [R-13 Sweatbath]	Early Naba?
11A-6-3 [Court 3, Acropolis]	Naba	19C1-1 [near K-23]	Late Naba or Balche
11A-6-4 [Court 3, Acropolis]	Naba	26A-8-5 (Balche) [F-2]	Naba or Balche, all brown monochromes
11A-7-2 [Court 3, Acropolis]	Naba		
11A-9-4 [Court 3, Acropolis]	Naba	34A-1-4, -1-5 [J-7 Terrace]	Naba
11A-11-2 [Court 3, Acropolis]	Naba	34A-3-5 – [J-7 Terrace]	Late Naba, Balche or mixed
11A-12-2 [Court 3, Acropolis]	Naba		
11E-1-2 [Court 3, Acropolis]	Naba, mixed with Yaxche	34A-11-3 [J-7 Terrace]	34A-7-1 is possible Naba
		34A-11-3 [J-7 Terrace]	Naba
11E-2-2 [Court 3, Acropolis]	Naba, mixed with Yaxche and Chacalhaaz	RS 6A-2 [BS 23]	Naba
		RS 6A-20 [BS 23]	Naba
11F-1-5 [Court 3, Acropolis]	Naba		
11F-1-7 [Court 3, Acropolis]	Naba		
11F-1-8 [Court 3, Acropolis]	Naba		
11F-1-9 [Court 3, Acropolis]	Naba		
11F-2-4 [Court 3, Acropolis]	Naba		
11F-2-5 [Court 3 Acropolis]	Naba		

The Early Classic ("Naba") period at Piedras Negras (Holley 1983:78) represents a veritable explosion of population and its more direct measures, such as building. Before this time, Piedras Negras had rather modest masonry architecture; now, structures appear in many parts of the site, at a monumental scale. Natural hillsides are concealed behind terraces, as on the Acropolis, near three Late Classic sweatbaths (Structures J-17, N-1, and O-4), below a Late Classic cemetery (near R-20), and underneath a group that housed, it seems, a family of subroyal elite (Structures C10–C14, to the northeast of the Northwest Group Plaza). Masonry is highly distinctive, with hard, dressed stone of rectangular shape and a propensity for inclusion in steeply sloping, but not vertical, walls. Plastering is dense and used to patch irregular surfaces; on floors, the plaster achieves a deep luster from burnishing. The leveling impulse applies to large parts of the South Group Court, Court 3 of the Acropolis, and much of the West Group Court, where excavations reveal a series of destroyed platforms disposed into patio arrangements (Garrido 1998:fig. 5). The destruction is not fully explained, since it may be related to acts of destructive warfare (Houston et al. 2000). In any case, the damage takes place at the end of the Early Classic period. What attracts our interest is the short period involved in constructing these platforms, for they exhibit only one major and a few minor modifications, in buildings constructed on or close to bedrock. Subsequent changes in layout are small, occurring in modified facades and patio outlines, and a reoriented building with so-called apron molding, a Z-shaped outline that produces a play of shadow and creates the illusion of a floating platform on which the Maya placed perishable buildings.

More modest structures also contain deposits, although in surprisingly limited quantities. The University Museum documented Early Classic ceramics in Structures V-1 and Q-1 (Holley 1983:80), and the current project has augmented these with finds within Structures F-2, K-23, S-8, and S-11. Most lie close to larger buildings of known Early Classic date. The fact that Piedras Negras has now had archaeological test-pits in or near most mound groups suggests strongly that this sample expresses a paradox: the presence of large-scale early constructions, but little evidence of ancillary settlement. Early Classic materials are found in the periphery of Piedras Negras, often as building fill (Amy Kovak, personal communication 1999), yet only in small numbers. It seems, then, that Piedras Negras not only came into existence as a monumental center within a short period of time, circa A.D. 400–450, but that it flourished initially with only modest amounts of surrounding settlement, in a strong pattern of "urbanization" (Huot et al. 1990:131).

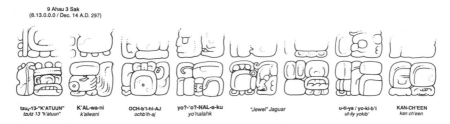

tzu$_r$-13-"K'ATUUN"   K'AL-wa-ni   OCH-b'i-hi-AJ   yo?-'o?-NAL-a-ku   *"Jewel" Jaguar*   u-ti-ya / yo-ki-b'i   KAN-CH'EEN
tzutz 13 'k'atuun"   *k'alwani*   *ochb'ih-aj*   *yo'nalahk*   *ut-iiy yokib'*   *kan ch'een*

Figure 9.3. Early Classic ruler, Altar 1, Piedras Negras (drawing: Stephen Houston).

If the test pits in the periphery can be taken at face value, the city scape of Piedras Negras coalesced *before* the full-bore occupation of its surrounding landscape, which consisted of scattered patio groups and house mounds. Only during the first phase of the Late Classic period, beginning about A.D. 600, did the population burst across this rural landscape, in a second phase of urban transformation.

Such results require further study, for there is a chance that sampling errors lurk behind them. There may have been considerable attrition of earlier remains, now surviving only as patches of sherd scatter. The results also raise perplexing historical questions. The first attested personage at Piedras Negras appears at A.D. 297, albeit anachronistically, on a much later monument labeled Altar 1 (figure 9.3). This date, well before the onset of monumental construction at Piedras Negras, poses a problem because it fails to accord with ceramic chronology and the rapid urbanization we perceive between A.D. 400 and 450. Altar 1 carries a final date of precisely one *baktun* (a cycle of 440 years) later, 9.13.0.0.0, hinting at some forced historical contrivance. An earlier mythological date, involving hearths and heavenly locales, also mentions, in a passage of unlikely historicity, an entity using the royal title of Piedras Negras. Yet, research at other sites, including Copan and Palenque, indicates that some of these backward-looking allusions must be taken seriously, particularly when they fall within the range of the Early Classic period (yet earlier dates are another matter). Regrettably, the relevant passages of Altar 1 are highly eroded, although the sculptors emphasized their importance by taking pains to prepare a long section of text. But, real or not, this early lord falls well before the beginning of inscriptional history at Piedras Negras, which begins to take more concrete form only after A.D. 500. This second pattern *does* accord roughly with ceramic dates.[9]

We are left, then, with a view of Early Classic and Late Classic settlement that bespeaks notable shifts, from a city-focused settlement, initiated with great rapidity after desultory and limited occupation during the Preclassic and the first years of the Early Classic period, to what Southall (1998:17) has called a "ruralized city," "run by the owners of rural land who were its chief resident citizens."[10] The rapidity of settlement points to a radically different signature from one of slow growth, systematic investment in ancestral shrines and appeals to primordial title over land or recurrent "genealogies of place" (McAnany 1995:110). Instead, one imagines a different set of claims based on "first occupancy," in which the first settlers gravitated to the land that best suited their needs (McAnany 1995:97). Because of the scale of settlement, these claims would need to be negotiated in a way contrasting with those required of low-level occupancy by dispersed farmers. Moreover, for this period, which corresponds to "Naba" ceramics at Piedras Negras, modes clearly differ from those of the Preclassic: *pace,* rapid, with great density of settlement; *scale,* great; *direction,* growth; *quantity,* high, but uncertain; *palaeodemography,* uncertain, but involving an order of magnitude greater than early phases, and forms of social organization that incorporated numerous households and people without direct kinship relation. These same patterns continue in the Late Classic.

These modes raise several questions. Where did this surge of people come from? Why and how did they get to Piedras Negras? Who encouraged or facilitated this movement? The mystery deepens when one recognizes there is some formal and stylistic continuity in ceramics between the Preclassic and Naba periods, so the population could not have supplanted completely any preexisting local population. The presence of ceramics from middle years of the Early Classic period from El Cayo, within 12 kilometers of Piedras Negras, supports this view (Lee and Hayden 1988:31–35), as does the early lord on Altar 1.[11] Long ago, Satterthwaite (1937:169) noted the close resemblance of early temples at Piedras Negras to examples from the central Petén, 150 kilometers to the east. This is equally true, in general, of ceramics of Piedras Negras, although it is impossible at present to establish any close material links with particular parts of the central Petén. Rather, as we suggest next, one must seek analogies and evidence elsewhere to account for the phenomenon of rapid settlement at Piedras Negras.

LATE PIEDRAS NEGRAS

Before speculating about the nature of the Early Classic explosion at Piedras Negras, we must mention another, related feature of settlement at Piedras Negras: the

Stephen Houston, Héctor Escobedo, Mark Child, Charles Golden, and René Muñoz

Figure 9.4. Kumche vessels found on collapse of the P-7 sweatbath (drawing: Mark Child).

rapidity of urbanization—in the sense of envelopment within large-scale population clusters served by diverse architecture—complements an equally abrupt denouement at the end of the Classic period. What is often described as "Terminal Classic" material at other sites is poorly attested at Piedras Negras (Holley 1983:211–215). The remains that occur, from the so-called Kumche phase, can only be described as remnants of "squatter" occupation, when much of the architecture at the site had fallen into ruins or was rapidly losing any coherent building program. After four seasons of large-scale excavation, our project has found only small numbers of the Fine Orange pottery that characterizes the Terminal Classic period, including a find on the front terrace of the R-5 pyramid, along with other sherds from the area of Structure J-24 and R-2. Other contexts include a sporadic scattering of ceramics on the terraces around the South Group Court and an earlier building, O-7, awkwardly modified by the addition of cylindrical altars or columns (Satterthwaite 1954:38–40); and habitation debris, surprisingly noisome after 1,200 years, in the R-11 ballcourt (Holley 1983:211). In the 2000 field season Mark Child found a painted gourd or wooden object (of which there remained only curving flecks of pale-green stucco) and two inverted plates with their supports hacked off (figure 9.4). The red-slipped plates date to the Kumche period and were carefully stacked atop a layer of wall debris from the collapse of P-7. Obviously, this building had collapsed in part by about A.D. 830, when the Kumche period approximately began at Piedras Negras. The overriding impression is that these deposits show little continuity with elite and urban practices of the Late Classic period.

Whatever problems beset Piedras Negras made themselves felt around A.D. 800.[12] Epigraphic evidence indicates that the last known ruler of the site, Ruler 7, was taken captive by the neighboring, historically antagonistic city of Yaxchilan (Houston et al. 1999). Circumstantial evidence plausibly correlates this event with the destruction of Throne 1 in the royal palace—an act thought by Eric Thompson (1966:108, fig. 9) to constitute evidence of class warfare—and the burning of Structure J-12, also in the royal palace (Holley 1983:202–207, fig. 10). Bracketing dates for this destruction come from the last firm monument of his reign, Stela 12 (A.D. 795), and the reference at Yaxchilan to Ruler 7's status as a captive (A.D. 808). The sole hieroglyphic date thought to come later, a reference on Altar 3 to 9.19.0.0.0 (A.D. 810), is problematic. Whatever was seen by earlier epigraphers, principally Sylvanus Morley (1937–1938:pl. 141)—who was not always so proficient with worn texts—is no longer visible in this irretrievably eroded and poorly documented text. Unfortunately, the lone available photograph does not clarify matters. Yet this date should still be taken seriously as possible counterevidence or, at least, information that Piedras Negras may have had another king after Ruler 7. Whatever the outcome of this debate, it is increasingly certain that the collapse of Piedras Negras as a city took place within a period of about 20 years.

The evidence for this assertion comes from a variety of sources. First, there is the historical datum of the royal capture and the consequent destruction of the palace. As mentioned before, the latest artifacts at the site (Kumche phase) are rare. (Altar 3 must be seen as introducing a disconcerting note into these patterns, although by any reckoning it would fall early in the late Chacalhaaz period.) Then there is the curious nature of ceramics of the time and their distribution. The late Chacalhaaz phase is still under review, but it evidently includes a changed basin form with red-slipped interiors, thick (>2 centimeters) bolstered rims, and relatively thin walls (<1 centimeter); bases are flat and slightly pedestaled. Another feature is a greater number of what may be comales, hinting at changes in diet or food preparation at the time (tamales to tortillas?). The fact that some are almost basin-like is disquieting in comparison with other comales. Nonetheless, many seem to show evidence of burning on the bottom, suggesting direct contact with hearths.

The late Chacalhaaz materials do not appear to have any Fine Gray (i.e., Telchac Composite or Chicxulub Incised), a kind of temperless ceramic that seems rather to date to the earlier phase of Chacalhaaz. Stratigraphically, these late Chacalhaaz deposits occur in the uppermost levels of the J-24 area, within and above structures of poor construction, and in the J-17 sweatbath. The absence of the Fine Gray implies an interruption in regional commerce, since these ceramics were certainly manufactured elsewhere. Moreover, the late Chacalhaaz deposits possess only small quantities of Fine Orange (indeed, they are far less numerous than earlier finds of Fine Gray), pointing to a date of about A.D. 830, when such finds became more common at other sites in the Usumacinta and Pasión areas (Sabloff 1975:17). At the same time, there was no obvious disruption in *local* manufacture, although those systems of production did begin to unravel within a few decades.

Pending further analysis, late Chacalhaaz ceramics seem limited to a few places at Piedras Negras, especially the J-17 sweatbath, along with upper deposits from several locations, such as C-10 and J-24. Before the royal palace was abandoned, this sweatbath had fallen into disuse, and trash was tossed in copious amounts over the surface of the abandoned structure.[13] Thus far, it appears that only a few examples of late Chacalhaaz come unambiguously from building fill (e.g., a rural site, RS 28; Amy Kovak, personal communication 2000), meaning that most deposits postdate major construction at the site. An attempt at public architecture may be represented by an unfinished or poorly constructed room on Structure R-8, with benches and crude colonnades. These features indicate that (1) the late component of Chacalhaaz was short and extended from circa A.D. 810 to 830 and perhaps a few decades later, as Kumche graded from that phase; (2) it presumably postdated the reign of Ruler 7, the last ruler known to have commissioned buildings and sculpture at Piedras Negras; (3) parts of his palace had fallen into disrepair just after his reign; and (4) late Chacalhaaz appears within a limited number of secure contexts, connected with shoddy construction. The pattern is less of a systematic contraction to the core, however, then a patchwork weakening of distribution in comparison with earlier phases. Yet, undeniably, the city was dying after the capture of Ruler 7.

Here is where controversy intrudes. It may be that late Chacalhaaz is everywhere present in humus and superficial deposits at Piedras Negras; poor preservation has, however, stripped ceramic sherds of diagnostic attributes. This would fatally underrepresent their profusion at the site. Moreover, future analysis may show its presence in most parts of the site and ambient settlement, pointing to the collapse of

Piedras Negras as large-scale and comprehensive. But available data do show one unassailable fact: just as the city came into existence with relative speed, so did it expire within a single generation, or perhaps two. Royal architecture, such as the J-17 sweatbath, suffered almost immediately at the hands of the remaining population, which made no effort to patch or restore destroyed sculptures and burned buildings. From this we can infer that kingship at the site, or at least its recognizable correlates in structures and artifacts, quickly came to an end. Within a short time, so did the city that had once been ruled by the holy lords of Piedras Negras.[14]

DISCUSSION

The evidence presented thus far underlines the peculiar occupational history of Piedras Negras: slight preexisting population during Preclassic times and the first centuries of the Early Classic period, followed by an explosion of population within the city, and then, apparently, the surrounding landscape (although more work remains to be done in analyzing the suburban ceramics), culminating in the sustained populations of the full Late Classic period. Present chronologies suggest that this dramatic change took place within a short term, certainly less than 100 years in duration and probably a briefer span than that. Subtle continuities exist in ceramics before and after this singular event, along with a poorly attested personage, but the breaks are even more profound. Afterward there appear new classes of architecture, a fuller historical sequence, and an immense ambition expressed in monumental construction and large-scale modifications of natural hill forms. Preexisting populations, even at older centers like El Cayo, are insufficient to account for this change by any model of local gathering (*reducción*) or natural increase within the general area (see the next section). Similarly, the urban collapse, if we understand the chronology correctly, took place within another short span.

The rapidity of these shifts implies that urban origins at Piedras Negras cannot be explained solely in ecological terms, that is, through the slow infilling of propitious farming land that would eventually generate, in good time, an urbanized zone. It is true that Piedras Negras lies within a hour's walk of attractive and ample potential farmland in valleys to the north and south (Hardin et al. 1998). But the fact remains that the immediate location of the city would hold little appeal to pragmatic farmers or traders. It sits athwart cockpit karst topography with, at best, isolated pockets of decent soil (Houston et al. 1999). As discussed before, its location is epidemiologically hazardous, and transport and fording are made arduous by the fury of the river that runs by Piedras Negras; in our opinion, the rapids of the Usumacinta deterred rather than facilitated long-distance movement. In both respects (agriculture and human movement), El Cayo and El Porvenir, both known to have Preclassic settlement, present more attractive milieux for population centers, since they lie near open lands with rich soil. Sleepy stretches of the river adjoin these sites. One of the few apparent advantages of Piedras Negras is that, as a location, it surveys a narrow stretch of river that could be monitored and controlled. The rapidity and violence of the Usumacinta near Piedras Negras may also have protected the city from what is now the Mexican side of the river.

The collapse is just as complex a phenomenon, but here an ecological explanation may weigh more favorably. Research by David Webster (personal communication 1999) and his students documents, in our opinion, relatively little evidence of stress, although this may change with further research. Areas to the south of Piedras Negras with good soil and water resources have negligible settlement; nor has Webster discovered any signs of terracing, check dams, or other markers of intensification. But the very drawbacks described for those living at Piedras Negras may have diminished safety margins during the moments of severe drought thought to have afflicted the southern lowlands during this time (Hodell et al. 1995). Other, better-favored cities such as Yaxchilan, adjacent to large areas of accessible farmland across the Usumacinta River, survived longer. (All such scenarios are necessarily speculative until such time as local climatic and erosional effects can be explored in relation to agriculture.) What the chronology does suggest, however, is that the local collapse at Piedras Negras could not have involved mass death so much as populations departing the middle reaches of the Usumacinta for more hospitable zones, leaving the dust and debris of a disintegrating city.

MORAL AUTHORITY AND HOLY LORDS

The seen and unseen operators behind this urban system are, we propose, the royal family and its principal, quasi-divine axis, the "holy lord" who presided over Classic Maya kingdoms of the southern lowlands as priest, chief warrior, dynastic procreator, palace manager, and principal recipient of tribute (Houston and Stuart 1996:295; see also Brüschweiler 1983:198). It is in terms of royal strategies and their failures that Piedras Negras can be understood, along with settlement transformations and volatile population shifts in other major centers (Fry 1990:296). The first concept to consider is "moral authority," the combination of claims to control and obedience with internalized notions of responsibility and virtuous conduct. This is decidedly *not* a system that possesses an "amoral [note: not immoral!] dependence on purely rational legal codes, enforceable by coercion and utilitarian calculations" (Wuthnow 1987:68). Rather, it requires a "moral object" or an "object of commitment," be it God, the family, the environment, or, in Classic Maya idiom, the holy lord and the order he sustains (Durkheim 1961:8, 29, 90). The moral object in turn necessitates a program of behavior; from that arises an ethical order in which authority can act. The order, naturally, necessitates belief and presupposes that people do not see the moral system as a lie (Durkheim 1965:14). Public and private rituals dramatize collective values and help nurture a moral "economy" of values and reciprocal obligations (Scott 1976:165, 167–173; Wuthnow 1987:167). Within this economy such obligations conform, in near-contractual terms, to "covenants" that may involve both supernatural and natural entities (Monaghan 1995:222–226, 2000; for an Islamic case, see Insoll 1999:9, 208–211). Pre-industrial cities often embody such ritual systems, within which people learn to become moral actors through collective worship and the evocation of moods (e.g., Parish 1994:21; see also Redfield and Singer 1954:57).[15] This is not to say, however, that all dwellers in the city perceive it the same way; only that they take part in a system that creates "commitments and orientations to action," internalized as a human desire for obligation that "shap(es) the experience of relatedness"; from this comes an impulse to social duty (Parish 1994:73–87). Transgressions will, and do, exist, but may be neutralized or justified by sundry expedients. The system collapses when the "subsistence claims" of peasants are violated irremediably. Elite claims to peasant production are thereby forfeit and rebellion or migration ensues (Scott 1976:188–189).

Such concepts would seem not to be controversial. Yet they run counter to common sentiments in archaeology, which tends instead to emphasize cleavages, factional tensions, resistance, individualism, variable loyalty contestation, and exploitative elites—in short, a worldview in which "religion" equates to "ideology" and other symbolic instruments of elite cunning (Wolfe 1999:B5–B6). This is not only a matter of emphasis, but of a different perspective on Maya society. One perspective, the dominant one, sees division and individual calculation, another sees community and collective effort, and of symbolic structures that matter.[16] Whether such attitudes in fact express the relative absence or presence of religious beliefs among scholars looking at the past is a matter of debate (Houston 1999). Both tendencies are necessary to encompass the totality of ancient communities, since the tension between them is primordial to human society, operating as the disquiet between individual and group needs, between that which splinters and that which binds. An ideal moral order, whatever its concrete or surface expressions, bridges such needs and tendencies through joint explanations and expectations.

There is strong evidence that, if people believed in holy lords, and the long history of Classic dynasties suggest that they did, then this would leave tangible expressions, not only in royal texts and iconography, but in other behaviors. The holy lord would, in fact, mute the countless frictions of everyday life by emphasizing cooperation at all levels, much like the Jero Gde, a mediator of water rights in Bali (e.g., Lansing 1991:82–88). Lest this sound too much like a parroting of Geertz's "theatre state" (Geertz 1980), in which symbolic projection becomes political reality, there is no doubt that "messiness" existed as individual rulers succeeded or failed at filling their appointed roles (Webster 1997:3)—the final reigns at Piedras Negras are a case in point (Houston et al. 2000). Moreover, it may be that such variance can be detected in the acutely episodic building programs at sites like Piedras Negras, in which some kings seem to have commissioned major works, others relatively few (Houston et al. 2000). This does not mean that one should assume a schism between moral order and "reality" (a distinction that may be difficult to sustain subjectively in any event), since this would be as difficult as splitting structures or codes from their overt expressions. The interaction between the two realms, one abstract and intangible, the other observable, is by definition complex. One cannot exist without the other. It may be that the nexus between them lies in the shadowy political economy of Classic kings: that is, in systems of tribute and redistribution, through which collective and self-interest find their most stable balance.

There are other implications for the nature of Classic cities. They were basically "mono-ethnic" in the sense of recognizing a joint identity as followers of a holy lord, as custodians of local gods, and as participants in a moral community (Houston and Stuart 1996). Once it had accumulated a population, the relatively small Maya city did not, as in Medieval Europe, provide a heady atmosphere of individual liberty—"City life makes free" (*Stadt Luft macht frei,* Sennett 1994:159)— but offered instead watchful eyes, behavioral constraint, and a shared moral order that transcended small kin and household groups (McAnany 1997; see also Levy 1990:23, drawing on Erving Goffman's [1956] notion of a "total institution"). That such an order was believable, that it provided answers and, through public ritual, an entertaining and emotionally rewarding spectacle, made the city attractive despite its intrinsic unhealthiness and, as one scholar argues, the heightened levels of stress induced by excessive, daily interaction (Fletcher 1995:70–71). The appeal of the moral order and belief in its royal predicates, the availability of a supernaturally sanctioned mediator, the ready accessibility of spectacle and a few, limited products—all of these made cities "enchant." (Maya cities have never been convincingly defined as trading centers or market locations, *pace* Jones 1996:91.) Such things made people want to live in them. And it made people accessible to one another for communal activities, as part of what Kostoff has called "energized crowding" (Kostoff 1991:37–38; see also Hannerz 1980:243), under an umbrella of both control *and* protection by the king, and as channeled through a political economy of tribute and redistribution. For many scholars, the very definition of a city is less in its absolute size than in its intense concentration of relationships (Southall 1983:10). Among the Classic Maya, those relationships would involve gods, rulers, and other occupants, "natural" and "supernatural," of the ancient city (cf. the Roman ritual of *lectisternium,* and the public feeding of gods, Stambaugh 1988:219).

MORAL COMMUNITIES AND SITE SIZE

Such a moral community, based on obligation and covenant, worked well at the scale of a city like Piedras Negras. Conceivably, smaller dynastic capitals were limited not only by how many people could be fed, but by their ability to absorb immigrants and yet maintain close, daily, face-to-face interaction between the majority of the urban populace. That so many Classic Maya cities remained fairly small (ca. 2,000 to 5,000 people in size) intimates that there were absolute, intrinsic limits on the number of people who could be fed effectively and, more to the point, that could be countenanced sociologically. Larger numbers would potentially undermine and endanger systems of patrimonial, morally authoritative rule. This may explain the size of open, civic spaces at cities such as Copan, Piedras Negras, and Dos Pilas (Houston 1993: figs. 2–4). The total population of these cities could assemble in such spaces for communal rituals. This also implies that a few larger cities, certainly Tikal and Calakmul, and perhaps Caracol, operated according to different arrangements that did not rely so heavily on moral authority as a device for governance and template for community organization.

A credible argument can be made that these communities affected other landscapes (Chase and Chase 1996b:805), transforming them into regional, socioeconomic hierarchies spanning large parts of the Yucatán peninsula (e.g., Folan et al. 1995:281).[17] In such a world, moral authority would count for less. But this pan-

Stephen Houston, Héctor Escobedo, Mark Child, Charles Golden, and René Muñoz

Mayan statist organization has yet to be proved in its economic and bureaucratic aspects, although an excellent argument can be made for hegemonic macropolities centered on a few sites like Calakmul and Tikal (Grube and Martin 1998). From bureaucratic states? Roads? None exist at this scale in the southern lowlands, although those in the northern lowlands may indeed point to such regional integration. Regional centers of substantial size that might be subordinate to yet larger centers? No such patterns have ever been shown in much of this zone. Caracol, a city nestled close to the Maya mountains, is a case in point. Its excavators suggest, on plausible grounds, a large population of some 115,000 to 150,000 people over a considerable area around the city (Chase and Chase 1994:5, 1996b:805). They also state, however, that the population continues without cease in all transects mapped so far (Chase and Chase 1994:5). Although none of the published maps have contours and hence their interpretation is difficult, it is evident that mound groups generally cluster on hilltops, and that the karst topography indicates a background of such settlement in all directions, without, however, any signs of greater intensity in the core (Chase and Chase 1998:fig. 2). That is, rather than making a case for a densely occupied city, one can construct an alternative argument for a densely settled *rural* landscape on which a moderately large (ca. 1–2 square kilometers) royal and ceremonial core has developed. Within a few kilometers of the core, the city extended limited control by means of causeways or crude roads. The presence of the city does not seem to have had any effect on density, as one would expect in a centralized system.[18]

The relation of these small sites and their elaborate agricultural terracing to the core remains unclear. The excavators argue for the "large-scale organized . . . nature of the terrace systems," but this is not conclusively supported by their published data, other than by the observation that the terraces possess great "magnitude and formality" (Chase and Chase 1998:72, 73) or "regularity . . . (in their) alignment and organization" (Chase and Chase 1996b:808). In fact, the outlines of terraces appear to follow the contours of local topography, connecting to local causeways it is true, but perhaps for purely practical reasons, as a means of accessing the terraces along cleared routes. Can one dismiss the possibility that this system is entirely under local, kin- or household-based control? Have the systems been compared with those in other parts of the zone, especially those across the Guatemala border that are not at the doorstep of a large center (Laporte 1994:5)? What is one to make of the large-scale "formality," "alignment," and "organization" of gigantic Ifugao terraces of Luzon in the Philippines, constructed by nonstate levels of social organization, or comparable works in the Lake Titicaca Basin of South America (Conklin 1980:5–6; Erickson 1993)? Or the implausibility of applying bureaucratic models to systematic agriculture in the densely settled rice fields of Bali (Lansing 1991:127)?[19] In short, at Caracol the initial, guiding premise of centralization and hierarchical control has, perhaps, dictated interpretation. We must add that the excavators of Caracol, with their abundant experience of the area and its data, may well be correct in their interpretations: it is just that alternative views must be decisively or credibly eliminated, since much hinges on the interpretation of Caracol and its landscape.

A second, more important point is that, even in such cases, one cannot easily reject the existence of the "king-based" systems that are dismissed with alacrity by the excavators of Caracol (Chase and Chase 1996b:810). What is taken for transparent evidence of bureaucracy and administrative complexity is seldom unambiguous. Rather, as David Webster (2001) notes, cities seem coterminous with royal courts, in the center of which reside, of course, the holy lords. Explanations that do not deal convincingly with such lords or their ontology as sacred rulers or the obvious centrality of their palaces will not result in solid arguments for Classic Maya cities.[20]

MORAL AUTHORITY AND SETTLEMENT TRANSFORMATION

The pieces are now in place to understand the interrelation of moral authority and the distinctive settlement history of Piedras Negras. We propose that movements of this scale, as seem well documented at Piedras Negras, can be understood as an *organized* activity that follows a royal strategy based on the moral authority of the monarch.[21] Scholars working in the Valley of Oaxaca have described a similar process underlying the abrupt creation of Monte Alban as a regional center (Blanton et al. 1996:62; Marcus and Flannery 1996:139–146), although debate continues as to whether the motivation for resettlement was political or determined largely by attractive agricultural resources near the ancient city (Marcus Winter, personal communication 2000). There is mounting evidence of such movements in the ancient Petén, Guatemala, and elsewhere in the Classic Maya region. The origins of the Yaxchilan dynasty at El Zotz, Bejucal, and other sites around it in the central Petén (David Stuart, personal communication, 1995), the beginnings of the Tonina dynasty in what may have been El Peru, as well as the better-understood instance of Dos Pilas rulers as cadet issue of the august Tikal dynasty (Houston 1993:99–101).[22] Recently, Sharer and his colleagues (Sharer, Traxler et al. 1999:19) have made a powerful argument in favor of an abrupt dynastic founding at the site of Copan during the Early Classic period. In sum, there are strong data pointing to the "seeding" of new dynastic seats from far older, more established centers, with which they did not necessarily retain good relations in the long term. The El Zotz/Yaxchilan example is particularly illuminating, for it suggests how an ancient dynasty from the central Petén spun off a branch to occupy or control a site on the Usumacinta (the various scenarios of, and reasons for, such movements are discussed in Houston 1993:100; intradynastic strife and competition may have been the strongest motivation). There are clues that many dynasties in this and other zones can be divided into two categories, those with long-standing dynasties and high counts-of-rulers (cumulative tabulations from the founder), such as Altar de Sacrificios and Tamarindito (Houston 1993:figs. 4–17), and those that appear to be intrusive, with known founders in historical (i.e., post–8.13.0.0.0 [A.D. 297]) time. Yaxchilan and Piedras Negras fit into this category. Other sites, such as Palenque, refer to apparent migrations from Early Classic locales to Late Classic ones (Stuart and Houston 1994:31).

Such information suggests that at least some organized population movements were involved, and that the reasons for moving seem to have resided in several factors, principally the search for new and better opportunities by lord and peasant in tandem.[23] In the nineteenth century, "caciques" or important personages and landlords of the Mixteca in Mexico are known to have brought settlers to new areas with promises of land at the personal disposal of the cacique (John Monaghan, personal communication 1999). Even "traveling" or "migratory" populations of the Chalca of central Mexico were supposedly led by kings during their peregrinations (Schroeder 1991:4). Closer to home, there is strong historical evidence of the founding of new towns and wholesale organization of political regions in highland Guatemala during the Postclassic period (Carmack 1981:129), including strong, corroborative evidence from documents and settlement archaeology for "rapid and well-organized *entradas* or migrations" (Hill 1998:233, 250–251, our translation). The rituals for such new establishments are described in loving detail and involved the display of sacred emblems, dances, drinking, and gift-giving (Recinos 1957:43). It seems clear that the motivations for these highland movements came from conflicts in home territories (Carmack 1981:130), although there also exist many supernatural tropes that blur or structure the historical record (e.g., Gillespie

1989:219–220). The founding of Tenochtitlan (or Salt Lake City!) on the basis of prophetic vision is an excellent example of how such movements find their endpoint.

Yet such migrations or gatherings of people must have taken place in the idiom of moral authority and by means of royal strategies by particular individuals. (Another approach to migration prefers to see it in terms of " 'push-pull' economic factors," perhaps involving landless tenants know as *terrazagüeros,* Blanton et al. 1996:17, 36). It is difficult to believe that systems of holy lordship were not implicated in such movements, since they had been in existence for some centuries before the beginnings of Piedras Negras as a city. Founding metaphors for Classic dynasties typically refer to "houses" (**wi-te-NA:H,** David Stuart, personal communication 1997), which suggests that the primordial act of constructing a royal dwelling or temple was an important part of this process in conceptual terms (Traxler 2001). A ruler led as moral object; subjects followed through moral practice, according to their joint understandings of mutual obligations. The ruler was honored and obeyed because of his special relations with the supernatural and because he was the head and embodiment of a moral community. Among the "settlers" there might even have been tutelary deities, as was certainly true among the Aztec (Codex Boturini 1964:2). The rapid construction and grandeur of Early Classic buildings at Piedras Negras indicates that such a moral community was in place, not before the population growth after A.D. 400–450—although the personage at A.D. 297 remains a mystery—but *afterward,* as an intangible social artifact imported with migratory parties (see Kopytoff 1999:88). With the king came a city, and an elaborate moral system involving not villagers but populations many times larger.[24] Cities may kill, but kings attract additional settlers with a community life that cushions and satisfies; it would be surprising if they did not also have the ability to allot land and evict social undesirables, and to provide protection in the uncertain landscapes of the Classic period.[25] To our regret, however, the glyphic evidence is notably silent about the geographic origin of the first migrants to Piedras Negras.

The abrupt collapse at Piedras Negras can be explained in similar ways. The failures of covenants, particularly in palpable ways such as famine or failure to adjudicate the tensions within a complex society, may have resulted from processes beyond royal control, but that would not have been the interpretation by Classic Maya. Perceived vulnerability in moral orders prompts crises of faith and subjective feelings of deprivation and betrayal (Wuthnow 1987:154–155).[26] The subsistence claims of peasants, thus violated by tribute impositions on an increasingly precarious agrarian ecology, would logically result in a debilitation of covenant, and a pronounced *ésprit frondeur* (Scott 1976:197).[27] In this sense, the collapse at Piedras Negras, and perhaps the Maya collapse in general, must be perceived as, among other things, a crisis of *faith* (e.g., Houston 1999; Webster 1997:17). If the moral community no longer observes its covenants, or if expectations have been dramatically breached, then the holy lord can no longer retain his people. Conservative impulses to stay on ancestral property would be weakened if no effective hope emanated from the royal family.

In such instances, the moral community, now inverted as a community of despair, would potentially transform itself into an expulsive force. The fact that people did not so much die as leave Piedras Negras within a short span, just after the catastrophic events at the end of Ruler 7's reign, corroborates this hypothesis. At other communities, with more adept leaders, the moral communities that *were* the Classic Maya cities stayed a little longer. The evaporation of the moral center of the polity would be equally destructive to the continued maintenance of urban settlement. Alongside these matters existed intensely practical ones. Without kings and their cadre of warriors, organized protection might have been less effective, and the community left undefended and open to attacks. Where there are no kings, a sustaining political economy would fail. A web of mutual obligations and reciprocity in goods and services would lose its connection to any organizing center. These changes do not, of course, exclude one another, nor do they deny the existence of a destructive moral vacuum when kingship itself disappears.

CONCLUSION

In this chapter, we have taken a sociological and cultural tack in explaining a perplexing pattern of settlement at the Classic Maya city of Piedras Negras. We have interpreted settlement, both in rapid growth and precipitous decline, not in familiar terms of agricultural potential, land tenure, and natural increase, but within a framework of belief and the moral predicates of social life that persuaded people to move from somewhere else. The tone of our discussion is partly rhetorical, for it would be unwise and imbalanced to ignore other, economic bases of power that involved control over tangible resources (McAnany 1997) or the practical advantages of following powerful lords. In essence, agrarian communities must remain systems of land tenure and use, opaque as they are for the Classic period. Nonetheless, we have argued for several points of view: that matters of meaning and culture should not be ignored in discussing settlement transformation, that the urban cycles of Piedras Negras need to be conceived first and foremost within a Maya idiom, and that purely ecological explanations, while crucial to discerning patterns of subsistence and collective maintenance, do not in and of themselves suffice in explaining *why* cities exist and *when* cities exist, although they do help determine *where* cities may flourish. Kingship and kings must have played a role in all such communities, regardless of the pragmatic decisions that influenced decisions to settle or depart by individual families or lineages. At Piedras Negras, we hope in the future to combine our perspective, which commandeers a preeminent place for kings, with more detailed studies of the agrarian bases that supported this important Pre-Columbian settlement.

ACKNOWLEDGMENTS

This chapter exists because of an invitation by Monica Smith to evaluate Maya cities from socially oriented perspectives, which we have endeavored to supply. She also supplied useful advice and leads on sources. A first reading took place at her invitation, as a paper presented at the Society for Archaeology Meetings in 1999, building on an earlier presentation by Houston at the Complex Society Meetings, held at T. Patrick Culbert's kind invitation in Tucson, Arizona. Simon Martin commented usefully on several points, particularly the need to pay closer attention to Piedras Negras Altar 3, as did William Sanders, Michael E. Smith, and David Webster, who provided perceptive criticisms and useful sources. Arthur Joyce was equally helpful in this regard. The excavations reported on here took place under a permit granted by the Instituto de Antropología e Historia de Guatemala and its directors and the Consejo de Arqueología. Funding came from generous private donations, and from a variety of foundations: the Foundation for the Advancement of Mesoamerican Studies, Inc., the Ahau Foundation, the Rust Trust, the National Geographic Society (for work by David Webster and team), the Fulbright fellowship program, the National Science Foundation, and our respective universities, most notably the College of Family, Home, and Social Sciences at Brigham Young University, under the direction of Dean Clayne Pope. A generous sabbatical during the 1998–1999 academic year gave Houston the time to write the body of this essay.

NOTES

1. "Royal strategy" derives from the term "Grand Strategy," conceived to describe the Roman and Spanish Habsburg empires (Luttwak 1976; Parker 1998.). We prefer "royal" because it does not carry

the imperial connotations of the policies described for Rome and Phillip II. Such a strategy implies the existence of a plan or overall program for a dynasty or reign, involving systematic use of manpower and moral resources to further the aims and interests of the ruler (Parker 1998:1). The most effective strategies are those that rely less on force than other kinds of inducements (Luttwak 1976:196)

2. The only general term for location, often in association with maximal or "holy" lords, reads *KAB-CH'E:N*, "earth-cave" (David Stuart, personal communication 1998). This locative expression is not, in our opinion, an abstract concept for "dominion," "city," or "kingdom," but a concrete reference to Maya places, which combine earth and rocky outcrops and caves—the very image of a karstic landscape.

3. These estimates come from mapping under the supervision of Jennifer Kirker and are reckoned by us from a rough outline of areas of highest settlement density. They are likely to be modified or refined in Kirker's Ph.D. dissertation at Pennsylvania State University.

4. As mapped by the University of Calgary Project, El Cayo is surrounded by small mound groups without any particular orientation to the massive patio group that forms its center. But in one respect El Cayo seems strikingly different from Piedras Negras. Some mound groups exist on the opposing side of the Usumacinta River, doubtless reflecting the gentle nature and ample sand beaches in the vicinity of El Cayo (Mathews and Aliphat Fernández 1998:fig. 2). Reconnaissance by Charles Golden, Alejandro Guillot, and Jacob Parnell in 2000 found large terraces with modest buildings on the Guatemalan side of the river. In contrast, the river as it courses by Piedras Negras becomes far more violent and uncongenial to fording (see the discussion that follows). As a result, the settlement does not appear to span both sides of the river, as it does at El Cayo.

5. It is interesting to speculate as to how many extended kin groups or "families" would have existed within this hypothetical number. In Colonial Yucatan, "a larger Maya family or household" would have contained an "occupancy of six to twelve people" (Restall 1997:100). If one defines "family" in this fashion, that is, as a unit of coresidence, then Piedras Negras would have had a total in the neighborhood of 200 to 250. The fact that there are considerably fewer patio groups than this number suggests either a lower population than presumed here or an alternative, more inclusive pattern of coresidence.

6. Sharlin's study suggests that, in early Modern Europe (seventeenth through eighteenth centuries A.D.), patterns of mortality varied dramatically between permanent residents of cities and relatively new immigrants. The former did relatively well, and even experienced a slight natural increase; the latter did badly and their mounting deaths skewed overall mortality rates. The balance between the two mortality patterns could be unstable, sometimes favoring growth, at other times not. Whether such a model fits Piedras Negras is still uncertain. It remains unclear whether comparisons can be made between two such varied epidemiological systems, one tropical, the other not, the first (Piedras Negras) based largely on a sudden influx of new immigrants, the second on continuous immigration. In a personal communication (2000), Linda Manzanilla raises the useful point that Storey's study of Teotihuacan may not easily be generalized to the city as a whole, as her own research has found indications of robust health in sectors occupied by elites.

7. Michael Smith (personal communication 2000) suggests that the problem with viewing cities as unhealthy places is that there are few data from contemporary *rural* areas. Skeletal samples from sites well away from Piedras Negras are needed to clarify this issue.

8. Our excavation system follows common practice in the Maya region: operation (a general locus, often covering a residential sector, a pyramid, or palace courtyard), suboperation (a locus within the

operation), unit (usually a 2-by-2-meter area within the suboperation), and a lot (a collection unit always equal to, or less than, a stratigraphic stratum). Discrete finds such as caches, burials, or other special deposits are piece-plotted and drawn to scale.

9. Yaxchilan's first historical date, a reference to the first royal accession at the city, is 8.16.2.9.1, or A.D. 359 (Mathews 1988:table 1–3). The second reconstructible date, 8.17.1.17.16 (A.D. 378), marks another royal accession (the third at Yaxchilan) and is several months after the apparent arrival of new, Teotihuacan-related rulers at Tikal (Stuart 2000). At Tikal, too, this arrival seemed to lead to dramatic changes in the dynasty, of which this may be another example. Nonetheless, Werner Nahm has posited far earlier dates for the dynasty, beginning about 8.13.0.0.0 (Simon Martin, personal communication 2000).

10. This view looks at the city from the perspective of the people and activities that feed it. Another approach would describe the entire landscape as "urbanized," emphasizing that both function within a single system (Smith 1995:1–2). But the flow is strongly unidirectional in meanings if not in goods: "messages which flow outwards to the rest of society are . . . impregnated with urban norms"; the city "contrives, prescribes, modulates, and disseminates order throughout the subsystems of that society" (Wheatley 1983:9). Archaeologists working in other regions have also addressed the subject of *les villes nouvelles* and their problematic signatures (Huot et al. 1990:211–212). Above all, such new cities involve the creation of obvious "symbols" of the city, particularly ramparts. In the case of Piedras Negras, the "urban symbol" would be a palace and mortuary pyramids.

11. Aristotle called such fusions of villages "synoecisms" ("living together" in Greek), essentially the result of administrative decisions (Kostoff 1991:59–62; see also Marcus and Flannery 1996:140–141, and, more recently, Blanton et al. 1999:63). For Piedras Negras, this process is possible but hypothetical. In no case does one see clear evidence of regional abandonment as people cluster in the new city.

12. Two historical details suggest turbulence even before Ruler 7 came to office. First, the introduction of fraternal succession and new regnal names in the preceding reign intimate some sort of rupture with established practices at Piedras Negras. Second, Ruler 7's immediate predecessor, Ruler 6, abdicated under mysterious circumstances. This led to an interregnum of slightly more than one year (Houston et al. 2000).

13. We think it doubtful that J-17 is simply an example of arrested construction, the fill representing an attempt to level the platform before further building. In other such cases, the sweat chamber is left intact and cleared, obviously not the case here. Yet there are other instances of arrested construction at Piedras Negras: Structures F-2, O-17, and possibly J-3. All consist of formless heaps of masonry and, in O-17, there is faint evidence of retention walls visible on the surface.

14. Yaxchilan soldiered on somewhat longer. Little has been published of the Mexican excavations at Yaxchilan, despite 15 years of almost continuous excavation. But the project ceramicist has mentioned the ubiquity of Fine Orange ceramics at the site (López Varela 1989:142, 144, 151, 153). More than 20,583 sherds of fine paste ceramics have been documented so far, which suggests that these ceramics emanate from the Yaxchilan (López Varela n.d.:8). Nonetheless, Lintel 10, the monument that mentions the capture of Ruler 7, is in itself the last at the site and notorious for its sloppy execution. The "small acropolis," including Structures 42–52, yielded a large number of chert points in collapsed fill (Kaneko 1998:262). From this, Kaneko, the excavator, contrives a dramatic if somewhat implausible tale of internecine warfare. The excavator provides no other chronological information, nor does he pinpoint, through sections and precise plans, the location of the points, which may potentially come from late midden debris.

Stephen Houston, Héctor Escobedo, Mark Child, Charles Golden, and René Muñoz

15. This is conceptually distinct from a system based on charismatic authority or "great men" (cf. Demarest 1992:156), a notion that explains matters only in terms of individuals and their rhetorical or strategic skills. A better explanation is one that emphasizes, not gullible underlings and manipulative leaders, but a community of shared precepts (Freidel 1992:128).

16. Much research on pre-industrial cities persistently focuses on their replication and reduction of cosmic models (e.g., Lynch 1981:81) or their position as points of mediation—"mesocosms"—between cosmic order and everyday experience (Levy 1990). Such is undoubtedly true in Maya cities, but the emphasis on ancestors and rulers counterbalances heavy-handed cosmic models.

17. The problem with satellite-generated images of Maya roads, intriguing as they are, is that they may illustrate not so much sociopolitical hierarchies as ritual connections or purely utilitarian paths over swamps (cf. Folan et al. 1995). Around Calakmul, where such roads have been detected, there is the added problem of chronology, since one system appears to head toward the Preclassic city of El Mirador and thus suggests a date that has little to do with sociopolitical networks of the Classic era.

18. Clues from other Classic sites suggest disconnections between settlement and center, as in Río Amarillo, Honduras, which appears suddenly without, however, having much impact on local settlement (Marcello Canuto, personal communication 1999).

19. The centralized aspects of Balinese agriculture come from reliance on irrigation systems, an issue that is not relevant to Caracol.

20. It is beyond the scope of this discussion, but other comments can be made. The authors use potentially anachronistic terms such as "garden city" (derived from Ebenezer Howard's 1898 book, *To-Morrow, A Peaceful Path to Social Reform*) and "middle class," in many ways less a technical label than a notion of the industrial age (e.g., Chase and Chase 1996a). The modern resonances of these terms can be misleading.

21. French and Italian scholars have commented extensively on the phenomenon of the urban *fondation* or *fondazione*, focusing on the necessity of economic preconditions (Margueron 1994:4) and human actors *(le prince fondateur)* (Mazzoni 1991:319–321). It is interesting that, in the Maya case, the *forma urbis* of new foundations do not have the regularity of planning evident in the ancient Near East (Mazzoni 1991:329).

22. The evidence from Tonina comes from a recently excavated, undesignated monument that refers to the primordial 4 Ahau 8 Kumku date, or some later version thereof. The text contains an explicit reference to someone who descends, twelfth in line, from a lord of what appears to be El Peru. The early style of the monument—it must date to the latter part of the Early Classic period—suggests that the dynasty must have come from El Peru during roughly 200 or more years before. The ceramic chronology approximately fits the projected beginnings of the dynasty (Becquelin and Baudez 1979:199–202). Nonetheless, Tonina seems largely to date to the beginnings of the Late Classic period, during which time the number of sherds increases exponentially (Protoclassic: 271 sherds; Early Classic: 514 sherds; Late Classic: 20,592 sherds).

23. The literature on migration theory is vast (e.g., Adams et al. 1978; Rouse 1986:13–18). After some years of disrepute in archaeology, the topic has been revisited with new sophistication (Anthony 1990, Beekman and Christensen n.d.; Boone 1991:121–122). Anthony effectively encapsulates the range of possible migrations and their complexities (Anthony 1990:909). In his terminology, we are describing for Piedras Negras a pattern of rapid "long-distance migration" (often linked with farmers) coupled with in-gathering of preexisting local groups; there must have been intelligence of the location beforehand (as evidenced by shared ceramic styles); and a "migration stream" rather than "leap-frogging"

populations was probably involved, yet, to an unusual extent, with little evidence of "return migration" (Anthony 1990:902–905). The "intervening obstacle" (Anthony 1990:fig. 1) would have been the nearly impassable Sierra Lacandón. Anthony is persuasive in suggesting that the precise reasons for such migrations are often impossible to reconstruct in the absence of reliable historical data (Anthony 1990:898).

24. Elisséeff (1983:151) labels such a city the *ville créée: "l'agglomération humaine c'est développée dans un cadre artificiel suivant un plan imposé par la volonté d'un homme."*

25. Nonetheless, the notion of a migrating community sponsored by holy lords does not imply city planning, as such population movements certainly did in the Mediterranean (Owens 1991:34–35). Rather, one sees "an orderly arrangement" rather than "a preconceived, regular pattern" (Owens 1991:35). Even among the Romans, city planning involved little more than arranging a city layout, without the comprehensive meanings of "town planning" in the modern sense of the term (Laurence 1994:12, 19).

26. The collapse of moral authority recalls the case of Peter III of Russia (Wallace 1984:297–298). During his brief life, Peter attempted to rescind *noblesse oblige*—paternalistic obligations toward peasants—without, however, eliminating serfdom itself. This led to a popular revolt during the reign of his immediate successor, Catherine II. Rather than reforging these bonds, she chose to grow yet closer to nobility. One wonders whether the same process is expressed in Late Classic history, when nobility achieved an unprecedented prominence in the textual record.

27. Scott's study of peasant rebellions has much to say with respect to the Maya collapse. Although acknowledging the difficulty of "easy generalizations," Scott (1976:202) suggests that "peasantries with strong communal traditions and few sharp internal class divisions" tend to be more explosive in revolt than "peasantries with weak communal traditions and sharper class divisions." Nonetheless, communities with strong collective traditions may also be able to "'redistribute pain' in such a way as to avoid or postpone subsistence crises." Alternatives to rebellion would include forms of "self-help" and localist strategies aimed at maintaining steady supplies of food. The most drastic step would be regional abandonment, the ultimate form of conflict avoidance. What is important in Scott's study is his subtle qualification of standard Marxist views of "mystification" and "false-consciousness"—there may well be congruence in peasant and elite values and attitudes as long as tribute exactions fall within a mutual zone of comfort (Scott 1976:233-234).

REFERENCES

Adams, W. Y., Dennis P. Van Gerven, and Richard S. Levy
    1978   The Retreat from Migrationism. *Annual Review of Anthropology* 7:483–532.
Anthony, D. W.
    1990   Migration in Archaeology: The Baby and the Bathwater. *American Anthropologist* 92:895–914.
Becquelin, P., and C. F. Baudez
    1979   *Tonina, une cité maya du Chiapas (Mexique)*. Etudes Mésoaméricaines, vol. 6, tome 1. Mission Archéologique et Ethnologique, Mexico City.
Beekman, C. S., and A. F. Christensen
    n.d.   A Synthetic Analysis of the Nahua Migrations. Manuscript in possession of authors.

Blanton, R. F., G. M. Feinman, S. A. Kowalewski, and L. M. Nicholas

1999 *Ancient Oaxaca.* Cambridge University Press, Cambridge.

Blanton, R. F., L. Finsten, S. A. Kowalewski, and G. M. Feinman

1996 Migration and Population Change in the Prehispanic Valley of Oaxaca, Mexico. In: *Arqueología Mesoamericana: Homenaje a William T. Sanders, II,* edited by A. G. Mastache, J. R. Parsons, R. S. Santley, and M. C. Serra Puche. Instituto Nacional de Antropología e Historia, Mexico City.

Boone, E.

1991 Migration Histories as Ritual Performance. In *To Change Place: Aztec Ceremonial Landscapes,* edited by Davíd Carrasco, pp. 121–151. University Press of Colorado, Niwot.

Brady, J. E., J. W. Ball, R. L. Bishop, D. C. Pring, N. Hammond, and R. A. Housley

1998 The Lowland Maya "Protoclassic": A Reconsideration of Its Nature and Significance. *Ancient Mesoamerica* 9:17–38.

Brüschweiler, F.

1983 La ville dans les textes littéraires sumériens. In *La ville dans le proche-orient ancien: Actes du Colloque de Cartigny 1979,* edited by F. Brüschweiler, Y. Christe, R. Martin-Achard, B. Urio, and J. Vicari, pp. 177–198. Editions Peeters, Leuven.

Carmack, R. M.

1981 *The Quiché Mayas of Utatlán: The Evolution of a Highland Guatemala Kingdom.* University of Oklahoma Press, Norman.

Castells, M.

1977 *The Urban Question: A Marxist Approach.* MIT Press, Cambridge, Mass.

Chase, A. F., and D. Z. Chase

1994 Details in the Archaeology of Caracol, Belize: An Introduction. In *Studies in the Archaeology of Caracol, Belize,* edited by D. Z. Chase and A. F. Chase, pp. 1–11. Pre-Columbian Art Research Institute Monograph 7. San Francisco.

1996a A Mighty Maya Nation: How Caracol Built an Empire by Cultivating Its "Middle Class." *Archaeology* 49(5):66–72.

1996b More than Kin and King: Centralized Political Organization among the Late Classic Maya. *Current Anthropology* 37:801–810.

1998 Scale and Intensity in Classic Period Maya Agriculture: Terracing and Settlement at the "Garden City" of Caracol, Belize. *Culture and Agriculture* 20(2/3):60–77.

Codex Boturini

1964 Códice Boturini. In *Antigüedades de México, basadas en la recopilación de Lord Kingsborough,* vol. 2, pt. 1, edited by J. Corona Núñez. Secretaría de Hacienda y Crédito Público, Mexico City.

Conklin, H.

1980 *Ethnographic Atlas of Ifugao: A Study of Environment, Culture, and Society in Northern Luzon.* Yale University Press, New Haven, Conn.

Demarest, A. A.

1992 Ideology in Ancient Maya Cultural Evolution: The Dynamics of Galactic Polities. In *Ideology and Pre-Columbian Civilizations,* edited by A. A. Demarest and G. W. Conrad, pp. 135–157. School of American Research Press, Santa Fe, N.M.

Durkheim, E.

1961   *Moral Education.* Free Press, New York.

1965   *The Elementary Forms of the Religious Life.* Free Press, New York.

Elisséeff, N.

1983   Urbanisme et urbanisation des *amṣār.* In *La ville dans le proche-orient ancien: Actes du Colloque de Cartigny 1979,* edited by F. Brüschweiler, Y. Christe, R. Martin-Achard, B. Urio, and J. Vicari, pp. 151–160. Editions Peeters, Leuven.

Fletcher, R.

1995   *The Limits of Settlement Growth: A Theoretical Outline.* Cambridge University Press, Cambridge.

Folan, W. J., J. Marcus, and W. F. Miller

1995   Verification of a Maya Settlement Model through Remote Sensing. *Cambridge Archaeological Journal* 5(2):277–301.

Forsyth, D. W.

1993   The Ceramic Sequence of Nakbe, Guatemala. *Ancient Mesoamerica* 4:31–53.

Forsyth, D. W., and Z. Hruby

1997   Análisis de la cerámica arqueológica de Piedras Negras: Temporada de 1997. In *Proyecto arqueológico Piedras Negras: Informe preliminar no. 1, primera temporada 1997,* edited by H. Escobedo and S. D. Houston, pp. 207–212. Report presented to the Instituto de Antropología e Historia de Guatemala (IDAEH).

Freidel, D. A.

1992   The Trees of Life: *Ahau* as Idea and Artifact in Classic Lowland Maya Civilization. In *Ideology and Pre-Columbian Civilizations,* edited by A. A. Demarest and G. W. Conrad, pp. 115–133. School of American Research Press, Santa Fe, N.M.

Fowler, W. R. Jr.

1989   *The Cultural Evolution of Ancient Nahua Civilizations: The Pipil-Nicarao of Central America.* University of Oklahoma Press, Norman.

Fry, R. E.

1990   Disjunctive Growth in the Maya Lowlands. In *Precolumbian Population History in the Maya Lowlands,* edited by T. P. Culbert and D. S. Rice, pp. 285–300. University of New Mexico Press, Albuquerque.

Garrido, L.

1998   PN 12: Excavaciones en la plaza del grupo oeste. In *Proyecto arqueológico Piedras Negras: Informe preliminar no. 2, segunda temporada 1998,* edited by H. Escobedo and S. D. Houston, pp. 55–81. Report presented to the Instituto de Antropología e Historia de Guatemala (IDAEH).

Geertz, C.

1980   *Negara: The Theatre State in Nineteenth-Century Bali.* Princeton University Press, Princeton, N.J.

Gillespie, Susan D.

1989   *The Aztec Kings: The Construction of Rulership in Mexica History.* University of Arizona Press, Tucson.

Goffman, Erving

1956   *Asylums.* Doubleday Anchor Books, Garden City, N.Y.

Gottdeiner, M.

1985   *The Social Production of Urban Space.* 2d ed. University of Texas Press, Austin.

Grube, N., and S. Martin

1998   *Notebook for the XXIInd Maya Hieroglyphic Forum at Texas: Deciphering Maya Politics.*
           Maya Workshop Foundation, Austin.

Hammond, N.

1991   Inside the Black Box: Defining Maya Polity. In *Classic Maya Political History: Hiero-*
           glyphic and Archaeological Evidence, edited by T. P. Culbert, pp. 253–284. Cambridge
           University Press, Cambridge.

Hannerz, U.

1980   *Exploring the City: Inquiries toward an Urban Anthropology.* Columbia University Press,
           New York.

Hansen, R. D.

1998   Continuity and Disjunction: The Pre-Classic Antecedents of Classic Maya Architec-
           ture. In *Function and Meaning in Classic Maya Architecture,* edited by S. D. Houston,
           pp. 49–122. Dumbarton Oaks, Washington, D.C.

Hardin, P., J. Parnell, and R. Terry

1998   Las comunidades rurales y los suelos de Piedras Negras. In *Proyecto arqueológico*
           Piedras Negras: Informe preliminar no. 2, segunda temporada 1998, edited by H. Escobedo
           and S. D. Houston, pp. 383–388. Report presented to the Instituto de Antropología e
           Historia de Guatemala (IDAEH).

Hill, R. M. II

1998   Los otros kaqchikeles: Los chajomá vinak. *Mesoamérica* 35:229–254.

Hodell, D. A., J. H. Curtis, and M. Brenner

1995   Possible Role of Climate in the Collapse of Classic Maya Civilization. *Nature* 375:
           391–394.

Holley, G. R.

1983   Ceramic Change at Piedras Negras. Unpublished Ph.D. dissertation, Department of
           Anthropology, Southern Illinois University, Carbondale.

Houston, S. D.

1993   *Hieroglyphs and History at Dos Pilas: Dynastic Politics of the Classic Maya.* University of
           Texas Press, Austin.

1999   Classic Maya Religion: Beliefs and Practices of an Ancient American People. *BYU*
           Studies, 38(4):43–72.

Houston, S. D., H. Escobedo, M. Child, C. Golden, R. Muñoz, and M. Urquizú

1998   Monumental Architecture at Piedras Negras, Guatemala: Time, History, and Mean-
           ing. *Mayab* 11:40–56.

Houston, S. D., H. Escobedo, M. Child, C. Golden, R. Terry, and D. Webster

2000   In the Land of the Turtle Lords: Archaeological Investigations at Piedras Negras,
           Guatemala, 2000. *Mexicon* 22:97–110.

Houston, S. D., H. Escobedo, D. W. Forsyth, P. Hardin, D. Webster, and L. Wright
1998   On the River of Ruins: Explorations at Piedras Negras, Guatemala, 1997. *Mexicon* 22:16–22.

Houston, S. D., H. Escobedo, P. Hardin, R. Terry, D. Webster, M. Child, C. Golden, K. Emery, and D. Stuart
1999   Between Mountains and Sea: Investigations at Piedras Negras, Guatemala, 1998. *Mexicon* 21:10–17.

Houston, S. D., H. Escobedo, R. Terry, G. Veni, D. Webster, and K. Emery
2000   Among the River Kings: Archaeological Research at Piedras Negras, Guatemala, 1999. *Mexicon* 22:8–17.

Houston, S. D., and D. Stuart
1996   Of Gods, Glyphs, and Kings: Divinity and Rulership among the Classic Maya. *Antiquity* 70:289–312.

Hruby, Z.
1998   Análisis de la Lítica: Temporada 1998. In *Proyecto arqueológico Piedras Negras: Informe preliminar no. 2, segunda temporada 1998,* edited by H. Escobedo and S. D. Houston, pp. 373–381. Report presented to the Instituto de Antropología e Historia de Guatemala (IDAEH).

Huot, J.-L., J.-P. Thalmann, and D. Valbelle
1990   *Naissance des cités.* Éditions Nathan, Paris.

Insoll, T.
1999   *The Archaeology of Islam.* Blackwell, Oxford.

Johnston, K. J.
1994   *The "Invisible" Maya: Late Classic Minimally-Platformed Residential Settlement at Itzán, Petén, Guatemala.* Unpublished Ph.D. dissertation, Deptartment of Anthropology, Yale University.

Jones, C.
1996   *Tikal Report No. 16: Excavations in the East Plaza of Tikal,* vol. 1. University Museum Monograph 92. University Museum, University of Pennsylvania, Philadelphia.

Kaneko, A.
1998   La pequeña acropolis de Yaxchilan, Chiapas. In *XI Simposio de investigaciones arqueológicas en Guatemala, 1997,* edited by J. P. Laporte and H. Escobedo, pp. 261–270. Ministerio de Cultura y Deportes, Guatemala City.

Kopytoff, I.
1987   The Internal African Frontier: The Making of African Political Culture. In *The African Frontier: The Reproduction of Traditional African Societies,* edited by I. Kopytoff, pp. 3–84. Indiana University Press, Bloomington.
1999   Permutations in Patrimonialism and Populism: The Aghem Chiefdoms of Western Cameroon. In *Beyond Chiefdoms: Pathways to Complexity in Africa,* edited by S. K. McIntosh, pp. 88–96. Cambridge University Press, Cambridge.

Kostoff, S.
1991   *The City Shaped: Urban Patterns and Meanings through History.* Bulfinch Press, Boston.

Lansing, J. S.

1991   *Priests and Programmers: Technologies of Power in the Engineered Landscapes of Bali.* Princeton University Press, Princeton, N.J.

Laporte, J. P.

1994   *Ixtonton, Dolores, Petén: Entidad política del noroeste de las Montañas Mayas.* Atlas Arqueológico de Guatemala No. 2. Ministerio de Cultura y Deportes, Guatemala City.

Laurence, R.

1994   *Roman Pompeii: Space and Society.* Routledge, London.

Lee, T. A. Jr., and B. Hayden

1988   *San Pablo Cave and El Cayo on the Usumacinta River, Chiapas, Mexico.* Papers of the New World Archaeological Foundation, No. 53. Brigham Young University, Provo, Utah.

Levy, R.

1990   *Mesocosm: Hinduism and the Organization of a Traditional Newar City in Nepal.* University of California Press, Berkeley.

López V., S. L.

1989   *Análisis y clasificación de la cerámica de un sitio maya del clásico: Yaxchilán, México.* British Archaeological Reports, International Series 535. Oxford.

n.d.   The Ceramics of Pomoná, Tabasco: A Classic Site Example on the Northwestern Lowlands, under the Realm of the Yaxchilan and Palenque Sphere. Unpublished manuscript in possession of author.

Luttwak, E. N.

1976   *The Grand Strategy of the Roman Empire from the First Century A.D. to the Third.* Johns Hopkins University Press, Baltimore.

Lynch, K.

1981   *Good City Form.* MIT Press, Cambridge, Mass.

McAnany, Patricia A.

1995   *Living with the Ancestors: Kinship and Kingship in Ancient Maya Society.* University of Texas Press, Austin.

1997   Shamans and Kings and the Politics of Authority. Paper presented at the Field Museum conference, "Leaders to Rulers: The Development of Political Centralization," Chicago.

Marcus, J.

1983   On the Nature of the Mesoamerican City. In *Prehistoric Settlement Patterns: Essays in Honor of Gordon R. Willey,* edited by E. Z. Vogt and R. M. Leventhal, pp. 195–242. University of New Mexico Press, Albuquerque.

Marcus, J., and K. V. Flannery

1996   *Zapotec Civilization: How Urban Society Evolved in Mexico's Oaxaca Valley.* Thames and Hudson, London.

Margueron, J.-C.

1994   Fondations et refondations au Proche-Orient au Bronze Récent. In *Nuove Fondazioni nel Vicino Oriente Antico: Realtà e Ideologia,* edited by Stefania Mazzoni, pp. 3–27. Giardini, Pisa.

Mathews, P. L.

1988   *The Sculpture of Yaxchilan.* Unpublished Ph.D. dissertation, Department of Anthropology, Yale University.

Mathews, P., and M. M. Aliphat Fernández

1998   *Informe de la temporada de campo 1993, Proyecto El Cayo.* Report presented to the Consejo de Arqueología, Instituto Nacional de Antropología e Historia (INAH).

Mazzoni, S.

1991   Aramaean and Luwian New Foundations. In *Nuove fondazioni nel Vicino Oriente antico: realtà e ideologia,* edited by S. Mazzoni, pp. 319–340. Giardini Editori, Pisa.

Monaghan, J.

1995   *The Covenants with Earth and Rain: Exchange, Sacrifice, and Revelation in Mixtec Sociality.* University of Oklahoma Press, Norman.

2000   Theology and History in the Study of Mesoamerican Religions. In *Handbook of Middle American Indians: Supplement 6, Ethnography,* edited by John Monaghan, pp. 24–49. University of Texas Press, Austin.

Morley, S. G.

1937–1938   *The Inscriptions of Peten.* 5 vols. Carnegie Institution of Washington, Publication 437. Washington, D.C.

Owens, E. J.

1991   *The City in the Greek and Roman World.* Routledge, London.

Parker, G.

1998   *The Grand Strategy of Philip II.* Yale University Press, New Haven, Conn.

Parish, S. M.

1994   *Moral Knowing in a Hindu Sacred City: An Exploration of Mind, Emotion, and Self.* Columbia University Press, New York.

Proskouriakoff, T.

1960   Historical Implications of a Pattern of Dates at Piedras Negras, Guatemala. *American Antiquity* 25:454–475.

Recinos, A.

1957   *Crónicas indígenas de Guatemala.* Editorial Universitaria, Guatemala City.

Redfield, R., and M. Singer

1954   The Cultural Role of Cities. *Economic Development and Cultural Change* 2(1):53–73.

Restall, M.

1997   *The Maya World: Yucatec Culture and Society, 1550–1850.* Stanford University Press, Stanford, Calif.

Rouse, I.

1986   *Migrations in Prehistory: Inferring Population Movement from Cultural Remains.* Yale University Press, New Haven, Conn.

Sabloff, J. A.

1975   *Excavations at Seibal, Department of Peten, Guatemala: Number 2, Ceramics.* Memoirs of the Peabody Museum of Archaeology and Ethnology, Harvard University, vol. 13, No 2. Cambridge, Mass.

Satterthwaite, L. Jr.

    1937   Identification of Maya Temple Buildings at Piedras Negras. In *25th Anniversary Studies,* edited by D. S. Davidson, pp. 161–177. Publication of the Philadelphia Anthropological Society, vol. 1. University of Pennsylvania Press.

    1943   Introduction. *Piedras Negras Architecture, Pt. 1, No. 1.* University Museum, Philadelphia.

    1954   *Piedras Negras Archaeology: Architecture, Part VI, Unclassified Buildings and Substructures, No. 4: Structure O–7.* Philadelphia: University Museum.

Schroeder, S.

    1991   *Chimalpahin and the Kingdoms of Chalco.* University of Arizona Press, Tucson.

Scott, J. C.

    1976   *The Moral Economy of the Peasant: Rebellion and Subsistence in Southeast Asia.* Yale University Press: New Haven, Conn.

Sennett, R.

    1994   *Flesh and Stone: The Body and the City in Western Civilization.* W. W. Norton, New York.

Sharer, R. J., W. L. Fash, D. W. Sedat, L. P. Traxler, and R. Williamson

    1999   Continuities and Contrasts in Early Classic Architecture of Central Copan. In *Mesoamerican Architecture as a Cultural Symbol,* edited by J. K. Kowalski, pp. 220–249. Oxford University Press, Oxford.

Sharer, R. J., L. P. Traxler, D. W. Sedat, E. E. Bell, M. A. Canuto, and C. Powell

    1999   Early Classsic Architecture beneath the Copan Acropolis: A Research Update. *Ancient Mesoamerica* 10:3–23.

Sharlin, A.

    1978   Natural Decrease in Early Modern Cities: A Reconsideration. *Past and Present* 79:126–138.

Smith, M. E.

    1995   The Mesoamerican Urban Landscape from Teotihuacan to the Aztecs. Paper presented at the conference, "Archaeology of Complex Societies: Centripetal and Centrifugal Forces," California State University, San Bernardino.

Smith, M. E., and F. F. Berdan

    1996   Introduction. In *Aztec Imperial Strategies,* edited by F. F. Berdan, R. E. Blanton, E. H. Boone, M. G. Hodge, M. E. Smith, and E. Umberger, pp. 1–9. Dumbarton Oaks, Washington, D.C.

Southall, A.

    1983   Towards a Universal Urban Anthropology. In *Town-Talk: The Dynamics of Urban Anthropology,* edited by G. Ansari and P. J. M. Nas, pp. 7–21. E. J. Brill, Leiden.

    1998   *The City in Time and Space.* Cambridge University Press, Cambridge.

Stambaugh, J. E.

    1988   *The Ancient Roman City.* Johns Hopkins University Press, Baltimore, Md.

Storey, R.

    1992   *Life and Death in the Ancient City of Teotihuacan: A Modern Paleodemographic Synthesis.* University of Alabama Press, Tuscaloosa.

Stuart, D.

    1998   "The Fire Enters His House": Architecture and Ritual in Classic Maya Texts. In *Func-*

tion and Meaning in Classic Maya Architecture, edited by S. D. Houston, pp. 373–425. Dumbarton Oaks, Washington, D.C..

2000 The Arrival of Strangers: Teotihuacan in Classic Maya History. In *The Classic Heritage: From Teotihuacan to the Templo Mayor,* edited by D. Carrasco, L. Jones, and S. Sessions, pp. 465–513. University of Colorado Press, Boulder.

Stuart, D., and S. D. Houston

1994 *Classic Maya Place Names.* Studies in Pre-Columbian Art and Archaeology No. 33. Dumbarton Oaks, Washington, D.C.

Thompson, J. E. S.

1966 *The Rise and Fall of Maya Civilization.* University of Oklahoma Press, Norman.

Traxler, L.

2001 The Royal Court of Early Classic Copan. In *Royal Courts of the Ancient Maya,* edited by T. Inomata and S. D. Houston, pp. 46–73. Westview Press, Boulder, Colo.

Turner, B. L. II

1990 Population Reconstruction of the Central Maya Lowlands, 1000 B.C. to A.D. 1500. In *Precolumbian Population History in the Maya Lowlands,* edited by T. P. Culbert and D. S. Rice, pp. 301–324. University of New Mexico Press, Albuquerque.

Wallace, D. M.

1984 *Russia: On the Eve of War and Revolution.* Princeton University Press, Princeton, N.J.

Webster, D.

1997 Maya Divine Kingship: Issues and Comparisons. Paper presented at the Brigham Young University conference, "Classic Maya Religion: A New Synthesis," Provo, Utah.

2001 Spatial Dimensions of Maya Courtly Life. In *Royal Courts of the Ancient Maya,* edited by T. Inomata and S. D. Houston, pp. 130–167. Westview Press, Boulder, Colo.

Webster, D., and J. Kirker

1997 Arqueología del paisaje: Transecto entre Piedras Negras y El Porvenir. In *Proyecto arqueológico Piedras Negras: Informe preliminar no. 1, primera temporada 1997,* edited by H. Escobedo and S. D. Houston, pp. 185–205. Report presented to the Instituto de Antropología e Historia de Guatemala (IDAEH).

Webster, D., J. Kirker, A. Kovak, and T. Murtha

1998 El reconocimiento: Investigaciones de población y ecología en la periferia de Piedras Negras. In *Proyecto arqueológico Piedras Negras: Informe preliminar no. 2, segunda temporada 1998,* edited by H. Escobedo and S. D. Houston, pp. 289–307. Report presented to the Instituto de Antropología e Historia de Guatemala (IDAEH).

Webster, D., and A. Kovak

1998 RS 6: Excavaciones en la periferia de Piedras Negras. In *Proyecto arqueológico Piedras Negras: Informe preliminar no. 2, segunda temporada 1998,* edited by H. Escobedo and S. D. Houston, pp. 309–331. Report presented to the Instituto de Antropología e Historia de Guatemala (IDAEH).

Weatley, P.

1983 *Nāgara and Commandery: Origins of the Southeast Asian Urban Traditions.* Research Paper Nos. 207–208. Department of Geography, University of Chicago, Chicago.

Wolfe, A.

1999   Morality in the Social Sciences. *The Chronicle of Higher Education* 46(2):B4–B6.

Wuthnow, R.

1987   *Meaning and Moral Order: Explorations in Cultural Analysis.* University of California Press, Berkeley.

Urban Social
Transformations and
the Problem of the
"First City"
New Research from Mesopotamia

GEOFF EMBERLING

A city, according to the etymological dictionary *Origins,* is simply "an aggregation of citizens" (Partridge 1983:101). This definition, however brief and however circular, highlights three elements of urbanism. First, a city is a community of
people, with forms of social, political, and economic organization that distinguish
it from pre-urban or nonurban communities. Second, this aggregation happens in a
particular location—the city—that takes its place not only within an economic geography, but also in the conceptual map of urban residents and their neighbors. Third,
the inhabitants of a city—its citizens, more or less—in some important way identify themselves with it. A city thus defines a community, a place, and an identity.

This chapter sheds light on the origin of cities in Mesopotamia of the fourth
millennium B.C. by presenting new data on the Uruk-period settlement at Tell Brak,
ancient Nagar, in northern Mesopotamia. After defining the notion of a city and

discussing explanations of their origins, I review evidence for prehistoric cities in the ancient Middle East from Jericho and Uruk to Tell Brak. The new data suggest revisions in our explanations of this fundamental transformation in human social life.

DEFINITIONS OF THE CITY

Most archaeologists, as social scientists, have focused on the city as a community. In his construct of the "Urban Revolution," Childe (1950) directed attention to the economic specialization required for a settlement to grow to urban dimensions; given the limitations of premodern agriculture and transportation, only intensive irrigation agriculture could produce enough food to feed a city. The surplus food would support not only the growing population of the city, but also a growing urban elite, dependent specialist artisans, and public construction projects. Childe notoriously included writing among his criteria for cities: a community is a city if some of the people living there can write, he argued. While one can criticize various of Childe's 10 criteria that "exhaust the factors common to the oldest cities" (Childe 1950:16), his fundamental notion that a city is a community constructed on and bound by specialization has itself been extremely productive.

Cities, of course, are not simply specialized communities; they are places with physical properties including a certain size, density, and contiguity of settlement, although it has proven impossible to define cross-culturally the size at which a town becomes a city. One threshold is the size at which the population is too large to provide its own food, given the constraints of daily travel to and from fields. A city is thus a community with an inherent link to a rural support network. While there is no absolute population size at which this transformation occurs, given variations in crop yields and transportation limitations, many archaeological sequences show quantum leaps in site size that reduce the ambiguity of our classifications.

Cities do not exist in isolation. In conceptual terms, the notion "urban" requires the contrasting and defining category "rural" (Yoffee 1995:284). The urban-rural distinction reflects an economic and social basis: a proportion of city residents depend on rural farmers for food, whether agricultural or animal-based (Zeder chapter 7), and a still larger proportion require wood or other fuel from outside the city itself. In this sense, rural production can constrain urban growth (e.g., Wilkinson 1994). In many settlement systems, rural farmers, herders, and hunters can conversely acquire some crafted products only in cities, although itinerant merchants and artisans alleviate this need in some settings. Activities conducted exclusively in one or the other location would come to have distinct social value attached to them. Central Place Theory and related theories of geography predict the location of centers within their rural hinterlands according to economic efficiency, and naturally the degree to which cities, towns, and villages are interconnected varies greatly among settlement systems. Furthermore, most cities also exist within a network of other cities. The specialization characteristic of the urban economy thus extends beyond the interdependence of a city and its hinterland.

Rural hinterlands are only one part of the culturally constructed landscape within which cities are located. The centrality of cities in this landscape, however, predisposes them to serve as foci of identity. The link between urbanization and alterations in constructed social identities was not emphasized by Childe or by subsequent scholars such as R. McC. Adams (whose comparative work is among the few attempts at explaining urban origins), and receives too little attention from scholars today.

ORIGINS OF CITIES

For better or worse, cities are a striking development in human history. On the one hand, the concentration of specialized labor in cities, including specialized administration and control, made possible the accumulation of great wealth and provides the context for invention and development in a variety of technological, artistic, and intellectual endeavors. On the other hand, the concentration of population leads to new kinds of diseases (Cohen 1989) and to a reduced standard of living for a majority of the population. Yet, like the compromise-laden adoption of agriculture that preceded it, urbanism too has proven to be an irreversible transformation.

Explanation depends on definition, and explanation of urban origins has depended on definitions proposed for "the city." In his extensive work on Mesopotamia, Adams (1966) shares Childe's perspective on the city as a kind of specialized society. He explains the origin of cities by identifying the origin of specialization, which he sees as the coordination of disparate local ecological zones and trade for distant raw materials. Wheatley (1971), in a similar vein, argues that early cities functioned as ceremonial centers, with priests as the first specialists in urban society. As recent archaeological theory has shown, a weakness of evolutionary explanations like these is that they fail to consider the active participants in the process. Who were these priests, and to what extent were they aware of the changes as they took place? Did they have competitors, or was control ceded entirely to them by their grateful subjects?

To augment and alter the explanations of Adams and Wheatley, we can first ask how and by whom cities were constructed as geographical foci in the landscape as a means of identifying a construction of place. One can hope for archaeological studies of how space within cities is divided and segregated and how activities are distributed over it (see Keith this volume). Second, we may want to inquire into the construction of identity surrounding the origin of the city. While textual sources may make this type of analysis more accessible, it may be visible in excavated material culture, just as it is increasingly argued that ethnicity may be (Emberling 1997).

CITIES IN THE ANCIENT MIDDLE EAST

A brief review of the development of central settlements in the ancient Middle East—as well as of claims for the world's oldest city—shows that there is no difficulty in identifying major thresholds in urban development. The earliest site for which urban status has been claimed is Jericho in the valley of the Jordan River (figure 10.1; summary in Holland and Netzer 1992). During the Pre-Pottery Neolithic A period, now dated to circa 10,000–8500 cal B.C., the settlement was composed of a series of small, single-roomed round houses dispersed over an area of perhaps 2.5 hectares. There is no evidence of craft specialization or any houses or burials of higher status than others. The inhabitants also built a stone town wall and associated stone tower as large as 8 meters high and 8.5 meters in diameter; the top of the tower would have projected more than 20 meters above the level of the surrounding plain. The excavator, Kathleen Kenyon (1956, 1981), believed the communal labor represented by the tower reflected an urban social organization, most likely for defense. Bar-Yosef (1986; 1995:193) has suggested that the stone construction served as a defense against flooding rather than against enemies. While such an interpretation would change Kenyon's understanding of the social environment within which the inhabitants of Jericho lived, it does not alter the fact that the economy and society were relatively undifferentiated, and thus that the settlement should not be considered a city.

Çatal Höyük on the Anatolian Plateau, a Pottery Neolithic site now dated to circa 7000–6000 cal B.C., was an unwalled settlement of approximately 12 hectares that has been called the "World's First City" (Shane and Küçük 1998; also Mellaart

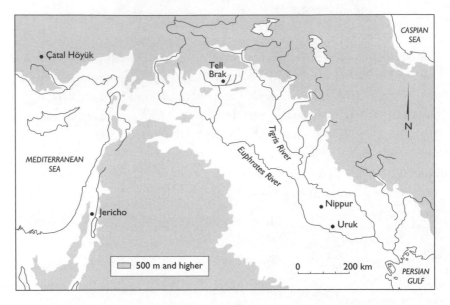

Figure 10.1. Map of the ancient Near East.

1967). Houses at Çatal Höyük seem to have been densely packed together over most of the mound, with relatively little open space. Some of these houses were decorated with wall paintings and plastered features. Mellaart proposed that the painted houses were shrines or priests' houses, arguing that some of the artifacts found at the site, particularly some of the obsidian tools, were so finely made that they had to be products of specialized artisans. More recent reanalysis by Hodder and his team has cast doubt on Mellaart's claims for separate shrines at the site, showing that the houses differed along a continuum of complexity (Hodder 1996; Ritchey 1996). Furthermore, recent work has shown that the material culture at the site is similar to that of other contemporary sites in Anatolia and is not likely to be specialist-produced. The settlement itself, rising some 17.5 meters above the surrounding Konya plain, would have been a prominent feature of the cultural landscape during the Neolithic. It was certainly the largest settlement of its time in the region, but it did not generate a differentiated rural hinterland; rather, it was surrounded by a number of small villages, as archaeological surveys have shown (Baird 1996).

The next major leap in settlement size recognized by archaeologists took place in the Middle and Late Uruk periods of southern Mesopotamia, circa 3800–3100 cal B.C.; the site of Uruk itself is the best-known example. Uruk is located in southern Iraq. While the region lacks metal and significant timber resources, the local environment could support farming in irrigated fields, fishing in river and marsh, and herding on the margins of these areas. During the Middle Uruk period, settlements of 50–75 hectares developed at Nippur and Uruk (Adams 1981:71). Because these estimates are based mainly on surface survey and limited soundings, little is known about the spatial layout of these earliest cities.

As the Tigris and Euphrates changed course during the Late Uruk period, large numbers of people migrated south from the Nippur area to Uruk and its hinterland (Adams 1981:61ff.; Pollock 1999:59ff.). Adams estimated that the settlement covered 100 hectares in this period; a more recent survey of the site suggests that it occupied some 250 hectares by the Late Uruk period (Finkbeiner 1991:194), with further expansion to as much as 550 hectares in the early third millennium B.C. (Finkbeiner 1991:195; Nissen 1972:793). In the Late Uruk period, the city was spatially and administratively dominated by a complex of public buildings 7 hectares in area and 25 meters above plain level known in later times as Eanna, the dwelling of the goddess Inanna. The function of these buildings is not certain because they contained few objects when excavated and because we have few parallels of this period, although Forest (1996:133) has made the unorthodox suggestion that the whole formed elements of a palace. In any case, it is abundantly clear that the city at Uruk formed a specialized urban economy, with specialized mass production of ceramics (Nissen 1970) and administrative tools that included the first cuneiform writing on clay tablets and cylinder seals, which verified the authority of an official to perform one of a number of transactions. The newly developing specializations included writing (by scribes), and among the early texts are the Standard Professions list, which lists titles of a number of occupations (summarized in Nissen et al. 1993:110–111), and the Cities list (Englund and Nissen 1993).

The notion that Uruk was the first city in the Middle East presumes a model of urban development summarized in a recent review: "Cities appeared in southern Mesopotamia . . . [and then] the concept spread further north" (van de Mieroop 1997:28–29). This model has been codified in the theory of the Uruk Expansion, in which inhabitants of Uruk moved into the distant resource-rich mountains to procure metals, stones, and timber for the city (Algaze 1993; see also Rothman 2001).

Settlement in the first cities may have been prompted by an environmental accident—changes in the Tigris and Euphrates watercourses—and the resulting concentration of people around Uruk—or perhaps by exceptional control exerted by an early ruler of the city, or again by a developing surplus and the opportunities it created, but the first city was in this view a unique event. With the large increase in population in the city of Uruk during the Late Uruk period, possibly composed largely of migrants, as Bernbeck (1999) has suggested, it is perhaps surprising that there is no recognizable evidence for distinct ethnic identities in the city. Later cities, after all, are well known as loci of social differentiation through prolonged, close interaction among their inhabitants. Late Uruk material culture is strongly homogenized through most of Mesopotamia, although we do not know whether to associate this material with a state or a city. Work on distinguishing styles within Uruk artifacts may make it possible to distinguish these identities.

In subsequent millennia, Mesopotamia was the population center of the Middle East, and cuneiform texts present Mesopotamian views of their cities. In literature of the late third millennium B.C., the city was depicted as the seat of political power. One such composition, the "Sumerian King List," presents an ideological vision of history in which Mesopotamia was ruled from one city at a time: "After the Flood had swept thereover, when the kingship was lowered from heaven, the kingship was in Kish . . . [after 23 kings reigned,] Kish was smitten with weapons; its kingship to Eanna was carried" (Jacobsen 1939:77, 85). Indeed, cities were considered to have been created by their individual city-gods; if a city were to be deserted by its god, it would be destroyed (Brüschweiler 1983).

Jacobsen (1943) long ago suggested that early Mesopotamian cities were ruled not only by kings but also by assemblies of "citizens" (Sumerian *dumu*). Although participation in the assembly—and therefore citizenship in one sense—was presumably limited to a small subset of the urban population, even foreign laborers working for public institutions were identified in administrative texts by their city of origin in the mid-third millennium B.C. By contrast, these laborers were not identified by their membership in or service to a temple, king, or state. It has even been suggested that the names of some Sumerian cities refer in fact to a kind of city or clan emblem (Jacobsen 1967).

In Mesopotamia, a single term designated a settlement, whether a small village or a large center (Sumerian *uru;* Akkadian *alum;* Oates 1983; van de Mieroop 1997). The architectural form of large Mesopotamian cities, however, with a central temple on a high platform, made them visible from great distances in the flat plains and made them focal points on the landscape. The settled area as a whole, defined by walled cities and areas of agricultural and pastoral production in between, came to represent order, while the steppe (Sumerian *edin*) and mountain areas (Sumerian *kur*) were foreign, chaotic, and dangerous—the home of wild beasts, nomads, spirits, and demons (Brüschweiler 1983; Limet 1978). There is no Sumerian or Akkadian term for state, however; in contrast, the Maya (Houston et al. this volume) recognized the state, but had no term for city.

Mesopotamian cities of the third and second millennium B.C. had a distinctive spatial organization, as the work of Elizabeth Stone demonstrates (1995, 1997; see also Keith this volume; Postgate 1992–1993, 1994). They were often walled, containing the temple of the city-god on a high platform and a palace and administrative center spatially separated from it. The cities were subdivided by canals or major roads as well as by internal walls. Surprisingly, there is little evidence for localization of craft production in specific craft quarters; rather, each neighborhood seems to have been largely self-sufficient, including within it a mix of crafts as well as elite and nonelite residential architecture. Early Mesopotamian cities had few large open spaces that could have served as marketplaces, but city gates or harbors may have fulfilled those economic functions. The applicability of these observations to cities of other distant cultures has yet to be assessed in detail. A literary description of the city of Uruk composed in the Kassite period emphasized orchards and clay pits in addition to walls and central temple: "One square mile is city, one square mile is orchards, one square mile is claypits, as well as the open ground of Ishtar's temple. Three square miles and the open ground comprise Uruk" (Gilgamesh I and XI; Dalley 1989:50, 120). A further description characterizes the city as "Uruk, the sheep-fold of holy Eanna, the sacred storehouse" (Gilgamesh I, 11–12).

Rather than being economically independent (cf. Charlton and Nichols 1997:1), Mesopotamian cities certainly depended on their rural hinterlands (Klengel 1990; Powell 1990) and also imported valuable raw materials from the distant mountains, and may have specialized locally in producing different subsistence products. Although an attempt has been made to study such specialization among Mesopotamian cities (Crawford 1973), such relationships have yet to be thoroughly documented.

To summarize, early Mesopotamian cities were communities whose specializations—ruler, priest, trader, artisan—had distinct traces in physical urban form. The city was an indigenous category, conceived as the home of the god, served by a king, and inhabited by people who, to greater or lesser degrees, identified themselves with it. Our analytical category "the state," by contrast, has little direct reflection in the practices of early Mesopotamians, and in fact homogenizes a series of disparate political and administrative institutions.

Figure 10.2. Tell Brak from the southeast.

TELL BRAK: AN EARLY CITY IN
NORTHERN MESOPOTAMIA

Recent work at Tell Brak, a city of the Uruk period in northeastern Syria more than 700 kilometers distant from Uruk, has begun to suggest that the unicentric model for Middle Eastern urbanism is not correct. Finds from excavation, survey, and resulting reappraisal of earlier work at the site show that Tell Brak, ancient Nagar, was a city comparable to Uruk in its size and complexity in the mid-fourth millennium B.C., before the extensive contacts of the Uruk period had taken place.

Tell Brak is located on a small tributary of the Khabur River, the Wadi Jaghjagh, on the edge of the modern limit of dry farming. While the current location of the Jaghjagh is some 3 kilometers from Brak, it is possible that a wadi ran closer to the site in antiquity. In spite of its relatively marginal location for agriculture, the settlement was occupied for more than 4,000 years, attesting to the significance of its location on two important routes, that from southern Mesopotamia through the Jebel Sinjar and into the mineral resources of the Taurus Mountains, and that across the plains of northern Mesopotamia, from the Tigris ultimately to the Mediterranean. Its importance over a long period of time is demonstrated by its accumulated height of 43 meters, which makes it dominate the surrounding landscape (figure 10.2). Like Uruk, Brak had the potential of integrating ecological

Figure 10.3. Rendering of the Eye Temple on its platform with reconstructed site contours; image from the virtual reality computer model reconstruction of the site by Learning Sites, Inc. Image copyright, Learning Sites, Inc. (reprinted with permission).

zones (the agricultural plains and the steppe to the south), which also undoubtedly contributed to its importance.

The site was first excavated in 1937–1938 by Max Mallowan (1947). Among his discoveries were three superimposed temples that he named the Eye Temple because thousands of amulets or idols with engraved eyes had been mixed in the bricks of the intermediate level. The temple was quite rich, including an altar embellished with a frieze of gold with silver nails, stone rosettes, and small human heads that may have been used as architectural ornaments. The temple on its platform stood well above the existing settlement and as much as 15 meters above the surrounding plain (figure 10.3), although later occupation at the site obscures its prominence. Mallowan originally dated the earliest of these structures to the Jemdet Nasr period, but recent finds of eye idols in a stratified domestic sequence through the Uruk period show that eye idols were being made in the "Northern Middle Uruk period" of the mid-fourth millennium B.C. (Area TW, Level 16; Oates and Oates 1993:176–177).

A more recent program of excavation by David Oates and Joan Oates begun in

1976 has recovered several intact contexts of Uruk date. Among their finds have been cylinder seal impressions earlier in date than any found at Uruk (Oates and Oates 1993:178). Most strikingly, excavation in 1997 revealed a fragment of a massive gateway—with stone door sill and door socket stone—and associated walls of Northern Middle Uruk date in Area TW (Levels 18–19). A fragment of a wall of identical construction had been found halfway around the mound in Area HS6 (Matthews 1996:66–68). Stratigraphically above this gateway was a large structure with niched walls (see Emberling and McDonald 2001), a mark of elite or public architecture in the Uruk period.

In the 1998 season, a topographic survey and program of test pits were conducted to identify the limits of settlement on the main mound as well as possible connections with a ring of outlying smaller mounds that had previously been dated to the Uruk period (Emberling et al. 1999). This work suggests, first, that the main mound itself may have covered an area of 65 hectares. Test pits on the outer mounds show occupation over a 45-hectare area during the Early Uruk period and over an area of perhaps 100 hectares during the Northern Middle Uruk period, although settlement is not continuous—extensive clay borrow pits in the intervening area may have removed traces of earlier settlement (Wilkinson et al. 2001). Brak was clearly a large settlement before southern Uruk settlers arrived.

We do not yet have a detailed understanding of Uruk-period settlement pattern around Brak. A recent survey may show aspects of the pattern but cannot be regarded as comprehensive, not least because the surveyors did not distinguish Middle from Late Uruk (Eidem and Warburton 1996). Furthermore, the gap in settlement in the northwestern portion of their survey map is at least in part due to the existence of the modern village of Tell Brak, and the linear concentration of sites along the present watercourses may have more to do with the survey methods than with ancient settlement patterns. In any case, the survey provisionally suggests the existence of a large "empty zone" 3–4 kilometers in width outside the "suburbs" of Brak during the Uruk period, with a series of evenly spaced small settlements, none larger than 4 hectares, further away. The "empty" zone may have been devoted to agriculture in antiquity, as it is in modern times, and may just have been sufficient to provide food for the city, given conservative estimates of population density and agricultural yields. It in any case corresponds to the length of radial hollows identified around many sites in Northern Mesopotamia, plausibly interpreted as roads (Wilkinson 1994:492–493), as well as to ethnographically derived estimates of the distance farmers are able to walk to their fields on a daily basis (Adams 1981:87). Detailed studies of the economic interrelationship of Brak and its surrounding settlements have yet to be undertaken.

CONCLUSION

To summarize, the first Mesopotamian cities developed during the Uruk period. While it has long been presumed that Uruk itself was the first true city in Mesopotamia, recent work at Tell Brak shows it to have been a large, complex settlement in the Middle Uruk period, approximately contemporary with the first growth of Uruk itself. While there can be little doubt that Uruk soon grew to much larger size and wealth than Tell Brak, perhaps because of environmental limitations on the growth of cities in the north (Wilkinson 1994), our explanations for the origin of Mesopotamian cities must now accommodate at least two burgeoning centers.

While most details of such an explanation remain to be assessed, it is striking that Adams's explanation of urban origins holds true in its outline form. Both of these cities are located in positions that integrate different ecological zones (if anything, Brak more than Uruk). Yet we still need to know more about competing factions, the changing organization and use of space, the construction of the center, and the changing role of urban citizenship and other social identities to give us a fuller understanding of the transformative effect of urbanization.

ACKNOWLEDGMENTS

I would like to thank Monica Smith for organizing the symposium in which this essay was originally given and for the continuing discussion since; Robert McC. Adams for some pointed comments in the symposium; and Norman Yoffee and Joan Oates for reading the manuscript.

REFERENCES

Adams, R. McC.
    1966   *The Evolution of Urban Society.* Aldine, Chicago.
    1981   *Heartland of Cities: Surveys of Ancient Settlement and Land Use on the Central Floodplain of the Euphrates.* University of Chicago Press, Chicago.
Algaze, G.
    1993   *The Uruk World System.* University of Chicago Press, Chicago.

Baird, D.

1996   Konya Plain. *Anatolian Archaeology* 2:12.

Bar-Yosef, O.

1986   The Walls of Jericho: An Alternative Interpretation. *Current Anthropology* 27:157–162.

1995   Earliest Food Producers—Pre-Pottery Neolithic (8000–5000). In *The Archaeology of Society in the Holy Land,* edited by T. E. Levy, pp. 190–201. Facts on File, New York.

Bernbeck, R.

1999   Landflucht und Ethnizität im alten Mesopotamien. In *Fluchtpunkt Uruk. Archäologische Einheit aus methodischer Vielfalt,* edited by H. Kühne, K. Bartl, and R. Bernbeck, pp. 296–310. Marie Leidorf, Espelkamp (Germany).

Brüschweiler, F.

1983   La ville dans les textes littéraires sumériens. In *La ville dans le Proche-Orient ancien,* edited by F. Brüschweiler et al., pp. 181–198. Les Cahiers du CEPOA 1. Peeters, Leuven.

Charlton, T. H., and D. L. Nichols

1997   The City-State Concept: Development and Applications. In *The Archaeology of City-States: Cross-Cultural Approaches,* edited by D. L. Nichols and T. H. Charlton, pp. 1–14. Smithsonian Institution Press, Washington, D.C.

Childe, V. G.

1950   The Urban Revolution. *Town Planning Review* 21(1):3–17.

Cohen, M. N.

1989   *Health and the Rise of Civilization.* Yale University Press, New Haven, Conn.

Crawford, H.

1973   Mesopotamia's Invisible Exports in the Third Millennium B.C. *World Archaeology* 5:232–241.

Dalley, S.

1989   *Myths from Mesopotamia: Creation, The Flood, Gilgamesh, and Others.* Oxford University Press, Oxford.

Eidem, J., and D. Warburton

1996   In the Land of Nagar: A Survey around Tell Brak. *Iraq* 58:51–64.

Emberling, G.

1997   Ethnicity in Complex Societies: Archaeological Perspectives. *Journal of Archaeological Research* 5(4):295–344.

Emberling, G., J. Cheng. T. Larsen, H. Pittman, T. Skuldboel, J. Weber, and H. Wright

1999   Excavations at Tell Brak 1998: Preliminary Report. *Iraq* 61:1–41.

Emberling, G., and H. McDonald

2001   Excavations at Tell Brak 2000: Preliminary Report. *Iraq* 63:21–54.

Englund, R. K., and H. J. Nissen

1993   Die lexikalischen Listen der archaischen Texte aus Uruk. Archaische Texte aus Uruk 3. Gebr. Mann, Berlin.

Finkbeiner, U.

1991   *Uruk, Kampagne 35-37, 1982–1984: Die archäologische Oberflächenuntersuchung (Survey).* Ausgrabungen in Uruk-Warka Endberichte 4. Philipp von Zabern, Mainz.

Forest, J.-D.

1996   *Mésopotamie. L'Apparition de l'état (VIIᵉ–IIIᵉ millénaires).* Méditerranée, Paris.

Hodder, I.

1996   *On the Surface: Çatalhöyük 1993–95.* British Institute of Archaeology at Ankara Monograph 22. British School of Archaeology at Ankara, London.

Holland, T. A., and E. Netzer

1992   Jericho. *Anchor Bible Dictionary* 3:723–740.

Jacobsen, T.

1939   *The Sumerian King List.* Assyriological Studies 11. University of Chicago Press, Chicago.

1943   Primitive Democracy in Ancient Mesopotamia. *Journal of Near Eastern Studies* 2:159–172.

1967   Some Sumerian City-Names. *Journal of Cuneiform Studies* 21:100–103.

Kenyon, K.

1956   Jericho and Its Setting in Near Eastern History. *Antiquity* 30:184–197.

1981   Excavations at Jericho 3: *The Architecture and Stratigraphy of the Tell,* edited by T. A. Holland. British School of Archaeology in Jerusalem, London.

Klengel, H.

1990   Introduction. In *The Town as Regional Economic Centre in the Ancient Near East,* edited by E. Aerts and H. Klengel, pp. 3–6. Leuven University Press, Leuven.

Limet, H.

1978   Étude sémantique de ma.da, kur, kalam. *Revue d'Assyriologie* 72:1–12.

Mallowan, M. E. L.

1947   Excavations at Brak and Chagar Bazar. *Iraq* 9.

Matthews, R. J.

1996   Excavations at Tell Brak, 1996. *Iraq* 58:65–77.

Mellaart, J.

1967   *Çatal Hüyük: A Neolithic Town in Anatolia.* Thames and Hudson, London.

Nissen, H. J.

1970   Grabung in den Quadraten K/L XII in Uruk-Warka. *Baghdader Mitteilungen* 5:101–191.

1972   The City Wall of Uruk. In *Man, Settlement, and Urbanism,* edited by P. J. Ucko, R. E. Tringham, and G. W. Dimbleby, pp. 793–798. Duckworth, London.

Nissen, H. J., P. Damerow, and R. K. Englund

1993   *Archaic Bookkeeping: Early Writing Techniques of Economic Administration in the Ancient Near East.* University of Chicago Press, Chicago.

Oates, D., and J. Oates

1993   Excavations at Tell Brak 1992–93. *Iraq* 55:155–199.

Oates, J.

1983   Urban Trends in Prehistoric Mesopotamia. In *La ville dans le Proche-Orient ancien,* edited by F. Brüschweiler et al., pp. 81–92. Les Cahiers du CEPOA 1. Peeters, Leuven.

Partridge, E.

1983   *Origins: A Short Etymological Dictionary of Modern English.* Greenwich House, New York.

Pollock, S.

1999   *Ancient Mesopotamia: The Eden That Never Was.* Cambridge University Press, Cambridge.

Postgate, J. N.

1992–1993   A Sumerian City: Town and Country in the 3rd Millennium B.C. *Scienze dell'Antichità* 6/7:409–435.

1994   How Many Sumerians per Hectare? Probing the Anatomy of an Early City. *Cambridge Archaeological Journal* 4(1):47–65.

Powell, M. A.

1990   Urban-Rural Interface: Movement of Goods and Services in a Third Millennium City-State. In *The Town as Regional Economic Centre in the Ancient Near East,* edited by E. Aerts and H. Klengel, pp. 3–6. Leuven University Press, Leuven.

Ritchey, T.

1996   Note: Building Complexity. In *On the Surface: Çatalhöyük 1993–95,* edited by I. Hodder, pp. 7–18. British Institute of Archaeology at Ankara Monograph 22. British School of Archaeology at Ankara, London.

Rothman, M. S. (editor)

2001   *Uruk Mesopotamia and Its Neighbors: Cross-Cultural Interactions and Their Consequences in the Era of State Formation.* School of American Research Press, Santa Fe, N.M.

Shane, O. C. III, and M. Küçük

1998   The World's First City. *Archaeology* 51(2):43–47.

Stone, E. C.

1995   The Development of Cities in Ancient Mesopotamia. In *Civilizations of the Ancient Near East,* edited by J. M. Sasson, pp. 235–248. Charles Scribner's Sons, New York.

1997   City-States and Their Centers: The Mesopotamian Example. In *The Archaeology of City-States: Cross-Cultural Approaches,* edited by T. H. Charlton and D. L. Nichols, pp. 15–26. Smithsonian Institution Press, Washington, D.C.

van de Mieroop, M.

1997   *The Ancient Mesopotamian City.* Clarendon, Oxford.

Wheatley, P.

1971   *The Pivot of the Four Quarters: A Preliminary Enquiry into the Origins and Character of the Ancient Chinese City.* Aldine, Chicago.

Wilkinson, T. J.

1994   The Structure and Dynamics of Dry-Farming States in Upper Mesopotamia. *Current Anthropology* 35(5):483–520.

Wilkinson, T. J., C. French, W. Matthews, and J. Oates

2001   Tell Brak: Geoarchaeology, Landscape and the Region. In *Excavations at Tell Brak 2,* by D. Oates, J. Oates, and H. McDonald. McDonald Institute for Archaeological Research, Cambridge and British School of Archaeology in Iraq, London.

Yoffee, N.

1995   Political Economy in Early Mesopotamian States. *Annual Review of Anthropology* 24:281–311.

ELEVEN

Early Walled Cities of the Indian Subcontinent as "Small Worlds"

MONICA L. SMITH

For urban residents, the advantages of city life consist of two interrelated opportunities that are found in zones of concentrated population: the opportunity to create improved social networks, and the opportunity to display those networks through material possessions and the organization of social space. Cities as repositories of goods and information are highly effective interaction loci in networks of communication; these networks become particularly valued during periods of increasing social complexity, when individuals and households seek to maximize their effectiveness in maintaining their bases of social and biological subsistence.

The rapid expansion of the urban form is linked to the efficiency of networks in fixed places, a phenomenon that can occur in two ways. One of them is encapsulated in the concept of "small worlds" as the establishment of links in dispersed populations results in improved communication and contacts (Watts and Strogatz 1998). The second manifestation of this phenomenon is due to sheer numbers, as exemplified by Metcalfe's Law, which proposes that the potential value of a network is "proportional to the square of the number of nodes in the network" (Gentry 2001:20; see also Metcalfe 1995). In human terms, this means that as the number of interlocutors increases, each new participant gains access to an already existing network and thereby exponentially increases potential contacts. The view of cities as social phenomena that, regardless of their initial point of growth, are maintained as the focus of a social network provides a powerful explanation for the workings of cities across time and space.

Network analysis involves the mathematical prediction of improved connectivity as distances between interlocutors are shortened. In social terms, this shortening affects the efficiency of communicating not only economic information, but also the compelling ephemera of ritual and symbolism. The analysis of social networks is a formal discipline that incorporates the general aspects of networks into social terms using basic propositions: that actors in social systems are interdependent; that links between actors enable the channeling of physical or psychological resources; and that the structure of social relations affects the ease and manner in which action is taken (Wetherell 1998:126). While the study of social networks has traditionally relied on personal interviews and other techniques in which individual actors (or their actions) can be traced and mapped, the understanding of the importance of links between people, and the material correlates of such links, makes the insights provided by network analysis particularly suited to archaeological case studies.

URBANISM AND
"SMALL-WORLD" EFFECTS

Watts and Strogatz (1998) have suggested that links created within large populations result in "small worlds," in which the existence of a few random nodes greatly increases the connectivity between a large number of points (see also Kochen 1989; Milgram 1967). Applying this principle to human societies, the desire to establish small-world networks as a means of increasing social stability may help to explain why urban systems become attractive to large numbers of people despite the negative aspects of urban life. In times of increased population and social uncertainty, the city becomes a way for people to gain a desired small-world perspective as it incorporates individuals whose origins include numerous rural and outlying areas.

As applied to human groups, the small-world phenomenon is one manifestation of the social networks active in any scale of human society. Early in the formal delineation of the discipline of sociology, researchers became interested in the graphic representation of social relations to illustrate how people became connected in a social group (e.g., Kapferer 1969; Lundberg and Lawsing 1937). These graphic representations (which can be viewed as an early type of geographic information system, or GIS) were a dramatic indicator of the way in which large numbers of people could be interconnected through one or two nodes of communication. These could be hierarchical relations, involving, for example, a person who is an employer to many, as well as people such as bankers, plumbers, and grocers who had contact with individuals of all social ranks. Social network analysis continues to be utilized by anthropologists to provide a graphic illustration of the way in which individuals become connected (Schweizer 1997). Because urban areas and dense social networks are found to consistently coexist, social network analysis has become an integral component of urban sociology and urban anthropology, starting with the seminal work of J. Clyde Mitchell (1969; Boissevain and Mitchell 1973; see also Klovdahl 1989).

As Kochen (1989:xii) has observed, "A city is by its nature a means for creating and activating personal contact." Cities have a large number of people in comparison with the number in the surrounding hinterland, usually accompanied by a high population density per unit of space. The dense populations attract and support economic specialists who provide products that villagers might require too rarely to support them full-time (Childe 1950:7). The higher resultant degree of specialization promotes interdependence (Blanton et al 1981; Zeder 1991:20 and this volume). Thus the concentrated and relatively dense populations that characterize urban areas *enable* a greater number of social contacts, while the increased number of interactions *compel* a greater number of social contacts.

The examination of ancient cities illustrates that the creation of social networks is not merely a by-product, but a fundamental reason for the displacement of people into urban environments. Watts and Strogatz (1998:441) propose that the small-world phenomenon "might be common in sparse networks with many vertices, as even a tiny fraction of short cuts would suffice" to create a high level of connectivity. Cities in a landscape of dispersed population under conditions of increasing sociopolitical complexity represent exactly this kind of network, in which any initial impetus for the creation of a population center (ceremonial, defensive, or economic) is sustained by social interaction under conditions where the greater ease of information exchange is deemed valuable. Information is manifested into physical surroundings, in which material goods and space are used by interlocutors to project identity and reaffirm status (Gottdiener 1995; see also Douglas and Isherwood 1996 [1979]; Miller 1987, 1990; Wilk 1990). Especially in the network of concentrated population represented by urban zones, consumption activities resulting in the acquisition and display of goods are the most effective means of demonstrating the small-world connections sustained by individuals and households.

DISPLAYING SOCIAL NETWORKS: AN
ARCHAEOLOGICAL APPROACH

In a recent volume, Michael Schiffer (with Miller 1999) evaluated the way in which human behavior is fundamentally and inextricably tied in with the material world. This volume, particularly notable for its emphasis on the way in which communication actions are *received,* follows a line of anthropological reasoning focused on the way in which the human social realm is manifested in the material world (Campbell 1995; Douglas and Isherwood 1996 [1979]; Glennie 1995; Gottdiener 1995; Miller 1985, 1987, 1990, 1995; Smith 1999a). Since personal interactions and communications of all kinds are signaled through the movement and placement of physical objects as well as the configuration of space, the presence of archaeologically recoverable patterns of space and objects permits us to reconstruct the parameters of social actions.

A diversity of goods enables individuals to demonstrate membership in cross-cutting social groups based on status, ethnicity, age, gender, and profession (Smith 1999a; Turner 1980). While the use of material possessions as a part of information exchange is found at all levels of social organization, this activity increases under conditions of increasing social uncertainty and/or increasing population density (see Hamilton and Lai 1989). As they migrate to cities, individuals express new social relations through an increased consumption of material goods supplied by the marketplace (Abu-Lughod 1969; see also Brewer and Porter 1993; Fine and Leopold 1993). At the same time, urban residents continue to maintain (albeit with modifications) old social relations, such as ethnic ties, which are also manifested in consumption activities (see Attarian this volume).

The activities of city-dwellers in the conscious creation and development of small worlds is not limited to the consumption of portable objects, but also involves the consumption of space (see Gottdiener 1985; Knox 1995; Lefebvre 1979). Indeed, the consumption of space and of objects is closely intertwined, as noted by Castells (1975:176): "Urban organization is not then a simple arrangement of spatial forms, but rather these forms as the expression of the process of collective treatment of the daily consumption patterns of households." Central places foster increased contact between inhabitants in part because of the diminished physical space between larger numbers of individuals (Ambrose 1969; Johnson 1975; Smith 1976). There are two ways for inhabitants to manage this space: through the development of ever-smaller worlds, such as neighborhoods (e.g., Abu-Lughod 1969; Myers 1996; Raben 1995; see also Keith this volume), and through the development of supra-neighborhood focal points that cultivate a sense of urban identity, such as monumental constructions.

Political leaders presented with a small world in the making can use supra-neighborhood arrangements of social space as a cost-effective strategy for the demonstration of their own status. When only limited resources are available for infrastructure, one-time labor inputs such as monumental architecture and fortification walls suffice to make a long-standing statement of central authority. This statement of authority need not be crushingly unilateral. While some scholars see urban planning as a simplistic "façade for power" (Gottdiener 1985:18), these elements of planning are often undermined by the actual configurations of real cities, both ancient and modern (e.g., Colombijn 1994; Myers 1996; Shen 1994). Instead, it is more appropriate to see sponsored inputs by a political and economic elite as symbolic manifestations of status that are often modified or co-opted by residents. In this way, both residents and leaders make use of monuments as a tangible focus of the city, itself a collective "repository of people's memories and of the past" (Urry 1996:50).

Ancient cities are often regarded as having required significant political investment, whether those cities were economically specialized (Wright 1977; Zeder 1991), were the focus of ritual space (Fritz et al. 1984; O'Connor 1993), or acted simply as "centers of power" (Hassan 1993:557). However, the connections between levels of political hierarchy and concentrations of population are not always straightforward (Crumley 1976; Pollock et al. 1996). The presence of cities in the premodern world did not require a state level of political organization, only an initial impetus for settlement, some level of highly visible labor investment, and a sustainable social network afterward. Such networks could only thrive when there was a communal perception of benefit; once the perceived advantages of urban life were outweighed by its disadvantages, urban demographic collapse could be extremely rapid (see, e.g., Houston et al. this volume).

The understanding of premodern social and political activities in the Indian subcontinent has been heavily conditioned by literary traditions, despite their limited scope. Indeed, the description of the early centuries B.C./A.D. as the "Early Historic" period is somewhat misleading, since there are few secular documents related to social and economic organization, and no descriptive indigenous texts that contain quantified economic data. As a result, literary texts broadly dated to the Early Historic period—such as the Sangam literature of southern India, the Pali Canon, and the political treatise *The Arthasastra of Kautilya* (Sastry 1988)—have often dictated the interpretation of archaeological data (Erdosy 1988; see also Kenoyer 1997). These texts are generally prescriptive and offer an idealized, elite-centered view of social life; moreover, the specific descriptions of town planning are rarely paralleled in the archaeological record. F. R. Allchin (1995:222) offers one particularly relevant example when he notes that the *Arthasastra* "recommends three concentric moats, although we know of no surviving fortification which displays this feature." Lacking detailed data, those explaining the success of cities in the Early Historic period have produced static descriptions, such as those based upon V. G. Childe's (1950) urban trait-list, or have relied upon modern parallels to promote the idea of a timeless "agrarian city" (e.g., Misra 1991; Sarkar 1987).

Cities and states of the Early Historic period are also often seen as intertwined. This assumption, and the presence of archaeologically identifiable urban zones and evidence for substantial labor investment, has led some scholars to label political entities from this era as "states" and even "empires" (see, for example, Allchin 1995; Liu 1988; Morrison 1995; Subramanian 1972; Thapar 1990 [1984]). Indian historians have begun to reassess the meaning of such terms when applied to early first-millennium polities (Parasher-Sen 1993a, 1993b; see also Mirashi 1981). Archaeological evidence suggests the presence of multiple ruling entities, as indicated by the simultaneous presence of coinage ascribed to a variety of contemporary rulers (e.g., Bajpai 1991; Chumble 1991; Srivastava 1991). The study of actual urban systems from this period provides the opportunity to understand urban dynamics decoupled from state-level political formations.

The Early Historic period was a time of social and economic growth. By the first century B.C., the Indian subcontinent was part of an elaborate trade network that touched the entire northern littoral of the Indian Ocean and included links to the Roman Mediterranean and to Han China (Begley and DePuma 1991; Liu 1988; Ray and Salles 1996). In addition to participating in long-distance exchange, the subcontinent sustained thriving networks of local and regional exchange. As a result, material culture became uniform throughout large regions (Smith 2001a). Politically, the subcontinent was the home of numerous political entities, each with shifting control over territory and resources (Casson 1989; Mirashi 1981).

Large sites (over 50 hectares) were already present in the Ganges Valley by the early sixth century B.C., and the number of such sites grew in the following centuries (figure 11.1; Allchin 1995; Chakrabarti 1995; Erdosy 1988). These population centers accommodated political, social, and administrative activities, although religious activities appear to have retained a separate sphere outside urban zones. By the second century B.C., major Buddhist pilgrimage sites such as Sanchi, Bharhut, and Amaravati were located outside of population centers; similarly, minor Buddhist constructions in the vicinity of smaller towns were located away from actual habitation zones (for examples from central India, see IAR 1988–1989:51; Nath 1992; Parasher 1991). Buddhist establishments throughout the subcontinent became the focus of economic activities such as markets and stopping points for traders (Ray 1986). These religious sites received some political patronage from local leaders, but the majority of donations came from a wide sector of the public, including nuns and monks, individuals, and whole towns (Sarkar 1987; Schopen 1997).

Large urban sites varied in form, and the proportion of walled sites appears to be greater in the northern subcontinent than in the south. The walled cities of the north were not uniform in plan, and most appear to adapt to the landscape, especially to nearby rivers (figure 11.2; Deloche 1992). In a few cases, such as at Sisupalgarh and Mahasthangarh, tributaries were canalized to form a moat around the urban zone. The actual number of walled sites of this period is unknown, as several factors make it difficult to assess site sizes and locations. Many Early Historic period sites were favorable locales for subsequent occupation, and fortifications of the early centuries A.D. have been obscured by later constructions, especially of the medieval period, when it appears that warfare was more prevalent (particularly in the western region of the subcontinent; see Kamalapur 1961). Another difficulty is that comprehensive survey data are lacking for much of the subcontinent. Although preliminary reconnaissance surveys in a number of regions have produced presence-absence documentation for Early Historic sites (published principally in the

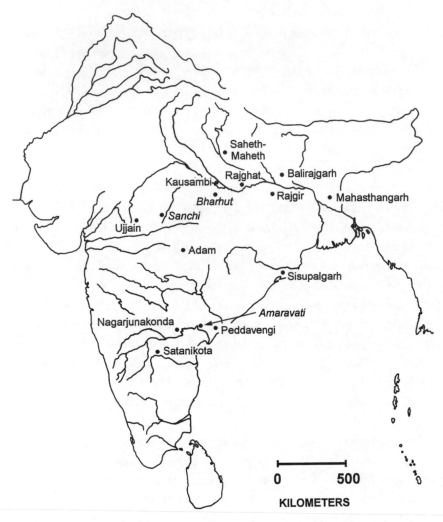

Figure 11.1. Sites of the Early Historic period mentioned in text. Religious sites are noted in italics.

government periodical *Indian Archaeology—A Review* [*IAR*]), survey data seldom indicate site sizes and configurations.

An important exception is George Erdosy's (1988) regional survey in the area around the large Gangetic urban site of Kausambi. By 100 B.C., the site of Kausambi had increased in size to 150 hectares and was surrounded by a number of "suburbs" in the 50-hectare size range (Erdosy 1988). Did other walled sites in the subcontinent also have a well-developed and well-populated hinterland, as

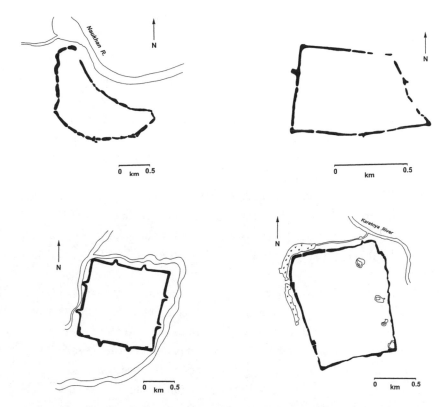

Figure 11.2. Forms of walled settlements in the Indian subcontinent (clockwise from top left: Saheth-Maheth, Balirajgarh, Sisupalgarh, Mahasthangarh).

Erdosy suggests on the basis of his survey data from the Kausambi region? According to Lal (1949:64), the immediate vicinity of Sisupalgarh shows numerous traces of habitation outside the walls. Similarly, in the area of Mahasthangarh, there are many small sites between the fortification walls and an outlying group of Buddhist monasteries 5 kilometers to the northwest. Many of these mounds are quite small, under 0.25 hectares, and may represent house mounds rather than whole villages (Smith 2001b). Aside from these examples, there have been too few surveys of this time period to establish the relationships between cities and their hinterlands in the region. Nonetheless, it does appear that the majority of archaeologically documented large sites in the northern subcontinent were walled sites, and that these walled sites were the central focus of population in the Early Historic period.

Archaeological investigations of walled sites such as Sisupalgarh (Lal 1949) and Satanikota (Sarkar 1987) suggest that the construction of encircling ramparts predates the development of regional political authorities. At sites such as Rajgir, an initial occupation phase predated the initial phases of rampart construction in the sixth to fifth century B.C. This initial phase consisted of a mud rampart built from the matrix carved out from an adjacent moat (*IAR* 1961–1962:7–8). In a subsequent period, a brick fortification wall was added to the top of the rampart. The same pattern of construction (initial occupation, a mud rampart, and a later brick wall) is also noted at Sisupalgarh (Lal 1949) as well as at Nagarjunakonda (*IAR* 1957–1958:5), Rajgir (*IAR* 1961–1962:7–8, 1962–1963:5–6), and Saheth-Maheth (Uesugi 1997:28).

What was the purpose of these labor-intensive ramparts? Warfare can prompt the development of elaborate fortifications, as seen in the archaeological and ethnohistoric records of the Maya region (Inomata 1997), Andean South America (Hyslop 1990; Valkenier 1998), West Africa (Connah 2000:40), and early Europe (Randsborg 1991). For South Asia, Erdosy (1995:107) suggests that competition and concentrations of power led to the proliferation of sites with ramparts in the early centuries B.C., and that warfare was a principal impetus to the development of increased social complexity in this period (see also Erdosy 1988). Allchin (1995) disputes this interpretation, observing that warfare and competition were present at least by the end of the Harappan period in the second millennium B.C. and thus were not unique to the Early Historic period.

Warfare is certainly attested in the literary record of this era, most notably in the inscriptions of Asoka Maurya, who credited his conversion to Buddhism to a sense of shock over the loss of life in wars against the Kalinga (Orissa) region in the third century B.C. (Habib and Habib 1989–1990; Thapar 1990 [1966]). However, this dramatic literary event is difficult to substantiate in the archaeological record. In his report of the excavations at Sisupalgarh, in the heart of the Orissa region, Lal (1949:68) noted that the earliest defenses dated to no earlier than the second century B.C. It appears, therefore, that the fortifications at Sisupalgarh cannot be identified simply as a response to Mauryan aggression as it is known from the literary tradition. Finally, the fortifications of this era do not strongly suggest a defensive role: there are often a large number of formal gateways (Sisupalgarh has eight), and a single rampart that could be easily breached. Many of the sites are located on flat alluvial terrain, even when there are nearby hills or outcrops that could have provided additional elevation (one exception is the site of Satanikota in the southern subcontinent, which is a walled site on a natural outcrop; see *IAR* 1977–1978:3–11).

In the absence of compelling evidence for chronic warfare, other explanations for the development of Early Historic walled cities are more plausible. Flooding appears to have been a considerable problem at many Early Historic sites, and in many cases of excavated ramparts the excavators also note that the area was affected by floods, with evidence for waterborne deposits of silt and freshwater shells both against the ramparts and in the adjacent habitation areas (e.g., at Balirajgarh, *IAR* 1962–1963; Mahasthangarh, Ahmed 1981; and Rajghat, *IAR* 1960–61:35–39). Mate (1969–1970) suggests that for the Ganges Valley, the earliest earthen ramparts surrounding sites represent attempts at flood control, and that formal fortifications constructed with bricks or stone, or both, did not appear until after the initial occupation of the sites (see also Thakur 1981:296–305).

Studies of walled cities elsewhere suggest a growing consensus that walls should be considered a form of monumental, labor-intensive architecture that is used for a variety of purposes simultaneously. The mere existence of a wall in and of itself demonstrates a level of organizational capacity (Pollock et al. 1996:689). Graham Connah (2000:36) has noted that in Africa, city walls "varied in function from domestic protection to formal military defence, as well as serving a variety of other functions." McIntosh and McIntosh (1993:632) observe that for the site of Jenne-jeno, these other functions might have included flood protection, civic identity, and the restriction or control of outsiders' access to markets. By viewing ramparts as a form of monumental architecture, our understanding of city walls encompasses both daily activities and extraordinary events: those associated with the city as a lived entity, as well as the occasional but significant incursions of floods and invaders that are deterred by those formal perimeters.

In the Indian subcontinent, a large number of walled urban zones are located precisely in regions where there are few other data to support an interpretation of hierarchical social organization. Archaeological evidence of long-distance trade and pilgrimage in the Early Historic period indicates that it was a time of high social mobility when population growth may have provided some pressure on resources but also opportunities for social action when population was concentrated. Emergent political leaders sought a variety of ways to demonstrate authority, including the development of coins and seals. The installation of fortifications and gateways as a focal point of community labor in urban areas would also have provided a cost-effective investment of authority.

The building programs that resulted in the augmentation of fortification walls would have required some level of direction and social cohesion for successful implementation. At Sisupalgarh, the excavations across the rampart wall indicate that the first ramparts were put up in a relatively short time, with repeated augmentation in later phases (Lal 1949). A process of repeated augmentation and reinforcement is also seen at the site of Balirajgarh (*IAR* 1962–1963); at Mahasthangarh, cuts across the rampart wall at different parts of the site show slightly different construction sequences, as though the augmentation was carried out piecemeal throughout the site's occupation. Evidence such as this suggests that the formal boundaries of the city provided a convenient way for local leaders to add their contribution to the city's status by using previously built ramparts as a base.

Throughout the period of occupation, these monumental walls also served as a symbol of community and labor identity. Recent and ongoing research at Sisupalgarh (Smith 2000, 2001c, 2002) shows that the area within the rampart walls has the remnants of many levels of wealth indicators. Architectural distinctions include a range of types from large colonnaded buildings to the remains of stone and brick structures. There is also a considerable variation in use of different categories of wares that indicate the residents' ability to acquire fancy vessels and fill extra storage vessels with supplies of food. One thing that is certain is that the city was fully occupied, a factor that again reinforces the idea that the ratio of leaders to occupants was low and that the per capita assessment of labor for rampart maintenance and augmentation was probably seen by the inhabitants as a reasonable level of shared obligation, given the city's benefits in terms of social and economic opportunities.

DISCUSSION

The transition between the initial construction of ramparts for flood protection and subsequent augmentations for defensive or symbolic purposes, or both, illustrates how cities in landscapes of dispersed population can be used as building blocks of subsequent integration. The initial construction of an earthen embankment for flood protection was likely to have been the result of single-event coordination that did not require the imposition of a permanent leadership (for comparative examples see Kolb and Snead 1997). However, the subsequent qualitative shift to baked-brick fortification walls on top of the earthen rampart were conducted on a larger scale and in a multistage process that involved greater allocations of fuel, raw materials, and labor. This qualitative shift requiring a greater level of sustained coordination can be described as a transition to "collective consumption," or the centrally guided provision of social services (Castells 1975, 1977; Forrest 1991; Gottdiener 1985).

Although guided by a central authority, the provision of social services and infrastructure can only be successfully implemented if there is a perception that the required labor investments are mutually beneficial and can be achieved at a relatively low cost. The provision of marketplaces, for example, allows an opportunity for central authorities to impose order, as well as to assure the distribution of production (including specialized production). At the same time, marketplaces also allow city dwellers to gain access to a wide variety of goods and services and a forum for consumption that enables households to express both new and old social alliances. Similar observations can be made about the organization of all types of social space in a city, not just marketplaces. Monumental constructions such as fortification walls constitute a form of labor investment that benefits both urban inhabitants and those who aspire to local leadership, by providing both a symbolic delineation of the city and protection against attack.

The walled cities of the Early Historic period in the Indian subcontinent provided what can be characterized as the largest stable territorial unit of that era. Moreover, the experience gained by local leaders in the cost-effective aggrandizement of urban sites provided the basis upon which subsequent state-level political formations were achieved. Long-lived states appear in the archaeological record of the peninsular Indian subcontinent after the Early Historic period in the fourth century A.D., with the rise of polities such as the Guptas in the north and the Vakatakas in the central subcontinent (Smith 1999b). These polities are distinct from those that preceded them for a number of reasons, as best illustrated by the Guptas, whose rule grew to encompass the entire Ganges Valley. This continuity in administration permitted the steady accumulation of surplus at the central level that could be utilized to support new religious developments and additional city-based trade infrastructure.

Several significant administrative changes were put into effect under the Guptas: the adoption of copper-plate grants for recording land records and temple donations, the shift away from Buddhism in a return to a pre-Buddhist Vedic (Hindu) tradition, and the revival of Sanskrit as the principal language for monumental inscriptions, land-grants, seals, and coins (Gokhale 1983; Miller and Eaton 1992;

Sharma 1989; Williams 1982). These developments were integrated into the Gupta territories as they grew through historically documented military conquests and alliances. The overt sponsorship of new religious constructions by political entities supplanted both the ideology and the communal support base of Buddhist institutions. The Guptas and Vakatakas prominently sponsored the development of Hindu temples and shrines unaided by other private parties, so that leaders came to be closely identified with a hierarchically organized religious authority (Williams 1982).

CONCLUSION

In the late first millennium B.C. in the Indian subcontinent, cities developed as a response to increased social and economic activity, prompted by factors such as population growth, the rise of trading activity within the subcontinent and throughout the Indian Ocean, and possibly, warfare. Urban areas provided opportunities for the increased consumption of both information and material goods that permitted households to establish and maintain their identities during a period of increasing uncertainty as well as increasing social and political complexity.

With people coming together into larger population units, elites who aspired to political power converted small investments in labor-management and materials into significant monuments that embellished the city and made it into an ever-more attractive zone of settlement. Fortifications walls, monumental gates, and other forms of labor-intensive architecture were a means of exhibiting strength to a city's neighbors, with which it was in competition for land, labor, or other resources. At the same time, these landscape modifications served as a symbol of containment, reinforcing otherwise ephemeral concepts of urban identity. At numerous walled sites in the Indian subcontinent, the embankments originally built for flood control were regularized and enhanced by brick fortification walls and elaborate gateways. As multipurpose embodiments of civic investment by both leaders and followers, these ramparts constituted an architecture of consensus in which individuals traded away labor that could have been used for other (household or domestic) purposes for a sense of collective participation. When these cities became the locus of greater activity, it became possible at the moment of state formation to link cities and their hinterlands together into large territorial units under political dynasties such as the Guptas and Vakatakas. Making use of the small-world connections that thrived in cities, and of the expertise gained through the management of urban zones, political leaders extended these networks across a landscape to create larger territories administered by state-level bureaucracies. The subsequent displacement of religious centers to urban zones, representing a rejection of Buddhism and a return to an earlier hierarchical Hindu tradition, proved to be the final link in the establishment of center-dominated states after the fourth century A.D.

REFERENCES

Aboshi, Y., and K. Sonoda (editors)
  1997   *Excavations at Jetavana.* Kansai University, Tokyo.
Abu-Lughod, J.
  1969   Migrant Adjustment to City Life: The Egyptian Case. In *The City in Newly Developing Countries,* edited by G. Breese, pp. 376–388. Prentice-Hall, Englewood Cliffs, N.J.
Ahmed, N.
  1981   *Mahasthan: A Preliminary Report of the Recent Archaeological Excavations at Mahasthangarh,*
  [1975]   3d ed. Department of Archaeology and Museums, Government of Bangladesh.
Allchin, F. R.
  1995   *The Archaeology of Early Historic South Asia: The Emergence of Cities and States.* Cambridge University Press, Cambridge.
Ambrose, P. J.
  1969   Central Place Theory. In *Analytical Human Geography,* edited by P. J. Ambrose, pp. 121–134. Longman, London.
Archaeological Survey of India (cited in text under title *IAR*)
Various years   *Indian Archaeology—A Review.* Delhi.
Bajpai, K. D.
  1991   Trade and Coinage in Ancient Madhya Pradesh. In *Coinage, Trade and Economy,* edited by A. Kumar Jha, pp. 1–15. Indian Institute of Research in Numismatic Studies, Nasik.
Begley, V., and R. D. De Puma (editors)
  1991   *Rome and India: The Ancient Sea Trade.* University of Wisconsin Press. Madison.
Blanton, R. E., S. A. Kowalewski, G. Feinman, and J. Appel
  1981   *Ancient Mesoamerica: A Comparison of Change in Three Regions.* Cambridge University Press, Cambridge.
Boissevain, J., and J. C. Mitchell (editors)
  1973   *Network Analysis: Studies in Human Interaction.* Mouton, The Hague.
Brewer, J., and R. Porter (editors)
  1993   *Consumption and the World of Goods.* Routledge, London.
Campbell, C.
  1995   The Sociology of Consumption. In *Acknowledging Consumption,* edited by D. Miller, pp. 96–126. Routledge, London.
Casson, L. (editor)
  1989   *The Periplus Maris Erythraei.* Princeton University Press, Princeton, N.J.

Castells, M.

1975   Advanced Capitalism, Collective Consumption, and Urban Contradictions. In *Stress and Contradictions in Modern Capitalism*, edited by L. Lindberg. D. C. Heath, Lexington Mass.

1977   *The Urban Question: A Marxist Approach.* Translated by A. Sheridan. Edward Arnold, London.

Chakrabarti, D. K.

1995   *The Archaeology of Ancient Indian Cities.* Oxford University Press, Delhi.

Childe, V. G.

1950   The Urban Revolution. *Town Planning Review* 21:3–17.

Chumble, P. D.

1991   Rare Satavahana Coins. *Numismatic Digest* 15:41–50.

Colombijn, F.

1994   *Patches of Padang: The History of an Indonesian Town in the Twentieth Century and the Use of Urban Space.* Centre of Non-Western Studies, Leiden University, Leiden.

Connah, G.

2000   African City Walls: A Neglected Source? In *Africa's Urban Past,* edited by D. M. Anderson and R. Rathbone, pp. 36–51. James Currey, Oxford.

Crumley, C. L.

1976   Toward a Locational Definition of State Systems of Settlement. *American Anthropologist* 78:59–73.

Deloche, J.

1992   Etudes sur les fortifications de l'Inde I: Les fortifications de l'Inde ancienne. *Bulletin de l'Ecole Française d'Extrême-Orient* 79.1:89–131.

Douglas, M., and B. Isherwood

1996   *The World of Goods.* Routledge, London.
[1979]

Erdosy, G.

1988   *Urbanisation in Early Historic India.* British Archaeological Reports Internatonal Series 430, Oxford.

1995   City States of North India and Pakistan at the Time of the Buddha. In *The Archaeology of Early Historic South Asia: The Emergence of Cities and States,* edited by F. R. Allchin, pp. 99–122. Cambridge University Press, Cambridge.

Fine, B., and E. Leopold

1993   *The World of Consumption.* Routledge, London.

Forrest, R.

1991   The Privatization of Collective Consumption. In *Urban Life in Transition,* edited by M. Gottdiener and C. G. Pickvance, pp. 169–195. Sage Publications, Newbury Park, Calif.

Fritz, J. M., G. Michell, and M. S. Nagaraja Rao

1984   *Where Kings and Gods Meet: The Royal Centre at Vijayanagara, India.* University of Arizona, Tucson.

Gentry, J.

2001   Metcalfe's Law and Data Marts. *Enterprise Systems Journal* 16(5):20.

Glennie, P.

    1995   Consumption within Historical Studies. In *Acknowledging Consumption,* edited by D. Miller, pp. 164–203. Routledge, London.

Gokhale, B. G.

    1983   Buddhism in the Gupta Age. In *Essays on Gupta Culture,* edited by B. L. Smith, pp. 129–153. Motilal Banarsidass, Delhi.

Gottdiener, M.

    1985   *The Social Production of Urban Space.* University of Texas, Austin.

    1995   *Postmodern Semiotics: Material Culture and the Forms of Postmodern Life.* Blackwell, Oxford.

Habib, I., and F. Habib

1989–1990   Mapping the Mauryan Empire. *Proceedings of the Indian History Congress* 50:57–79.

Hamilton, G. G., and C.-K. Lai

    1989   Consumerism without Capitalism: Consumption and Brand Names in Late Imperial China. In *The Social Economy of Consumption,* edited by H. J. Rutz and B. S. Orlove, pp. 253–279. University Press of America, Lanham, Mass.

Hassan, F. A.

    1993   Town and Village in Ancient Egypt: Ecology, Society and Urbanization. In *The Archaeology of Africa: Food, Metals, and Towns,* edited by T. Shaw, P. Sinclair, B. Andah, and A. Okpoko, pp. 551–569. Routledge, London.

Hyslop, J.

    1990   *Inka Settlement Planning.* University of Texas, Austin.

IAR   *See* Archaeological Survey of India.

Inomata, T.

    1997   The Last Day of a Fortified Classic Maya Center: Archaeological Investigations at Aguateca, Guatemala. *Ancient Mesoamerica* 8:337–351.

Johnson, G. A.

    1975   Locational Analysis and the Investigation of Uruk Local Exchange Systems. In *Ancient Civilization and Trade,* edited by J. A. Sabloff and C. C. Lamberg-Karlovsky, pp. 285–339. University of New Mexico Press, Albuquerque.

Kamalapur, J. N.

    1961   *The Deccan Forts.* Popular Book Depot, Bombay.

Kapferer, B.

    1969   Norms and the Manipulation of Relationships in a Work Context. In *Social Networks in Urban Situations: Analyses of Personal Relationships in Central African Towns,* edited by J. C. Mitchell, pp. 181–244. Manchester University Press, Manchester.

Kenoyer, J. M.

    1997   Early City States in South Asia. In *The Archaeology of City-States: Cross-Cultural Approaches,* edited by D. L. Nichols and T. H. Charlton, pp. 51–70. Smithsonian Institution Press, Washington, D.C.

Klovdahl, A. S.

    1989   Urban Social Networks: Some Methodological Problems and Possibilities. In *The Small World,* edited by M. Kochen, pp. 176–210. Ablex, Norwood, N.J.

Knox, P. L.

1995 World Cities in a World-System. In *World Cities in a World-System,* edited by P. L. Knox and P. J. Taylor, pp. 3–20. Cambridge University Press, Cambridge.

Kochen, M. (editor)

1989 *The Small World.* Ablex, Norwood NJ.

Kolb, M. J., and J. E. Snead

1997 It's a Small World After All: Comparative Analyses of Community Organization in Archaeology. *American Antiquity* 62(4):609–628.

Lal, B. B.

1949 Sisupalgarh 1948: An Early Historical Fort in Eastern India. *Ancient India* 5:62–105.

Lefebvre, H.

1979 Space: Social Product and Use Value. Translated by J. W. Freiberg. In *Critical Sociology: European Perspectives,* edited by J. W. Freiberg, pp. 285–295. Irvington, New York.

Liu, X.

1988 *Ancient India and Ancient China: Trade and Religious Exchange, A.D. 1–600.* Oxford University Press, Delhi.

Lundberg, G. A., and M. Lawsing

1937 The Sociography of Some Community Relations. *American Sociological Review* 2(3):318–335.

Macdonald, S.

1996 Introduction. In *Theorizing Museums: Representing Identity and Diversity in a Changing World,* edited by S. Macdonald and G. Fyfe, pp. 1–18. Blackwell, Oxford.

McIntosh, S. K., and R. J. McIntosh

1993 Cities without Citadels: Understanding Urban Origins along the Middle Niger. In *The Archaeology of Africa: Food, Metals, and Towns,* edited by T. Shaw, P. Sinclair, B. Andah, and O. Okpoko, pp. 622–641. Routledge, London.

Mate, M. S.

1969–1970 Early Historic Fortifications in the Ganga Valley. *Puratattva* 3:58–69.

Metcalfe, R. M.

1995 Metcalfe's Law: A Network Becomes More Valuable as It Reaches More Users. *InfoWorld* 17(40):53.

Milgram, S.

1967 The Small-World Problem. *Psychology Today* 1(1):61–67.

Miller, B. S., and R. Eaton

1992 Introduction. In *The Powers of Art: Patronage in Indian Culture,* edited by B. S. Miller, pp. 1–16. Oxford University Press, Delhi.

Miller, D.

1985 *Artefacts as Categories.* Cambridge University Press, Cambridge.

1987 *Material Culture and Mass Consumption.* Basil Blackwell, London.

1990 Fashion and Ontology in Trinidad. *Culture and History* 7:49–77.

1995 Consumption and Commodities. *Annual Review of Anthropology* 24:141–161.

Mirashi, V. V.

1981 *The History and Inscriptions of the Satavahanas and the Western Kshatrapas.* Maharashtra State Board for Literature and Culture, Bombay.

Misra, S. C.

1991   Urban History in India: Possibilities and Perspectives. In *The City in Indian History*,
            edited by I. Banga, pp. 1–7. South Asian Publications, Columbia, Missouri.

Mitchell, J. C.

1969   The Concept and Use of Social Networks. In *Social Networks in Urban Situations:
            Analyses of Personal Relationships in Central African Towns*, edited by J. C. Mitchell,
            pp. 1–50. Manchester University Press, Manchester.

Morrison, K. D.

1995   Trade, Urbanism, and Agricultural Expansion: Buddhist Monastic Institutions and
            the State in the Early Historic Western Deccan. *World Archaeology* 27(2):203–221.

Myers, G. A.

1996   Naming and Placing the Other: Power and the Urban Landscape in Zanzibar. *Journal
            of Economic and Social Geography* 87(3):237–246.

Nath, A.

1992   Adam: An Index to Vidarbha Archaeology. In *New Trends in Indian Art and Architecture,
            Felicitation to Dr. S. R. Rao*, edited by B. U. Nayak and N. C. Ghosh, pp. 69–79. Aditya
            Prakashan, New Delhi.

O'Connor, D.

1993   Urbanism in Bronze Age Egypt and Northeast Africa. In *The Archaeology of Africa:
            Food, Metals, and Towns*, edited by T. Shaw, P. Sinclair, B. Andah, and A. Okpoko,
            pp. 570–586. Routledge, London.

Parasher, A.

1991   Social Structure and Economy of Settlements in the Central Deccan (200 B.C.–
            A.D. 200). In *The City in Indian History*, edited by I. Banga, pp. 19–46. South Asia
            Publications, Columbia, Mo.

Parasher-Sen, A.

1993a   Culture and Civilization. In *Social and Economic History of Early Deccan*, edited by A.
            Parasher-Sen, pp. 66–114. Manohar, New Delhi.

1993b   Introduction: Problems of Interpretation. In *Social and Economic History of Early Dec-
            can*, edited by A. Parasher-Sen, pp. 1–65. Manohar, New Delhi.

Pollock, S., M. Pope, and C. Coursey

1996   Household Production at the Uruk Mound, Abu Salabikh, Iraq. *American Journal of
            Archaeology* 100(4):683–698.

Raben, R.

1995   Facing the Crowd: The Urban Ethnic Policy of the Dutch East India Company
            1600–1800. In *Mariners, Merchants, and Oceans: Studies in Maritime History*,
            pp. 209–245. Manohar, New Delhi.

Randsborg, K.

1991   *The First Millennium A.D. in Europe and the Mediterranean.* Cambridge University Press,
            Cambridge.

Ray, H.

1986   *Monastery and Guild: Commerce under the Satavahanas.* Oxford University Press, Delhi.

Ray, H. P., and J.-F. Salles (editors)

1996   *Tradition and Archaeology: Early Maritime Contacts in the Indian Ocean.* Manohar, New Delhi.

Salles, J.-F.

    1995   Les fouilles de Mahasthangarh (Bangladesh). *Comptes Rendus de l'Academie des Inscriptions et Belles-Lettres,* Avril–Juin 1995, pp. 531–560. Diffusion de Boccard, Paris.

Sarkar, H.

    1987   Emergence of Urban Centres in Early Historical Andhradesa. In *Archaeology and History,* edited by B. M. Pande and B. D. Chattopadhyaya, pp. 631–641. Agam Kala Prakashan, Delhi.

Sastry, R. S. (translator)

    1988   *Kautilya's Arthasastra.* 9th ed. Padam Printers, Mysore.

Schiffer, M. B., with A. R. Miller

    1999   *The Material Life of Human Beings: Artifacts, Behavior, and Communication.* Routledge, London.

Schopen, G.

    1997   *Bones, Stones, and Buddhist Monks.* University of Hawai'i, Honolulu.

Schweizer, T.

    1997   Embeddedness of Ethnographic Cases: A Social Networks Perspective. *Current Anthropology* 38(5):739–752.

Sharma, T. R.

    1989   *A Political History of the Imperial Guptas.* Concept Publishing, New Delhi.

Shen, C.

    1994   Early Urbanization in the Eastern Zhou in China (770–221 b.c.): An Archaeological View. *Antiquity* 68:724–44.

Smith, C. A.

    1976   Exchange Systems and the Spatial Distribution of Elites: The Organization of Stratification in Agrarian Societies. In *Regional Systems,* vol.2: *Social Systems,* edited by C. A. Smith, pp. 309–374. Academic Press, New York.

Smith, M. L.

    1999a   The Role of Ordinary Goods in Premodern Exchange. *Journal of Archaeological Method and Theory* 6(2): 109–135.

    1999b   "Indianization" from the Indian Point of View: Trade and Cultural Contacts with Southeast Asia in the Early First Millenium C.E. *Journal of the Social and Economic History of the Orient* 42(1):1–27.

    2000   Sisupalgarh 2000 Field Reconnaissance Report. Manuscript on file, Archaeological Survey of India, New Delhi.

    2001a   *The Archaeology of an Early Historic Town in Central India.* BAR International Series 1002, British Archaeological Reports, Oxford.

    2001b   The Archaeological Hinterlands of Mahasthangarh: Observations and Potential for Future Research. In *France-Bangladesh Joint Venture Excavations at Mahasthangarh First Interim Report 1993–1999,* edited by Md. S. Alam and J.-F. Salles, pp. 61–73. Bangladesh Department of Archaeology, Dhaka.

    2001c   Sisupalgarh 2001 Field Report. Manuscript on file, Archaeological Survey of India, New Delhi.

    2002   Sisupalgarh 2001 (Second Season): Field Report. Manuscript on file, Archaeological Survey of India, New Delhi.

Srivastava, O. P. L.

 1991 *Archaeology of Erich: Discovery of New Dynasties.* Sulabh Prakashan, Varanasi.

Subramanian, N.

 1972 *History of Tamilnad (to A.D. 1336).* Koodal Publishers, Madurai.

Thakur, V. K.

 1981 *Urbanisation in Ancient India.* Abhinav Publications, New Delhi.

Thapar, R.

 1990 *A History of India,* vol.1. Penguin, London.
 [1966]

 1990 *From Lineage to State: Social Formations in the Mid-First Millennium B.C. in the Ganga Valley.*
 [1984] Oxford University Press, Delhi.

Turner, T. S.

 1980 The Social Skin. In *Not Work Alone,* edited by J. Cerfas and R. Lewin, pp. 112–140.
    Temple Smith, London.

Uesugi, A.

 1997 *Brief Report of Excavations at Saheth-Maheth, India, 1986–96.* Archaeological Research
    Institute, Kansai University, Osaka.

Urry, J.

 1996 How Societies Remember the Past. In *Theorizing Museums: Representing Identity and Di-*
    versity in a Changing World, edited by S. Macdonald and G. Fyfe, pp. 45–65. Black-
    well, Oxford.

Valkenier, L. K.

 1998 Early Fortifications on the Central and North Coast of Peru. Paper presented at the
    38th Annual Meeting of the Institute of Andean Studies, Berkeley, Calif.

Watts, D. J., and S. H. Strogatz

 1998 Collective Dynamics of "Small-World" Networks. *Nature* 393:440–442.

Wetherell, C.

 1998 Historial Social Network Analysis. *International Review of Social History* supplement
    6:125–144.

Wilk, R.

 1990 Consumer Goods as Dialogue about Development. *Culture and History* 7: 79–100.

Williams, J. G.

 1982 *The Art of Gupta India: Empire and Province.* Princeton University Press, Princeton.

Wright, H. T.

 1977 Recent Research on the Origin of the State. *Annual Review of Anthropology*
    6:379–397.

Zeder, M. A.

 1991 *Feeding Cities.* Smithsonian Institution Press, Washington D.C.

T W E L V E

Compromises and Conflicts

Production and Commerce in the Royal
Cities of Eastern Zhou, China

CHEN SHEN

In China, urbanization was a gradual process, with two phases occurring before the end of the first millennium B.C. The first phase corresponds with the rise of the first state, Xia (ca. 2100 B.C.). According to K. C. Chang (1976, 1983, 1985, 1986), this process was the result of social evolution, during which most of the Neolithic walled settlements became administrative or religious centers, or both, occupied mainly by royal families and the ruling class. The second urbanization did not occur until the eighth century B.C., at the beginning of the Eastern Zhou dynasty, as a result of a series of integrated social changes among feudal states (Shen 1994). Urbanization gave rise to full-scale commercially based production and marketplaces within royal *centers,* which transformed them into *cities.* Although substantial archaeological evidence has been collected from dozens of Eastern Zhou city sites, until now there have been few archaeological interpretations of

urban production and commerce (e.g., Liu and Chen in press). In this study I concentrate on archaeological data relating to urban activities from the site of Yan-
Xiadu and provide new perspectives on Eastern Zhou urbanization. The central
question addressed here is how did city rulers deal with the transformation of their
religious and administrative centers into commercially driven cities with large urban
populations? The answer is, through compromises and conflicts.

Recent archaeological evidence suggests that the earliest Neolithic settlements with
walled structures appeared in the Middle Yangtze Valley about 6,000 years ago
(Hunan 1993). Nearly 50 such walled sites have been identified (Cao 2000; Ren
1998; Zhang and Okamura 2000). Owing to long-standing ambiguities surrounding the definition of a "city," debate continues as to whether these walled
settlements qualify as "cities" (Chen 1998; Gao and Yang 1993; Ma 2000; Wiesheu
1997; Zhou 1992). Between 6,000 and 4,000 years ago these walled settlements
were clearly not just simple occupational sites with enclosure features. Many large-
scale structures (e.g., gates, platform foundations, public facilities) make them distinct from other late Neolithic sites. Although the function of these walled sites
needs to be further explored, many archaeologists believe that they represent aggregated communal centers with defensive features, where elites performed religious ceremonies (Ren 1998; Zhou 1992).

During the subsequent Xia, Shang, and Western Zhou dynasties, walled settlements became larger and regular in plan. These sites, the first that can clearly be
called "cities," encompassed strong political and religious elements. Large complexes of palaces and temples appeared as central structures for the first time, although there was not yet a regular city plan in terms of divisions of palatial, residence, and workshop areas. Kinship-based settlements were scattered within cities
while workshops were generally located outside the city (Xu 1999). Chang (1976:
69, 1983:17–18, 1986:418–19) has described the city form before the eighth century D.C. as a political nucleus and administrative locus. Others consider these population centers merely "farmland with walls" (Fu 1980:321–386, 1981:280). In Fu's
view, these walled settlements were not a "city" in the sense that they had not resulted from a natural aggregation of population for commercial purposes. Nevertheless, archaeological discoveries of palace or temple foundations on stamped-

earth platforms suggest that such sites functioned as royal centers. Because evidence for production and marketplaces within cities has not yet been recovered from this period, some scholars have concluded that it might be most accurate to call these Shang and Western Zhou cities "King's Cities" (Wang 2000).

In the Eastern Zhou dynasty (771–221 B.C.), which is further divided into the Spring and Autumn period (771–482 B.C.) and the Warring-States period (481–221 B.C.), the number of cities dramatically increased, and urban population grew rapidly (Wu 1999; Yang 1998). These changes were the direct result of political reforms and social transformations in this period (Hsu 1965, 1999; Lewis 1999; Tu 1980). This second urbanization phase occurred when the individualized production of agricultural products, new technological innovations of iron manufacture, private production, and markets, along with frequent civil wars, became important parts of social life (Shen 1994).

While the principles of city construction continued to accord with the regulations of royal construction set forth by the Zhou royal system, in fact the inhabitants of Eastern Zhou cities to a large degree reshaped city layout and changed city function in a variety of ways (Shen 1994). First, with the great increase in urban population, the city became larger and city layout became more complex. Second, the form of the city was influenced by surrounding topographic features so as to make good use of natural resources (such as water) and to build up defensive elements. Third, the palatial city (with an inner wall) or area (without an inner wall) was no longer positioned in the center of the city. The function of the city expanded to include specialized urban handicrafts and designated residential areas. For the first time, Eastern Zhou cities integrated royal administration with general public affairs, including production and market exchanges. As a result of the Eastern Zhou urbanization, the "King's City" was transformed into a truly commercial-based urban city aggregating a large number of residents with a wide variety of skills.

URBAN ECONOMY AND
URBANIZATION IN EARLY CHINA

Textual sources illustrate the growing importance of market-based activities as an aspect of political economy and help to substantiate the notion of economic specialization as a key criterion for identifying cities in the archaeological record (see also Zeder this volume). In fact, the two characters that make up the Chinese word "city" are *Cheng* (city) and *Shi* (marketplace). Although marketplaces did not emerge exactly in parallel with urban development in early China, they appear to have increased in importance in the first millennium B.C. The earliest text referring to *Shi* is from the *Zhouli.Kaogongji,* a book on construction and craftsmanship written in the Eastern Zhou period. It recorded that, according to regulations, city marketplaces must be built at the "back" (north) of the palace/royal court, which was usually designed to be in the center of the city.

Other texts include a cluster of bamboo-slip books recovered from the Han Tomb of Mt. Yinqueshan at Linyi city of Shandong Province in 1972 (Shandong 1975). One of these books contained incomplete sections entitled *Shi Fa* (regulations of the marketplace), written in the Warring-States period. According to the inscriptions, marketplaces during the Eastern Zhou were well organized and managed. The *Shi Fa* regularized the size and layout of the marketplace, placement of vendors, organization of market administration, and market operation. According to other Classic texts, every marketplace in a different state had its unique name; for example, the Zhang state had *Yang Shi;* the Lu state had *Zhou Shi* and *Hsu Shi;* and the Chu state had *Er Shi.* Some of these same names also appear in the impressed marks of pottery vessels. The book of *Regulations of Marketplace* also listed strict by-laws to control market officers' possible misconduct. The earliest record mentioning market officers appeared in *Zuozhuan,* a chronicle book of the Spring and Autumn period. According to the chapter titled *Royal Regulations* of the Book *Xunzhi,* the duty of the market officer in earlier times included only street maintenance and cleaning, traffic control, security patrols, and price controls. However, when marketplaces later became larger and fully developed, market officers had additional duties, notably, vendor management, merchandise inspection, dispute settlement, and loan arrangement. One of the major tasks of market officers in the Warring-States period was to collect sales, property, and import taxes. According to records, these commercial taxes became a very important part of state revenues in the Eastern Zhou (Tu 1980:684–685; Yang 1998:129).

Although the type of city prescribed by the *Zhouli.Kaogongji* has yet to be fully documented archaeologically, in the 1980s archaeologists discovered a "marketplace" in the ruin of Yongcheng, the ancient capital of the Qin state during the eighth to fifth century B.C. (now in Fengxiang County of Shaanxi Province; Shang and Zhao 1989). The site was located at the northeastern corner of the 3.4-by-3.1-kilometer city ruin, and the marketplace was enclosed by a wall running 180 meters east-west and 160 meters north-south. A gate structure was found at the middle of each side, with a walkway paved with large regular bricks. Streets running north-south and east-west were arranged regularly, where remains of likely shops were located. According to recovered artifacts, including Qin bronze coins, roof tiles, and pottery bases impressed with marks, the excavators identified it as a marketplace previously known only in the textual records. However, this interpretation cannot be verified until the full report of this discovery is published. If the Qin site from Yongcheng city does turn out to be a marketplace, this would be the first archaeological evidence of urban commercial activities in the Eastern Zhou period.

The subsequent development of marketplaces in the Eastern Zhou was to a great extent closely related to the rapid growth of private production within cities. Before the Eastern Zhou, craft production in the city served mainly the royal courts; therefore production was controlled and managed by the state. The products were mainly bronze, ceramic, bone/ivory, and textiles, items made only for the lavish lifestyles of the royal family and upper-class members who lived in cities (Xu et al 1994). Because of that, very few products were exchanged in the market. By contrast, the Eastern Zhou period was one of private production fostered by state administration. From extensive analyses of Classic texts, Yang (1998) summarized four types of productive operation within the Warring-States cities. The first type was household craft workshops. These evolved directly from farmer families with particular skills that migrated into cities for permanent settlement and relied on exchanging goods. Their operation was rather small but self-sufficient. The second type was specialized craft production for goods made of ceramic, leather, metal, and wood. The craftsmen are referred to in the record as *Bai Gong,* indicating an unprecedented class of nonfarming residents. Their products were mainly sold in markets. The third type was private cooperative production of merchandise on a large scale. These manufacturing establishments were mainly iron foundries and salt production operations, which required systemic production flows. Both kinds of production had previously been managed by states (see Liu and Chen in press) but later, some entrepreneurs were given permits of operation under certain (i.e., tax) conditions (Yang 1998:108–109). The last type of production in the city was state production, managed by state representatives. The products, including weapons, ritual bronzes, and coins, were mainly for state or royal court use, not for sale. Most state foundries were administered by a three-level hierarchy: master craftsmen, who were responsible for casting; supervisors, who were in charge of the daily operation of the foundries; and inspectors, or king's designates, who inspected and accepted products. The name and title of officers were normally cast on the products, which have been identified from archaeological findings (Huang 1974).

Production and commerce clearly became a very important part of the urban economy during the Eastern Zhou. Political centers, such as capitals of states, quickly turned into commercial cities that attracted a large number of migrants (Shen 1994). Importantly, some small cities also emerged for the sole function of market exchanges, given that their locations provided easy access to major cities. A famous commercial city of this kind, according to texts, was Dingtao of the Song state in present Henan Province. Because of its vigorous market activities, most of the powerful neighboring states attempted to conquer the Song state in order to collect tax revenues from Dingtao (Yang 1998; Xu et al. 1994). Ironically, frequent warfare mobilized populations, which in part stimulated exchanges of goods in marketplaces.

To sum up, textual records show that Eastern Zhou urbanization consisted of a sudden rise of marketplaces along with the development of private production, an unprecedented social phenomenon. In the following section I examine a single archaeological urban site in order to provide archaeological perspectives on the Chinese urban economy during the sixth to third centuries B.C.

THE STATE OF YAN AND THE
YAN-XIADU SITE

Yan was one of the most important northern feudal states of the Zhou dynasty (Li 1985). Upon the establishment of that state in the tenth century B.C., its first capital was founded at Jin, near the present-day city of Beijing. Because of conflicts with northern nomads, Yan was later confined to the southern part of its original feudal territory in most parts of present Hebei Province, some in Inner-Mongolia district and Liaoning Province (figure 12.1). Yan also mobilized its military forces to the south, where its fort was built at Yi, in present-day Yixian County of Hebei Province. In the early Warring-States period, the rulers of Yan also moved their court to Yi, which became the secondary capital of the state. Yi was then renamed Xiadu, meaning the Lower Capital, to distinguish it from the Upper Capital, Jin, which was about 85 kilometers away in the northeast. It appears that the reason for the formal establishment of Yan-Xiadu during the sixth century B.C. was defense and administration. It was bounded by two rivers, one to the north and the other to the south, and moats were dug to protect the east and west sides.

The urban ruin was first surveyed in the 1930s, when archaeological remains came to light (Fu 1955). Extensive investigations and a series of excavations were carried out during the 1960s and 1970s. A final report of these investigations was

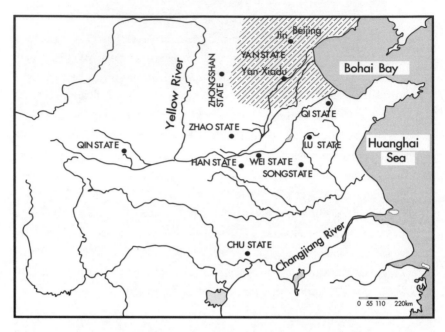

Figure 12.1. Map showing location of the Yan-Xiadu site and major states of the Warring-States period in northern China.

published in 1996 (Hebei 1996). This discussion provides a reanalysis of the published data, focusing on modes of production and trading patterns.

The plan of the city is roughly a rectangle about 8 kilometers east-west and about 4 kilometers north-south (figure 12.2). In the middle was an ancient river canal running from north to south, along with a wall dividing the city into two parts: the East and West Cities. In the northern part of the East City, a barrier wall 4.4 kilometers long east-west cut across the city. Three city gates have been identified, along with streets. There appears to be a division between the royal court areas in the north and the workshop/habitation area in the south; and the two river canals played a role in separating the royal areas from other parts of city. Most of the archaeological features and remains were found in the East City. According to the excavators, a concentration of earthen platforms and structural foundations was identified in the north-central section of the East City. Thirty-three elite tombs were found in the northwestern corner of the East City, as well as in the northern part of the West City. On the basis of cultural remains, the other 30 sites were classified into three categories: workshops, habitation sites, and other sites, such as streets, gates, graves, and defensive structure sites.

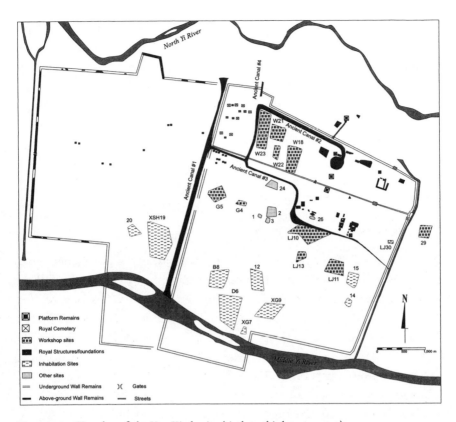

Figure 12.2. City plan of the Yan-Xiadu site (sixth to third century B.C.).

Archaeological investigations show that there was a preexisting population at the site before the founding date noted in textual sources. The D6 habitation site, in the southern part of the city, is the only one dated to as early as the late Shang dynasty, which indicates that the area was already considered favorable for habitation. By the end of the Spring and Autumn period (in the middle of the fifth century B.C.), a few settlements had expanded and occupied some areas later encompassed in the central to southern parts of the city. The settlements include two habitation sites (XG7 and B8) and a workshop (LJ13). A majority of occupational sites within the city were dated to the Warring-States period, notably all of the large structure complexes in the north. When the Yan royal family moved to Yan-Xiadu during the early Warring-States period, the royal court or elite residences were confined within the northern part of the city by an additional inner wall and river canals. Increased population at this time is evident, as a large number of workshop and residential sites appeared surrounding the royal court area. The archaeological sequence points to a later date (the middle to late Warring-States period) for the construction of the West City wall compared with that of the East City. It has been suggested that the West City wall had been added later for defensive purposes (Hebei 1996:874). Because there is no direct evidence of additional defensive elements but only a couple of urban habitation sites in the south and a few cemeteries in the north, I suspect that this area had been prepared for expansion of the city because of population pressure in the east side but was never occupied owing to the sudden collapse of the state in 222 B.C.

ROYAL RUINS AND CITY RULERS

Seven earthen platforms were found on the north side of the city. Among these, the *Wuyang Tai* platform is the largest one, measuring 80 by 50 meters at the base and preserved today to a height of 11 meters. In 1971, a ritual bronze vessel *zun*, clearly indicative of a noble's luxury object, was found at the *Wuyang Tai*. Bronze inscriptions on the vessel displayed *youfuyi*, literally "right-mansion master" (Li 1985:112–114). It is believed that the *Wuyang Tai* was the remaining foundation of a large mansion or palace complex. Surrounding the *Wuyang Tai*, a number of structural remains or foundations were found in association with platforms, forming five clusters of royal complexes in this part of the city (Shi 1992).

Although the exact functions and layouts of these structures need to be further explored, archaeological evidence suggests that the structures atop the *Wuyang Tai* platform might have been a large open courtyard compound (Shi 1992). In addition to findings of architectural elements such as pottery pipes, roof-titles, bricks, attachments, and nails, the most fascinating discovery from this area was a large number of exotically decorated semicircular eaves-tiles (Hebei 1996). The decorations on these tiles are similar to motifs shown on many ritual vessels of that time, which represent symbols of noble utilization (see So 1995). Motifs of dragons, clouds, geometrics, or animal-faces were distinctive forms of art linked to the lavish lifestyle of the Yan noble family (Wang and Shi 1998). Furthermore, some tiles as well as pottery fragments were impressed with marks showing inscriptions such as *Yougon Mou* (literally "so-and-so of the Right Palace") and *Zuogong Mou* ("so-and-so of the Left Palace"), which suggest the nature of these complexes.

The northern portion of the city was the site of not only royal living quarters, but also royal cemeteries. Two cemeteries, *Xuliangzhong* and *Jiunutai,* were identified in the northeastern corner of the East City. While the *Xuliangzhong* cemetery site includes 13 tombs, the *Jiunutai* cemetery site has 10 tombs, all arranged in rows of three or four. An additional cemetery, named *Xinzhangtou*, was located in the northern part of the West City. Eight tombs were identified in pairs. Each of these tombs has a large earthen mound, some as high as 10 meters. According to the survey data, most of the tombs have two ramps running north-south (for example, the XLM8 tomb has south tomb ramps 73 meters long). Tombs JM14, JM15, and JM16 at *Jiunutai* were found in association with horse-and-chariot pits. At *Xingzhangtou* tomb XZHM30, grave goods included bronze-imitation ritual pottery vessels (such as *ding, dou, gui,* and *hu*), pottery musical instruments made to look like bronze, bronze weapons, and gold and silver ornaments. Other items included bronze horse fittings, bronze buckles, bronze mirrors, jade and stone ornaments, and bone objects (Hebei 1996:684–731). Eighty-six gold ornaments in various geometric or animal shapes were also recovered, 20 of which were impressed with value marks (see the next section). A large quantity of bronze-imitation pottery vessels was also recovered from tomb XLM8. On the basis of comparative data, Li (1985:117) suggested that "the use of bronze-imitating pottery for grave furnishing was probably a custom dating to the state of Yan in the early part of the Warring-States period." It is clear, then, that all of these tombs belonged to the Yan royal family or noble-class members.

To date, the investigations of the structures and cemeteries of Yan-Xiadu have been very limited. However, the complexity of royal ruins in this urban site clearly indicates that Yan-Xiadu was first built for royal residential and administrative purposes. Unlike many other royal cities of the Eastern Zhou period, Yan-Xiadu had no separate enclosed palatial city (Shen 1994), although the northern concentration of royal ruins is obvious. Most workshops and other urban habitation sites were located in the central to southern parts of the city, where urban production and commerce apparently took place.

PRODUCTION AND COMMERCE

Archaeological evidence of production at Yan-Xiadu comes directly from workshop sites. Eleven workshop sites were identified on the basis of discoveries of clay moulds, raw materials, kilns, tools, by-products, and waste materials. The recovery of different types of raw materials and products led the excavators to further recognize one iron-making foundry (G5), one bronze-casting foundry (W21), four weapons manufacturing factories (LJ13, W23, W18, and LJ10), one coin-minting factory (G4), one coin-mould workshop (LJ30), two pottery workshops (LJ11 and LJ29), and one bone workshop (W22) (Hebei 1996:85–434). All of these workshop sites were distributed along river canals in the central to northern parts of the city, suggestive of good use of water resources. Only one workshop is located outside the east wall, and none are found in the West City. Their location close to the royal court implies that some of the foundries were controlled by the state. At present, sites LJ13, W21, W18, W23, and G4 may be interpreted to be state-operated foundries.

These state-operated foundries specialized in the production of bronze weapons, bronze ritual vessels, and coins. During this period warfare was endemic, weapons were in great demand, and their manufacture was strictly controlled by the state. At site W23, about 208 *Ge* halberds, long-shafted killing weapons, were collected in the southern part of the workshop site in 1973. Subsequently the area was test-excavated, and an additional 108 pieces of *Ge* were recovered from an area measuring 50 square meters. Such density of *Ge* weaponry was clearly indicative of mass production.

Evidence of state involvement in manufacture is confirmed by inscriptions on weapons recovered from these sites. As already mentioned, a study of weapon inscriptions suggests that the manufacture of weapons during the Warring-States period involved three levels of management (Huang 1974). There were some stylistic variations in how and what inscriptions were made among the states. In the Yan state, only the king's name was cast on the weapons, indicating that the weapons were state property. All but one of the 108 pieces of *Ge* from the W23 site had the king's name cast on it (Hebei 1996:185–190; Li 1959).

Other archaeological evidence of state-controlled production comes from official seals recovered from these sites, which give the names and ranks of officers in charge of the production. One seal has the inscription *Wai Si Lu Duan,* which is believed to be the title of an official in charge of coin-minting (Shi 1980). Other official seals have inscriptions containing the words *Jinding,* which may be related to metal manufacturing. Some of the more elaborate foundations could be the remains of administrative buildings associated with the foundry sites. At the LJ13 site, there are a large number of decorated semicircular eaves-tiles with styles similar to those found in the royal complex. This suggests that similar structures must have been at this weaponry manufacturing workshop.

Finally, consistent with historical records indicating that state-controlled production was also usually large in scale, the sites that we identified to be Yan state workshops are relatively large, especially the W18, W21, and W23 sites, all of which were located adjacent to the royal courts. While the LJ13 site is rather small, a study of artifacts from this well-stratified site suggests that it had been a small habitation site before it turned into a state-controlled foundry specializing in the manufacture of weapons during the fourth century B.C. (Hebei 1996:127).

Historical texts mention that private production sprang up in large urban cities during the Eastern Zhou. Although it is a challenge to identify privately operated workshops from archaeological contexts, there should be some difference in forms of manufacturing between state-controlled and private production in both managerial styles and a resultant variety of technological approaches. Therefore, lack of official manufacturing seals or stamps on products and great variation in the products from workshops can be reasonably assumed to be features of private production. According to historic records, private producers were usually engaged in generalized manufacture of daily utensils and farming tools; accordingly, archaeologists would expect these types of workshop sites to be limited in scale and the artifacts recovered to lack elaborate materials. At present, four sites—W22, LJ10, LJ11, and LJ30—can be interpreted to be workshops of private production in the Yan capital. More extensive excavation is needed at the other two sites, G5 and LJ29, to assess the production mode. In their preliminary report (Hebei 1996), the excavators suggested that G5 may have been a state-run iron-tools manufacturing foundry and LJ29 a privately run pottery workshop.

Artifacts from these workshops are not made of elaborate materials, and the sites are relatively small. Artifact assemblages are dominated by pottery vessels and iron handicraft or agricultural tools as well as architectural elements. A study of artifact typology indicates that the LJ10 site may have been a household-level workshop specializing in stone working in the early phase of its use, then may have developed into a large-scale multifunction workshop in the later phase. Most of the artifacts from the early Warring-States phase of the site are limited to pottery utensils and stone objects. No house foundation was identified, although a number of roof-tiles and other architectural elements were recovered. Nearly 300 stone objects were recovered from a single earthen pit, H729, in the shape of a rectangle measuring 0.90 meter long, 0.60 meter wide, and 0.30 meter deep. All of the stone objects are ornaments, including *bi* rings, *bei* cowries, and open-worked phoenix-design and other pendants. Most important, these objects were of standardized production. Such delicate objects must have been made for market exchange.

The recovery of a few house foundations from the middle Warring-States period indicates that the size of the workshop had expanded. Bronze and iron products are found in layers corresponding to this time, in addition to an increased number of pottery utensils. Clay moulds also suddenly appear in large quantity, which suggests that the workshop appeared to have specialized in the production of moulds.

By the end of the Warring-States period, the site had developed into a full-scale commercial operation. The house structures also became more elaborate. While a round-shaped subterranean structure was the only form in both early periods, two additional large rectangular houses with multiple rooms were identified from the later period and the frequencies of earthen architecture elements increased. In addition to pottery vessels, iron, bronze, and bone objects (which were rarely found from the two underlying deposits) were substantial components of the artifact assemblage. The types of bone products were predominantly delicate hairpins, tubes, and some bone sticks, probably used as game counters. Given that bone debris and raw materials were found at the site, this workshop may have functioned as a location of bone manufacturing. Note, too, that a new group of artifacts—coins—appeared from this occupation. The coins were primarily the Yan's knife-shaped coins but also included shade-shaped coins from neighboring states. This may suggest that some kind of exchange using coins took place at the site.

Pottery vessels constituted the main component of artifact assemblages throughout the three phases at the LJ10 site. Frequencies increased dramatically between the early and later periods, and forms, including jars, pots, and containers, became standardized. However, because no kilns were positively identified from the site, it is hard to assess whether the ceramic standardization was a result of on-site production. Rather, these vessels may have been personal items used by workshop craftsmasters. Whatever the case, it is clear that these ceramic wares were merchandise from the market, suggested by impressed marks on the vessels. A majority of these vessels (unfortunately, no statistical data are provided from the report of Hebei 1996) were impressed with characters or symbols indicating some properties of pottery manufacturing. In general, there are three kinds of impression style. The first one is a line of three characters indicating a potter's name. The first two characters are always *Taogong* (meaning "Potter") and the last symbol stands for the name of the potter, together suggesting that the vessel was made by "Potter so-and-so." The second kind of impression shows a single character, probably standing for the name of a "workshop" or "shop." The third kind of impression consists of symbols of value, such as "three," "five," "seven," "ten," "twenty," and so forth. The standardization of these goods is also evident from the location of the impressed marks on the vessels. Almost all of the jars have marks on the shoulder, while all of the basins have marks on the rim. Another type of ceramic ware, the *Dou* stemmed cup, displays impressed marks on the stem. All of these pottery vessels bearing marks appeared after the beginning of the Warring-States period, which clearly suggests the timing of the development of market exchanges.

While the weapons, luxurious ritual bronze vessels, and coins appear to come from the state-controlled foundries for the exclusive use of the royal court, items including various daily-life utensils must have been produced in some private workshops whose products were for the marketplace. Such goods include the aforementioned ceramic wares with value marks, stone ornaments and pendants, and bone ornaments. Pottery vessels recovered from urban residential sites in the southern part of city, such as D6 and XG9, had forms and marks similar to those from the LJ10 workshop. Interestingly, most pottery vessels from residential sites display marks of value or a place name, while a majority of pottery vessels from the LJ10 workshop were impressed with potter's names. It is not clear what this contrast means without additional spatial analysis of pottery assemblages. However, the large quantity of valued-marked pottery in the residential sites indicates that people were actively involved in market exchanges. For example, the symbol *Tu*, presumably standing for the name of a place (shop or workshop?), was found on the same type of vessel: the *Dou* stemmed cup at both the LJ10 workshop site and the D6 habitation site. This may suggest that somewhere in Yan-Xiadu there was a place called *Tu*, where this type of *Dou* stemmed cup was produced or sold.

A previous study suggests that there were only two iron foundries in the Yan State: one at Yan-Xiadu and the other at Dafujianggou of Xingnong in present Inner-Mongolia district (Shi 1985:113–115). The one identified at Yan-Xiadu was the G5 workshop site. Although the sites were not systematically excavated and studied, G5's function as an iron foundry is confirmed by the large quantity of iron raw materials and waste found there, along with remains of kilns. Iron tools were recovered from most of the workshops, although they were not necessarily manufactured by those workshops. Since iron tools were necessary and effective handicraft implements at many types of workshops, such tools must have been acquired through market exchange. Iron farming tools were commonly found at farming settlement sites outside the Yan-Xiadu city (Shi 1985). These tools are similar in form and size to those found at the workshop site LJ10. Because iron production required special procedures and equipment, it could not be made by the average farming household; therefore iron tools used by farmers outside the city were probably also traded in marketplaces.

The more than 30,000 coins recovered from the Yan-Xiadu site are also direct evidence of the extensive trading activities that took place in the marketplaces of the Yan capital city (Shi and Shi 1996). These "ming" knife coins, an official type of Yan state coin, were cast locally, to judge by the many coin moulds found in workshop sites. The fact that many coins belonging to neighboring states were also found suggests that the Yan state markets attracted people from distant locations. The open-worked phoenix-design stone pendants, the manufacturing by-products of which were surface-collected from the urban site, are identical to those from pit H729 of the LJ10 site. The pendants also appeared in one of the lower-class tombs outside the city, YNXM2. This suggests that the grave owner must have obtained these items from markets and guarded them with his or her life.

COMPROMISE AND CONFLICTS

Archaeological evidence from Yan-Xiadu clearly suggests that commercial production accompanied by market exchanges occurred for the first time between the sixth and third centuries B.C. This development in the urban economy corresponded to social transformations in all aspects of the Zhou world from the onset of the Spring and Autumn period, as described by Hsu (1999:585, emphasis added):

> Among the many developments that mark the Spring and Autumn period, the following are perhaps the most important: the establishment of the *ba* system of recognized leadership among the states; the assimilation of the southern state of Chu (and, later, the states of Wu and Yue) into the political order, such that an unprecedented degree of cultural pluralism was achieved; the concentration of authority in the states, both through the recruitment of capable ministers and also through new governing structures such as the *xian* county organization; *the gradual emergence of private land ownership; the beginning of iron casting; far-flung commercial activities;* and perhaps the most important of all, the rise of the *shi* class and, with it, the dramatic intellectual breakthrough brought about by Confucius.

In all of these aspects, the two and a half centuries of the Spring and Autumn period brought changes with profound effects both for the following Warring-

States period and, indeed, for all subsequent Chinese civilization. Changes in land tenure and production brought about during the Eastern Zhou allowed peasants to own a piece of land if they paid taxes in kind. This change stimulated an increase in productivity. Innovation, more efficient tools such as iron tools, and an advanced irrigation system all came into play then. As a result, the agricultural surplus became sufficient to supply populations of nonfarming classes such as those *Bai Gong* craftsmasters in urban areas. On the other hand, frequent interstate conflicts required a large number of military personnel, who were stationed in most cases within major cities or nearby. Most supplies for military institutions, including weapons, arms and armor, and subsistence goods, must have been obtained through urban production. Under such circumstances, city rulers had to reorganize the managerial structure for urban development to deal with substantial and continuous migrations into urban areas.

If the city was regarded as a royal family residence and administrative center prior to the Eastern Zhou, a question arises: how did city elites deal with the rapid development of urban economic activities within their territory? They could still physically confine their royal courts and residences to one corner of the city, which could account for the appearance of double-enclosed royal cities (Shen 1994; Wang 2000; Wu 1999). At the same time, the city ruler would not tolerate unrestricted commercial activities by the general population. Therefore it became necessary to create a management organization to oversee production and marketplace activities. The rulers certainly benefited from commercial taxes as an additional, but important, part of state revenue. Yan's official seals as well as inscriptions from bronze and pottery products confirmed the existence of managerial officials and facilities responsible for state and private production, as well as marketplace activities. These inscriptions indicate that Yan's management organizations of urban production had two divisions: "Right so-and-so," and "Left so-and-so," and subdivisions to administer the production of items such as pottery, weapons, iron, and coins (Shi and Shi 1996:178). One previously collected Yan seal displays inscriptions suggesting that the seal belonged to an official in charge of a marketplace named *Danyou*. Similar inscriptions from other official seals indicate that there were several marketplaces in the Yan state (although their exact location may never be known).

There is other archaeological evidence suggesting compromises between the state administration and private production. While river canals had served as a barrier to separate the royal court from production and residential areas in the city, they also transported water resources into the city and served as a compromising gesture by city rulers offering support in the establishment of production facilities. We have no doubt that coin-minting was strictly a state affair, from production to distribution. However, an overwhelming number of coins found at the Yan-Xiadu site indicate that the minting processes required a corresponding number of moulds. At the LJ10 and LJ13 sites, archaeologists found hundreds of clay moulds for making the state standard "ming" knife coin. The small LJ30 workshop contains nothing but clay coin moulds, which suggest that this small private workshop had once supplied coin moulds to the state-controlled mints. At the relatively large workshop, LJ10, not only coin moulds but also weapon moulds were supplied for state production. It appears that private operations were supported by the state, which in turn stimulated the development of commercial production. As Zeder (this volume) has suggested, this involvement at the stage of distribution (rather than production) may mark a more effective way for elites to control access to certain goods.

The royal elites certainly enjoyed the benefits of a blooming urban economy. Archaeological evidence for this can be drawn from tomb XZHM30. The gold ornaments recovered were only from this upper-class nobleman's tomb, and 20 of them were marked with values. Shi (1982) suggests that the value marked on the back of each gold object is consistent with its actual weight according to Yan's measuring system at the time. Because the ornaments are gold, the value of the weight also reflects the market value of the objects, suggesting that they might have been produced locally and acquired by the noble family at market values. In addition, a pile of finely made bone items, probably gaming counters, that were found in this tomb are identical to ones from the LJ10 site, a private workshop. These items imply that city elites patronized the city markets.

Although the rapid growth of the urban economy might suggest a loosening of the boundaries between city elites and the general public, there were challenges to city elites' authority. The dramatic increase in urban populations directly affected the stability of royal cities. According to the *Shiji,* the historic record, urban unrest and rebellion in Yan-Xiadu lasted several months during the early fourth century B.C. and resulted in the massacre of tens of thousands of civilians. In the south, beyond the urban site, archaeologists identified 14 mass graves. One of the graves, which is in fact a very shallow pit 23 meters long, 0.6 meter wide, and 0.7 meter deep, contained over 2,000 skulls and no other skeletal remains. The skulls are probably the remains of a massacre; cutting marks on the neck were clearly evident. The excavators believe that the 14 mass graves are plausibly linked to the massacre of civilians described in the text (Hebei 1996:768–774), but archaeologically there is no proof of the status of the dead. They could just as well have been war captives. Nevertheless, conflicts between the two classes within the royal cities in all likelihood existed, brought about by the processes of urbanization and the eroding of the authority of the ruling class. This could reasonably be considered one of the inevitable outcomes of urbanization. It must be noted that the discord resulting from class struggles did not discourage further migration into the city. Nor was there a withholding of private production and commercial activities, simply because the urban economy during the Warring-States period had grown to a point of no return.

CONCLUSION

Cities in ancient China first developed as settlement aggregations of royal families and administrative centers during the Shang and Western Zhou dynasties. The physical forms as well as social context of these early royal cities had changed greatly by the time private production and marketplace exchange rapidly developed in the Eastern Zhou. In the case of Yan-Xiadu, the royal family and its followers first established the city for court and defensive purposes. The social transformations and technological innovations of the Eastern Zhou allowed agricultural productivity to increase, which resulted in surplus and the mobilization of farming households. As this tide of new urbanization gathered strength, private production expanded from small-scale household operations to full-scale commercial operations. Commercial production stimulated the creation of marketplaces that were regulated and monitored by state agencies. Compromising efforts by city elites provided a foundation for the steady growth of private production, marking a new height in the urban economy of Eastern Zhou cities.

ACKNOWLEDGMENTS

An earlier draft of this chapter was presented at the 64th annual meeting of the Society of American Archaeology. I thank Monica Smith for inviting me to participate in the symposium and for her comments on the early draft. I especially thank all of my Chinese colleagues who provided assistance during my writing. They are Professors Fang Hui, Xie Fei, Wei Qi, Chen Xingcan, Xu Hong, and Wang Guanghao.

REFERENCES

Cao, G.

2000   Exploring the Ancient Cities of China. In *The Second Proceedings of Henan Archaeology Association Conference,* edited by Henan Archaeology Association, pp. 77–86. Zhongzhou Guji Publishing House, Zhengzhou.

Chang, K.-C.

1976   *Early Chinese Civilization: Anthropological Perspectives.* Harvard University Press, Cambridge, Mass.

1983   *Art, Myth, and Ritual.* Harvard University Press, Cambridge, Mass.

1985   On the Concept of "City" in Early China. *Wen Wu* 2:61–67.

1986   *Archaeology of Ancient China.* Yale University Press, New Haven, Conn.

Chen, C.

1998   A Study of the Origin of City. *Wen Wu Ji Kan* 2:58–64.

Fu, Z. F.

1980   The Position and Role of Chinese Ancient City in Socio-Economic Development. In *Selected Papers on History of Chinese Economy,* edited by Z. Fu, pp. 321–386. Shanghai People's Publishing House, Shanghai.

Fu, Z. L.

1955   Preliminary Analysis and Study of Artifacts from Yan-Xiadu. *Kaogu Tongxun* 4:18–26.

1981   *History of Economy in Chinese Feudal Society.* People's Press, Beijing.

Gao, S., and C. Yang

1993   Preliminary Discussions on the Origin of Chinese Early City. *Wen Wu Ji Kan* 3:48–54.

Hebei Provincial Institute of Archaeology and Cultural Relics

1965   Excavation Report on the W22 site from Yan-Xiadu. *Kaogu* 11:562–570.

1996   *Yan-Xiadu.* Cultural Relics Publishing House, Beijing.

Hsu, C.-y.

1965   *Ancient China in Transition: An Analysis of Social Mobility, 722–222 B.C.* Stanford University Press, Stanford, Calif.

1999   The Spring and Autum Period. In *The Cambridge History of Ancient China: From the Origins of Civilizations to 221 B.C.,* edited by M. Loewe and E. L. Shaughnessy, pp. 545–586. Cambridge University Press, Cambridge.

Huang, S.

1974   The Dating of the Bronze Weapons of the States of Han, Zhao, Wei, and Some Related Problems. *Kaogu Xuebao* 1:13–44.

Hunan Provincial Intstitute of Archaeology and Cultural Relics

1993   Survey and Test-Excavation at the Chengtoushan Site, a Qujialing-Culture Walled Settlement from Lixian County. *Wen Wu* 12:19–30.

Lewis, M. E.

1999   Warring States: Political History. In *The Cambridge History of Ancient China: From the Origins of Civilizations to 221 B.C.,* edited by M. Loewe and E. L. Shaughnessy, pp. 587–650. Cambridge University Press, Cambridge.

Li, X. Q.

1959   Introduction to the Warring-State Inscriptions. *Wen Wu* 7:50–54.

1985   *Eastern Zhou and Qin Civilization.* Yale University Press, New Haven, Conn.

Liu, L. and X. Chen

In press   Cities and Towns: The Control of Natural Resources in Early States, China. In *Population and Preindustrial Cities: A Cross-Cultural Perspective,* edited by G. Storey. University of Alabama Press.

Ma, S.

2000   New Insights on the Origin of City. In *The Proceedings of the 2d Henan Archaeology Association Conference,* edited by Henan Archaeology Association, pp. 72–76. Zhongzhou Guji Publishing House, Zhengzhou.

Ren, S.-N.

1998   A Survey of Chinese Prehistoric City Sites. *Kao Gu* 1:1–16.

Shandong Provincial Museum

1975   Four Tombs of the Western Han from Mt. Yinqueshan in Linyi County. *Kao Gu* 6:363–379.

Shang, Z., and C. Zhao

1989   The Yongcheng City in Fengxiang County. *Zhongguo Kaoguxue Niangjiang,* 252–253.

Shen, C.

1994   Early Urbanization in the Eastern Zhou in China (770–221 B.C.): An Archaeological View. *Antiquity* 68:724–744.

Shi, Y.

1982   The Measuring System of the Yan State. In *The Proceedings of the 2d Annual Conference of Chinese Archaeology Association,* pp. 172–175. Cultural Relics Publishing House, Beijing.

1985   Agricultural Development of the Yan State during the Warring-States Period. *Nong Ye Kao Gu* 1:113–121.

1992   A Study of Palatial Architectures at Yan-Xiadu and Related Problems. *Wen Wu Chun Qiu* (supplementary issue):171–186.

Shi, Y., and L. Shi

1996   *The Eastern Zhou Coin Collections from Yan-Xiadu.* Cultural Relics Publishing House, Beijing.

Shi, Z.

1980   Notes on Interpretations of Ten Seals from the Warring-States Period. *Zhongguo Lishi Bowuguan Guankan* 2:108–113.

So, J.

1995   *Eastern Zhou Ritual Bronzes from the Arthur M. Sackler Collection.* Arthur M. Sackler Foundation, in association with the Arthur M. Sackler Gallery, Smithsonian Institution, New York.

Tu, C.-S.

1980   The Characteristics and Development of Chinese Cities in the First Millennium B.C. *Bulletin of the Institute of History and Philology Academia Sinica* 51(4):615–747.

Wang, S., and Y. Shi

   1998   Artistic Forms of the Semicircular Eaves-Tiles from Yan-Xiadu. *Wen Wu Cun Qiu* 4:44–49.

Wang, T.

   2000   A City with Many Faces: Urban Development in Pre-modern China. In *Exploring China's Past: New Discoveries and Studies in Archaeology and Art,* edited by R. Whitfield and T. Wang, pp. 111–121. Saffron Books, London.

Wiesheu, W.

   1997   China's First Cities: The Walled Site of Wangchenggang in the Central Plain Region of North China. In *Emergence and Change in Early Urban Societies,* edited by L. Manzanilla, pp. 87–105. Plenum Press, New York.

Wu, H.

   1999   The Art and Architecture of the Warring-States Period. In *The Cambridge History of Ancient China: From the Origins of Civilizations to 221 B.C.,* edited by M. Loewe and E. L. Shaughnessy, pp. 651–744. Cambridge University Press, Cambridge.

Xu, H.

   1999   Natures of Cities in the Xia, Shang, and Western Zhou Dynasties. In *Studies of the Three Dynasties: Proceedings of 1998 Xingtai Intearnational Conference of the Shang / Zhou Study Association,* edited by E. Board, pp. 286–295. Science Press, Beijing.

Xu, X., W. Si, and D. Yang

   1994   *General History of China,* vol. 3: *Ancient Part 2.* Shanghai People's Publishing House, Shanghai.

Yang, K.

   1998   *History of the Warring State Period.* 3d ed. People's Press, Beijing.

Zhang, C., and H. Okamura

   2000   Excavations of Cities: Shijiahe and Yingxiangcheng. In *Exploring China's Past: New Discoveries and Studies in Archaeology and Art,* edited by R. Whitfield and T. Wang. Saffron Books, London.

Zhou, H.

   1992   The Early City in Ancient China. In *Proceedings of the 32d International Congress for Asian and North African Studies,* pp. 111–114. Franz Steiner Verlag Stutigart, Hamburg.

Index

Brak (Tell Brak or Nagar), 27, 254–255, 262–265

brewers, 71

bronze-imitation pottery vessels, 299

Brumfiel, Elizabeth, 189

Buddhist religious sites, India, 275, 277, 278, 281, 283

Buenavista, 131, 135

burials: China, 293, 296, 298–299, 306–307; Elmina, Ghana, 10; Mesoamerica, 42, 43, 84, 88, 91, 95–97, 217, 219, 224; Mesopotamia, 65, 66, 257

butchers, 74

Byzantine cities, 17–18

caciques, 94, 237

Cahal Pech, 135

Cairo, 20

Calakmul, 234, 235

Calancha, Antonio, 93, 94

camels, 164

canals: Old Babylonian neighborhoods, 62–64, 77, 261; Yan-Xiadu, 296, 297, 300, 305

caprines. See sheep and goats

Caracol, 234, 235, 236

Casma Valley, Peru, 82

Castells, M., 7, 273

Castillo, Xunantunich, 126, 127, 130, 133, 137

Castillo Incised pottery, 190, 199–204, 200

Çatal Höyük, 11, 257–258

cattle, 74, 164–166, 171, 173

caves, sacred, 47

cemeteries. See burials

ceramics. See pottery and ceramics

Cerén, 45

Cerro Mayal, 195, 196

Cerro Portezuelo, 38

Ceterni, 94

Chacalhaaz period, 217, 228, 229

Chan Chan, 84–86, 229; ciudadelas, 84, 88–93, 95–97; Inka conquest, 96–97; maps, 83, 85; sociospatial organization, 91–93

Chang, K. C., 112, 290, 291

Chao Valley, Peru, 82

chapels, 64, 65, 66, 72–73, 77

charity, 22

Cheng, 292

Cheng-chou, 112

chert workings, 132, 138, 219

Chicago School, 188

Chicama Valley/Mocollope, 26–27, 139, 184–211; maps, 192, 193; methodologies and data sets, 191–204; pottery style and ethnogenesis, 189–190, 199–204; settlement history, 190–191; social/material correlates, 194, 197–198, 204

chickens, 167

Chicxulub Incised pottery, 229

Child, Mark, 221, 227

Childe, V. G., 9, 12, 105, 184, 255, 256, 271, 274

Chimú empire, 25, 84, 196; ciudadelas, 89; class differences, 91–96, 97; Inka conquest of, 93, 96–97; Lambayeque culture, 91; sociospatial organization, 91–93, 97–98

China, 5, 10, 21, 105, 112, 117, 275. See also Yan-Xiadu

Chot, 94

Chucuito, 96

Chu state, 304

Ciernuncacu, 95

circulation patterns: Old Babylonian neighborhoods, 62–64, 77

cities. See urbanism

Ciudadela, Teotihuacan, 40

ciudadelas, Chan Chan, 84, 88–93, 95–97

Ciudadela Velarde, Chan Chan, 90

Cium, 94

civic-ceremonial structures, 19, 255, 256; Chinese Neolithic settlements, 291; Indian subcontinent, 279–282; Mesopotamia, 59, 259, 260, 264; Moche, 84; Piedras Negras, 216, 220–222, 224, 225, 229–230; San Lorenzo, 141–143; Teotihuacan, 38, 40–41, 43, 45; Xunantunich, 126, 132–134, 136

"civilization," concept of, 12, 121

cladistics and cladograms, 113–114, 113, 116

Clark, Mary, 106, 109–110

class and authority, 1, 7–8, 16–19, 22–23, 27, 195–197, 273; Chimú empire and Chan Chan, 91–96, 97; domesticated animals, 163–167, 175–178; Eastern Zhou dynasty cities, 290–291, 292–295, 299–307; heterarchy vs. hierarchy, 114, 115, 117; hunting and game, 161, 176; Indian subcontinent, 275–283; Mesopotamia, 257, 259, 260; middle-level approach, 145; Middle Niger, 105, 114–117; origins of cities, 257, 259, 260; pastoral economies, 163–164, 165, 175–176, 177–178; Piedras Negras, 214–215, 231–240; production and distribution control, 159, 232, 235–236, 238, 294, 300–301, 303, 305–307; San Lorenzo, 137, 139–144; Teotihuacan, 43–44, 46; Xunantunich, 131–137, 142–144

Classic (Chinese) texts, 293, 294

Classic (Maya) period, 213, 219, 222, 227, 232–234, 236, 238, 239

Classical (European) period, 5, 6, 14, 15, 17, 22, 234, 275

clay mould production, Yan Xiadu, 299, 300, 302, 306

climate. *See* agriculture and food supply; environment and ecology; irrigation and water

coercive urbanism, 2, 51, 124, 135

Cohen, Abner, 186, 188

coins, 294, 300, 302–306

Colombijn, F., 5, 7, 17, 19

conflict between social groups, 23, 306–307

Conklin, William, 92

Conrad, Geoffrey, 95–96

consumption patterns, 21–22, 27–28, 272–273, 281, 282

cookshops and taverns, 64, 66, 71, 77

Copan, 225, 234, 237

corvée labor, 21, 143

cosmogonies. *See* origin myths

cosmogram, Xunantunich as, 132–133

Cowgill, George L., 17, 21, 25, 195

Coyotlatelco, 38

craft activities: China, 294; family and kinship patterns, 21; Mesopotamia, 65–68, 74–75, 77, 257, 261; origins of cities, 255, 257; specialization, 157, 159, 160, 177, 186–187; Teotihuacan, 38, 40, 41; Xunantunich, 131–132

creation myths. *See* origin myths

Cuicuilco, 45–46

Curacas, 94

Cuzco, 93, 96, 97

Dafujianggou, 303

deer, 161

defensive sites. *See* military significance, sites with

defining cities, 8–11; Chicama Valley/Mocollope, 189; China, 291–292; Mesopotamia, 254–256; Middle Niger, 105–106; Piedras Negras, 215, 234; Xunantunich, 121–122

Deioces the Mede, 81–82, 98

demography. *See* population

Dia, 109, 110, 112

Dingtao, Song state, 295

Di Segni, L., 17–18

districts. *See* neighborhoods

dogs, 161

domesticated animals, 156–183; archaeological remains,

usefulness of, 167–168; class and authority issues, 163–167, 175–178; fodder, 163, 165; Middle Niger, 108; New World vs. Old World, 161; Old Babylonian neighborhoods, 62, 69, 73–74; production and control, 160, 163, 177–178; separation of farming and herding economies, 162; specialization, 161–164, 165. *See also* Khabur Basin pastoral economies; *specific animals*

Donnan, Christopher, 91, 94

Dos Arroyos polychrome pottery, 222

Dos Pilas, 234, 237

Douglas, Mary, 87, 89, 91, 92

draft animals, 164–165

Drehem (Puzrish Dagan or Tell Drehem), 163, 165

Dumuzi-gamil, 69

Dursagene garden gate district, Nippur, 73

Eanna, 255, 260

Early Classic or Naba (Maya) period, 220, 222, 223, 224, 225, 226, 230, 237

Early Historic period walled cities of Indian subcontinent, 27, 269–289; configuration, 274–277, **277**; map, **276**; social investment, as locus of, 278–282

Early Intermediate Period (EIP), 185, 196, 199

Early Uruk period, 264

Eastern Zhou dynasty cities of China, 10, 290–310. *See also* Yan-Xiadu

Ecbatana, 82

economy, 9–10, 21–23, 27–28, 156–157, 195–197; Eastern Zhou dynasty cities, 290–291, 292–295, 299–307; Mesopotamia, 261, 265; Middle Niger, 106–108; San Lorenzo, 139; surplus wealth, labor, and food, 187, 255, 259; warfare and, 295, 305; workforce availability, 18–19, 21, 135, 137, 140, 143, 187, 274; Xunantunich, 131–132, 135. *See also* craft activities; specialization; *specific commodities*

Ecuador, 94

Elamites, 168

El Brujo complex, 191

El Cayo, 216–217, 220, 226, 230, 231

Elmina, Ghana, 10

El Peru, 236

El Pilar, 131

El Porvenir, 216, 231

El Zotz, 236, 237

Emberling, Geoff, 16, 27

empty space, 73, 264

environment and ecology, 3, 256; domesticated animals, 164–165, 166, 167, 169–171, 172; integration of ecological zones, 262–263, 265; Khabur Basin, 169–171, 172, 173, 175; Middle Niger, 103–114, 116; Piedras Negras, 230–231, 240; Tell Brak (Nagar), 265. *See also* agriculture and food supply; irrigation and water

Ephesus, 23

Erdosy, George, 276, 278

Erh-li-t'ou, 112

Escobedo, Héctor, 184–211

Ešnunna (Eshnunna), 21, 62

ethnicity and ethnogenesis, 26, 184–211; defined and described, 185–188; diversity of ethnicity, 42–43, 111, 260; mono-ethnicity, 233, 275; origins of cities, 257; pottery styles and, 189–190, 199–204; wealth and class distinguished from, 195–197

Euphrates River. *See* Mesopotamia

exotic/rare raw materials, 140–141, 159, 256, 261, 294, 299

Eye Temple and eye amulets, Tell Brak (Nagar), 27, **263**

family and kinship patterns, 21; Chinese Neolithic settlements, 291; ethnogenesis and, 188; Middle Niger cluster cities, 111; Old Babylonian neighborhoods, 63, 65, 75, 77–78; Piedras Negras, 235; Teotihuacan, 41–42, 48–49

Farfán, 89

farming. *See* agriculture and food supply

feasting, 136, 139, 140

Fine Gray pottery, 229

Fine Orange pottery, 227, 229

the "first city," 11, 27, 255, 257–259

fish, 161

flooding, walled cities as response to, 257, 279, 280, 282

flour mills, 60, 66, 70

food supply. *See* agriculture and food supply

Fortin, M., 171, 172

Fox, Richard, 122, 134

fullers: Old Babylonian neighborhoods, 66, 72, 77

funerary sites. *See* burials

Galindo, 89, 190–191

Gallinazo culture and ceramic phase, 185, 190, 191, 192, 195, 199, 204

game. *See* hunting and game

Ganges Valley, India, 14–15, 275, 279, 281

gazelle, 169, 171, 173, 176

geographic information system (GIS), 271

geometry: Teotihuacan, 45

Ghana, 10

Gilgamesh, 261

"global cities," 5

goats. *See* sheep and goats

Goffman, Erving, 233

Gottdiener, Mark, 4, 7

government. *See* class and authority

graphic representation of social relationships, 271

greenstone, 140

grid and group, 87–88, 89, 91, 92, 98

group interaction boundaries, 186

Gudeda, 171, 172, 173

guinea pigs, 161

Guitarra Incised pottery, 220

Gulf Lowlands: Teotihuacan affiliations, 38, 42

Guptas, 281–282

Han period, China, 275, 293

hares, 161

Hassi el-Abiod, 108

Hats' Chaak phase: San Lorenzo, 138–141, 143; Xunantunich, 126, 128, 133, 135, 143

health and sanitation, 3, 49–50, 219, 230, 233, 256

Hellenistic period, 5, 6, 14

Herodotus, 81–82

heterarchy vs. hierarchy, 114, 115, 117

hierarchies. *See* class and authority

Hinduism, 281–282, 283

hinterlands, 2, 4, 5, 10, 11, 13, 18, 26; food provisioning, 157–158; Indian subcontinent, 276–277, 282; Mesoamerica, 38, 122–124, 132, 135–142, 143, 216, 224, 234–235; Mesopotamia, 261, 264–265; Middle Niger, 103–104, 106, 108, 112–114; origins of cities, 255–256, 258

horses, 164

houses. *See* residential compounds

Houston, Stephen, 17, 27, 132

Hsing-T'ai, 112

Huaca de la Luna, Moche, 84

Huaca del Sol, Moche, 84

Huanaco Pampa, 96

Huaynuná, 82

hunting and game, 160, 161, 176; Khabur Basin, 168–173; Middle Niger, 108

identity, 184–185, 257; Classic Maya cities, 233–234; material expressions of, 187, 189–190, **194,** 195–205,

197–198, 204, 272; walled cities, 279–282; Xunantunich, 123–124, 135–144. *See also* ethnicity and ethnogenesis

Inanna, 255

IND (Inland Niger Delta), 108–109

India. *See* Early Historic period walled cities of Indian subcontinent; *specific sites*

Industrial Revolution, 2, 3, 4

Indus Valley, 26

Inka empire, 93, 94, 96–97, 187

Inland Niger Delta (IND), 108–109

innkeeping, 64, 66, 71, 77

Iranian highlands, 167–168

irrigation and water, 255; animal requirements, 164, 166; Eastern Zhou dynasty cities, 292, 305; Khabur Basin, 169–171; Piedras Negras, 216, 219, 231; Teotihuacan, 47. *See also* canals

Isbell, William, 97

Ishtar's temple, Uruk, 261

Isin, 75

isochrestic style, 189

jade and jadeite, 140, 299

Jaghjagh (Wadi), 262

Jebel Abd al-Aziz, 171

Jebel Singar, 262

Jemdet Nast period, 263

Jenne-jeno, 106–110, **107,** 112, **113,** 115, 279

Jequetepeque Valley, Peru, 89

Jericho, 11, 255, 257

Jero Gde, 233

Jin, 295

Jiunutai, Yan-Xiadu, 298–299

Juvenal, 6

Juventud Red pottery, 220

Kalinga (Orissa) region, 278

Kamalapur, 275

Kanchipuram, 6

Kano, 105

karst topography, 230, 235

Kassite period, 261

Kausambi, 276–277

Keith, Kathryn, 19, 20, 25, 261

Keller, S., 57–58

Kenyon, Kathleen, 257

Khabur Basin pastoral economies, 22–23, 26, 157,

167–178; class distinctions, 175–176; map, **169;** northern vs. southern regions, 168–170, 175; pre-urban animal economy, 168–170; specialization, 173–175; urbanization of region, 170–175

Khabur River, 262

"King's Cities," Chinese Neolithic settlements, 292

kinship patterns. *See* family and kinship patterns

Kish, 72, 260

Knox, Paul, 5, 7

Kobadi, 108

Kofyar people, Nigeria, 19

Konya plain, 258

Kopytoff, Igor, 214

Kostoff, S., 212, 234

Koumbi Saleh, 20

Kovak, Amy, 224, 229

Kumche phase, **227,** 227–228, 229

labor. *See* workforce, availability of

Lagash, 167

Laguna Verde Incised pottery, 220

Lake Titicaca Basin, 196, 236

Lambayeque culture, 91, 94, 95

Larsa, 63, 64, 68, 72, 75

Late Classic (Maya) period, 213, 217, 220, 222, 224, 225, 226, 230, 237

Late Preclassic (Maya) period, 220, 221, 222

Late Uruk period, 258, 259, 260, 264

La Ventilla district, Teotihuacan, 38, 41

leadership. *See* class and authority

Leilan (Tell), 158, 171, 174–176, 178

Leventhal, Richard M., 125

livestock. *See* domesticated animals

llamas, 161

London, 6, 22

Lo-yang, 112

Lubaantun, 222

Lugard, Frederick, 105

MacDonald, Kevin, 111

Mahasthangarh, 275, **277,** 279, 280

Malian Sahara, 108

Mali empire, 116

Mallowan, Max, 66, 263

Manchan, 89

Mande, 111, 114–117. *See also* Middle Niger clustered cities

Qin state, 293–294

rabbits, 161
Rajghat, 279
Rajgir, 278
Rapoport, Amos, 60, 86
Raqa'i (Tell), 171, 172
rare/exotic raw materials, 140–141, 159, 256, 261,
    294, 299
residential compounds, 20; *ciudadelas,* Chan Chan,
    88–93; middle-level approach to urban sites, 145;
    North Coast Peru, 84, 88–93, 92, 95–97; Old Baby-
    lonian neighborhoods, 62, 63, 64–65, 73, 76, 77;
    Piedras Negras, 216, 217; San Lorenzo, 139, 140;
    Teotihuacan, 40–42, **42**, 48–49; Xunantunich, 125,
    131; Yan-Xiadu, 296, 297, 298
Rome and Roman period cities, 5, 6, 14, 15, 17, 22, 23,
    234, 275
Rowe, John H., 91, 93, 94
Rubinos y Andrade, J. M. de, 94, 95

Sackett, James, 189, 190
sacral aspects, 15–17; ancestor worship, 42, 43; chapels,
    Old Babylonian neighborhoods, 64, 65, 66, 72–73,
    77; Chinese urbanization, 290–291; Indian subconti-
    nent, 275–283; Mesopotamia, 14, 27, 261, **263**; Mid-
    dle Niger, 109, 114–117; migratory histories, 237–238;
    origins of cities, 260, 273; Piedras Negras, 214–215,
    231–240; San Lorenzo, SL-13 site, 141–143; shaman-
    ism, 117; Teotihuacan, 43, 44–47; Xunantunich,
    132–133, 134, 136
Šaduppum, 61, 62, 66, 72
sahel, 105
Saheth-Maheth, **277**, 278
sajal, 216
Salinar ceramic phase, 191
Salinas de Chao, 82
Salinas drainage, 219
salt production, 294
Samal ceramic phase: San Lorenzo, 138, 139; Xunantu-
    nich, 126
Šamaš, 74
Sanchi, 275
Sangam literature, 274
sanitation. *See* health and sanitation
San Lorenzo, 130, 132, 137–144, **138**. *See also* Xunantunich
Sanskrit, 281

Santa Valley, Peru, 191
Satanikota, 278, 279
Satterthwaite, L., Jr., 226
Schafer, E. H., 5
Schmidt, J., 62–63
Schwartz, G. M., 171, 172
separation, ideology of: Chimú empire, 93
servants, 71, 76
shamanism, 117
Shang dynasty, 112, 291, 292, 297, 307
sheep and goats: Khabur Basin, 171, 172, 173, 174, 176;
    Mesopotamia, 74, 162–164; Old Babylonian neigh-
    borhoods, 74; separation of herding from farming and
    urban control, 163–164; Tell Leilan, 176
shell ornaments, 140, 301
Shen, Chen, 8, 10, 21, 23, 27–28
shops: Old Babylonian neighborhoods, 60, 64, 66, 72
Sippar, 63, 71
Sisupalgarh, 275, **277**, 278, 280
slate carving, 131
slaughtering, 74
slaves, 71, 76
"small worlds," 269–273, 282–283
social conflict, 23, 306–307
social network analysis, 269–273
sociospatial organization, 1–2, 9, 19–22, 27–28; con-
    sumption of space, 272–273; grid and group, 87–88,
    89, 91, 92, 98; Mesopotamia, 57, 59–61, 261; Middle
    Niger, 106; North Coast Peru, 82, 86–88, 91–93,
    96–98; San Lorenzo, 143; Teotihuacan, 37–44;
    Xunantunich, 132–133
Song state, 295
specialization: agriculture and food supply, 156–161;
    craft activities, 157, 159, 160, 177, 186–187; domestic
    animals, 161–164, 165, 177–178; Eastern Zhou dy-
    nasty cities, 292; exotic/rare raw materials, 159; mate-
    rial expression of social effects of, 187, 188, 193, 194,
    204; Mesopotamia, 173–175, 259, 261; origins of
    cities, 255–256, 258, 259, 271, 273; urbanism and,
    156–159
spinning, 174
Spring and Autumn period, Eastern Zhou dynasty, 292,
    293, 297, 304
Stanish, Charles, 196
states and cities, relationship between, 12–16, 25, 26,
    103–105, 260–261, 274, 281–283
Stone, Elizabeth, 14, 62, 63, 65, 261